Film
Review
1987-8

Film Review
1987-8

INCLUDING VIDEO RELEASES

F. Maurice Speed

in association with
James Cameron-Wilson

COLUMBUS BOOKS
LONDON

First published in Great Britain in 1987 by
COLUMBUS BOOKS LIMITED
19-23 Ludgate Hill
London EC4M 7PD

Copyright © 1987 F. Maurice Speed

British Library Cataloguing in Publication Data
Film review: including video releasees. —
1987-8
1. Moving-pictures — Periodicals
791.43'05   PN1993

ISBN 0–86287–364–9
ISBN 0–86287–365–7 Pbk

Designed by Fred Price

Phototypeset by Falcon Graphic Art Ltd
Wallington, Surrey

Printed and bound by R. J. Acford,
Chichester, Sussex

Contents

Introduction

F. MAURICE SPEED surveys the cinematic year

There's little difficulty in selecting the three topics which have dominated the film scene during the twelve-month period coming to a close as I write these lines.

Although it remains to be seen what the full and lasting effects will be of Britain's David Puttnam taking over the production reins as head of the Coca-Cola-owned Hollywood giant, Columbia Pictures, his initial impact has certainly been considerable – the cold winds of change are blowing right through the film colony and the breeze has not been universally welcomed.

Secondly, there has been a considerable uproar – still going on, with a number of legal actions pending or promised – following the news that several companies are in the business of 'colourizing' old black-and-white movies with a view to giving them a new lease of life, not only on television but also in the cinema. Protests have been wide-ranging and vociferously expressed by many distinguished figures on both sides of the Atlantic. Indeed, the sound and strength of these protests have obviously astonished, not a little dismayed and often considerably irritated the would-be colourizers. Everyone concerned with the idea has quite a lot to think about.

Thirdly, there is the continuing and often sensational Cannon saga: the acquisitive and lively Israeli duo of Menahem Golan and Yoram Globus, with their chains of cinemas in Britain, France, Italy and the United States, and their major output of movies, suddenly find themselves running out of petty cash and having to switch roles from buyers to sellers in an effort to refill their depleted coffers.

Of the three, by far the most important story concerns Puttnam and Columbia. This sane-thinking, straight-talking, feet-on-the-ground idealist can and most probably will, in his new and very important position, have a major impact on film production generally in Hollywood. He has already said enough about Hollywood methods and personalities to set many manes bristling. For instance, at a press conference given on 17 November 1986 with his chief aide, David Picker, soon after he had moved into the Columbia hot seat, Puttnam announced that no fewer than 57 films had been withdrawn from the existing development schedule, and a further 64 projects were being held over for further examination. Two films close to actual production were shelved, perhaps to be sold off to other studios, because Puttnam found them 'too exploitative for my taste'.

At this conference Puttnam revealed that Coca-Cola had

Nicolas Roeg during the making of his Cannon release Castaway.

given him virtually *carte blanche* with regard to productions, at least all those with a budget below $30 million. He also disclosed that the future Columbia production schedule would be limited to about 15 features a year; the most expensive of these would be costed at about $13 million or under with others down to $7 million or even lower, adding that under his regime Columbia films would be costed perhaps $1½ million less than comparable pictures made elsewhere. He made no bones about criticizing the spend-thrift methods now and recently common in Hollywood, describing the average 1986 cost of a Hollywood production at just under $16½ million as insane.

Puttnam insisted that his aim would be to make good movies and good profits and he castigated Hollywood for many of its ways; in particular he criticized 'lazy movie-making', and the prevalent 'package deal' by which a book would be sold to a studio along with a star player, often someone not suited to the role.

Puttnam said he intended to use directors who loved the screenplay rather than the cash the film would bring them. He also slammed production credits, citing ludicrous cases where a movie included credits for three or even four producers while 'the one poor soul who actually knows how to produce the film isn't even named', with the three who are named maybe being the agent or the friend of the writer, or the writer's mother: 'I find it grossly offensive and really very, very upsetting.'

Puttnam pledged to moviegoers that he would be far more demanding of those who worked for him: in order not to short-change the public, he would challenge directors to direct better, players to act better, and technicians to work better, adding, 'We're all a little bit lazy and we've got away with not giving audiences enough. If there's been a breach of faith in the last five years between the audience and the filmmakers, I have to say that it's been on the side of the filmmakers.'

With the words went deeds. In the spring of 1987 Puttnam announced that arrangements with nine producers who had deals with Columbia were to lapse, a decision said to have particularly annoyed Norman Jewison. Three of his productions in the Columbia pipeline, including *The Man Who Could Work Miracles*, were shelved, though subsequently Jewison made alternative arrangements for production of this and other titles. Puttnam had said he was not going ahead with *Miracles* because although he loved the story he didn't care for the script. He may also have already decided that in future there were to be more 'inside' and fewer, more

Andrei Konchalovsky explains to star Julie Andrews how he wants her to do the next scene in his Cannon release Duet for One.

costly, 'outside' productions. After the announcement of September 1987 that Columbia were merging with Tri-Star and denials that Puttnam would be affected by this, the shock news on 16 September was that Puttnam had resigned.

Puttnam was one of those bitterly opposed to the colouring of old black-and-white films. Strong words on the subject also came from the Directors' Guild of Great Britain, with Fred Zinnemann calling the idea 'a cultural crime'. The Guild's anti-colourization campaign was led by such imposing figures as Sir Richard Attenborough, Lindsay Anderson, John Boorman, Alan Parker and John Schlesinger. The Directors' Guild of America joined in the condemnation: 'cultural butchery' and 'artistic desecration' were among its accusations. The American Film Institute (Milos Forman, Sidney Lumet, Arthur Hiller, etc.) added its powerful voice to the controversy, and horrified opposition was also voiced by The American Society of Cinematographers, who claimed the idea represented an unwarranted intrusion into 'the artistry of the cinematographers who originally photographed the film . . . to tamper with [the old films] amounts to sacrilege tantamount to altering . . . Beethoven's 9th Symphony'. Other big guns lined up to shoot colourization down included The United Actors'

Guild, The Writers' Guild of America and the National Arts Council. Big guns indeed.

Meanwhile, apparently oblivious to all the clamour, the Hal Roach Studios – the parent company of Colorization Inc – went steadily ahead with colouring two of the late Otto Preminger's features (*Advise and Consent* and *St Joan*). Another of the companies involved, Colour Systems Technology, threatened legal action against the complainers. That they were annoyed was understandable, I suppose, when one realizes that this company apparently had a contract to colour no fewer than 100 old black-and-white MGM films.

Seemingly unmoved and certainly ignoring all the uproar, including the actual and threatened lawsuits, another company, American Film Technologies, announced on 1 April (a suitable date?) that they were offering a new, faster and more economical colouring system called Digichrome. More about this in Anthony Slide's Hollywood contribution on page 126.

While the Cannon saga ironically enough wasn't as explosive a subject as colourization, it made plenty of good stories for the media during the period. Initially Buy, Buy, Buy in terms of cinemas, and Produce, Produce, Produce in terms of moviemaking*, by the end of our twelve-month period, the words had changed to Sell, Sell, Sell. Already owners of the old Classic Circuit and the EMI chain of British ABC cinemas – totalling 587 screens on this side of the Atlantic – Cannon acquired the sixth largest cinema chain in the United States with the purchase of the 425-screen Commonwealth Theatre Circuit. The story began to change when whispers circulated about financial bothers for the Menahem Golan-Yoram Globus firm. The Israeli whiz-kids (well, maybe not exactly kids, but certainly whizzy and bouncy) had to call a meeting of financial journalists in Paris to explain the company's financial position, claiming stability and painting a rosy picture of the firm's future. But by November 1986 Cannon were said to be ready to sell the American cinemas they had bought only a few months earlier. Undoubtedly at least some of the reason for this sale was that, with several of the major American film companies avidly anxious to purchase cinema outlets for their films, Cannon expected to make a quick, handsome and unexpected profit by the deal.

Another Cannon sale in 1987 was the Thorn-EMI Film Library – which had been part of their EMI cinema chain purchase – for some $90 million. The sale caused consternation in many quarters, but alarm was somewhat allayed when it was revealed that the 2,000-odd movies were likely to remain in Britain, stored in the vaults of the National Film Archive at Berkhamsted. Purchaser Jerry Weintraub is also almost certain to buy the old Elstree Studios, sold by Thorn-EMI to Cannon about a year ago, a deal which will further replenish the Cannon coffers by around $25 million. Warner Bros also helped Cannon to surmount their financial troubles: for $50 million, they acquired a two-year option on a half-interest in Cannon's European chain of cinemas.

So, the highly complicated and – to this writer – confusing Cannon crisis story continues right up to the moment of going to press, and is likely to make showbiz headlines long after it. *Variety* published an interesting story quoting Cannon's words to the US Government, namely: '. . . its ability to continue to function as a going concern is dependent upon, among other factors, the immediate completion of these objectives [in essence the raising of a vast amount of finance] and there can be no assurance that these objectives will be realized.' And just two weeks later they announced that Cannon's 'co-toppers' Golan and Globus were acquiring the 29-screen South African CIC circuit of cinemas ('a deal that doesn't involve their acutely distressed Cannon Group') and another item about the two Cannon chiefs arriving in Moscow to talk co-production deals and the acquisition of ten Russian features for Israeli release! With a sense of inevitability one read, right next to the South African story, that the Group were acquiring something like a $11½ million cash infusion from the Luxembourg company Intercorporation – a company, incidentally, which is 25 per cent owned by Mr Golan and 25 per cent owned by Mr Globus. To many people, I am sure, it is all quite logical and easy of explanation but to me it sounds like an updated Alice's tea party. Perhaps a clearer picture of the situation will emerge in next year's annual.

In America, the year has seen a quite extraordinary number of cinemas changing hands and, significantly, a

![Steven Spielberg with his star Whoopi Goldberg on the set of The Color Purple.]

Steven Spielberg with his star Whoopi Goldberg on the set of The Color Purple.

forceful entry into the market by the major Hollywood production companies. For instance, Gulf + Western, parent company of Paramount Pictures, acquired no fewer than three cinema circuits, joining Universal and Columbia as production-distribution-cinema-owning giant conglomerates. (This, of course, was the pattern of the past, broken

Glaswegian director Charles Gormley seems very happy to make Scene 1 Take 1 of his Recorded Releasing feature Heavenly Pursuits.

* At the Cannes Film Festival in May 1987, Cannon showed 42 new films and announced future product with stars like Meryl Streep, John Travolta, Peter Ustinov, Lauren Bacall, John Gielgud, Hayley Mills and many others.

9

Director David Jones with writer Helene Hanff while making Columbia's 1987 Royal Command Performance film 84 Charing Cross Road; *and with one of the stars, Anthony Hopkins.*

will be shown widely; and they don't have to pay any percentages to the cinema owners. And just think of all that extra cash to be made on the side from the sale of chocolate, cigarettes and mountains of popcorn.

Also in America, in stark, sad contrast to Great Britain, film production hit new heights in 1986 and looks like going even higher throughout 1987: the fact that an incredible 79 feature films were started there between 1 January and 28 February suggests that the end-of-year total might well merit an entry in the *Guinness Book of Records*.

In the month of April the major Hollywood companies started shooting some 29 feature films, a far higher figure than any single month for many years. Though some of this rush may be due in part to fears of a threatened Directors' Guild of America strike in July, *Variety* has already made an inspired guess that the final figure for the year will be something like 550 features, representing *more than 10 new films being offered for release every week!*†

On the British scene, all the signs are that 1987 might well achieve the distinction of being one of the worst years on record, and this in spite of the success British films have recently been enjoying world-wide.

Pinewood Studios, Britain's largest, which started the year with only one film in production (and when this was completed apparently had only one TV feature on its books) bowed to the situation in late spring 1987 by announcing that 60 per cent of its 409 staff were being laid off. Jim Daly, MD of Rank's Film Services, said the blank order book was without precedent in the 51 years the studio had been operating. Part of the blame, said Mr Daly, lay at the door of the British Government, which had imposed new taxes on foreign performers and removed tax allowances for film investment.

At Elstree Studios, also, things were not too happy; the year started with only one film on the floor (Disney's *Who Framed Roger Rabbit?*), though they did have three more productions scheduled to start some time during 1987. The story was no better at Shepperton, and the smaller studios had to rely on commercials and similar work to keep them going. In bright contrast to the general gloom were the British Film Institute's plans to make six – obviously modestly budgeted – productions during 1987. Modest, because the Government contributed only just over £½ million to the BFI production fund, though it must not be forgotten that the total subsidy to the BFI now exceeds £10 million. In fact, the BFI would be in a far less healthy financial state were it not for their dependable 'angel', American film enthusiast Paul Getty Jr, who during the past five years has donated some £15 million to the BFI coffers. Among Mr Getty's 1986 gifts was the major expense of the smart new BFI headquarters building in London, as well as the Conservation Centre at Berkhamsted and the Museum of the Moving Image on the South Bank, next to the Institute's National Film Theatre. Incidentally, the BFI-staged Lon-

only by the 1948 Paramount consent decree forcing the major studios to sell off their cinema interests.) The advantages for companies making, distributing and showing their films in their own cinemas are obvious; they can show their films when and as they please; they can be certain that they

† The long-feared, headline-hitting threat of this strike, with its potentially disastrous consequences, lasted a fraction over three hours, for at five minutes past 6 am on the morning of 14 July a new agreement was settled with the producers and a new three-year contract signed with them, a contract which apparently in most respects is the same as the one in operation for the previous three years. Most of the changes agreed relate to TV, especially the re-running of small-screen shows.

don Film Festival, always one of the main events of the British Film Year, was generally agreed to be one of the most, if not actually the most, successful yet.

Writing of success reminds me of the quite wonderful news that the Merchant/Ivory film *A Room With a View* in 1987 topped the £2 million gross revenue mark *in Britain* and is anticipated to take up to $50 million world-wide, heartening support for those of us who maintain that an outstanding artistic achievement *can* also be a financial success.

The long-running Goldcrest story continued from 1986 into 1987 with a British *v.* American battle emerging for control of the ailing company. Negotiations for the sale are still proceeding tortuously in hiccups as I write, but who finally wins what of this celluloid lame duck distribution-producing company is sure to have been settled by the time you read this.

Now for a few of those miscellaneous items which are worth recording though unlikely to have any real impact on the cinema story. One such item was the battle to keep London's – indeed, Britain's – oldest purpose-built cinema from being knocked down or otherwise 'vandalized'. Starting life as The Imperial Cinema in Portobello Road in 1905, it has had all the usual ups and downs but was well down when Mainline Pictures' Romaine Hart fell in love with the place and purchased it in 1983. But love was not enough; all the policies tried out at The Imperial failed and so finally it was sold to a property company. They have to tread carefully, however, for the cinema is a Grade One Listed Building. As I write, the former staff and all kinds of cinema enthusiasts are fighting to keep the building as a cinema, but I would guess there is only a slim chance of this.

Typecasters beware! During the year the Supreme Court of Italy gave a ruling that in future 'actors [and presumably actresses] must not be stereotyped by producers or directors'.

Great news for Orson Welles fans was the discovery that, having long since been accepted as lost forever, the greater part of the maestro's unfinished semi-documentary that he made in Brazil in 1942 has turned up – something like 20 hours of fascinating film. A 22-minute 'teaser' shown at the Venice Film Festival gave an exciting promise of the remarkable standard of the film, which was being made under the title of *It's All True* when RKO pulled out of the project.

In Italy, *Day of Hell* (a film about secret arms deals with Iran, made before the real story hit the headlines) seems to have been particularly aptly titled; during a heated argument between the producer and the distributor, the former hit the latter on the head so effectively that the distributor had to be taken off to hospital while the producer was carted off to jail.

The American release of the Sylvester Stallone film *Over the Top* was set for 12 February 1987, a date decided upon before the first scene was even started in the studio. The reason was that this was the date Stallone's astrologer stipulated would ensure the film's success at the box-office. Producer Menaham Golan subsequently divulged that the actor-writer was an astrologer nut, never starting a film unless assured by 'his' stars that the timing was propitious.

A new addition to the crowded Film Festival Calendar this year was the first Funny Film Festival, unveiled in the Dolomites in the autumn of 1986. With 16,000 tickets sold for the four days of the festival, everyone concerned judged it a big, hilarious success. Incidentally, the festival's theme was 'Laugh To Live Better'. Another new festival was staged at Brighton in May, planned as an annual event.

The laughter courted by Michael Winner's 1976 comedy *Won Ton Ton, the Dog Who Saved Hollywood* was somewhat muted when *Variety* revealed that for thirteen of the cast it was their last screen appearance before their death, while fourteen others, though they did subsequently make a film, also died. A further dozen of the cast do still survive (as of now) but have never had another engagement since the movie.

And a happy news note for feminists: the Academy of Canadian Cinema and Television is now run entirely by women, who, since taking over the annual Canadian Film Awards (known as The Genies) seven years ago, have appropriately enough re-named them the 'Gennies'.

The EEC has designated 1988 'European Cinema and Television Year', but at the moment have not revealed what this will mean in practical terms. It appears likely that suitable projects during the period may be backed by EEC cash handouts.

Now there appears to be some dispute about the date of the birth of Hollywood. In 1954 a 'Time Capsule' was buried at the corner of Sunset and Vine to celebrate what was then taken to be the film colony's 100th birthday. But this year the Hollywood Chamber of Commerce has launched a well publicized Hollywood Centennial celebration. The former date was adopted because it was the one on which the cameras first rolled on the first film ever made in Hollywood, *The Squaw Man*, whereas the latter date is the date of the registration of a real estate sub-division named Hollywood which took place on 1 February 1887. The argument proceeds!

Odd bagfellows! Dino de Laurentiis, whose idea it appears to have been, is going into partnership with rubbish bag makers, Glad, to make a film called *The Million Dollar Mystery*. It is about a race to discover the whereabouts of a missing $4 million. The gimmick is that only three-quarters of the amount is found by the cast; the other million, thanks to clues to be found in the film and on the sides of Glad's bags, has to be found by you, the audience. You find the gold and you get the gold! As was said when the story was published in *The Standard*: 'A brilliant idea, which surely deserves an Oscar, for purity of commercial vision.'

According to a report made by the director of the Motion Picture and Television Fund and quoted in *Variety*, 'An estimated 35 per cent of those employed in the motion picture and television industries, not excluding executives, have substance abuse [drug] problems.'

Old actors never die, they just go on acting and they don't even fade away. So suggests the news that, at 91, George Burns has just signed a contract to star in a new film entitled *Eighteen Again*, inspired by the nonagenarian's 1980 hit song, 'I Wish I was Eighteen Again'.

If by now you are wondering what happened to my usual diatribe against foul language and lavatory humour in the modern film, I decided on this occasion to give the subject – and you – a rest. But that doesn't mean I don't still maintain that foul language and vulgarity spoil many an otherwise splendid movie. Happy movie-going.

Releases of the Year

In this section you will as usual find details of all the films released in Great Britain from 1 July 1986 to the end of June 1987 – the period covered by all the reference features in the book. The precise dating of some of these releases is a little tricky in view of the current lack of any rigidity in the release pattern, but dates given refer to the general release and not pre-release.

In the case of films sent out on a 'floating' release I have added the date of the film's first London showing because usually this is also the first British showing.

The normal abbreviations operate as follows: Dir – for Director; Pro – for Producer; Assoc Pro – for Associate Producer; Ex Pro – for Executive Producer; Pro Ex – for Production Executive; Pro Sup – for Production Supervisor; Co-Pro – for Co-Producer; Pro Co-Ord – for Production Co-Ordinator; Ph – for Photographer; Ed – for Editor; Art – for Art Director; Pro Des – for Production Designer; M – for Music; and a few others which will be obvious.

Abbreviations for the name of film companies are also pretty obvious when used, such as Fox for 20th Century-Fox, Rank for Rank Film Distributors, UKFD for United Kingdom Film Distributors and UIP for Universal Interna-tional Pictures. Where known, the actual production company is given first, the releasing company last.

When it comes to nationality of the film, you will find that this is noted wherever possible – those films without any mention of country of origin can be taken as being American – but in these days of increasing international co-productions between two, three and even four countries it is sometimes a little difficult to sort out where the premier credit is due.

Finally, unless otherwise specified (i.e. in black-and-white), it can safely be taken that the film is made in Technicolor or some similar colour process.

Censorship certificates: *U* represents films suitable for persons of any age; *PG* (Parental Guidance) represents films which some parents might consider unsuitable for their children; *15* means no persons under that age will be admitted; and films certified with an *18* (approximately the old 'X' certificate) means that nobody under that age will be admitted to the cinema while that film is showing.

Note: 'No cert' means that no certificate had been issued by the *initial showing of the film* but this does not mean that one will not be issued at a later date.

About Last Night . . . Screen expansion of David Mamet's one-act stage play *Sexual Perversity in Chicago*. It emerges as a lightly amusing, easily forgettable comedy mainly concerned with the on-again-off-again romance of a couple of pretty superficial characters for whom any sort of commitment appears something to be avoided like the plague. Apparently the switch from stage to screen not only changed the title but also cut out the more serious side of the original.

Cast: Rob Lowe, Demi Moore, Jim Belushi, Elizabeth Perkins, George DiCenzo, Michael Alldredge, Robin Thomas, Donna Gibbons, Megan Mullally, Patricia Duff, Rosana de Soto, Sachi Parker, Robert Neches, Joe Greco, Ada Maris, Rebecca Arthur, Tim Kazurinsky, Kevin Bourland, Dean Bastounes, Charlotte Maier, Marjorie Bransfield, Kimberly Pistone, Lindy Huddleson, Raffi DiBlasio, Sheenika Smith,

Jim Belushi as the wise-cracking Bernie in Tri-Star's light comedy About Last Night . . . *The stage play on which it was based was more titillatingly entitled* Sexual Perversity in Chicago.

Heath Wagerman, Brie O'Banion, Dawn Arnemann, Catherine Keener, Steven Eckholdt, Robert D. Durkin, Ray Wohl. Dir: Edward Swick. Pro: Jason Brett and Stuart Oken. Assoc Pro: E. Darrell Hallenbeck. Ex Pro: Arnold Stiefel. Screenplay: Tim Kazurinsky and Denise DeClue, based on the play by David Mamet. Ph: Andrew Dintenfass. Ed: Harry Keramidas. Art: William Elliott. Pro Des: Ida Random. M: Miles Goodman. (Tri-Star). Rel: 3 October 1986. 113 mins. Cert 18.

Aliens. A remarkable addition to the major science-fiction films: 137 minutes of sustained tension and seat-edging spectacular thrills in a triumphal follow-up to the far less lavish 1979 thriller of the same title (except *sans* the new, final s). Sigourney Weaver gives an unceasingly high-key and Oscar-worthy performance as she fights the Things that have taken over and wiped

Expedition leader Sigourney Weaver discusses a scaring situation with her skyship crew (Michael Biehn, left; Bill Paxton, right; Lance Henriksen, background) and the orphaned Newt (Carrie Henn) in Fox's Aliens.

out the workers on one of earth's planetary colonies. Technically outstanding in all departments, so much so that it is easy to overlook any gaps in credibility that there may be in the script.

Rest of cast: Carrie Henn, Michael Biehn, Paul Reiser, Lance Henriksen, Bill Paxton, William Hope, Jenette Goldstein, Al Matthews, Mark Rolston, Ricco Ross, Colette Hiller, Daniel Kash, Cynthia Scott, Tip Tipping, Trevor Steedman, Paul Maxwell, Valerie Colgan, Alan Polonsky, Albie Parsons, Blain Fairman, Barbara Coles, Carl Toop, John Lees, Louise Head, Kiran Shah. Dir and Screenplay: James Cameron, based on a story by Cameron, David Giler and Walter Hill. Pro: Gale Anne Hurd. Ex Pro: Gordon Carroll, David Giler and Walter Hill. Ph: Adrian Biddle. Ed: Ray Lovejoy. Assoc Ed: Peter Boita. Pro Des: Peter Lamont. M: James Horner. (James

Cameron/Brandywine Pro-Fox). Rel: 26 September 1986. 137 mins. Cert 18.

Almost You. One of the funniest films of the year. Erica and Alex are an adjusted, intelligent and loving married couple living in Manhattan. One day, out of the blue, cracks in their relationship appear and outside forces do everything to widen them. An adult New York comedy which, unlike Woody Allen's portrayals of urban paranoia, has *warmth*. Brooke Adams and Griffin Dunne shine in the two leads, and Karen Young (in a difficult role) is excellent as their foil. Art and editing are first-rate, but the script's the thing (by 29-year-old New Yorker Mark Horowitz). Very witty, very real.

Rest of cast: Marty Watt, Christine Estabrook, Josh Mostel, Laura Dean, Dana Delany, Miguel Pinero, Joe Silver, Joe Leon, Daryl Edwards, Suzzy Roche, Spalding Gray, Stephen Strimpell, Suzanne Hughes, Wendy Creed, Harvey Waldman, Karsen Lee Gould, Mark Metcalf, Steve Deluca, Jim Phelan, Seth Allen, Will Hussung, Harry Madsen. Dir: Adam Brooks (no relation

to the star). Pro: Mark Lipson. Ex Pro: Charles C. Thieriot, Sandy Climan and Stephen J. Levin. Screenplay: Mark Horowitz. Ph: Alexander Gruszynski. Ed: Mark Burns. Art: Nora Chavoosian. M: Jonathan Elias. (Wescom-Recorded Releasing Co.). Rel: floating; first shown London (Metro) 17 April 1987. 96 mins. Cert 15.

Alpine Fire – Höhenfeuer. Slow-paced, almost documentary-styled Swiss film about the isolated and introverted life of six people, a family living high on the mountain tops of the Swiss Alps. The story that emerges is about the deaf-mute, sexually frustrated son, and the almost inevitable seduction of his sister: having gone off alone to an alpine hut to escape the wrath of his forbidding, narrow-minded father, she visits him with food and stays the night. Lovely scenic backgrounds and possible allegorical meanings more than make up for weakness in other directions, such as marring overlength.

Cast: Thomas Nock, Johanna Lier, Dorothea Moritz, Rolf Illig, Tilli Breiden-

Director-producer-star and writer Henry Jaglom with his real ex-wife, Patrice Townsend, left, playing herself, and Melissa Leo as her sister in the Mainline Pictures release Always.

bach, Jorg Odermatt. Dir and Screenplay: Fredi M. Murer. Pro: Bernard Lang. Ph: Pio Corradi. Ed: Helena Gerber. Art: Bernhard Sauter. M: Mario Beretta. (Lang Pro-Rex Films-Electric). Rel: floating; first shown London (Everyman) 10 October 1986. 117 mins. No cert.

Always. Director-producer-writer-star Henry Jaglom's movies are always 'different' and this one is no exception. The story, based largely on his own experiences, centres on a strange weekend when his separated wife (played by Jaglom's own ex-wife Patrice

Townsend) turns up with the divorce papers to sign. She stays on to make it with the various friends who turn up to a 4 July party, during which they tirelessly discuss love, relationships, sex and life in general while indulging liberally in the sex part. Amusing, technically rough, with Jaglom dangerously self-indulgent in regard to the length of his movie which, with typical extravagance, Orson Welles called 'the bravest film ever to come out of Hollywood'.

Rest of cast: Joanna Frank, Alan Rachins, Melissa Leo, Jonathan Kaufer, Amnon Meskin, Bud Townsend, Bob Rafelson, Michael Emil, Andre Gregory. Dir, Pro and Screenplay: Henry Jaglom. Assoc Dir: Judith Wolinsky. Ph:Hanania Baer. M: Miles Kreuger. No other credits. (Jaglom/International Rainbow Pictures-Mainline

Pictures). Rel: 27 March 1987. 105 mins. Cert 15.

Angelos. Highly prized Greek film (Best Film, Actor, Script etc. at the Thessalonika Film Festival) based on a true story about a young homosexual whose exploitation by his lover leads to his sinking into prostitution and worse.

Cast: Michael Maniatis, Dionyssis Xanthos, Katerina Chelmi, Maria Alkaiou, Vasilis Tsanglos, Yorgos Bartis, Aleka Toumazatou, Eleni Kourkoula, Aliki, Tasos Papadakis, Babis Sariyannidis, Nikos Kouros, Stelios Lionakis, Michalis Yannatos, Michalis Angelidakis, Yannis Silignakia, Paulos Kontoyannidis, Mennelaos Daflos, Simon Patroklos, Tasos Polychronopoulos, Sakis Samartsis, Takis Moschos, Kristos Pantzalis, Spiros Bibilas, Nikos Mandas, Rosa,

Daisy, Nadia, Zoe, Lotretta, Stephania, Mina, Ion, Vangelis, Petros. Dir, Pro and Screenplay: Yorgos Katakouzinos. Ph: Tasos Alexakis. Ed: Aristide Karydis-Fuchs. Art: Marilena Aravandinou. M: Stamatis Spanoudakis. (Greek Film Centre-Cannon). Rel: floating; first shown London (Cannon, Piccadilly and Première) 21 November 1986. 118 mins. Cert 18.

The Assault–De Aanslag. Powerful and gripping Dutch film which in a unique way is something of a whodunit, centring on a horrific event which took place in Holland in 1945. A Dutch Nazi cop was murdered and his body found dumped outside the Steenwijk family home; in reprisal the Germans burnt down the house, and 19 villagers, including the Steenwijk family, were shot. Sole exception was 12-year-old Anton Steenwijk, who went on to become superficially happy and successful but whose life is understandably coloured by his 1945 trauma. Gradually, by chance events and meetings, Anton learns the full story of that tragic night. It makes for gripping cinema under the expert producing/directing of Fons Rademakers, and won the 1987 Best Foreign Film Oscar as well as the Golden Globe and Seattle International Film Festival awards.

Cast: Derek de Lint, Monique van de Ven, John Kraaykamp Sr, Huub van der Lubbe, Marc van Uchelen, Elly Weller, Ina van der Molen, Mies de Heer, Frans Vorstman, Edda Barends, Caspar de Boer, Wim de Haas, Hiske van der Linden, Piet de Wijn, Akkemay, Kees Coolen, Eric van Heijst, Oliver Domnick, Amadeus August, Matthias Hell, Horst Reichel, Ludwig Haas, Mike Bendig, Michel Van Rooij. Dir and Pro: Fons Rademakers. Ex Pro: Joss van der Linden. Screenplay: Gerard Soeteman, based on the novel by Harry Mulisch. Ph: Theo van der Sande. Ed: Kees Linthorst. Art: Dorus van der Linden. M: Jurrian Andriessen. (Rademakers-Cannon). Rel: floating; first shown London (Cannons Baker Street and Prèmiere) 17 April 1987. 140 mins. Cert 18.

At Close Range. An increasingly brutal, violent and finally sickeningly nasty story – based on truth– about some extremely repellent characters, a gang of travelling thieves led by a smooth, smiling villain who, when the crunch comes, quite ruthlessly kills his younger son and his pals, then tries to murder his elder, admiring son and his girl-friend, in the latter case succeeding.

Cast: Sean Penn, Christopher Walken, Mary Stuart Masterson, Christopher Penn, Millie Perkins, Eileen Ryan, Tracey Walter, R. D. Call, David Strathairn, J. C. Quinn, Candy Clark, Jake Dengel, Kiefer Sutherland, Stephen Geoffreys, Crispin Glover, Noelle Parker, Alan Autry, Paul Herman, Gary Gober, Marshall Fallwell Jr, Doug Anderson, Nancy Sherburne, Terry Baker, Michael Edwards, Myke R. Mueller, Bob McDivitt, Bonita Hall, Terri Coulter, Anna Levine, Janie Draper, Charles 'Tatoo' Jensen, E. R. Davies. Dir: James Foley. Pro: Elliott Lewitt and Don Guest. Ex Pro: John Daly and Derek Gibson. Screenplay: Nicholas Kazan, based on a story by Lewitt and Kazan. Ph: Juan Ruiz Anchia. Ed: Howard Smith. Art: Peter Jamison. Pro Des: Peter Jamison. M: Patrick Leonard. (Hemdale-Rank Film Dist.). Rel: floating, first shown London (Cannon Haymarket) 12 September 1986. 115 mins. Cert 18.

Back to School. The appropriately named Thornton Melon is an over-ripe, middle-aged millionaire who made his fortune in the rag trade, producing clothes for the overweight. He has everything he could want: money, friends and a loving son; everything, that is,

Sean Penn and his screen girlfriend (Mary Stuart Masterson) realize that they have become prime targets for the lad's smooth but completely ruthless gang-leader dad in Orion-Rank's At Close Range.

except an education. So he decides to buy his way into the Grand Lakes University to become the oldest freshman in scholastic history. He pays NASA to do his astronomy homework and bribes Kurt Vonnegut Jr to write his thesis on the work of, er, Kurt Vonnegut Jr. However, Melon's tutors become suspicious and force the jovial fraud to undergo a devastating oral exam. Constructed in much the same way as Rodney Dangerfield's first starring vehicle *Easy Money*, *Back to School* is fun: the jokes hardly stop for an instant, but when the going gets a little too tedious, the story steps in to save the day.

Rest of cast: Sally Kellerman, Burt Young, Keith Gordon, Robert Downey Jr, Paxton Whitehead, Terry Farrell, M. Emmet Walsh, Adrienne Barbeau, William Zabka, Ned Beatty (as Dean Martin), Severn Darden, Sam Kinison, Robert Picardo, Kurt Vonnegut Jr, Edie McClurg, Sarah Abrell, Dana Allison, Boris Aplon, Nora Boland, Kimberlin Brown, Lisa Denton, Bob Drew, Holly Hayes, Jason Hervey, Leslie Huntly, James Ingersoll, Michael McGrady, Santos Morales, Beth Peters, Phil Rubenstein, Timothy Stack, Steve Sweeny, Stacey Toten, John Young, Brad Zutaut, Josh Saylor, William Grauer, Kristen Aldrich, Beck LeBeau, Tricia Hill, Jill D. Merin, John James, Eric Alver, Theresa Lyons. Dir: Alan Metter. Pro: Chuck Russell. Ex Pro: Estelle Endler, Michael Endler and Harold Ramis. Screenplay: Steven Kampmann, Will Porter, Peter Torokvei and Harold Ramis, based on a story by Rodney Dangerfield, Greg Fields and Dennis Snee. Ph: Thomas E. Ackerman. Ed: David Rawlins. Pro Des: David L. Snyder. M: Danny Elfman. (Orion Pictures/Paper Clip Pro/Rank

Bad boys turned good boys, led by Tiger (Stephen Lang, 4th from left), do battle against the drug-dealers in Tri-Star/Columbia's Band of the Hand.

In Basil, The Great Mouse Detective, *a Walt Disney cartoon feature, the mouse hero searches for clues while his Dr Watson watches with admiration.*

Film Dist.). Rel: 27 February 1987. 96 mins. Cert 15.

Ballet Black. 16mm documentary about the Ballets Nègres, Europe's first all-black ballet company, which was formed in 1946 and became very popular before disbanding in 1952. The story is told through the dancers, in-

vited to a get-together more than 30 years later, exchanging reminiscences.

Dir, Pro, Ph, Ed and written by Stephen Dwoskin. (Dwoskin/Urbane-Arts Council). Rel: floating; first shown London (ICA) 10 January 1987. 83 mins. No cert.

Band of the Hand. Having knocked his quintet of troublesome Miami street urchins into physical and moral shape in the Everglades, Vietnam Vet Joe Tiger (Stephen Lang) sets up headquarters with them in a less than salubrious district of Miami and takes up arms against the local drugs baron. This story of rehabilitation the hard way marked the interesting directing debut of Paul Michael Glaser, who as actor is no stranger to screen roughstuff.

Rest of cast: Michael Carmine, Lauren Holly, John Cameron Mitchell, Daniele Quinn, Leon Robinson, Al Shannon, Danton Stone, Paul Calderon, Larry Fishburne, James Remar, Tony Bolano, Frank Gilbert, Erla Julmiste, Deborah King, Jimi Ruccolo, Bill Amitrovich, Luis Valderrama, Roy Datz, James Eros, Ken Calman, Carl Cofield, T. R. Durphy, Eddie Edenfield, Matt Butler, Dan Fitzgerald, Christopher Berry, Peter

Fournier, Julian Byrd, Joan Murphy, Allyson Garret, Michael Gregory, Sandy Mielke, D. L. Blakely, Jim Zubiena, Nelson Oramus, Antoni Corone, Joe Petrullo. Dir: Paul Michael Glaser. Pro: Michael Rauch. Assoc Pro: Don Kurt. Ex Pro: Michael Mann. Screenplay: Leon Garen and Jack Baran. Ph: Reynaldo Villalobos. Ed: Jack Hofstra. Pro Des: Gregory Bolton. M: Michael Rubini. (Tri-Star-Columbia). Rel: 5 June 1987. 65 mins. Cert 18.

Basil, the Great Mouse Detective. One of the Disney studio's best, most winning works for quite a while, reminiscent of their memorable earlier animated features. About a mouse replica of the great Baker Street sleuth (living upstairs) who, with the help of roly-poly Dr Dawson, defeats the dastardly plot of London's underworld rodent boss, Professor Ratigan, to unseat Queen Victoria and take over the country.

With the voices of Vincent Price (villain), Barrie Ingham (hero), Val Bettin, Susanne Pollatschek, Candy Condido, Diana Chesney, Eve Brenner, Alan Young, Basil Rathbone (as Holmes), Laurie Main (as Watson), Shani Wallis, Ellen Fitzhugh, Wayne Allwine, Tony Anselmo, Walker Edmiston. Dir: John Musker, Ron Clements, Dave Michener and Burny Mattinson. Pro: Mat-

Controversial college coach Gene Hackman urges his basketball team to rise to the big occasion in Orion-Rank's Best Shot.

tinson. Screenplay: Pete Young, Vance Gerry, Steve Hulett, Ron Clements, John Musker, Bruce M. Morris, Matthew O'Callaghan, Burny Mattinson, Dave Michener and Melvin Shaw. Based on the book *Basil of Baker Street* by Eve Titus. Anim Ph: Ed Austin. Sup Anim: Mark Henn, Glen Keane, Robert Minkoff and Hendel Butoy. Ed: Roy M. Brewer Jr and James Melton. Art: Guy Vasilovich. M: Henry Mancini. (Walt Disney-UK Film Dist.). Rel: 19 December 1986. 74 mins. Cert U.

The Berlin Affair. One of the worst films of the year, *The Berlin Affair* was directed, surprisingly, by Liliana Cavani Based on Junichiro Tanizaki's novel *The Buddhist Cross* but transported from 1932 Japan to 1938 Berlin, the film is a tiresome, unwieldy melodrama about a precocious Oriental *femme fatale* who in turn ensnares the affections of an art teacher, his female student and the student's weak husband. Appallingly acted and scripted, the film is about as erotic as a walk in the rain on Brighton beach.

Cast: Gudrun Landgrebe, Kevin McNally, Mio Takaki, Hanns Zischler, Massimo Girotti, Philippe Leroy, William Berger, Andrea Prodan, Tomoko Tanaka, Claudio Lorimer, Edward Farrelly, John Steiner, Enrica Maria Scrivano, Clara Algranti, Benedetta Fantoli, Pieter Daniel, James Crompton, Sarah Blum, Silke Meyer, Jusaburo Tsujimura. Dir: Liliana Cavani. Pro: Menahem Golan and Yoram Globus.

Gudrun Landgrebe, one of the victims of Japanese femme fatale *Mitsuko (Mio Takaki) in Liliana Cavani's Cannon release* The Berlin Affair.

Screenplay: Liliana Cavani and Roberta Mazzoni. Ph: Dante Spinotti. Ed: Ruggero Mastroianni. Art: Luciano Ricceri. M: Pino Donaggio; conducted by Natale Massaro. (Cannon Films-Cannon Film Dist.). Rel: several Cannon cinemas, 9 January 1987. 96 mins. Cert 18.

Best Shot. Somehow the combination of director David Anspaugh, writer–co-

Some of those involved (l. to r.: Dennis Dun, Donald Li, Kurt Russell, Kim Cattrall and Kate Burton) in Fox's Big Trouble in Little China. *Inset: Miss Cattrall and Suzee Pai (left) are put to the 'Test of the Burning Sword' by James Pax in preparation for their marriage.*

producer Angelo Pizzo and star Gene Hackman manages to inject new, exciting and even occasionally genuinely moving life into that tired old story about the team of Nobodies who are enthused into beating the highly favoured Somebodies in the heartcatching final few minutes of a cup final – in this case, college basketball. Gene Hackman gives a particularly fine performance as the once-famous coach who, after a ten-year absence from the game, for dubious reasons turns up in 1951 Hickory and with his strong, abrasive personality licks the local lads into prize-winning shape – and wins the pretty girl in the process. Simple but endearing schmaltz.

Rest of cast: Barbara Hershey, Dennis Hopper, Sheb Wooley, Fern Persons, Chelcie Ross, Robert Swan, Michael O'Guinne, Wil Dewitt, John Robert Thompson, Michael Sassone, Gloria Dorson, Mike Dalzell, Cal-

vert L. Welker, Eric Gilliom, Robert Boyle, Jerry D. Petro, Sam Smiley, Tom McConnell, Dennis Farkas, Tim Fogarty, Don Stratigos, Ken Strunk, Jerry D. Larrison, Thomas D. Marshall, Gary Long, C. W. Mundy, Jeff Moster, Ralph H. Shively, Rich Komenich, Scott Miley, Robert Sutton, Ray Crowe, Ray Craft, Tom Carnegie, Hillard Gates, Geoff Brewer, Dean Ferrandini, Gary Jensen, Laura Robling, Nancy Harris, Libbey Schenck, The Hickory Huskers. Dir: David Anspaugh. Pro: Carter de Haven and Angelo Pizzo. Assoc Pro: Graham Henderson. Ex Pro: John Daly and Derek Gibson. Screenplay: Angelo Pizzo. Ph: Fred Murphy. Ed: C. Timothy O'Meara. Pro Des: David Nicholls. M: Jerry Goldsmith. (Orion/Hemdale-Rank). Rel: 5 June 1987. 115 mins. Cert PG.

Betty Blue: 37.2 in the Morning – 37.2 Le Matin. Several steps beyond and above *Last Tango in Paris* in terms of passion, nudity (male and female), eroticism and performances, this third film from new French writer-director Jean-Jacques Beineix is in every way his best. It tells the story of an unambitious writer who is stirred into all kinds of action by the advent of a nubile youngster whose initial carnal satisfaction

turns to deeper feelings. Then, somewhat ambiguously, even puzzlingly, she tears her eye out and is judged to be incurably insane – a nightmare situation which her lover solves by smothering her, these final sequences being the least satisfactory of the film. Still, an artistic triumph and two superb performances from newcomers Béatrice Dalle and Jean-Hugues Anglade.

Rest of cast: Consuelo de Haviland, Gérard Darmon, Clémentine Celarié, Jacques Mathou, Claude Confortes, Philippe Laudenbach, Vincent Lindon, Raoul Billerary, Claude Aufaure, André Julien, Nathalie Dalyan, Louis Bellanti, Bernard Robin, Nicolas Jalowyj. Dir and Screenplay: Jean-Jacques Beineix. Ex Pro: Claudie Ossard. Ph: Jean-François Robin. Ed: Monique Prim and Yves Deschamps. Art: Carlos Conti. M: Gabriel Yared. (Constellation/Cargo Films-Fox). Rel: floating; first shown London (Screen, Gate and Cannon Tottenham Court Road) 12 September 1986. 121 mins. Cert 18.

Big Trouble in Little China. Lavish, fast-moving, incredibly and consistently noisy mish-mash of the *Indiana Jones* variety, just not as good. Adventure, broad comedy, Kung Fu action, thrills and special effects magic are thrown into an utterly confusing story about a truck driver, a Chinese magician and a young Chinese man teaming up to find the last-named's lovely fiancée and save her from becoming a sacrifice in San Francisco's city-beneath-the-city.

Cast: Kurt Russell, Kim Cattrall, Dennis Dun, James Hong, Victor Wong, Kate Burton, Donald Li, Carter Wong, Peter Kwong, James Pax, Suzee Pai, Chao Li Chi, Jeff Imada, Rummel Mor, Craig Ng, June Kim, Noel Toy, Jade Go, Jerry Hardin, James Lew, etc. Dir: John Carpenter. Pro: Larry J. Franco. Assoc Pro: Jim Lau and James Lew. Ex Pro: Paul Monash and Keith Barish. Screenplay: Gary Goldman and David Z. Weinstein, adapted by W. D. Richter. Ph: Dean Cundey. Ed: Mark Warner, Steve Mirkovich, Dennis Michelson and Edward A. Warschilka. Art: Les Gobruegge. Pro Des: John H. Lloyd. M: John Carpenter in assoc with Alan Howarth. (Taft/Barish/Monash Pro-Fox/UKFD). Rel: 21 November 1986. 100 mins. Cert PG.

Blood Red Roses. Long, British, leftwing sympathizing story of social and political struggles in Scotland, where brave Bessie fights the system. Almost certainly bound for the small screen.

Will she, won't she . . .? Isabella Rossellini and Kyle MacLachlan in the De Laurentiis-UKFD release Blue Velvet.

Cast: Elizabeth MacLennan, James Grant, Gregor Fisher, Dawn Archibald, Louise Beattie, Amanda Walker, Julie Graham, Caroline Paterson, Sandy Imach, Iain MacDonald, John Murray, Monica Brady, Finlay Welsh, Patricia Ross, Simon MacKenzie, Bill Johnstone, Mary Ann Coburn, Andy Barr, Vincent Friel, Joe Mulhaney, Eve Pearce, Ron Donachie, John McGlynn, Myra McFadyen, Doreen Cameron, Ian Sexon, David Neville etc. Dir and Screenplay: John McGrath. Pro: Steve Clark-Hall. Pro Co-Ord: Christine MacLean. Ph: Mark Littlewood. Ed: Jane Wood and Jo Nott. Art: Andy Harris. M: Eddie McGuire and Inti Illimani. (Freeway Films in assoc with Lorimar for Channel 4-The Other Cinema). Rel: floating; first shown London (Metro) 17 October 1986. 150 mins. Cert 15.

Blood Ties – Il Cugino Americano. First-rate, no frills, English-speaking, Italian-made thriller about the Mafia and its villainous ways, in this case forcing an honest, innocent young American to murder his cousin by holding the young man's father and threatening to do some nasty things to him . . . set in America and Sicily.

Cast: Brad Davis, Tony LoBianco, Vincent Spano, Barbara de Rossi, Arnoldo Foa, De-

lia Boccardo, Ricky Tognazzi, Michael Gazzo, Maria Conchita Alonso. Dir: Giacomo Battiato. Pro: Giovanna Genoese and Alessandro Fracassi. Assoc Pro: Robbie Little. Screenplay: Battiato and Corrado Augias. Ph: Romano Albani. Ed: Mario Morra. Art: Paolo Biagetti. M: Celso Valli. (Racing Pictures/RAI I-Palace Pictures). Rel: floating; first shown London (Electric) 17 April 1987. 98 mins. Cert 18. (American length was 120 mins and there is a TV version lasting four hours.)

Blue Velvet. Long, grim, dark, superbly crafted and imaginative film from David Lynch (*Eraserhead/Elephant Man*). Set in a quiet, sunny and outwardly serene mid-American small town where appearances are deceptive. When a pleasant and innocent young man finds a severed human ear on some wasteland and decides, against official advice, to find out whose it is, why and how it came to be there, the town reveals its warped, normally unseen, nightmarish reality. It is a quest which leads the young man to a dark and dreadful world of sexual perversion, bestiality and drugs, a world he finds perversely and insidiously attractive,

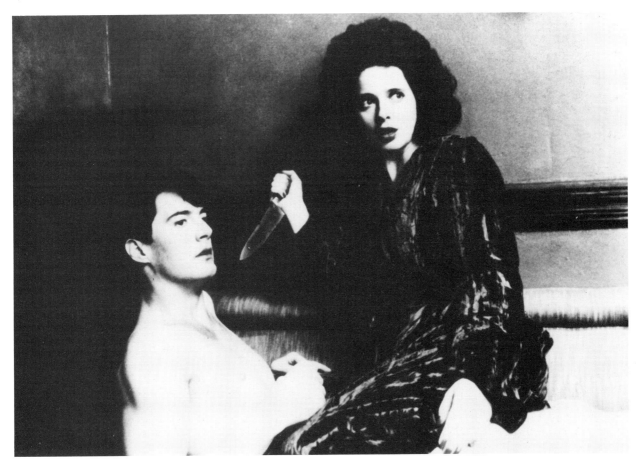

before achieving catharsis by killing the evil man at the centre of the web. Not always credible, often putting questions and failing to offer answers, the film is dramatically absorbing; it both repels and fascinates. Some excellent performances, notably by Kyle MacLachlan (the young man), Isabella Rossellini (the prostitute), Laura Dern (the wholesome girlfriend) and Dennis Hopper (the drug-crazed villain).

Rest of cast: Hope Lange, Dean Stockwell, George Dickerson, Priscilla Pointer, Frances Bay, Jack Harvey, Ken Stovitz, Brad Dourif, Jack Nance, J. Michael Hunter, Dick Green, Fred Pickler, Philip Markert, Leonard Watkins, Moses Gibson, Selden Smith, Peter Carew, Jon Jon Snipes, Andy Badale, Jean-Pierre Viale, Donald Moore, A. Michelle Depland, Michelle Sasser, Katie Reid, Richard Langdon. Dir and Screenplay:David Lynch. Pro: Fred Caruso. Ex Pro: Richard Roth. Pro Sup: Gail Kearns. Ph: Frederick Elmes. Ed: Dunwayne Dunham. Pro Des: Patricia Norris. M: Angelo Badalmenti, theme song sung by Isabella Rossellini. (De Laurentiis Entertainment Group-UKFD). Rel: 15 May 1987. 120 mins. Cert 18.

Boy Soldier – Milwr Bychan. The first film (at least that I can recall) which carries English sub-titles for the considerable amount of Welsh language dialogue. Set in Northern Ireland, it's the story of a young Welshman, a good 'boy' soldier who likes the Army but is trapped into a murder charge, brutal treatment, prison sentence and dishonourable discharge. The whole film has a ring of truth about it (the director claims it is based on truth) as well as a very obvious bias.

Cast: Richard Lynch, Dafydd Hywel, James Donnelly, Bernard Hill, Elmer Gillespie, Bernard Latham, Robert Pugh, Simon Coady, Ian Saynor, Roger Nott, Timothy Scott, Terry Jackson, Timothy Lyn, Dylan Davies, Russell Gomer, Dani Grehan, Elfred Davis, Kevin Staples, Isaac Maynard, Ian Rowlands, Stephen Kelly, David Wyn Roberts, Edward Thomas, Ian McLaren, W. J. Phillips, Menna Trussler, Eric Wyn, Mary Crofton, Peter Dinnion, Laurence Hynam, Marion McLoughlen, Patrick Waldron, Ciaren McIntyre, Brian Nash, Stephen Lyons, Jill Greenhaugh, Eamonn Collinge, Nicola Redmond, Siobhan Hadden, Dewi Savage, Nigel Watson, Moira Mouse. Dir, Screenplay and (with Hayden Pierce) Pro: Karl Francis. Co-Pro: Ruth Kenley. Ph: Roger Pugh Evans. Ed: Aled Evans. Pro Des: Hayden Pierce. M: Graham Williams. (Ciné Cymru

Pro/Channel 4 Wales-The Other Cinema). Rel: floating; first shown London (Metro) 30 January 1987. 100 mins. No cert.

The Boy Who Could Fly. Sad, serious and generally sombre, this thoughtfully directed and beautifully played film tells of the relationship between a sweet little teenager, Milly (played by Lucy Deakins) and her autistic neighbour (Jay Underwood) who is seen by nearly everyone else as a nutcase. In its own special way, quite a beautiful film.

Rest of cast: Bonnie Bedelia, Fred Savage, Colleen Dewhurst, Fred Gwynne, Louise Fletcher. Dir and Screenplay: Nick Castle. Pro: Gary Adelson. Assoc Pro: Brian Frankish. Co-Pro: Richard Vane. Ph: Steven Poster and Adam Hollander. Ed: Patrick Kennedy. Art: Graeme Murray. Pro Des: Jim Bissell. M: Bruce Broughton. (UKFD). Rel: floating; first shown London (Plaza) 26 June 1987. 114 mins. Cert PG.

The Boy Who Had Everything. He's Johnny, a school hero and athletic prodigy, someone his bullying, brutal and sadistic seniors at college decide to cut down to size. So, misery at college and not much better at home, with a mother

Real-life mother and son Diane Cilento and Jason Connery played in that relationship in the Enterprise release of Australia's The Boy Who Had Everything – seen here with Nique Needle as one of the unpleasant pupils not impressed by The Boy when he enters college.

who's a lush (he suffers somewhat from an Oedipus complex) and a very moral girl-friend sending him to prostitutes for his love-life. Intriguingly, mother and son are played by real life mother and son Diane Cilento and Jason Connery; junior hasn't yet developed dad's charisma and wit. Set in 1965, Vietnam year for young Australia, and with all the expected Australian production values, this film sadly neglects to pursue the many themes its story raises.

Rest of cast: Laura Williams, Lewis Fitz-Gerald, Ian Gilmore, Nique Needles, Michael Gow, Mark Wignall, Monroe Reimers, Tim Burns, Caz Lederman, Jo Kennedy, Matthew Todd, Toni Scanlan, Sno Norton-Sinclair, Denise Roberts, James Condon, Drew Tingwell, Vyvyan Black, David McPherson, Vanessa Downing, Jack Pross, Alan Faulkener, Greg Jones, John Plant, Howard Vernon, Barry Gray, Alan Penney, Alexander Broun, Dominic Thurn, Kati Edwards, Edmond Morley, Roxanne Moorhouse, Bernard Hart, Paul Barrie, Nick Biggin, Duncan Miller, Tony Brown, Matt Reed, Stewart Chandler, Adrian White, David Hirst, Brian White, Keith Leggett. Dir and Screenplay: Stephen Wallace. Pro: Richard Mason and Julia Overton. Ph: Geoff Burton. Ed: Henry Dangar. Pro Des: Ross Major. M: Ralph Schneider. (Multi Films/Alfred Road Films-Enterprise). Rel: floating; first shown London (Cannon Tottenham Court Road) 24 October 1986. 94 mins. Cert 15.

Brighton Beach Memoirs. Generally successful transfer to the big screen of one of Neil Simon's plays. While never

Isabelle Huppert, having lost one eye in an accident and losing her sight in the other, falls in love with totally blind Robert (Robert Menzies) in Paul Cox's Australian Blue Dolphin release Cactus.

uproariously funny, it has plenty of chuckles and quite a number of the writer's witty one-liners. Considerably and admittedly autobiographical, it's about a Jewish family living in a middle-class section of Brooklyn in 1937 and their various problems, mostly concentrating on teenager Eugene, who wants to be a writer but at the moment finds sex and baseball his main interests in life. A beautifully photographed, nicely polished production, and a warm Jewish family feeling about the whole affair.

Cast: Blythe Danner, Bob Dishy, Brian Drillinger, Stacey Glick, Judith Ivey, Jonathan Silverman, Lisa Waltz, Fyvush Finkel, Kathleen Doyle, Alan Weeks, Marilyn Cooper, Jason Alexander, Christian Baskous, Brian Evers, Ed Deacy, Wanda Bimson, Richard Bright, James Handy, Betty Henritze, Steven Hill, David Margulies. Dir: Gene Saks. Pro: Ray Stark. Assoc Pro: J. M. Caracciolo. Ex Pro: David Chasman.

Screenplay: Neil Simon, based on his stage play. Ph: John Bailey. Ed: Carol Littleton. Art: Paul Eads. Pro Des: Stuart Wurtzel. M: Michael Small. (Rastar/Universal-UIP). Rel: 29 May 1987. 110 mins. Cert 15.

Cactus. Easily the most unequivocally personal film to date by the always fascinating and intelligent Australian director Paul Cox. Here he takes a basically very simple situation and adorns it with some marvellous photography (surely the opening pan shot must be the longest on record?), literate asides, significant flashbacks and all sorts of visual excursions, while never straying too far from the central dramatic and romantic core of his story. A French girl (beautifully played by Isabelle Huppert) visits some Australian friends as an escape from her crumbling marriage. On the way she has a car accident, in which she damages an eye. The doctors want to remove it to save the other, affected optic, but she hesitates until she falls in love with and begins to understand a young blind man, whose significant hobby is the culture of cacti. Long, diverse and a good example of the true art of film.

Rest of cast: Robert Menzies, Norman Kaye, Monica Maughan, Banduk Marika, Sheila Florance, Peter Aanensen, Julia Blake, Lionel Kowal, Jean-Pierre Mignon, Elsa Davies, Ray Marshall, Maurie Fields, Sean Scully, Dawn Klingberg, Curtis Easton, Kyra Cox, Tarni James, Tony Llewellyn-Jones. Dir and (with collaboration of Norman Kaye and Bob Ellis) Screenplay: Paul Cox. Pro: Cox and Jane Ballantyne. Assoc Pro: Tony Llewellyn-Jones. Ex Pro: Jeannine Seawell. Ph: Yuri Sokol. Ed: Tim Lewis. Pro Des: Asher Bilu. M: (extracts from Pergolesi's 'Stabat Mater'). (Dofine Films/Blue Dolphin). Rel: floating; first shown London (Renoir cinemas) 13 February 1987. 105 mins. Cert PG.

La Cage aux Folles III – The Wedding. Third of the series of French film farces about a couple of 'gays' who run a famous homosexual night club in San Tropez, with Ugo Tognazzi and Michel Serrault again turning in brilliant performances. The by now familiar fun may have lost its initial sparkle – and this particular script, written by no fewer than five people, is not very good – but it is still amusing, very much so; and the story, that one of the partners inherits a Scottish estate and fortune if he will marry, is really no more daft

Captive Irina Brook and captor Hiro Arai reversing their situations in a somewhat odd result of British-French co-production, the Virgin-released Captive.

than that of many more ambitious films.

Rest of cast: Michel Galabru, Antonella Interlenghi, Benny Luke, Saverio Vallone, Stéphane Audran, Umberto Raho, Gianluca Favilla, Pierfrancesco Aielo, Roberto Posse, Flora Mastroianni, Roberto Cuccarini, Massimo Dicecco, Valter Esposito, Pasqualino Lancione, Claudio Meloni, Marco Paolantoni, Piero de Carlo, Renato de Montis, Fabio Albanesi, Nunzio Altobelli, Cesare Nizzica, Roberto Posse, Ippolita Santarelli, Ginestra Spinola. Dir: Georges Lautner. Pro: Marcel Danon. Screenplay: Michel and Jacques Audiard, Marcello Danon, Lautner and Gérard Lambelle. Pro Sup: Lamberto Palmieri. Ph: Luciano Tovoli. Ed: Michelle David, Elisabeth Guido and Lidia Pascolini. Pro Des: Mario Garbuglia. M: Ennio Morricone. (Da.Ma. Produzione, Rome/Columbia, Paris-Tri-Star). Rel: floating; first shown London (Cannon) 4 July 1986. 91 mins. Cert 15.

Captive. French-British co-production which is a subtle, fascinating oddity. The story is of a girl abducted from her father's castle by a trio of assorted kidnappers (a Frenchman, a Japanese and an English girl) whose aim is neither financial gain, sexual gratification nor otherwise criminal, but rather (and this, like so much else in the movie, is never very clear or definite) to mould her to their way of thinking. When they eventually free her and she returns home, she finds father having it off with a girl. Daughter's disgust sends her back to her former captors, and leads to some generally odd behaviour by all concerned, ending in the suicide of the trio and a jail sentence for the heroine. A very strange affair indeed, with considerable nudity, easy to fault but difficult to dismiss in view of the film's overall quality: and viewers will have their own ideas of what writer-director Paul Mayersberg is getting at.

Cast: Irina Brook, Oliver Reed, Xavier Deluc, Corinne Dacla, Hiro Arai, Nick Reding, Annie Leon, Michael Cronin, Marissa

Dunlop, Choyling-Man, Mark Tandy, Sarah Cam, Lucien Morgan, Benny Young, Sidney Livingstone, Geoff Harding, Arturo Venegas, Alan Turner. Dir and Screenplay: Paul Mayersberg. Pro: Don Boyd. Assoc Pro: David A. Barber. Ex Pro: Al Clark and Stanley Sopel. Co-Pro: Christian Ardan. Ph: Mike Southon. Ed: Marie-Thérèse Boiche. Art: George Djurkovic. Pro Des: Voytek. M: The Edge and Michael Berkeley. (Lawson Colgrave Pro, London/Les Productions Belles Rives, Paris-Virgin). Rel: floating; first shown London (ABC Fulham and Cannon cinemas) 19 September 1986. 99 mins. Cert 18.

Care Bears Movie II: A New Generation. While having everything it should to please, amuse and morally educate the kids, this second Canadian animated feature about the cuddlesome CBs somehow falls short. But at the very least, its object is highly commendable; so it's a pity the original charm – and voices and music – are missing.

With the voices of: Maxine Miller, Pam Hyatt, Hadley Kay, Cree Summer Francks,

*All of shapely screen newcomer Amanda Dono-
hoe was on view in Cannon's film of the Lucy
Irvine book* Castaway. *Sharing the desert island and the hug: Oliver Reed.*

Alyson Court, Michael Fantini etc. Dir:
Dale Schott. Pro: Michael Hirsh, Jack
Loubert and Clive A. Smith. Ex Pro: John
Bohach, Jack Chojnacki, Harvey Levin,
Carle MacGillvray and Paul Pressler.
Screenplay: Peter Sauder. Pro Sup: Dale
Cox. Anim Dir: Charles Bonifacio. Ed:
Evan Landis. M: Patricia Cullen. (Col-
umbia). Rel: 29 August 1986. 77 mins. Cert
U.

Castaway. Generally entertaining
adaptation by Nicolas Roeg (director of
the classic *Walkabout*) of Lucy Irvine's
best-seller about her life with husband-
for-convenience Gerald Kingsland during their one year together as voluntary
castaways on a desert island. Though it
does raise many of the physical and
mental problems of enforced intimacy,
it never digs very far below the intriguing ambiguity of the man-woman
relationship. Beautiful photography,
plenty of nudity from delightful, shapely screen newcomer Amanda Donohoe,
and a solid performance by Oliver
Reed.

Rest of cast: Georgina Hale, Tony Rickards,
Todd Rippon, Frances Barber, Len Peiho-
pa, Virginia Hey, Sarah Harper, Stephen
Jenn, Sorrel Johnson, John Sessions, Paul
Reynolds, Sean Hamilton, Arthur Cox,
Richard Johnson. Dir: Nicolas Roeg. Pro:
Rick McCallum. Ex Pro: Peter Shaw and
Richard Johnson. Screenplay: Allan Scott,
based on the book by Lucy Irvine. Ph:
Harvey Harrison. Ed: Tony Lawson. Pro
Des: Andrew Sanders. M: Stanley Myers.
(Cannon Screen Entertainment-Cannon).
Rel: floating; first shown London (Cannon
Shaftesbury Avenue) 20 February 1987. 120
mins. Cert 15.

Chan is Missing. From the makers of
that minor classic *Dim Sum*, this wholly
American-Chinese comedy was, incredibly, made on a budget of about
£15,000; at that price it is a major
triumph for all concerned. Set in San
Francisco's Chinatown and Manila-
town, it concerns the search by two
local cabbies for their missing partner
who has vanished with their money, a
search that introduces a long line of
highly individual and amusing characters. A major collector's piece, full of
subtlety, wit and the workings of the
Oriental mind.

Cast: Wood Moy, Marc Hayashi, Laureen
Chew, Judi Nehei, Peter Wang, Presco
Tabias, Frankie Alarcon, Ellen Yeung, Emi-
ly Yamasaki, George Woo, Virginia R. Cevi-
nio, Roy Chan, Leong Pui Chee. Dir and
Pro: Wayne Wang. Screenplay: Wang, Isaac
Cronin and Terrel Seltzer. Ph: Michael
Chin. Ed: Wang. M: Robert Kikuchi, with
Chinese pop music by Sam Hui. (CIM Pro-
Mainline Pictures). Rel: floating; first
shown London (Metro) 15 August 1986. 80
mins. No cert.

Children of a Lesser God. Whatever
success the original play may have had,
the film adaptation emerges as just
another Hollywoodian love story; the
fact that the girl is deaf and, apparently

23

Teacher William Hurt and his angry deaf pupil, with whom he is in love, played by Marlee Matlin in her screen debut, for UIP's Children of a Lesser God.

deliberately, dumb, thus entailing the need for the lovers to converse by sign language, seems almost incidental. Still, the performances of William Hurt, as a teacher at a school for the deaf who falls in love with an ex-pupil, now staff member, played by actually deaf, pretty newcomer Marlee Matlin, together make the whole thing memorable.

Rest of cast: Piper Laurie, Philip Boscoe, Allison Gompf, John F. Cleary, Philip Holmes, Georgia Ann Cline, William D. Byrd, Frank Carter Jr, John Limnidis, Bob Hiltermann, E. Katherine Kerr, John Basinger, Barry Magnani, Linda Bove, Ann Hanson, James H. Carrington, Max Brown, Maria Cellario, Jon-Paul Dougherty, Linda Swim, Lois Clowater, Allan R. Francis, Richard Kendall, Christopher Shay, Laraine Isa, Nanci Kendall, Marie Brazil, Charlene Legere, Pat Vaughan, Margaret Amy Moar, Leigh French, Archie Hahn III, Jack Blessing, Nicholas Guest, Gigi Vorgan, Lynne Marie Stewart. Dir: Randa Haines. Pro:

Burt Sugarman and Patrick Palmer. Assoc Pro: Candace Koethe. Screenplay: Hesper Anderson and Mark Medoff, based on the latter's stage play. Ph: John Seale. Ed: Lisa Fruchtman. Pro Des: Gene Callahan. M: Michael Convertino. (Paramount-UIP). Rel: 20 March 1987. 119 mins. Cert 15.

Chronicle of a Death Foretold – Cronaca di una Morte Annunciata. To some degree enigmatic, this Francesco Rosi opus is a sombre reflection on love, death and, more especially, inhumanity. It is set in a Colombian riverbank town where an antiquated code of honour demands death for anyone who deflowers and does not marry a virgin, the sentence to be carried out by the girl's kin. In this case twin brothers are the reluctant killers while the local populace, aware of what is happening, adopt the role of spectators and do nothing to stop this useless tragedy. Beautifully photographed with much potential symbolism in lush and lovely settings, dripping with atmosphere and heavy with passion, the film's quietly happy ending seems almost contrived, the more so by an unfortunate piece of casting in a leading

role. But, quibbles aside, a movie of power and artistry.

Cast: Rupert Everett, Ornella Muti, Gian Maria Volonte, Irene Papas, Lucia Bose, Anthony Delon, Alain Cuny, Sergi Mateu, Silverio Blasi, Carlos Miranda, Rogerio Miranda, Vicky Harnandez, Leonor Gonzales Mina, Caroline Lang, Carolina Rosi, Edgardo Roman, Lucy Martinez, Mariela Rivas, Yolanda Garcia, Maryilde Suescun, Gabriel Pazoz, Isabel de Leon, Denis Julio, Carlos Verela, Nelson Pineres, Pablo Soler, Dora Izquierda, Lina Botero, Divo Cavicchiola, Cesar Fernandez, Arquimedes Herazo, Bienvenida Chamorro, Carmencita de Rizo, Bill Moore, Antonio de la Vega, Regulo Ahumada, Maria Helena Castro, Fanny Sejin, Antonio Segovia. Dir and (with Tonino Guerra) Screenplay: Francesco Rosi, based on the novella by Gabriel Garcia Marquez. Pro: Yves Gasser and Francis von Buren. Assoc Pro: Xavier Gelin (France) and Felipe Lopez Caballero (Colombia). Ex Pro: Jean-Jose Richer. Ph: Pasqualino de Santis. Ed: Ruggiero Mastroianni. Pro Des: Andrea Crisanti. M: Piero Piccioni. (Italmedia Films, Rome/Soprofilms/Les Films Ariane/FR3 Films, Paris with co-operation of Rai Radio Televisione Italiana/Rete Due-Virgin Films). Rel: floating; first shown London (Lumière and Gate) 19 June 1987. 104 mins. Cert 15.

With a belt full of bombs – and Brigitte Nielsen – Sylvester Stallone prepares for the next bout of action in Warner's Cobra.

Cobra. Strong, tough, fast and highly competent *Dirty Harry*-style American cop thriller; with Sylvester Stallone (who also wrote the script) and Reni Santoni as the team given all the dirty, difficult police jobs to do and doing them successfully, if by unconventional and officially frowned-upon methods. Here the dutiful duo are faced with the case of a psycho killer and the 16 murders he appears to have committed within a month, only to uncover the fact that it's an army rather than one man they are facing. However, little things like that don't deter them from seeing – sometimes rough – justice done.

Rest of cast: Brigitte Nielsen, Andrew Robinson, Lee Garlington, John Herzfeld, Art La Fleur, Brian Thompson, David Rasche, Val Avery, Marco Rodriguez, Christine Craft, Bert Williams, Ross St Phillip, John Hauk, Nick Angotti, Nina Axelrod, Joe Bonny, Bradley Bovee, Kevin Breslin, Roger Aaron Brown, John Cahill, Malik Carter, Louise Caire Clark, Gregory Norman Cruz, Deborah Dalton, Harry B. Demopulos, Scott Dockstader, Laura Drake, Ken Hill, Arthur Kassell, Karen Kondazian, Fred Lucky, Robert Martini, Joe Masino Jr, Dorothy Meyer, Paul Monte, Joe Stone, Jim Wilkey, Leslie Morris, Clare Nono, Steve Lentz, Glenda Wina, Michael Bershad, Joe Fowler. Dir: George Pan Cosmatos. Pro: Menahem Golan and Yoram Globus. Assoc Pro: Tony Munafo. Ex Pro: James D. Brubaker. Screenplay: Sylvester Stallone, based on the novel *Fair Game* by Paula Gosling. Ph: Ric Waite with add ph by Nick McLean. Ed: Don Zimmerman and James Symons. Art: William Skinner and Adrian H. Gorton. Pro Des: Bill Kenney. M: Sylvester Levay. (Cannon Group/Golan-Globus-Warner). Rel: 1 August 1986. 87 mins. Cert 18.

The Color of Money. Twenty-five years after winning an Oscar nomination for his performance as Fast Eddie, the pool-playing *Hustler* in the 1961 film of that title, Paul Newman wins the Oscar for his work as the same character in the sequel; in which Eddie is lured back to the professional tables through a love-hate, basically jealous relationship with a young, flashy but brilliant player protégé. Some important loose ends (what about the death threat at the end of the original film which made Eddie hang up his cue *for good*?) but brilliant direction, and one

With mixed feelings, the old hustler (Paul Newman) watches protégé Tom Cruise show off his skill in Touchstone-UKFD's The Color of Money. Left: the youngster with girlfriend – exciting newcomer Elizabeth Mastrantonio.

outstanding mature (Newman) and two very promising performances (Tom Cruise as the youngster and Elizabeth Mastrantonio as his sexy, scheming girlfriend) add up to one of the best films of the year.

Rest of cast: Helen Shaver, John Turturro, Bill Cobbs, Robert Agins, Keith McCready, Carol Messing, Steve Mizerak, Bruce A. Young, Zlvin Anastasia, Elizabeth Bracco, Joe Guastaferro, Grady Matthews, Jerry Piller, Forest Whitaker, Vito D'Ambrosio, Randall Arney, Lisa Dodson, Ron Dean, Donald A. Feeney, Andy Nolfo, Paul Geier,

Cary Goldenberg, Lawrence Linn, Rick Mohr, Rodrick Selby, Jimmy Mataya, Peter Saxe, Briuan Sunina, Jim Widlowski, Paul Herman, Lloyd Moss, Michael Nash, Migeul Nino, Juan Ramirez, Mario Nieves, Ernest Perry Jr, Iggy Pop, Richard Price, Alex Ross, Charles Scorsese, Fred Squillo, Christina Sigel, Harold L. Simonsen, Wanda Christine, Zoe. Dir: Martin Scorsese. Pro: Irving Axelrod and Barbara de Fina. Assoc Pro: Dodie Foster. Screenplay: Richard Price, based on the novel by Walter Tevis. Ph: Michael Ballhaus. Ed: Thelma Schoonmaker. Pro Des: Boris Leven. M: Robbie Robertson. (Touchstone in assoc with Silver Screen Partners II-Walt Disney Pro-UKFD). Rel: 13 March 1987. 119 mins. Cert 15.

The Color Purple. Unusual in the sense this is one of the few major films ever to have been made with an almost all-black cast. Long, uneven, often somewhat melodramatically over-drawn; but, on the other hand, super-

bly acted story, sometimes extremely moving, always very watchable. The film focuses on 40 years in the life of a Deep South negro family in the early 1900s, more especially on the transformation during that period of the initially cowed and cruelly treated young girl – an outstanding performance by debuting Whoopi Goldberg – into a woman of considerable personality. All this characteristically handled by Steven Spielberg, right down to the emotional, fairy-tale ending. One of the year's more satisfying movies.

Rest of cast: Danny Glover, Margaret Avery, Oprah Winfrey, William Pugh, Akosua Busia, Desreta Jackson, Adolph Caesar, Rae Dawn Chong, Dana Ivey, Leonard Jackson, Bennet Guillory, John Patton Jr, Carl Anderson, Susan Beaubian, James Tillis, Phillip Strong, Larry Fishburne, Peto Kinsaka, Lelo Masamba, Margaret Freeman, Howard Starr, Daphaine Oliver, Jadili Johnson, Lillian Njoki Distefano, Donna Buie, Leon Rippy, John R. Hart, David Thomas, Thamsana R. Ngubeni, Carrie Murray, Juliet Poe, Katie Simon, Ethel Taylor, Marcus Covington, Marcus Liles, April Myers, Maurice Moor, Lechanda Latharp, Saunders Sonny Terry, Greg Phillinganes, Roy Gaines. The musicians: Paulinho Da Costa, Nana Yaw Asiedu, Clarence Avant, Bayo Martin, Ndugu Chancler, Jeffrey Kwashi, Pete Munzhi and Aniijia Rae Schockley; Margaret Avery's vocals performed by Tata Vega. Dir: Steven Spielberg. Pro: Spielberg, Kathleen Kennedy, Frank Marshall and Quincy Jones. Assoc Pro: Carol Isenberg. Ex Pro: Jon Peters and Peter Guber. Screenplay: Menno Meyjes, based on the novel by Alice Walker. Ph: Allen Daviau.Ed: Michael Kahn. Art: R.W. Welch. Pro Des: J. Michael Riva. M: Quincy Jones. (Amblin Entertainment in assoc with Quincy Jones-Gubert/Peters Co-Warner). Rel: 5 September 1986. 154 mins. Cert 15.

Come and See. In 1943 the German army advanced along the Russian/Polish border and burned down 4,885 peasant villages. *Come and See* is the story of one village, as seen through the eyes of a young boy, Florya (Alexei Kravchenko). A raw, unrelenting and unforgettable film, one of the most powerful anti-war tracts ever made. The imagery – a discarded pillow in an empty lane, Florya asleep in the shelter of a dead cow, German soldiers applauding a human conflagration – scorches itself into the heart and mind, reaffirming Elem (*Agony*) Klimov's standing as a world-class director. A masterful film, but not for the weak of stomach.

Rest of cast: Olga Mironova, Lubomiras Lauciavious, Vladas Bagdonas, Viktor Lorents. Dir and (with Alexander Adamovich) Screenplay, based on the works of Adamovich: Elem Klimov. Ph: Alexei Rodionov. Pro Des: Viktor Petrov. M: Oleg Yan-chenko. (Byelarusfilm/Mosfilm for Cannon Film Dist.). Rel: floating; first shown London (Curzon Phoenix) 20 March 1987. 143 mins. Cert 15.

Coming Up Roses – Rhosyn a Rhith. There are delightful echoes every foot of the way of those modest, marvellous Ealing comedies of the 1940s and 1950s in this captivating little Welsh-speaking comedy (with English sub-titles) about a doomed cinema in a small Welsh town, its staff (of two), and the way that inspiration and mushrooms prove

A lovely performance by Whoopi Goldberg helped to make the Warner release of Spielberg's The Color Purple *sheer cinematic delight.*

The two delightful stars, Iola Gregory and Dafydd Hywel, outside the doomed cinema at the centre of the action in Mainline's outstanding Welsh-speaking comedy Coming Up Roses – Rhosyn a Rhith.

equally important to the couple who find romance along the way. Lovely performances by Dafydd Hywel and Iola Gregory.

Rest of (splendid) cast: Olive Michael, Mari Emlyn, W. J. Phillips, Glan Davies, Gillian Elisa Thomas, Ifan Huw Dafydd, Rowan Griffiths, Bill Paterson, Clyde Pollitt. Dir: Stephen Bayly. Pro: Linda James. Screenplay: Ruth Carter. Ph: Dick Pope. Ed: Scott Thomas. Pro Des: Hildegard Bechtler. M: Michael Story. (Red Rooster/S4C Pro-Mainline Pictures). Rel: floating; first shown London (Screen-on-the-Hill) 20 February 1987. 94 mins. Cert PG.

Cop's Honour – Parole de Flic. More or less routine French crime thriller but with lots of fascinating side-issues, as well as all kinds of political and personal significance thrown in by the film's producer, star, co-scripter and even theme-song vocalist, Alain Delon. It's the story of a bitter, disillusioned cop who hands in his badge and goes into comfortable retirement in the Congo when his wife's murderer goes free on a legal loophole. But he returns when he hears that his daugher has been murdered in Lyons, and proceeds with remorseless and pretty revolting cruelty to track down, torture and kill her killers one by one. Lots of ground for controversy for those who know the Delon history.

Rest of cast: Jacques Perrin, Fiona Gélin, Jean-François Stévenin, Stéphane Ferrara, Vincent Lindon, Eva Darlan, Aurelle Doazan, Dominique Valéra, Sacha Gordine, J. Yves Chatelais, Bernard Atlan, Nandor Werl, W. Victor Foottit, Bertrand Migeat, Guy Viltard, Franck Brethes, Serge Ruben, Françoise Cretu, Manuel Farraz, Raphaël Aguilar, Thierry Carpentier, Fermin Pisias, Anne Roussel, François Montagut, Maria Martine, Christina Meyer, Gérard Ravet, André Obadia, Frédéric Deban, Joseph Niambi Moe, Philippe Lafont, Luis Marques. Dir: José Pinheiro. Pro: Jacques Bar. Ex Pro: Alain Delon. Screenplay: Delon, Pinheiro and Frédéric Fajardi, based on a story by Philippe Setbon. Ph: Jean-Jacques Tarbes. Ed: Claire Pinheiro-L'Heveder. Art: Théo Meurisse. M: Pino Marchese, theme song 'I Don't Know' sung by Delon and Phyllis Nelson. (Adel Pro-Guild). Rel: floating; first shown London (Cannons in Oxford and Panton Streets) 6 February 1987. 98 mins. Cert 18.

Crimes of the Heart. Three marvellous performances in a slim-storied but well written film that never strays far from its obvious theatrical origin, but is none the worse for that. A mixture of drama and often crazy comedy always on the point of turning into tragedy, it is about three sisters in North Carolina, all of whom are trying to come to terms with lives considerably shadowed by their father's abandonment of them when children, their mother's subsequent suicide, and an incipient trend towards mental instability. A perfect example of how to make basically unlikely material into outstanding screen entertainment.

Cast: Diane Keaton, Jessica Lange, Sissy Spacek (the trio), Sam Shepard, Tess Harper, David Carpenter, Hurd Hatfield, Beeson Carroll, Jean Willard, Tom Mason, Gregory Travis, Annie McKnight, Eleanor Eagle, Jessica Ezzell, Natalie Anderson, Connie Adams. Dir: Bruce Beresford. Pro: Freddie Fields. Assoc Pro: P. K. Fields Zimmerman. Ex Pro: Burt Sugarman. Screenplay: Beth Henry, based on her stage play. Co-Pro: Arlyne Rothburg and Bill Gerber. Ph: Dante Spinotti. Ed: Anne

Sisterly trio (l. to r.) Jessica Lange, Sissy Spacek and Diane Keaton find fun in an old photographic scrapbook in the De Laurentiis/Fox release Crimes of the Heart.

Goursaud. Art: Ferdinando Giovannoni. Pro Des: Ken Adam. M: Georges Delerue. (De Laurentiis Entertainment Group-Fox). Rel: floating; first shown London (Odeon Haymarket) 17 April 1987. 105 mins. Cert 15.

Critters. Yet more menace from Outer Space, this time from a group of creepy roller-ball criminals who have broken out of their planet's jail and fled to Earth – Kansas, in fact – hotly pursued by a couple of angry bounty hunters. These latter are able to change to any human likeness at will, and almost destroy the town trying to track down their quarry, who have settled on a farm in the vicinity, terrorizing the family after eating one of the farmer's cows for a snack. Well, all's well that ends . . . well?

Cast: Dee Wallace Stone, M. Emmet Walsh, Billy Green Bush, Scott Grimes, Nadine van der Velde, Don Opper, Billy Zane, Ethan Phillips, Jeremy Lawrence, Lin Shaye, Michael Lee Gogin, Art Frankel, Douglas Koth, Montrose Hagins, Roger Hampton, Chuck Lindsley, Terence Mann, David Strenstrom, Adele Malis-Morey. Dir and (with Dominic Muir) Screenplay: Stephen Herek. Pro: Rupert Harvey. Assoc Pro: Sara Risher. Ex Pro: Rober Shaye. Ph: Tim Suhrstedt. Ed: Larry Bock. Pro Des: Gregg Fonseca. M: David Newman. (New Line Cinema/Sho Films in assoc with Smart Egg Pictures-Palace Pictures). Rel: 28 November 1986. 86 mins. Cert 15.

These Kansas folk are not that keen on their visitors from outer space, as you will see, in Critters, *a Palace Pictures sci-fi thriller.*

One of the biggest box-office winners of the year in America and elsewhere, Australia's 'Crocodile' Dundee (a Fox release) had a great deal going for it, including the performance of its star Paul Hogan, seen with pretty co-star Linda Kozlowski.

'Crocodile' Dundee. Another gem of a movie from Down Under, a conventional comedy-romance with a corny ending which is both visually and verbally witty; delightfully acted, consistently chuckly, with a vein of satirical wisdom. A weatherbeaten crocodile hunter in the outback almost miraculously survives one of his victim's attacks and becomes the hero of a pretty New York reporter's Australian despatches, eventually accepting her invitation to go back to New York with her. The impact of the outback on her and the impact of New York on him form the core of the story.

Paul Hogan (Dundee), Linda Kozlowski (Sue Charlton) and John Meillon (Dundee's partner) make a marvellous trio, with (Australian) support from: David Gulpilil, Ritchie Singer, Maggie Blinco, Steve Rackman, Gerry Skilton, Terry Gill, Peter Turnbull, Christine Totos, Graham (Grace) Walker, David Bracks, Brett Hogan. New York cast: Mark Blum, Michael Lombard, Irving Metzman, Reginald Veljohnson, Rik Colitti, John Snyder, J. J. Cole, Gwyllum Evans, Jan Saint, Peter Bucossi, Sullivan Walker, Bobby Alto, Anne Carlisle, Anne Francine, Paige Matthews, Paul Greco, Caitlin Clarke, Nancy Mette, Barry Kivel, Tony Holmes, Dan Lounsbery, Dolores Messina. Dir: Peter Faiman. Pro: John Cornell. Line Pro: Jane Scott. Screenplay: Paul Hogan, Ken Shadie and John Cornell, based on an original story by Hogan. Ph: Russell Boyd. Ed: David Stiven. Pro Des: Graham (Grace) Walker. M: Peter Best. (Rimfire Pro-Fox). Rel: from 12 December 1986. 98 mins. Cert 15.

Crossover Dreams. Familiar story of the rise, fall and realization of what life is all about by a young Puerto Rico-born singer in New York's Spanish Harlem who makes the crossover from small-time dates to big-time discs, only to flop and end up down and broke before painfully beginning to climb back. Cynical in parts, sentimental in others, with lots of music; enthusiastic comment by one critic: '. . . terrific film, and you can dance to it.'

Cast: Ruben Blades, Shawn Elliot, Tom Signorelli, Elizabeth Pena, Frank Robles, Joel Diamond. Dir: Leon Ichaso. Pro: Manuel Arce. Screenplay: Ichaso and Arce. Ph: Claudio Clea. Ed: Garry Karr. Pro Des: Octavio Soler. (Crossover Films-ICA/NBD Pictures). Rel: floating; first shown London (ICA) 28 November 1986. 86 mins. No cert.

The Cure in Orange. As filmed rock concerts go, this is as straightforward as you can get. Shot in one night at the historic amphitheatre of Antique d'Orange in Provence, France, the film faithfully follows a performance by The Cure, an English band with a slew of hit singles and a handful of critically revered albums. To put it bluntly, as director Tim Pope did, it's 'just a bunch of long-haired herberts enjoying themselves and making a loud din'.

The Cure are: Robert Smith (vocals and guitar), Laurence Smith, Simon Gallup, Porl Thompson, Boris Williams. Dir: Tim Pope. Pro: Gordon Lewis. Ex Pro: Chris Parry. Ph: Chris Ashbrook. Ed: Peter Goddard. (Fiction Films in assoc with Polygram-Blue Dolphin). Rel: floating; first shown London (Cannon Oxford Street) 1 May 1987. 113 mins. Cert U.

Daemon. New Children's Film Unit production; a story about supernatural happenings in suburbia when an 11-year-old boy (Arnaud Morell) is left behind while his parents have to go to New York on a business trip. They leave him with his psychiatrist (Susannah York) as his only friend and defender.

Rest of cast: Bert Parnaby, Sadie Herlighy, Donna Glaser, Orlando Swayne, Faith Steemson, Neil Walker. Dir and Screenplay: Colin Finbow. With the crew of the Children's Film Unit. M: David Newson. (ICA Projects). Rel: floating; first shown London (ICA) 22 August 1986. 65 mins. Cert U.

Dancing in the Dark. A remarkable *tour de force* debut by director-writer Leon Marr in chamber-piece-style, with an outstanding performance by Martha Henry, a fine one by Neil Munro and some magnificent photography. This Canadian film is a concentrated psychological study of a nearly perfect housewife who after 20 years of marriage learns that her ever-loving husband is being unfaithful to her, picks up a kitchen knife and stabs him to death. The telling – largely by voice-over – is superbly economical, with almost every frame of the film essential and the overall effect mesmerizing.

Rest of cast: Rosemary Dunsmore, Richard Monette, Elena Kudaba, Brenda Bazinet, Anne Butler, Vince Metcalfe, Janet Baily, Carole Galloway, Marshal Margolis, Florence Catalano-Carenza, Barbara McMullen, Bob Shaw, John Shepherd, Amanda Smith, Olwyn Chipman, Alan Rose. Dir and Screenplay: Leon Marr, based on the novel by Joan Barfoot. Pro: Anthony Kramreither. Ex Pro: Don Haig. Co-Pro: John Ryan. Ph: Vic Sarin. Ed: Tom Berner. Pro

Martha Henry and Neil Munro as the supposedly happy, long-married couple who come to a tragic end in Entertainment's Canadian release Dancing in the Dark.

Des: Lillian Sarafinchan. (Brightstar Films/Film Arts/Film House Group in assoc with The Canadian Broadcasting Corp-Entertainment Films Dist.). Rel: floating; first shown London (Cannon Tottenham Court Road) 1 May 1987. 98 mins. Cert 15.

Day of the Dead. Third of George A. Romero's 'Dead' thrillers (previous: *Night of the Living Dead* in 1968 and *Dawn of the Dead* in 1979), this one shows the sands of inspiration running out, although everything points to a possible further addition to the series in the future. The last few humans argue and fight among themselves in their besieged underground silo while the now all-conquering 'deaders' assemble outside with the nastiest of intentions.

Cast: Lori Cardille, Terry Alexander, Joseph Pilato, Jarlath Conroy, Antone Di Leo Jr, Richard Liberty, Howard Sherman, Gary Howard Klar, Ralph Marrero, John Amplas, Philip G. Kellams, Taso N. Stavrakis, Gregory Nicotero, Don Brockett, William Cameron, Deborah Carter, Debra Gordon, Winnie Flynn, Jeff Hogan, David Kindlon, Bruce Kirkpatrick, William A. Laczko, Susan Martinelli, Kim Maxwell, Barbara Russell, Gene A. Saraceni, John Schwartz, Mark Tierno, Michael Trcic, John Vulich. Dir and Screenplay: George A. Romero. Pro: Richard P. Rubinstein. Ex Pro: Salah M. Hassanein. Ph: Michael Gornick. Ed: Pasquale Buba. Art: Bruce Miller. Pro Des: Cletus Anderson. M: John Harrison. (Laurel-Media Releasing). Rel: floating; first shown London (Cannon Royal) 12 September 1986. 102 mins. Cert 18.

Day of the Idiot. 1981 West German film about a beautiful rich girl who finds life too much for her. Described

Young scientist Matthew Laborteaux introduces his robotian creation 'Bee Bee' to pretty neighbour Kristy Swanson and best friend Michael Sharrett in Warner's Deadly Friend.

Olsen, William H. Faeth MD, Joel Hile, Tom Spratley, Jim Ishida. Dir: Wes Craven. Pro: Robert M. Sherman. Ex Pro: Patrick Kelley. Screenplay: Bruce Joel Rubin, based on the novel *Friend* by Diana Nenstell. Co-Pro: Robert L. Crawford. Ph: Philip Lathrop. Ed: Michael Eliot. Assoc Ed: John P. Morrisey. Pro Des: Daniel Lomino. M: Charles Bernstein. (Warner). Rel: 27 March 1987. 90 mins. Cert 18.

Death of a Soldier. For all its good intentions (and some rave press coverage), by no means a great film. The true story of a hunky GI in war-time Melbourne accused of murdering three Australian women, the film first shows us the brutality of these acts and then attempts to sway our loyalties by showing us the killer as just a nice, sweet American guy with a screw loose. The polemic is then whether or not the insane should hang.

Cast: James Coburn, Bill Hunter, Reb Brown (a dead-ringer for a built-up Ryan O'Neal), Maurie Fields, Belinda Davey, Max Fairchild, Jon Sidney, Michael Pate, Randall Berger, John Cottone, Nell Johnson, Mary Charleston, Jeanette Leigh, Rowena Mohr, Duke Bannister. Dir: Philippe Mora. Pro: David Hannay and William Nagle. Ex Pro: Oscar Scherl and Richard Tanner. Screenplay: William Nagle. Ph: Louis Irving. Ed: John Scott. M: Allan Zavod. (Scotti Brothers/Suatu Film Management/Vestron). Rel: floating; first shown London (Cannon Haymarket) 8 May 1987. 93 mins. Cert 18.

effect, and ending up with a completely ludicrous climax.

Cast: Matthew Laborteaux, Kristy Swanson, Michael Sharrett, Anne Twomey, Anne Ramsey, Richard Marcus, Russ Martin, Lee Paul, Andrew Roperto, Charles Fleischer, Robin Nuyen, Frank Cavestani, Merritt

Reb Brown as the American GI convicted of the murder of three Australian women in Vestron's Down Under drama Death of a Soldier.

as 'powerful' and 'hallucinatory', with some justice.

With Carole Bouquet, Ingrid Craven and Christine Kaufmann etc. Shown as part of The Festival of German Arts. Dir: Werner Schroeter. Screenplay: Schroeter and Dana Horakova. (ICA/Goethe Institute). Rel: floating; first shown London (ICA) 2 May 1987. 110 mins. No cert.

Deadly Friend. A Wes Craven flesh-creeper about a young scientific whiz-kid who builds a remarkable robot and, when it is destroyed, implants its brain into his murdered girl-friend with devastating results. Starting amusingly enough, it gets wilder, and woollier, and altogether more ridiculous as it goes along, sacrificing all vestige of credibility for the sake of chilling

The three wives – Dominique Michel, Dorothée Berryman and Louise Portal – loosen up physically and mentally in the gym while their husbands talk sex and prepare the disastrous dinner in Artificial Eye's Canadian import The Decline of the American Empire.

The Decline of the American Empire. Literate, stagey, witty, mordantly amusing but basically unpleasant comedy from Canada. In its study of a group of academics and their life style, the film presents almost endless talk of sexual matters. All is revealed at a dinner party for four couples, before which the men talk smut in the kitchen and their wives do something similar while 'working out' in the gym (sexual reversal – significance?). The fun goes sour when unexpected infidelities and betrayals are revealed during dinner.

Cast: Dominique Michel, Dorothée Berryman, Louise Portal, Geneviève Rioux, Pierre Curzi, Rémy Girard, Yves Jacques, Daniel Brière, Gabriel Arcand. Dir and Screenplay: Denys Arcand. Pro: René Malo and Roger Frappier. Ph: Guy Dufaux. Ed: Monique Fortier. Art: Gaudeline Sauriol. M: François Dompierre, from themes by Handel. (Corporation Image M&M Ltée/Office National du Film du Canada/Artificial Eye). Rel: floating; generally during September 1986. 95 mins. Cert 18.

The Decline of Western Civilization. Ironic or apt title for a 1979–80 documentary presenting some of the 'toughest and most aggressive' bands of the West Coast of America, including cult favourites 'The Circle Jerks' and 'Black Flag'. Of obviously specialized appeal.

Dir: Penelope Spheris. No other credits listed. (Shperis Films-ICA). Rel: floating; first shown London (ICA) 2 November 1986. 100 mins. No cert.

Desert Bloom. Intelligent, restrained and credible drama of difficult human relationships in a family of three young girls, a working mother, an unstable WWII-marked stepfather and the mother's glamorous sister. Set in Las Vegas in 1950, when everyone is tensely waiting for the forthcoming atmospheric atom bomb test. Careful direction and very good performances (especially by 13-year-old Annabeth Gish as the youngster through whose eyes we see

Mother (JoBeth Williams) comforts daughter (Annabeth Gish) after a fight with her unstable stepfather in the Columbia/Palace release Desert Bloom.

New Yorker Vivian (Helen Shaver) feels alienated in spite of the efforts of Alex McArthur when she arrives at the Reno dude ranch to await her divorce, in Mainline's Desert Hearts.

the mounting drama and whose voice provides the occasional commentary) make this one of the most successful modest movies of its period.

Rest of cast: Jon Voight, JoBeth Williams, Ellen Barkin, Jay D. Underwood, Desirée Joseph, Dusty Balcerzak, Allen Garfield, Tressi Loria, Laura Rasmussen, William Lang, Jim McCarthy, Ann Risley, Rick Scheiffer, Irene Goodnight, Eugenia Moran, Danica Remy, Bruce Weiniger, Armen Dirtadian, Molly Fontaine, Al Petito, Randy Harris, Chris Corr, Fred C. Smith, Steven Mastroieni, Bob Fish, Onna Young, Jesse Sloan, Kiysha Doty, Todd Barish, Sherry Allen, Doris Berman, Reynaldo Villalobos Jr, Judith Gish, Mike Stein, Ray Le Fre, Tamara Cooley, Patty Harbor, J. L. Watkins, Mark Jenkins. Dir and Screenplay: Eugene Corr, based on a story by Corr and Linda Remy. Pro: Michael Hausman.

Assoc Pro: Remy. Ex Pro: Richard Fishchoff. Ph: Reynaldo Villalobos. Ed: David Garfield, John Currin and Cari Coughlin. Art: Lawrence Miller. M: Brad Fiedel. (Carson Pro Group in assoc with The Sundance Institute-Palace Pictures). Rel: floating; first shown London (Barbican, Cannon Tottenham Court Road and Odeon Kensington) 22 May 1987. 106 mins. Cert PG.

Desert Hearts. A very feminine film about a lesbian love affair at a time (1959) when such things were frowned upon. Passion develops between a very much up-tight New York Professor of English staying at a near-Reno dude ranch while waiting for her divorce to come through, and a very outgoing young lady working at one of the casinos. It is all done – by a largely feminine production team – with a lot of sympathy and commendable good taste. Performances are all very good, too.

Cast: Helen Shaver, Patricia Charbonneau, Audra Lindley, Gwen Welles, Dean Butler,

James Staley, Kati la Bourdette, Alex McArthur, Anthony Ponzini, Denise Crosby, Tyler Tyhurst, Brenda Beck, Sam Minsky, Patricia Frazier, Sheila Balter, Tom Martin, Joan Mankin, Audra Akers, Frank Murtha, Dave Roberts, Bob Blanknan, Ron Fisher, Gene Skaug, Donna Deitch. Dir and Pro: Donna Deitch. Screenplay: Natalie Cooper, based on the book *Desert of the Heart* by Jane Rule. Ph and Ed: Robert Elswit. Pro Des: Jeannine Oppewall. M: Robert Estrin, period numbers by Patsy Cline, Buddy Holly and Elvis Presley etc. (Mainline). Rel: floating; first shown London (Screen-on-the-Hill, Cannon Tottenham Court Road and Electric Screen) 1 August 1986. 93 mins. Cert 18.

Distant Voices. Interesting, and in some ways experimental, first feature by writer-director Terence Davies, who reconstructs the story of a Liverpudlian family from their own memories, using time and space in a novel way to achieve quite an impact. Shot in five weeks in London and Liverpool in the autumn of 1985.

Cast: Freda Dowie, Peter Postlewaite, Angela Walsh, Dean Williams, Lorraine Ashbourne, Sally Davies, Nathan Walsh, Susan Flanagan, Debi Jones, Marie Jelliman, Anne Dyson, Jean Boht, Michael Starke, Chris Darwin, Terry Melia, John Thomalla, John Carr, John Michie. Dir and Screenplay: Terence Davies. Pro: Jennifer Howarth. Ex Pro: Colin MacCabe. Ex in charge of Pro: Jill Pack. Ph: William Diver. Ed: Diver in collaboration with Geraldine Creed and Toby Benton. Art: Miki van Zwanenberg, with Jocelyn James. (BFI). Rel: floating; first shown London (NFT) 22 July 1986. 46 mins. No cert.

Dona Herlinda and Her Son – Dona Herlinda y su Hijo.
A homosexual love story-cum-comedy from Mexico about a young surgeon, a young musician and the former's understanding mother.

Cast: Arturo Meza, Marco A. Trevino, Gustavo Meza, Guadalupe del Toro, Leticia Lupercio, Billy Alva, Angelica Guerrero, Donato Castaneda etc. Dir and Screenplay: Jamie Humberto Hermosillo, based on a story by J. L. Paez. Pro: Manuel Barbachano Ponce. Ph: Miguel Ehrenberg. Ed: Luis Kelly. Pro Des: Daniel Varela (Clasa Films Mundiales-Mainline). Rel: floating; first shown London (Cannon Piccadilly) 12 June 1987. 91 mins. Cert 15.

Down by Law.
Following up his first, odd little black-and-white comedy (*Stranger Than Paradise*), which won Festival awards and a cult following, writer-director-producer Jim Jarmusch comes up with another, funnier film, again made in black-and-white and again a highly individual effort. An unlikely trio of jail-breakers land up in an even more unlikely wayside café where one of them (Roberto Benigni – a delightful performance) finds unexpected romance. (Query: that title? It never seems to relate to anything in the film.)

Rest of cast: Tom Waits, John Lurie, Nicoletta Braschi, Ellen Barkin, Billie Neal, Rockets Redglare, Vernel Bagneris, Timothea, L. C. Drane, Joy Houck Jr, Carrie Lindsoe, Ralph Joseph, Richard Boes, Dave Petitjean, Adam Cohen, Alan Kleinberg, Archie Sampier, David Dahlgren, Alex Miller, Elliot Keener, Jay Hilliard. Dir and Screenplay: Jim Jarmusch. Pro: Alan Kleinberg. Ex Pro: Otto Grokenberger, Cary Brokaw and Russell Schwartz. Co-Pro: Tom Rothman and Jim Stark. Ph: Robby Muller. Ed: Melody London. Pro Des: Roger Knight. M: John Lurie. (Island Pictures/Black Snake/

Roberto Benigni and Nicoletta Braschi embrace in Jim Jarmusch's Palace Pictures-released comedy – made in black-and-white – Down by Law.

Grokenberger Films-Palace Pictures). Rel: 16 January 1987. 106 mins. Cert 15.

Duet for One.
Film version of Tom Kempinski's claustrophobic, oppressively dramatic play. Many were surprised when the female lead went to Julie Andrews. Miss Sugar and Spice to play a violinist stricken with multiple sclerosis? Nothing wrong there – Julie Andrews is a fine actress and pulls out all the stops to produce a credible, daunting picture of shattered dignity. The trouble lies in the film's attempt to leave the play behind, to open out the subject matter and to 'aerate' the claustrophobia. In spite of the fine performances (with Rupert Everett particularly memorable as a spoilt musical prodigy), the film leaves one strangely unmoved.

Rest of cast: Alan Bates, Max von Sydow, Margaret Courtenay, Cathryn Harrison, Sigfrit Steiner, Liam Neeson, Macha Meril, Janette Newling, John Delaney, Kevin Ranson, Dorothea Phillips, Marcia Linden, David Miller, Gary Fairhall, Nicola Davies, Pam Brighton, Nicola Perring. Dir: Andrei Konchalovsky. Pro: Menahem Golan and Yoram Globus. Screenplay: Tom Kempinski, Jeremy Lipp and Konchalovsky, based on the play by Kempinski. Ph: Alex Thomson. Ed: Henry Richardson. Pro Des: John Graysmark. M: Michael Linn. (Cannon). Rel: floating; first shown London (Cannons Shaftesbury Avenue and Fulham Road) 6 March 1987. 107 mins. Cert 15.

Dust.
A 'mood' film, a French-Belgian co-production made in English, shot in Spain, with Jane Birkin giving a brilliant performance of the descent into madness of a young woman living with her demanding father (Trevor Howard) on a very isolated farm in South Africa. Seeing her father seduce the young wife of their coloured farm hand disgusts the daughter to the point of murder, the beginning of her slide into insanity. Firmly controlled by ex-actress Marion Hansel, whose second film this is, in its way this is a quite brilliant effort at adapting a (filmically) extremely difficult subject.

Rest of cast: John Matshikiza, Nadine Uwampa, Lourdes C. S. Momoboko, René Diaz, Tom Vrebos, Jean Ackermans, Jean-Paul Bellemans. Dir and Screenplay: Marion Hansel, based on the novel *In the Heart of the Country* by J. M. Coetzee. Ex Pro: Michèle Tronçon. Ph: Walther van den Ende. Ed: Susana Rossberg. Pro Des: Pierre Thevenet. (Man's Films, Brussels/Daska International, Ghent/Flach Films and FR3 Films, Paris in assoc with Ministère de la Communauté Francophone de Belgique and the Ministerie van de Vlaamse Gemeenschap van Belgie-ICA Projects). Rel: floating; first shown London (ICA) 19 September 1986. 87 mins. Cert 18.

Eat the Peach.
Economically budgeted, highly original, completely delightful Irish film, with a warm and winning story about two brothers living in a small border town who suddenly decide, after seeing Elvis Presley's film *Roustabout* on TV, that they will build and operate a 'Wall of Death' and make their fortune with it. But the dream and the ramshackle wall end in smoke.

35

Stephen Brennan and Eamon Morrissey as the brothers who dream about making their fortunes from the ramshackle 'Wall of Death' they build and ride in the delightful Irish-UIP release Eat the Peach.

Beautifully drawn characters superbly played by Eamon Morrissey and Stephen Brennan as the crazy but dauntless brothers with lots of fine support from Catherine Byrne. A real gem of a gentle comedy.

Rest of (excellent) cast: Niall Toibin, Joe Lynch, Tony Doyle, Takashi Kawahara, Victoria Armstrong, Barbara Adair, Bernadette O'Neill, Paul Raynor, Martin Dempsey, Maeliosa Stafford, Jill Doyle, Don Foley, B. J. Hogg, Pat Kelly, Barry Kelly, Edmund Lynch, Jack Lynch, Frank Melia, Liam Sweeney, Ronan Wilmot, Robert Byrne, Mark Shelley, Dick Keating, Jim Reid, Frank Quinlan, John Gallagher, Fintan McKeown, David Nolan, Akiko Hoashi Kobayashi, Snu Miyoshi Hayashi, Patricia Jeffares, David Carey, Chris Dunne, Peter Gowan, Tim McDonnell, Noel Donovan, Stephan Ryan, Charles Winter. Dir: Peter Ormrod. Pro: John Kelleher. Ex in charge of Pro: David Collins. Pro Assoc: Jimmy O'Connor. Screenplay: Ormrod and Kelleher. Ph: Arthur Wooster.Ed: J. Patrick Duffner. Pro Des: David Wilson. M: Donal Lunny. (Strongbow Pro-UIP). Rel: floating; first shown London (Plaza) 5 December 1986. 95 mins. Cert PG.

84 Charing Cross Road. Almost miraculously successful transfer to the big screen of the London stage play (based on the TV production stemming from the published book of letters exchanged over a long period between New York writer Helene Hanff and the owner and staff of Marks and Co., the antiquarian bookseller in Charing Cross Road – now, alas, no more). The small, warm, and at times honestly moving account of a literary relationship (the principals never met) is a perfect example of the way inspiration and craftsmanship can translate the most unlikely material into drama. A shining performance by Anne Bancroft and a beautifully underplayed one by Anthony Hopkins.

Rest of cast: Judi Dench, Jean de Baer, Maurice Denham, Eleanor David, Mercedes Ruehl, Daniel Gerroll, Wendy Morgan, Ian McNeice, J. Smith-Cameron, Tom Isbell, Anne Dyson, Connie Booth, Ronn Carroll, Sam Stoneburner, Charles Lewsen, Bernie

American rare book collector Anne Bancroft in the 1978 Royal Command Performance film choice, 84 Charing Cross Road, *a Columbia release.*

Passeltiner, Michael John Mc Gann, Gwen
Nelson, Roger Ostime, John Bardon, Betty
Low, James Eckhouse, David Davenport,
Max Harvey, Rupert Holliday-Evans, Freda
Rogers, Marty Glickman, Tony Todd,
Kevin McClarnon, Janet Dale, Zoe Hodges,
Kate Napier Brown, Rebecca Bradley, Bar-
bara Thorn, Danielle and Lee Burns. Dir:
David Jones. Pro: Geoffrey Helman. Assoc
Pro: Randy Auerbach and Jo Lustig. Ex
Pro: Mel Brooks. Screenplay: Hugh White-
more, based on the book by Helene Hanff.
Ph: Brian West. Ed: Chris Wimble. Pro
Des: Eileen Diss (London) and Edward
Pisoni (New York). M: George Fenton.
(Brooksfilm-Columbia). Rel: floating; first
shown London (Curzon Mayfair) 24 March
1987. 99 mins. Cert U.

Eleni. A further addition to the spate of
'based on fact' films. This one is based
on the book by *New York Times* investigative reporter Nicholas Gage, about
his long and intercontinental search for
the Greek communistic killer of Cage's
mother: after torturing her, the man
had her executed by firing squad in the
Greek Civil War after WWII. It's an
intermittently absorbing story – understandably biased – which jumps a little
disconcertingly between the Grecian
past (filmed in Spain) and the American
present.

Cast: Kate Nelligan, John Malkovich, Linda
Hunt, Ronald Pickup, Oliver Cotton, Rosa-
lie Crutchley, Glenne Headley, Dimitra
Arliss, Steve Plytas, Peter Woodthorpe,
John Rumney, Alison King, Leon Lisseck,
Alfred Molina, Stefan Gryff, Andrea Las-
kari, Lisa Rose, Claudia Gough, Maria
Alvarez, Anhoula Vraca, Noam Almaz,
Norman Chancer, Leo Kharibian, Arlene
Mazerolli, Michael Zelniker, Keram Malicki
Sanchez, Adrienne Pocock, Anthony Stam-
boulieh, Christiana Fragou, Michael Ches-
den, Miguel Pedregosa, Vic Tablian, John
Eastham, Georgia Clarke, Avril Clark, Athe-
na Voyatzis, Aaron Schwartz, Patricia Car-
roll Brown, Theresa Tora, Lisa Jakub. Dir:
Peter Yates. Pro: Nick Vanoff, Mark Pick
and Nicholas Gage. Asso Pro: Nigel Wooll.
Screenplay: Steve Tesich, based on the book
by Nicholas Gage. Ph: Billy Williams. Ed:
Ray Lovejoy. Art: Steve Spence and Fernando Gonzalez. Pro Des: Roy Walker. M:
Bruce Smeaton. (CBS/Eleni Films Productions-Rank Film Dist). Rel: floating;
first shown London (Cannon Haymarket) 26
September 1986. 117 mins. Cert PG.

Eliminators. Minor science-fiction film
about a part-man, part-robot character
who, like Frankenstein before him,
turns upon his creator and with a small
crew of odd-bods sets out to confront

In Eleni, *a story of the Greek Civil War,
released by Rank Film Distributors, the innocent Eleni (Kate Nelligan) is condemned to
death by a communist commander (Oliver Cotton), while the man she once saved (Ronald
Pickup, at the table) looks uncomfortably on.*

him. Pretty mechanical mix of laughs
and thrills, all set to become something
of a cult movie . . . if it hasn't already.
Set in Mexico, made in Spain, American production.

Cast: Andrew Prine, Denise Crosby, Patrick
Reynolds, Conan Lee, Roy Dotrice, Peter
Schrum, Peggy Mannix, Fausto Bara, Tad
Horino, Luis Lorenzo. Dir: Peter Manoo-
gian. Pro: Charles Band. Screenplay: Paul
de Meo and Danny Bilson. Ph: Mac
Ahlberg. Ed: Andy Horvitch. Art: Gumer-
sindo Andres Lopez. Pro Des: Phillip Foreman. M: Bob Summers. (Charles Band/
Empire Pictures-Entertainment). Rel: floating; first shown London (ICA) 1 September
1986. 96 mins. No cert.

Emma's War. Leisurely paced, gentle
Australian period piece about the four
war-time years it takes for Emma
Grange (a charming performance by

*A picnic for mother Anne Grange (Lee Remick)
and daughters Emma (Miranda Otto) and
Laurel (Bridey Lee) in Curzon's Australian
release* Emma's War.

screen newcomer Miranda Otto) to grow from schoolgirl to assured young lady. Terence Donovan as the official war artist father who is for most of the time away with the Army in New Guinea (and brings problems on his return) and Lee Remick as the wife who misses him a lot, works in a factory and, beset with problems, is inclined to take refuge in the bottle. Lovely Sydney and Blue Mountains backgrounds, extremely ably recreated atmosphere of time and place; in its own particular, somewhat specialized way, something of a minor gem.

Rest of cast: Bridey Lee, Mark Lee, Pat Evison, Donal Gibson, Grigor Taylor, Rebel

Nightclub owner Ray McAnally rewards the winner of a no-holds-barred fight on the premises in the Virgin/Miracle release Empire State.

Penfold-Russell, Noeline Brown, Marvyn Drake, Kay Eklund, Jean Calver, Ashley Grenville, Tara Rajkumar, Jason West, Sky Carter, Annette Charter, David Hannay, Dennis Scott, Normal Galton. Dir, Co-Pro and (with Peter Smalley) Screenplay: Clytie Jessop. Assoc Pro: David Hannay. Ex Pro: Robin Dalton. Co-Pro: Andrena Finlay. Ph: Tom Cowan. Ed: Sonia Hoffman. Art: Jane Norris. M: John Williams. (Belinon Pro-Curzon Film Dist). Rel: floating; first shown London (Curzon Phoenix) 19 June 1987. 90 mins. Cert PG.

Empire State. Coarse, complicated and contrived London East End crime thriller about some very unpleasant characters, all more or less concerned with the corruption and conniving surrounding the plans to develop London's old Docklands. Though it starts promisingly, with some splendid backgrounds,

the film's poor script, indecisive direction, overdone violence, cardboard characters and hammy performances send all the good intentions – and good isolated sequences – down the sleazy drain.

Cast: Cathryn Harrison, Jason Hoganson, Elizabeth Hickling, Jamie Foreman, Lee Drysdale, Emily Bolton, Ian Sears, Jay Simpson, Roger Ashton Griffiths, David Lyon, Martin Landau, Tristram Wymark, Tim Brierley, Lorcan Cranitch, Ian McCurrach, Jenny Bolt, Alan Talbot, Eric Gold, Perry Fenwick, Jimmy Flint, Ray McAnally, Ron Berry, Josephine Melville, Glen Murphy, Debbie Killingback, Stuart Turton, David Rhule, John Levitt, Sadie Frost, Gary Webster, Clare McIntyre, Steve Ausden, Stanford Calaman, James Simmons, Michael Mueller, Ronan Vibert, Melita Clark, Doreen Taylor, Harry Walker, Terry Plummer, Dave Foreman. Dir: Ron Peck. Pro: Norma Heyman. Assoc Pro: Redmond Morris. Ex Pro: Mark Ayres. Screenplay: Peck and Ayres. Pro Ex: Anwar Kawadri. Ph: Tony Imi. Ed: Chris Kelly. Art: Val Wolstenholme. Pro Des: Adrian Smith. (British Screen/Cine-Film (UK(Ltd/Film Four Int/Team Pictures Pro-Virgin/Miracle). Rel: 29 May 1987. 104 mins. Cert 18.

Enemy Mine. Familiar theme – that of sworn enemies forced into mutual respect and finally friendship by having to face up to shared dangers – but this time seen against the less familiar background of a star wars future. Two warplane pilots, one human, the other a creature from the planet Dracon, shoot each other down and then must try to survive on an inhospitable planet. The ludicrous finale is aided by a ton of salt; you could call it 'spatial comedy', with great work from the special effects boys.

Cast: Dennis Quaid, Louis Gossett Jr, Brion James, Richard Marcus, Carolyn McCormick, Bumper Robinson, Jim Mapp, Lance Kerwin, Scott Kraft, Lou Michaels, Andy Geer, Henry Stolow, Herb Andress, Danmar, Mandy Hausenberger, Emily Woods, Barry Stokes, Tony Moore, Kevin Taylor, Colin Gilder, Charly Huber, Ulrich Günther, Frank Henson, Jazzer Jeyes, Dough Robinson, Mark McBride, Balog Menyert, Jack Luceno, Martin Grace. Dir: Wolfgang Petersen. Pro: Stephen Friedman. Ex Pro: Stanley O'Toole. Screenplay: Edward Khmara, based on the story by Barry Longyear. Ph: Tony Imi. Ed: Hannes Nikel. Pro Des: Rolf Zehetbauer. M: Maurice Jarre. (Fox). Rel: 11 July 1986. 93 mins. Cert PG.

Evening Dress – Tenue de Soirée. The controversial Bertrand Blier back

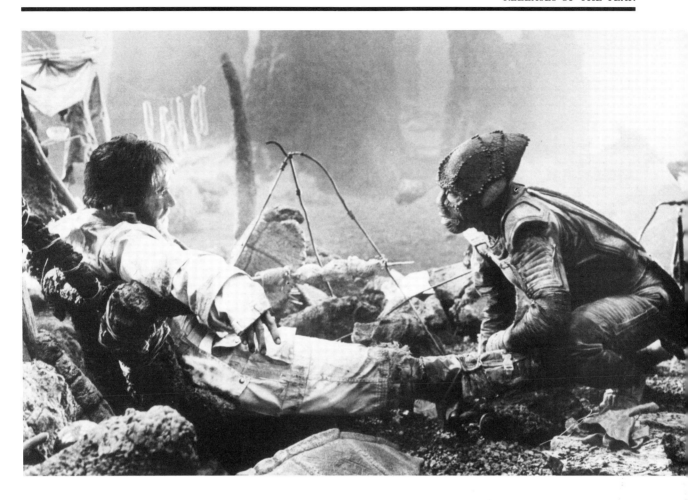

Enemies Earthman (Dennis Quaid) and Drac-onite Spaceman (Louis Gossett Jr) are forced into friendship as they struggle to survive after crash-landing on a hostile planet in Fox's Enemy Mine.

to provocative form in a weird story about a kind of *ménage à trois*, an unholy trio of burglars, two men and girl, whose sexual '*la ronding*' helps add to the effrontery of it all. An acidulous black comedy, the bad taste of which dares you to object. Heretofore roughly masculine Gérard Depardieu is cast as a homosexual and director-writer-star Michel Blanc is his lover.

Rest of cast: Miou-Miou, Michel Creton, Jean-François Stevenin, Mylene Demongeot, Caroline Sihol, Jean-Yves Berteloot, Bruno Cremer, Jean-Pierre Marielle, Dominique Besnehard, Bernard Fracy, Michel Pilorge, Michel Such, Maurice Travail. Dir and Screenplay: Bertrand Blier. Pro: Philippe Dussart. Pro Sup: Jacques Lacour. Pro Con: Michel Choquet. Ph: Jean Penzer. Ed: Claudine Merlin. Art: Theobald Meurisse. M: Serge Gainsbourg (Hachette Première/

DD-Pro/Ciné Valse/Philippe Dussart-Virgin). Rel: floating; first shown London (Screen-on-the-Hill etc.) 29 May 1987. 102 mins. Cert 18.

The Evil Dead 2. Way-out horror piece which is quite a lot of fun, with director Sam Raimi going gaily over the top time and time again and, one feels, having a lovely time doing it. Most of the action – and there's plenty – takes place in a remote cabin: Bruce Campbell battles against the forces of evil who have already got a nasty grasp on the girlfriend (Sarah Berry). For those who won't worry about the lavish use of tomato juice, flying eyeballs and moving severed hands, this is great stuff.

Rest of cast: Dan Hicks, Kassie Wesley, Theodore Raimi, Denise Bixler, Richard Domeier, John Peaks, Lou Hancock, Snowy Winters. And the voice of William Preston Robertson. Dir: Sam Raimi. Pro: R. G. Tapert. Ex Pro: Irvin Shapiro and Alex De Beneditti. Screenplay: Raimi and Scott Spiegel. Ph: Peter Deming (night ph by Eugene Schlugleit). Ed: Kaye Davis. Art: Philip Duffin and Randy Bennett. M:

Joseph Lo Duca. (Renaissance Pictures-Palace). Rel: floating; first shown London (several Cannons) 26 June 1987. 84 mins. Cert 18.

Explorers. Sci-fi fun for junior. Lavishly produced, computerized spectacular adventure of three young lads who, having achieved a home-made DIY spacecraft, set off in it into the high blue yonder, ending up on a planet where the bizarre jelly-baby inhabitants have obtained their ideas about earthlings from the American TV they pick up, with startling results. Once the routine school bullying, classroom confrontations and wet-behind-the-ears romantic dallying is past, and the nitty-gritty space stuff starts, it all becomes fine fun.

Cast: Ethan Hawke, River Phoenix, Jason Presson, Amanda Peterson, Dick Miller, Robert Picardo, Leslie Rickert, James Cromwell, Dana Ivey, Bobby Fite, Bradley Gregg, Georg Olden, Chance Schwass, Meshach Taylor, Brooke Bundy, Tricia Bartholome, Eric Luke, Taliesin Jaffe, Karen Mayo-Chandler, Robert Boyle, John

P. Navin Jr, Mary Hillstead, Simone Blue, Christa Denton, Angela Lee, Deborah A. Paddock, Elaine Pagnozzi. Dir: Joe Dante. Pro: Edward S. Feldman and David Bombyk. Assoc Pro: Tom Jacobson. Ex Pro:

Farrah Fawcett as the attacked housewife who turns the tables on her would-be rapist (James Russo) in Entertainment's aptly titled Extremities.

Michael Finnell. Screenplay: Eric Luke. Ph: John Hora. Ed: Tina Hirsch. Pro Des: Robert F. Boyle. M: Jerry Goldsmith. (Paramount-Blue Dolphin). Rel: 19 December 1986. 110 mins. Cert U.

Extremities. Playwright William Mastrosimone's own adaptation of his successful stage play which is concerned, in essence, with rape and the violent

The three youngsters (l. to r. River Phoenix, Ethan Hawke and Jason Presson) prepare to take off in their DIY spacecraft, in which they visit a planet and meet some very odd characters (above) in Paramount/Blue Dolphin's Explorers.

reactions of both raped and rapist. In this case, the actual rape does not occur but the effects of the humiliation and sexual violence do, and the film is sexually, psychologically and ethically controversial and disturbing. Though the movie always has its stage origin peeping through, it is still highly effective in a voyeuristic way and is well served by the cast, including a surprisingly assured performance as the victim by ex-Charlie's Angel, Farrah Fawcett.

Rest of cast: James Russo, Diana Scarwid, Alfre Woodard, Sandy Martin, Eddie Velez, Tom Everett, Donna Lynn Leavy, Enid Kent. Dir: Robert M. Young. Pro: Bert Sugarman. Ex Pro: Thomas Coleman and Michael Rosenblatt. Line Pro: G. W. Perkins and Scott Rosenfelt. Screenplay: William Mastrosimone, based on his stage play. Ph: Curtis Clark. Ed: Arthur Coburn. Pro Des: Chester Kaczenski. M: J. A. C. Redford. (Atlantis Rel Corp-Entertainment). Rel: 14 November 1986. 89 mins. Cert 18.

The Fantasist. Once again a killer is on the loose, but this time in Dublin, a refreshing change of location if not of subject matter. An educated art enthusiast gets his kicks by stripping women and getting them to pose in the style

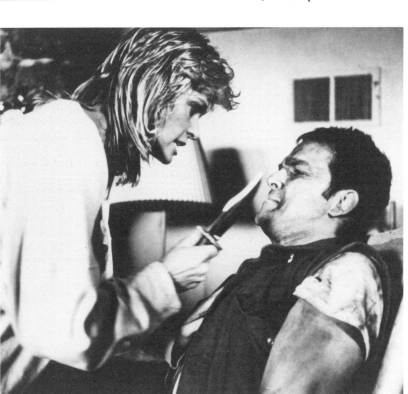

of his favourite painting (François Boucher's 'Louise O'Murphy') – and then knifing them in the back. A whodunit/slasher-movie from Robin Hardy, creator of the cult 1973 film *The Wicker Man*, this is a slow-moving, uncertain thriller that is redeemed by an impressive, assured debut from Moira Harris as the leading lady in distress.

Rest of cast: Christopher Cazenove, Timothy Bottoms (very good), Patricia Teeling, John Kavanagh, Mick Lally, Bairbre Ni Chaoimh, James Bartley, Deirdre Donnelly, Liam O'Callaghan, Ronan Wilmot, May Giles, Se Ledwidge, Gabrielle Reidy, Agnes Bernelle, Seamus Forde, Derek Halligan, Virginia Cole, Sean Rafferty, Pat Daly, Maeloisa Stafford, Ronan Smith, Frank Melia, Derry Power, Charlie Roberts, Des Nealon, Dearbhla Kirwan, Brendan Cauldwell, Michael Duffy, Denise Ryan, Simon Crane, Gerry Alexander, Tony O'Hehir. Dir: Robin Hardy. Pro: Mark Forstater. Assoc Pro: Vivien Pottersman. Screenplay: Hardy, based on the novel *Goosefoot* by Patrick McGinley. Ed: Thomas Schwalm. Ph: Frank Gell. M: Stanislas Syrewicz. (New Irish Film Pro-Blue Dolphin). Rel: floating; first shown London (Warner) 27 February 1987. 94 mins. Cert 18.

Farewell – Proshchanie. Long, indelibly classical Russian film (made in 1981) about the destruction of a village (one of several) in order to facilitate the flooding of a valley where a giant new hydro-electric power station is to be built. Differing reactions to the situation by members of the Pinegin family, ranging from baffled resignation to sad co-operation. Slow, sad and gloomy, with the usual concentration on marvellously patient peasant faces and moments of visual splendour, more especially at the conflagrationary finale.

Cast includes: Stefaniya Statiuta, Lev Durov, Alexei Petrenko, Vadim Yakovenko, Maiya Bulgakova. Dir: Elem Klimov. Pro: A. Razkazov and G. Sokolova. Screenplay: German Klimov, Larisa Shepitko and Rudolf Tyurin. Ph: Alexei Rodionov, Yuri Skhirtladze and Sergei Taraskin. Ed: V. Byelova. Art: V. Petrov. M: V. Artyomov and Alfred Shnitke. (Mosfilm Studios-Artificial Eye). Rel: floating; first shown London (Camden Plaza) 1 May 1987. 128 mins. Cert PG.

Making an impressive screen debut, Moira Harris faces up to the killer in a Warner thriller with an Irish background, The Fantasist.

Fatherland. Ken Loach, the Warwickshire-born director of such gritty low-life films as *Poor Cow, Kes* and *Looks and Smiles,* returns to main feature direction after an absence of four years. Unlike his previous bleak observations of English life, *Fatherland* is a bleak observation of Berlin, and for a large part of the film the dialogue is in German. Still, if Wenders and Herzog can film in English . . . The story, for

German singer Gerulf Pannach gets assistance in his search for father from French journalist Fabienne Babé in Ken Loach's heavily political Palace Pictures Anglo-German release, The Fatherland.

what its worth, is of a political song-writer who is forced to leave East Berlin for the Western sector, and prospects of money and freedom. Disillusioned with writing songs, he embarks on a search for his long-lost father, a classical musician, who defected from East Berlin 30 years earlier. But on every count expectations are disappointed, and he discovers that the only real freedom is in the soul. No doubt a terribly worthy effort, *Fatherland* is so dull that it defeats its single purpose – to enlighten us about the hypocrisy of so-called Western 'freedom'.

Cast: Gerulf Pannach, Fabienne Babé, Cristine Rose, Sigfrit Steiner, Robert Dietl, Heike Schrotter, Stephan Samuel, Thomas Oehlke, Patrick Gillert, Heinz Diesing, Eva Krutina, Hans Peter Hallwachs, Ronald Simoneit, Marlow Shute, Jim Raketa, Bernard Bloch, Winfried Tromp. Dir: Ken Loach. Pro: Raymond Day. Ex Pro: Irving Teitelbaum. Screenplay: Trevor Griffiths. Ph: Chris Menges. Ed: Jonathan Morris. Pro Des: Martin Johnson. M: Gerulf Pannach and Christian Kunert. (Film Four International/Kestrel in assoc with Clasart Film and MK2-Palace Pictures). Rel: floating; first shown London (ICA) 27 March 1987. 110 mins. Cert 15.

Ferris Bueller's Day Off. Writer-director-producer John Hughes, who has made a speciality out of movies about pupils (hmm!) at American high schools, goes once again to the same well. Results reveal that it is beginning to run dry in this story of a rich kid who goes to any lengths to prove to parents and school authorities that he's sick while actually he's having a fun day in Chicago. The tale is told against a heavy beating background of rock numbers.

Cast: Matthew Broderick, Alan Ruck, Mia Sara, Jeffrey Jones, Jennifer Grey, Cindy Pickett, Lyman Ward, Edie McClurg, Charlie Sheen, Ben Stein, Del Close, Virginia Capers, Richard Edson, Larry 'Flash' Jenkins, Kristy Swanson, Lisa Bellard, Max Perlich, T. Scott Coffey, The South Shore Drill Team, Lockport High School Band etc. Dir and Screenplay: John Hughes. Pro: Hughes and Tom Jacobson. Assoc Pro: Jane Vickerilla. Ex Pro: Michael Chinish. Ph: Tak Fujimoto. Ed: Paul Hirsch. Pro Des: John Corso. M: Ira Newborn. (Paramount-UIP). Rel: 13 February 1987. 103 mins. Cert 15.

A Fine Mess. One of Blake Edwards' least successful comedies, far less personal and far more mechanical than most of his better work, this is the story of an actor who overhears a plot by two small-time crooks to dope a horse and tries at his peril to cash in on it.

Cast: Ted Danson, Howie Mandel, Richard Mulligan, Stuart Margolin, Maria Conchita Alonso, Jennifer Edwards, Paul Sorvino, Rick Ducommun, Vic Polizos, James Cromwell, Dennis Franz, Brook Alderson, Key Luke, Ed Herlihy, Walter Charles, Tawny Moyer, Emma Walton, Carrie Leigh, Sharan Lea, Rick Overton, John Short, Theodore Wilson, Valerie Wildman, Larry Storch, C. James Lewis, Robert Hoy, John Davey, Frederick Coffin, Darryl Henriques, Sharon Hughes, Garth Wilton, Castulo Guerra, Sharon Barr, Jack O'Leary, Doug Cox, Elaine Wilkes, Jeffrey Lampert, Jim Byers, Shep Tanney, Danielle Antes, Tamara Barkley, Marcie Dinardo, Dierdre Dudley, Michelle Gerard, Derek London, David Rozier, Jim Sallenbach, Melanie Sims, Pam Stewart, David White. Dir and Screenplay: Blake Edwards. Pro: Tony Adams. Assoc Pro: Trish Caroselli. Ex Pro: Jonathan D. Krane. Ph: Harry Stradling. Ed: John F. Burnett and Robert Pergament. Pro Des: Rodger Maus. M: Henry Mancini. (Columbia Delphi V Pro/Columbia). Rel: floating; first shown London (Cannon Haymarket) 19 September 1986. 90 mins. Cert PG.

Flight of the Navigator. Entertaining Disney film about a 12-year-old Fort Lauderdale lad (played most pleasantly by Joey Cramer) who becomes involved with the 'crew' of a spaceship from another planet. He has a lot of fun in navigating it, but finds things less funny when, landing back on earth, he discovers that while he's still the boy he

Young Joey Cramer approaches the spacecraft with guarded curiosity in the Walt Disney fantasy Flight of the Navigator.

was when he took over the controls everyone else is 8 years older. Good fun for the youngsters, and oldsters with youngster hearts!

Rest of cast: Veronica Cartwright, Cliff de Young, Sarah Jessica Parker, Matt Adler, Howard Hesseman, Paul Mall, Robert Small, Albie Whitaker, Jonathan Sanger, Iris Acker, Richard Liberty, Raymond Forchion, Cynthia Caquelin, Ted Bartsch, Gizelle Elliot, Brigid Cleary, Michael Strano, Parris Buckner, Robyn Peterson, Tony Tracy, Philip Hoelcher, Julio Mechoso, Butch Raymond, Bob Strickland, Michael Brockman, Louis Cutolo, Debbie Casperson, Chase Randolph, John Archie, Tony Calvino, Rusty Pouch, Robert Goodman, Ryan Murray, Keri Rogers, Peter Lindquist, Jill Beach, Kenny Davis, Bruce Laks, Arnie Ross, Fritz Braumer. Dir: Randal Kleiser. Pro: Robby Wald and Dimitri Villard. Ex Pro: Jonathan Sanger, Mark Damon and John Hyde. Screenplay: Michael Burton and Matt MacManus, based on a story by Mark H. Baker. Co-Pro: David Joseph. Co-Ex Pro: Malcolm Harding. Ph: James Glennon. Ed: Jeff Gourson. Pro Des: W.J. Greber. M: Alan Silvestri. (Disney-UKFD). Rel: 10 April 1987. 90 mins. Cert U.

The Fly. Maybe they should introduce a new certificate category for this sort of movie . . . say 'R' for Revolting? Certainly this David Cronenberg re-make (well, sort of) of the 1958 horror classic is quite disgusting in parts, more especially when after an intriguing start the film dips into such blatant sensationalism that it becomes uneasily amusing. It's all about a scientist whose experiments go wrong and he gradually turns into an enormous housefly – much to the distress of his faithful girl-friend

Sam Shepard, star as well as scriptwriter for the Cannon film Fool for Love *(based on his own stage play) and Kim Basinger as his sister, sharing a forbidden love.*

when she hugs him and knocks his ear off. First-class production qualities and some remarkable work by the special effects department don't stop the nasty sensations when, for instance, a woman gives birth to a giant maggot.

Cast: Jeff Goldblum, Geena Davis, John Getz, Joy Boushel, Les Carlson, George Chuvalo, Michael Copeman, David Cronenberg, Carole Lazare, Shawn Hewitt. Dir and (with Charles Edward Pogue) Screenplay: David Cronenberg, based on a story by George Langelaan. Pro: Stuart Cornfeld. Co-Pro: Marc-Ami Boyman and Kip Ohman. Ph: Mark Irwin. Ed: Ronald Sanders. Pro-Des: Carol Spier. M: Howard Shore. (Brooksfilms/Cronenberg-Fox). Rel: 27 February 1987. 96 mins. Cert 18.

Fool for Love. Screen adaptation of a neatly engineered play by writer-actor Sam Shepard about gradually revealed, incestuous and other complicated relationships seen against the background of a seedy motel on the edge of the Mexican Mojave desert. Fascinating, if

stagily static until the climax, the film is far too long for its own good but splendidly acted, especially by Sam Shepard, Kim Basinger, and Harry Dean Stanton; dripping with dusty and sweaty atmosphere.

Rest of cast: Randy Quaid, Martha Crawford, Louise Egolf, Sura Cox, Jonathan Skinner, April Russell, Deborah Mac-Naughton, Lon Hill. Dir: Robert Altman. Pro: Menahem Golan and Yoram Globus. Assoc Pro: Scott Bushnell and Mati Raz. Ex in charge of Pro: Jeffrey Silver. Screenplay: Sam Shepard, based on his stage play. Ph: Pierre Mignot. Ed: Luce Grenenwaldt, and Steve Dunn. Pro Des: Stephen Altman. M: George Burt, songs written and performed by Sandy Rogers and Billy Joe Shaver. (Cannon). London Rel: 4 July 1986. 107 mins. Cert 15.

Foreign Body. The spirit of the 'Carry On' films *et al* is alive and well and thriving in this obnoxious, embarrassing moral comedy. The story of an unemployed Calcutta Indian making good in Harley Street is less a cousin of *My Beautiful Laundrette* than a stepson of British 1960s comedy at its worst. Victor Banerjee stars as Ram Das, a naive Indian who comes to London to

find his fortune and lose his virginity. Grateful for a job on the London buses, Ram puts his 'photographic' memory to good use, swotting up on library books, and eventually faking his way into a doctor's practice, a high social circle and the heart of the beautiful, aristocratic Amanda Donohoe. Implausible stuff, played over the top; a tragic waste of the talents of Geraldine McEwan, Denis Quilley, Anna Massey and Trevor Howard.

Rest of cast: Warren Mitchell, Eve Ferret, Stratford Johns, Jane Laurie, Rashid Karapiet, Sinitta Renet, Marc Zuber, Janet Henfrey, Ann Firbank, Timothy Bateson, Jack Galloway, Angela Morant, Richard Wilson, Patrick Godfrey, Miles Richardson, Harriet Thorpe, Roy Evans, Peggy Aitchison, John Rogan, Eric Mason, Terry Diab, Neville Phillips, Clive Mantle, Barry Upton, Stephen Rashbrook, Jenny Michelmore, Barrie Rutter, Peter Ellis, Meriel Brook, Peter Forbes-Robertson, Roger Hammond, Paul Rattee, Albert Moses, Edita Brychta. Dir: Ronald Neame. Pro: Colin M. Brewer. Ex Pro: Christopher Neame. Screenplay: Celine La Frenière, based on the novel by Roderick Mann. Ph: Ronnie Taylor. Ed: Andrew Nelson. Art: Diane Dancklefsen. Pro Des: Roy Stannard. M: Ken Howard. (Orion Pictures Corp/Christopher Neame-

Colin M. Brewer Production-Rank Films). Rel: floating; first shown London (Cannon Haymarket), 22 May 1987. 111 mins. Cert 15.

The Fourth Protocol. Slick, polished, attention-holding British screen adaptation by Frederick Forsyth of his convoluted spy thriller, with Russian and British top-brass espionage executives working as much to promote and protect themselves as to defend or attack each other's agent's work. Honest, hard-working and ill-used agent Michael Caine almost single-handedly tries to smash a Rusky plot to explode an atom bomb on an American air base in Britain. Not always easy to follow, and always pretty incredible, but nevertheless very good entertaining cinema, with some neat performances.

Rest of cast: Pierce Brosnan, Joanna Cassidy, Ned Beatty, Betsy Brantley, Peter Cartwright, Sean Chapman, Rosy Clayton, David Conville, Matt Frewer, Julian Glover, Michael Gough, Jerry Harte, John Horsley, Michael J. Jackson, Philip Jackson, Ray McAnally, Matthey Marsh, Alan North, James Older, Ronald Pickup, George Phillips, Ian Richardson, Anton Rodgers, Jiri Stanislav, Aaron Swartz, Octavia Verdin, Caroline Blakiston, Joseph Brady, Johnny Allan, Roy Alon, Michael Bilton, Sarah Bullen, Rebecca Burrill, Cyril Conway, Nancy Grane, Joanna Dickens, Sam Douglas, Mick Ford, Ronnie Golden, Steve Halliwell, Gordon Honeycombe, Boris Isarov, Julian Jacobson, Alexei Jawdokimov, Clare Kelly, Sally Kinghorn, Ronnie Laughlin, Renos Liondaris, Peter Manning, Kenneth Midwood, John Murtagh, William Parker, Stephen Persaud, Neville Phillips, Richard Ridings, Chris Walker, Mark Rolston, Michael Seezen, Patsy Smart, Phil Smeeton, Juanita Waterman, Tariq Tunus, George Zenios. Dir: John MacKenzie. Pro: Timothy Burrill. Ex Pro: Frederick Forsyth, Michael Caine and Wafic Said. Screenplay: Frederick Forsyth with George Axelrod and additional material by Richard Burridge. Ph: Phil Meheux. Ed: Graham Walker. Art: Tim Hutchinson. Pro Des: Allan Cameron. M: Lalo Schifrin. (Rank Film Dist.). Rel: 3 April 1987. 119 mins. Cert 15.

The Fringe Dwellers. Bruce Beresford's warmly affectionate and technically faultless adaptation of Nene Gare's Australian best-seller of the 1960s, about an aboriginal family living in a wretched shanty settlement on the

Underneath the Whitehall lamp-post, British agent Michael Caine in the Rank release The Fourth Protocol.

Strong-willed daughter – Kristina Nehm – persuades her reluctant father – Bob Maza – to sign on the dotted line in Virgin's Australian production, Bruce Beresford's The Fringe Dwellers.

fringe of a small Queensland outback town. A story of family fondness beneath occasional friction, with the more educated daughter rebelling against the living conditions and the underlying white man's racial prejudice. Some controversial undercurrents, racial, political and social and some marvellous natural performances from the whole cast. A delightful minor classic.

Cast: Kristina Nehm, Justine Saunders, Bob Maza, Kylie Belling, Denis Walker, Ernie Dingo, Malcolm Silva, Marlene Bell, Michelle Torres, Michele Miles, Kath Walker, Bill Sandy, Maureen Watson, Robert Ugle, Alan Dargin, Terry Thompson, Annie Saward, Dianne Eden, Wilkie Collins, Lisa-Jane Stockwell, Sandra Lehane, Theresa Stafford, Leo Wockner, Wilf Campagnoni, David Glendinning, Noanie Wood, Gabrielle Lambrose, Jack Mayers, Rob Johnston, Laurence Foel, Colin Martin, John McCollon, Kevin Dean, Rita the Wonder Dog. Dir and (with Rhoishin Beresford) Screenplay, based on the novel by Nene Gar: Bruce Beresford. Pro: Sue Milliken. Ex Pro: Damien Noland and Hilary Heath. Ph: Don McAlpine. Ed: Tim Wellburn. Pro Des: Herbert Pinter. M: George Dreyfus. (Fringe Dwellers Pro in assoc with Ozfilm-Virgin). Rel: floating; first shown London (Odeon Kensington) 12 September 1986. 98 mins. Cert PG.

By far the best of the youth-aimed movie releases at Christmas 1986 was Australia's ICA-released Frog Dreaming, *an imaginative thriller with* ET*'s young hero Henry Thomas giving a most attractive performance. Inset: the fearsome apparition that rises from the mysterious tarn.*

Frog Dreaming. Another notable Australian film, this time about, tailored for, and considerably acted by some youngsters; more especially the serious, brainy type who becomes obsessed with the mystery of a brooding, unmapped, forest-set mere – a place of magic for the aborigines – where a fisherman apparently dies from terror and strange apparitions periodically rise from the bubbling depths. It's a first-class atmospheric thriller with wonderful scenic backgrounds beautifully photographed, a lot of imagination in script and direction, in all, something like a more elaborate version of those wonderful old British CFF films. The boy is played by American Henry Thomas who, you may recall, was the boy in *ET*.

Rest of cast: Tony Barry, Rachel Friend, Tamsi West, John Ewart, Dennis Miller, Katy Manning, Dempsey Knight, Peter Cummins. Dir: Brian Trenchard-Smith. Pro: Barbi Taylor. Ex Pro: David Thomas and John Picton-Warlow. Screenplay: Everett de Roche. Ph: John McLean. Ed: Brian Kavanagh. Pro Des: John Dowding. M: Brian May. (Middle Reef Pro-ICA). Rel: floating; first shown London (ICA) 19 December 1986. 93 mins. Cert U.

From Beyond. A – sort of – sequel to *Re-Animator*; a pretty gruesome film that starts with a mad scientist's headless body being found in his laboratory, and goes on from there to log graphically a series of equally unpleasant endings. All the horrid hoopla stems from the scientist's invention, the 'Resonator', which 'stimulates the pina gland' and is the direct cause of either holes in or equally off-putting protuberances from the victims' heads. Ugh.

Cast: Jeffrey Combs, Barbara Crampton, Ted Sorel, Ken Foree, Carolyn Purdy-Gordon, Bunny Summers, Bruce McGuire, Del Russel, Dale Wyatt, Karen Christenfeld, Andy Miller, John Leamer, Regina Bleesz. Dir: Stuart Gordon. Pro: Brian Yuzna. Assoc Pro: Bruce Curtis. Ex Pro: Charles Band. Line Pro: Roberto Bessi. Screenplay: Dennis Paoli, based on the story by H. P. Lovecraft. Ph: Mac Ahlberg. Ed: Lee Percy. Pro Des: Giovanni Natalucci. M: Richard Band. (Taryn Pro/Empire Pictures-Westron). Rel: floating; first shown London (Scala) 5 June 1987. 85 mins. Cert 18.

F/X Murder by Illusion. Complicated, very competent, if puzzling, and generally exciting crime thriller, in which a movie special effects wizard (Aussie actor Bryan Brown) becomes the 'fall guy' in a ruthless plot by some crooked US Department of Justice characters. They are bribed by a gangster boss to free him from the threat of jail, and give him a new and comfy life abroad after his faked death . . .

Rest of cast: Brian Dennehy, Diane Venora, Cliff de Young, Mason Adams, Jerry Orbach, Joe Grifasi, Martha Gehman, Roscoe Orman, Trey Wilson, Tom Noonan, Paul D'Amato, Jossie DeGuzman, Jean de Baer, M'e Dowd, Tim Gallin, Patrick Stack, John Doumanian, Ray Iannicelli, Edward Crowley, Gibby Brand, Jim Elliott, Christopher Curry, James Lovelett, George Kodisch, Jim Cordes, Richard Hayes, Christopher McHale, James Pickens Jr, Michael Fischetti, Angela Bassett, Yolanda Lloyd, Marvin Beck, John McLoughlin, Jim Babchak, Bernie Friedman, Drummon Erskine, Joseph Petangelo, Gerald Campbell. Dir: Robert Mandel. Pro: Dodi Fayed and Jack Wiener. Ex Pro: Michael Peyser. Screenplay: Robert T. Megginson and Gregory Fleeman. Ph: Miroslav Ondricek. Ed: Terry Rawlings. Pro Des: Mel Bourne. M: Bill Conti. (Orion-Rank Film Dist.). Rel: 19 September 1986. 109 mins. Cert 15.

The Gate. Above-average chiller from Canada, about a couple of youngsters who by opening up a hole in the backyard while Mom and Dad are away, also open the door to the nether regions, through which come nasty little creatures and their Demon Lord with the idea of taking over our planet. With its two young leading characters, its careful avoidance of any really repulsive (though brilliantly created) characters, this is almost the nicest chiller to come around for some time – *almost* harmless enough to take the kids along with you.

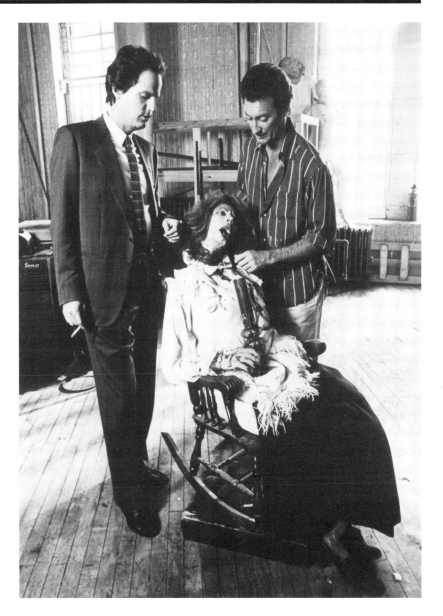

Special effects artist Bryan Brown shows visiting government agent Cliff de Young one of his macabre creations in Orion's FX Murder by Illusion.

Cast: Stephen Dorff, Christa Denton, Louis Tripp, Kelly Rowan, Jennifer Irwin, Deborah Grover, Scot Denton, Ingrid Veninger, Sean Fagan, Linda Govanson, Carl Kraines, Andrew Gunn. Dir: Tibor Takacs. Pro: John Kemeny. Screenplay: Michael Nankin. Co-Pro: Andras Hamori. Ph: Thomas Vamos. Ed: Rit Wallis. Pro Des: William Beeton. M: Michael Hoenig and J. P. Robinson. (Gate Films/Alliance Entertainment-Premiere/Medusa). Rel: 19 June 1987. 84 mins. Cert 15.

Ginger and Fred. Marvellously wrought Fellini movie, decorating a slim plot – about a couple of ex-dancers whose act was called 'Ginger and Fred' and who are lured out of retirement to appear in a big TV spectacular. A bitter, satirical view of TV at its mechanical and superficial worst; beneath the fun is a sadness and nostalgia culminating in the final magical climax: the partners survive their ordeal to win the audience's applause before separating for the last time to go their respective ways. Two magnificent performances from Mrs Fellini (Giulietta Masina) and Marcello Mastroianni surely put the film in line for more than one Oscar?

Rest of cast: Franco Fabrizi, Frederick von Ledeburg, Augusto Poderosi, Martin Maria Blau, Jacques Henry Lartigue, Toto Mignone, Ezio Marano, Antoine Saint Jean,

Frederich Thun, Antonio Ivorio, Barbara Scoppa, Elizabetta Flumeri, Salvatore Billa. Dir: Federico Fellini. Pro: Alberto Grimaldi. Screenplay: Fellini, Tonino Guerra and Tullio Pinelli, based on a story by Fellini and Guerra. Ph: Tonino Delli Colli and Ennio Guarnieri. Ed: Nino Baragli, Ugo de Rossi and Ruggiero Mastroianni. Art: Dante Ferretti. M: Nicola Piovani. (PEA Produzioni Europée Associates, Rome/Revcom Films in assoc with Les Films Ariane, FR3 Films, Paris/Stella Films in assoc with Anthea, Munich/with collaboration of RAIUno-Recorded Releasing). Rel: floating; first shown London (Gate and Cannon Tottenham Court Road) 7 November 1986. 127 mins. Cert 15.

Girl in a Boot – Einmal Ku'damm und Zurück. Based, it seems, on truth, this is an initially amusing, latterly rather sad but generally charming story of the romance between a lively East German girl and the Swiss Embassy's chauffeur. She persuades him to smuggle her across the East-West Berlin border in the official car's boot so that she can sample the delights of the decadent West, but an accident spoils the fun and the romance, as the escapade begets international intervention. A delightful performance by Ursula Monn as the girl won her the Berlin Journalists' Association's 1985 Max Lubitsch Award – and she certainly deserved some sort of accolade for her good work.

Rest of cast: Christian Kohlund, Evelyn Meyka, Peter Schiff, Peter Seum, Brigitte Mira. Dir: Herbert Ballman. Ex Pro: Axel Bar and Franz Thies. Screenplay: Jurgen Engert. Ph: Ingo Hamer. Ed: Hans Otto

Here they are, the good Gobots and their horrid enemies in Entertainment's animated feature for juveniles, Gobots: The Battle of the Rock Lords.

Eddie Murphy rescues the greatly revered young Tibetan religious leader (J. L. Reate) in Paramount-UIP's comedy The Golden Child.

Kruger and Ruth Kusche. Art: Hans Jürgen Kiebach. M: Jürgen Knieper. (Cinecom GmBH/Neue Filmproduction Berlin/Sender Fries, Berlin-Cannon Film Dist.). Rel: floating; first shown London (Cannon Premier) 28 September 1986. 96 mins. Cert PG.

Gobots: The Battle of the Rock Lords. Technically and storywise a superior animated feature based on the American TV series *Challenge of the Gobots*. The good Gobots come to the aid of the oppressed Rock People and topple their enemies (the horrid Rock Lords and their renegade Gobots allies). Aimed by the Hanna-Barbera animators at children, but any adults who go along with them should find plenty of simple fun too.

With the voices of Margot Kidder, Roddy McDowall, Michael Nouri, Telly Savalas, Arthur Burghardt, Ike Eisenmann, Bernard Erhard, Marilyn Lightstone, Morgan Paul, J ou Richards, Leslie Speights, Frank Welker, Dick Gautier, Foster Brooks, Michael Bell, Ken Campbell, Philip Lewis Clarke, Peter Cullen, Darryl Hickman, B. J. Ward, Kelly Ward, Kirby Ward. Dir: Ray Patterson, Don Lusk and Alan Zaslove. Pro: Kay Wright. Ex Pro: William Hanna and Joseph Barbera. Co-Ex Pro: Joe Taritero. Ex in charge of Pro: Jayne Barbera and Jean MacCurdy. Sup Anim Dir: Paul Sabella. Pro Sup: Bob Marples. Screenplay: Jeff Segal. Sup Ed: Larry C. Cowan. M: Hoyt Curtin. (Hanna Barbera/Tonka Corp in assoc with Cuckoo's Nest Studio and Wang Film Pro-

Entertainment). Rel: floating; first shown London (Cannon Oxford Street) 17 October 1986. 74 mins. Cert U.

The Golden Child. Eddie Murphy, below his best form, in an odd little film which is something of a mish-mash of Eastern mysticism, magical special effects, romance, kung-fu exercises and more. The story is about a Tibetan youngster apparently sent from Heaven(?) to be the new Christ and solve all the world's ills, and who is saved from the handsome devil's devices by heroic American social worker Murphy. Real weird!

Rest of cast: Charles Dance, Charlotte Lewis, Randall 'Tex' Cobb, James Hong, Shakti, Tau Logo, J. L. Reate, Tiger Chung Lee, Pons Maar, Peter Kwong, Wally Taylor, Eric Douglas, Charles Levin, Kenneth 'Fruity' Frith Jr, Bennett Ohta, Kinko Tsubouchi, Govind Chipalu, Chantara Nop, Phok Ok, Bob Tzudiker, Cliffy Magee, Jeff Soo Hoo, Bindra Joshi, Judy Hudson, Ron Packham, Marilyn Schreffler, Frank Welker, Victor Wong. Dir: Michael Ritchie. Pro: Edward S. Feldman and Robert de Wachs. Assoc Pro: Gordon A. Webb. Ex-Pro: Richard Tienken and Charles R. Meeker. Screenplay: Dennis Feldman. Co-Pro: Feldman. Ph: Donald E. Thorin. Ed: Richard A. Harris and Bill Kimberlin. Pro Des: J. Michael Riva. M: Michael Colombier. (Feldman/Meeker in assoc with Eddie Murphy Pro-UIP). Rel: 24 January 1987. 94 mins. Cert PG.

Golden Eighties. Chantal Ackerman's stylized Franco-Belgian-Swiss musical which, while below the standard, reminds one inevitably of those classic old Jacques Demy movies. Whereas Demy's work was light and charming, Ackerman introduces an almost savage, satirical bite into the story and (often sexually explicit) lyrics. Set in a shopping arcade, from which it moves only momentarily at the end, the film presents love in the 1980s as a hard and ruthless business, a superficial frill of life, easily interchangeable – a far cry from Demy's romantic characters. Imaginatively produced, effectively staged and well presented by a cast in which Delphine Seyrig shines out as bright and warmly human.

Rest of cast: Nicolas Tronc, John Berry, Lio, Fanny Cottençon, Charles Denner, Jean-François Belmer, Myriam Boyer, Pascale Salkin. Dir: Chantal Akerman. Pro: Martine Marignac. Screenplay: Ackerman, Pascal Bonitzer, Henry Bean, Jean Gruault and Leora Barish. Ph: Gilberto Azevedo and Luc Benhamou. Ed: Francine Sandberg. Art: Serge Marzolff. M: Marc Hérouet. (La Cecilia/Paradise Films/Limbo Films-Electric Pictures). Rel: floating; first shown London (Everyman) 27 March 1987. 92 mins. No cert.

The Good Father. Small, multilayered, sardonically amusing British film about the break-up of two marriages, and the fights for child custody which, apart from its disillusioning look at the British legal profession and its workings, offers the interesting suggestion that sometimes it is the advent of a first child that starts the marital rot. And that the subsequent legal battle for the offspring is often more important to one of the bitter contestants than the child. Brilliant performances by Anthony Hopkins and Jim Broadbent as the contrasting angry and rueful dads.

Rest of cast: Harriet Walter, Frances Viner, Simon Callow, Miriam Margolies, Joanne Whalley, Michael Byrne, Jennie Stoller, Johanna Kirby, Stephen Fry, Clifford Rose, Chris Bradshaw, Harry Grubb, Tom Jamieson. Dir: Mike Newell. Pro: Ann Scott. Screenplay: Christopher Hampton, based on the novel by Peter Prince. Ph: Michael Coulter. Ed: Peter Hollywood. Art: Alison Stewart-Richardson. Pro Des: Adrian Smith. M: Richard Hartley. (Greenpoint Films-Mainline Pictures). Rel: 3 October 1986. 90 mins. Cert 15.

The Good Fight. Feature documentary relating a little known page of history: about the Abraham

Anthony Hopkins as The Good Father *in the Mainline British film of that title.*

Lincoln Brigade, who fought a pretty hopeless but gallant battle against Franco's well-trained troops in the Spanish Civil War, then came home – those who were left, about half the original 3,200 – to face hostility and the fact that, branded as communists, they were unable to get work. It's as brave a film in its ironic and hard-hitting way as were the unfortunates who fought and often died in a lost cause.

Dir, Pro and Ed: Noel Buckner, Mary Dore and Sam Sills. Narrated by Studs Terkel. Made on 16mm film in colour and black-and-white. (Contemporary). Rel: floating; first shown London (Rio) 8 May 1987. 80 mins. No cert.

Good to Go. A latecomer to the by now almost deceased Go-Go dance-music cycle, presenting Art Garfunkel as a tippling reporter who for the sake of a badly wanted story allows himself to be framed. It's the music that comes out top, if you like that kind of music.

Rest of cast: Robert Doqui, Harris Yulin, Reginald Daughtry, Richard Brooks, Paula Davis, Richard Bauer, Michael White, Hattie Winston, Fred Braithwaite, Roderick Garr, Winston Jackson, Eric Delums, Terry Barnes, Chuck Byrd, Leslie Ross, Arthur Dailey, Albert Butler, Roosevelt Littlejohn, Linda Gravatt, Sid Bernstein, Gino Sullivan, Annie Allman, Mark Rowen, Guy Louthan, Kim Brown, Isabel Monk, Steve Blake, Laura White, Michelle Curtis, Anjelica Huston, Arthur Kay, Byron West, Franklyn Bullard, Bill Polk, Ron Canada, Joseph Pinkney, Cornell Williams, Ron Downing, Sergeant James Hunt, Bob Rafferty, Gray Kooritzky, Max Kidd. Dir and Screenplay: Blaine Novak. Pro: Douglas Dilge and Sean Ferrer. Ex Pro: Chris Blackwell and Jeremy Thomas. Ph: Peter Sinclair. Ed: Gib Jaffe, Kimberly Logan and D. C. Stringer. Art: Ron Downing. M Pro: Rob Fraboni. (Island Alive-Recorded Releasing). Rel: floating; first shown London (several Cannons) 3 October 1986. 89 mins. Cert 15.

Gothic. Britain's foremost filmic *enfant terrible*, Ken Russell, does it again in a movie which is a mixture of good ideas never developed, hysterical action, visual overkills (skulls, maggots, etc.) overlaid with large slices of ham, as Byron, Shelley and sundry others run up and down dim corridors, uttering shrieks, while outside the thunder and lightning never stop. This, suggests our Ken, tongue surely in cheek, was the night Frankenstein was born. And it does take talent to make all this drift into final boredom.

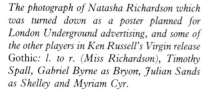

The photograph of Natasha Richardson which was turned down as a poster planned for London Underground advertising, and some of the other players in Ken Russell's Virgin release Gothic: l. to r. (Miss Richardson), Timothy Spall, Gabriel Byrne as Bryon, Julian Sands as Shelley and Myriam Cyr.

Cast: Gabriel Byrne, Julian Sands, Natasha Richardson, Myriam Cyr, Timothy Spall, Andreas Wisniewski, Alec Mango, Dexter Fletcher, Pascal King, Tom Hickey, Linda Coggin, Kristine Landon-Smith, Chris Chappell, Mark Pickard, Kiran Shah, Christine Newby, Kim Tillesley. Dir: Ken Russell. Pro: Penny Corke. Ex Pro: Al Clark and Robert Devereux. Screenplay: Stephen Volk. Ph: Mike Southon. Ed: Michael Bradsell. Pro Des: Christopher Hobbs. M: Thomas Dolby. (Virgin). Rel: floating; first shown London (Lumière) 27 February 1987. 87 mins. Cert 18.

The Green Ray – Le Rayon Vert. Another in his 'Comedies and Proverbs' series and a fascinating 'talk' film from Eric Rohmer. A slim story about a restless, unfulfilled, shy girl and her initially unhappy but finally more satisfactory *vacances* (she keeps going off to mountain or sea, only to change her mind and return almost immediately to Paris), this meanders along, taking time off to discuss such subjects as vegetarianism (a wonderful sequence) and the reason why an old Parisian taxi-driver doesn't take a holiday (with a lot of ex-tempore dialogue). As ever, the literate Rohmer, with his usual subtle-

ty, makes his thin material endlessly absorbing in a way few other directors working in the cinema could achieve.

Cast: Marie Rivière, Vincent Gauthier; (in Paris) Amira Chemakhi, Sylvie Richez, Lisa Hérédia, Basile Gervaise, Virginie Gervaise, René Hernandez, Claude and Alaric Jullien, Dominique, Laetitia and Isabelle Rivière, Béatrice Romand, Rosette and Marcello Pezzutto and Irène Skobline; (in Cherbourg) Eric Hamm, Gérard and Julie Quéré, Huger Foote, Brigitte Poulain, Gérard, and Liliane and Vanessa Leleu; (in La Plagne) Michel Labourre and Paulo; (in Biarritz) Marie Couto-Palos, Isa Bonnet, Yve Doyhamboure, Dr Friedrich Gunther, Paulette Christlein, Carita, Marc Vivas, Joël Comarlot and Vincent Gauthier. Dir and (with Marie Rivière) Screenplay: Eric Rohmer. Pro: Margaret Ménégoz. Ph: Sophie Maintigneux. Ed: Marie-Luisa Garcia. M: Jean-Louis Valero. (Les Films de Losange-Artificial Eye). Rel: floating; first shown London (Chelsea and Renoir cinemas) 13 March 1987. 98 mins. Cert PG.

Gung Ho. Comedy-farce about a Japanese firm taking over a failed American motor-car plant, with whatever fun to be had in the contrast between dedicated Orientals and slaphappy, less caring American workforce, ending up after routine friction in a happy-ever-after, mutually acceptable compromise. Too long and too predictable to be really successful, though Michael Keaton as the 'man between' gives his (funny) all to keep things going.

Rest of cast: Gedde Watanabe, George Wendt, Mimi Rogers, John Turturro, Soh

Yamamura, Sab Shimono, Rick Overton, Clint Howard, Jihmi Kennedy, Michelle Johnson, Rodney Kageyama, Rance Howard, Patti Yasutake, Jerry Tondo, Dennis Sakamoto, Stanford Egi, Martin Ferrero, James Ritz, Dock P. Ellis Jr, Richard M. McNally, Jean Speegle, Thomas Ikeda, Noboru Kataoka, Mariye Inouye, Juhachiro Takada, Linda Carola, Jun Lyle Kamesaki, Tamie Saiki, Charlie Samaha, Nann Mogg, Paul C. Nolan, R. Scott Peck, Josef Pilato, W. S. Bartman, Tommy La Fitte, James Cash, Kim Chan, Bill Dalzell, Tak Kubota, Frank Seals, Maria Barney, Neil A. Machlis. Dir and Ex Pro: Ron Howard. Pro: Tony Ganz and Deborah Blum. Assoc Pro: J. R. Lloyd, Lowell Ganz and Babaloo Mandel. Screenplay: Ganz and Mandel, based on a story by Blum, Ganz and Mandel. Ph: Don Peterman. Ed: Daniel Hanley and Michael Hill. Art: J. G. Taylor. Pro Des: James Schoppe. M: Thomas Newman. (Paramount-UIP). Rel: floating; first shown London (Plaza) 5 June 1987. 112 mins. Cert PG.

Half Life. Powerful, accusatory Australian documentary about the unfortunate native inhabitants of the Marshall Islands who were subjected by the Americans to the varying effects of some 66 nuclear bomb test explosions, including the first hydrogen bomb in 1954. These had horrific effects on the islanders and led to still-born monsters and the many misshapen and deformed adults of today. It is a record of broken official promises, excuses and lies, a formidable indictment both pictorial and oral which leaves you wondering why, if it is all true, it hasn't long since caused an international uproar.

Dir, Pro, Ph and Screenplay: Dennis O'Rourke. Ed: Tim Litchfield. (O'Rourke and Associates Filmmakers-The Other Cinema). Rel: floating; first shown London (Metro) 11 July 1986. 86 mins. Cert PG.

Half Moon Street. The sort of movie one can understand someone wanting to make – an adaptation of the Paul Theroux book *Dr Slaughter* – but can't understand their not making a better job of it than here. Sigourney Weaver is the attractive researcher who spins out her meagre grant by joining an escort agency and is soon deeply involved with a terrorist target, the fascinating milord (Michael Caine), the pair of them surviving to make a romantic fadeout.

Rest of cast: Patrick Kavanagh, Faith Kent, Ram John Holder, Keith Buckley, Annie Hanson, Patrick Newman, Niall O'Brien, Nadim Sawalha, Vincent Lindon, Muriel Villiers, Michael Elwyn, Ninka Scott, Jaspar Jacob, Donald Pickering, Maria Aitken, Hossein Karinbeik, Anita Edwards, Angus MacInnes, John Sinclair, Eiji Kusuhara, Togo Igawa, Rupert Vansittart, Anne Lambton, Judy Liebert, Brian Hawksley, Dulice Liecier, Judy Maynard, Andy Lucas, Haluk Bilginer, Dave Duffy, Kevork Malikyan, Philip Whitchurch, Hugo de Vernier,

Mac McDonald, Robert Lee, Andrew Seear, Janet McTeer, Rosemary McHale, Carol Cleveland, Katherine Schofield, Siobhan Redmond, Claude Villiers, Robert Guillermet, Joy Lemoine, Timothy Peters, Frank Henson, Steve James, Eddie Powell. Dir: Bob Swaim. Pro: Geoffrey Reeve. Assoc Pro: John Davis. Ed Pro: E. R. Pressman and David Korda. Screenplay: Swaim and Edward Behr, based on the novel *Dr Slaughter* by Paul Theroux. Pro Sup: Tom Sachs. Pro Co-Ord: Linda Rabin. Ph: Peter Hannan. Ed: Richard Marden. Art: Peter Williams. Pro Des: Anthony Curtis. M: Richard Harvey. (Geoff Reeve Enterprises for RKO Radio in assoc with Showtime/Movie Channel-Rank Dist.). Rel: 29 May 1987. 89 mins. Cert 18.

Hannah and Her Sisters. One of Woody Allen's major successes, achieving more – in terms of Bergmanesque philosophic thought – than his pretentious *Interiors* but doing it with a marvellous mixture of uproariously funny comedy, wry comment on the human condition and, at times, quite moving sisterly situations. Hannah and her sisters are on the fringe of New York artistic life. Allen gives us their husbands, love affairs and romantic ups and downs over a three-year period, from one annual Thanksgiving get-together to another; and his own hypochondriac, desperately faith-seeking character is both a gem of farcical comedy and shrewd observation of the human condition. Sparkling performances from Mia Farrow, Dianne Wiest, Carrie Fisher and Barbara Hershey as the sisters, a sad one by the late Lloyd Nolan as their dad and a subdued one by the possibly miscast Michael Caine.

Rest of cast: Maureen O'Sullivan, Daniel Stern, Max von Sydow, Sam Waterston, Lewis Black, Julia Louis-Dreyfus, Christian Clemenson, Julie Kavner, J. T. Walsh, John Turturro, Rusty Magee, Allen DeCheser, Artie DeCheser, Ira Wheeler, Richard Jenkins, Tracy Kennedy, Fred Melamed, Benno Schmidt, Joanna Gleason, Maria Chiara, Stephen De Fluiter, The 39 Steps Rock Band, Bobby Short, Rob Scott, Beverly Peer, Daisy Previn, Moses Farrow, Paul Bates, Carrotte and Mary Pappas, Bernie

One of Woody Allen's best films, the Rank release Hannah and Her Sisters, *co-starred him with four lovely ladies, as the sisters, three of whom (inset) were (l. to r.) Mia Farrow, Barbara Hershey and Dianne Wiest.*

A less than merry wedding reception in the Rank British film Haunted Honeymoon. *Newlyweds Gilda Radner and Gene Wilder are bottom left and right; others you may or may not recognize include Dom DeLuise (top, in drag).*

Leighton, Ken Costigan, Helen Miller, Leo Postrel, Susan Gordon-Clark, William Sturgis, Daniel Haber, Verna O. Hobson, John Doumanian, Fletcher Previn, Irwin Tenenbaum, Amy Greenhill, Dickson Shaw, Marje Sheridan, Ivan Kronenfeld. Dir and Screenplay: Woody Allen. Pro: Robert Greenhut. Assoc Pro: Gail Sicilia. Ex Pro: Jack Rollins and Charles H. Joffe. Ph: Carlo di Palma. Ed: Susan E. Morse. Pro Des: Stuart Wurtzel. M: a marvellously nostalgic collection of old numbers like 'You Made Me Love You' superbly arranged and played. (Orion-Rank). Rel: 29 August 1986. 107 mins. Cert 15.

Harem. English-speaking French romance which slowly unveils an unlikely story: one of those oil-rich sheiks drugs and abducts a girl in New York and adds her to his desert kingdom harem, where, at first rebellious, she soon accepts her lot, embarking on an affair with her captor which is always des-tined for a sad, romantic ending. Pulp fiction stuff against fascinating, beautifully photographed background, with Ben Kingsley as the aesthetic sheik and Nastassja Kinski as the girl.

Rest of cast: Dennis Goldson, Zohra Segal, Michel Robin, Juliette Simpson, Rosanne Katon, Maurice Lamy, Norman Chancer, Henry Sarde, Yaron Yaltan, Nadim Sawalha, Ibrahim Moussa, Bill Dunn, Jürgen Osterloh, Michael Morris, Guy Matchoro, Teco Celio, Myriam Tadesse, Karen Bowell, Daniel Emilfork, Maria Kaushan, Kamel Cehrif, Jack Davidson, Charmagne Eckert, A. Khelloufe. Dir: Arthur Joffe. Pro: Alain Sarde. Screenplay: Joffe and Tom Rayfiel, based on a story by Joffe. Ph: Pasqualino de Santis. Ed: Françoise Bonnot and Dominique Martin. Sup Ed: Ruggiero Mastroianni. Pro Des: Alexandre Trauner. M: Philippe Sarde. (Sara Films-Cannon). Rel: floating; first shown London (Cannon Shaftesbury Avenue) 12 December 1986. 97 mins. Cert 15.

Haunted Honeymoon. Typically wild Gene Wilder comedy (with Gene as co-scripter, director and star) in which he takes the familiar Old Dark House formula and wrings every possible laugh from it with mildly amusing re-sults. It's at least fast, furious and farcically well acted, with Wilder scoring top honours, though especially good support comes from Gilda Radner, Bryan Pringle and Ann Way. Something of a hybrid in that, although the setting is strictly American, the film was made in Britain.

Rest of cast: Dom DeLuise, Jonathan Pryce, Paul Smith, Peter Vaughan, Roger Ashton-Griffiths, Jim Carter, Eve Ferret, Julann Griffin, Jo Ross, Will Keaton, Don Fellows, Lou Hirsch, Christopher Muncke, Bill Bailey, David Healy, Howard Swinson, Edward Wiley, Andrea Browne, Matt Zimmerman, Francis Drake, Mac McDonald, William Hootkins, Barbara Rosenblat, Jon Bloomfield, Colin Bruce, Sally Osborn, Alastair Haley, Andy Ross, Svampi the Dog. Dir: Gene Wilder. Pro: Susan Ruskin. Asso Pro: Basil Rayburn and Emile Buyse. Screenplay: Wilder and Terence Marsh. Ph: Fred Schuler. Ed: Christopher Greenbury. Pro Des: Terence Marsh. M: John Morris. (Rank Film Dist.). Rel: 17 April 1987. 83 mins. Cert PG.

Heartbreak Ridge. Star and director, and producer too, Clint Eastwood triumphs over some very dodgy material; the all-too-familiar jingoistic story of a bunch of rag-tag recruits (in this case to the elite US Marine Corps) who are eventually knocked into highly efficient combat shape (for the Granada adventure) by Korea and Vietnam battle-honed Sergeant Clint, in the final phase of his martial career but to the end serving those stars and stripes faithfully and well in spite of military and personal problems.

Rest of cast: Marsha Mason, Everett McGill, Moses Gunn, Eileen Heckart, Bo Svenson, Boyd Gaines, Mario van Peebles, Arlen Dean Snyder, Vincent Irizarry, Ramon Franco, Tom Villard, Mike Gomez, Rodney Hill, Peter Koch. Dir and Pro: Clint Eastwood. Ex Pro: Fritz Manes. Screenplay: James Carabatsos. Ph: Jack N. Green. Ed: Joel Cox. Pro Des: Edward Carfagno. M: Lennie Niehaus. (Malpaso in assoc with Jay Weston Prods/Warner). Rel: 27 December 1986. 130 mins. No cert.

Heartburn. Intelligent, adult, true-to-life and sharply written film version of Nora Ephron's best-selling *roman-à-clef*. Ephron, thinly disguised here as doting wife and mother Rachel Sam-

Magic was created by two brilliant performances from Jack Nicholson and Meryl Streep in Paramount-UIP's Heartburn, *a memorable movie.*

Clint Eastwood as the veteran US Marines sergeant who could knock a platoon of apes into martial shape in Warner's Heartbreak Ridge.

stat, is played to perfection by Meryl Streep in a rare comic (but very real) performance. Jack Nicholson is the egotistical, cheating husband, a character apparently modelled on Watergate reporter Carl Bernstein. The two stars create magic and torment on-screen as Nicholson's extra-marital affair becomes apparent, but they never overshadow an excellent supporting cast, including Milos Forman (who directed Nicholson in *One Flew Over the Cuckoo's Nest*) in his acting debut. Very funny, very moving, very painful.

Rest of cast: Jeff Daniels, Maureen Stapleton, Stockard Channing, Richard Masur, Catherine O'Hara, Steven Hill, Natalie Stern, Karen Akers, Aida Linares, Anna Maria Horsford, Ron McLarty, Kenneth Welsh, Kevin Spacey, Mercedes Ruehl, Joanna Gleason, R. S. Thomas, Jack Gilpin, Christian Clemenson, John Wood, Sidney Armus, Yakov Smirnoff, Caroline Aaron, Lela Ivey, Tracey Jackson, Libby Titus, Angela Pietropinto, Cynthia O'Neal, Susan Forristal, Dana Ivey, John Rothman, Elijah Lindsay, Jack Neam, Kimi Parks, Salem Ludwig, Patricia Falkenhain, Margaret

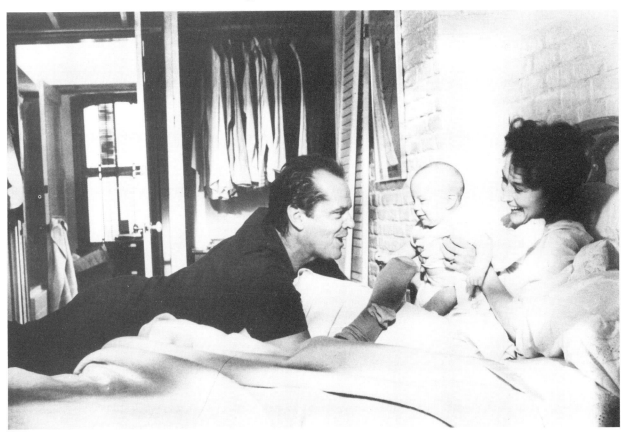

Miracle worker Tom Conti and sceptical girlfriend Helen Mirren in the Recorded Releasing comedy Heavenly Pursuits. *Left: sister Jennifer Black and Father Brian Pettifer conspire to make certain that miracles can and do still happen.*

Thomson, Charles Denney, Gregg Almquist, Garrison Lane, Ryan Hilliard, Dana Streep, Mary Streep, Cyrilla Dorn, May Pang, Michael Regan, Ari M. Roussimoff, Luther Rucker. Dir: Mike Nichols. Pro: Nichols and Robert Greenhut. Assoc Pro: Joel Tuber. Screenplay: Nora Ephron, based on her novel. Ph: Nestor Almendros. Ed: Sam O'Steen. Art: John Kasarda. Pro Des: Tony Walton. M: Carly Simon. (Paramount UIP). Rel: 9 January 1987. 110 mins. Cert 15.

Heavenly Pursuits. Sprawling and only intermittently amusing British comedy – with the fun largely due to Tom Conti's typically warm and winning performance – about a Catholic school teacher whose fall from the roof brings about a reversal of his medically certified fatal cancer of the brain. It carefully skirts the problem about miracles; do they or do they not occur?

Rest of cast: Helen Mirren, David Hayman, Brian Pettifer, Jennifer Black, Dave Anderson, Tom Busby, Sam Graham, Kara Wilson, Robert Paterson, John Mitchell, Ewen Bremner, Philip Maxwell, James Gibb, Grace Kirby, Juliet Cadzow, Jenny McCrindle, Paul Nolan, David McCormack, Ronnie McCann, John Sheddon, Margo Croan, Mel Donald, Sandy Neilson, Monica Brady, Ron Donachie, Jake D'Arcy, David McKail, Bill Denniston, Lawrie McNicol, Billy McElhaney, Jay Smith, Carey Wilson, Robert Carr, Doreen Cameron, Ann-Marie D'Agostino, Christopher Thomas Bryant, Tony Curran, Fiona Chalmers, Louise Duncan, William Fox, John Fraser, Michael Honan, Jeni Maxwell, Sarah Miller, Susan Nisbet, Kate Sandison, Pamela Wright. Dir and Screenplay: Charles Gormley. Pro: Michael Relph. Assoc Pro: Clive Reed. Ex Pro: Ann Skinner. Ph: Michael Coulter. Ed: John Gow. Art: Annette Gillies. Pro Des: Rita McGurn. M: B. A. Robertson. (Island Films in assoc with SKREBA for Film Four International with National Film Finance Corp-Recorded Releasing). Rel: 23 January 1987. 90 mins. Cert 15.

Highlander. Over-long, over-blown, over-loud and over-violent British film which, with its mixture of science-fiction, thriller, romance, period piece and spectacle, ends up something of a mess. Superficially a quite remarkable production and a triumph for the special-effects boys, who create some stunning sequences. The story jumps between 16th-century Scotland to today's Madison Square Garden, centred on some immortals condemned to fight down the centuries until only one is left to take all the power in the world . . . and Christopher Lambert never looks like being fit for the job. In fact, acting honours go to Sean Connery in a supporting role.

Rest of cast: Roxanne Hart, Clancy Brown, Beatie Edney, Alan North, Sheila Gish, Jon Polito, Hugh Quarshie, Christopher Malcolm, Peter Diamond, Billy Hartman, James Cosmo, Celia Imrie, Alistair Findlay, Edward Wiley, James McKenna, John Cassady, Ian Reddington, Sion Tudor Owen, Damien Leake, Gordon Stern, Ron Berglas, Louis Guss, Peter Banks, Ted Maynard, Anthony Mannino, Helena Stevens, Frank Dux, Prince Howell, Anthony Fusco, Ian Tyler, Corrinne Russell, Buckley Norris. Dir: Russell Mulcahy. Pro: Peter S. Davis and William N. Panzer. Assoc Pro: Harold Moskovitz, John Starke and Eva Monley. Ex Pro: E. C. Monell. Screenplay: Gregory Widen, Peter Bellwood and Larry Ferguson, based on a story by Widen. Ph: Gerry Fisher and Tony Mitchell. Ed: Peter Honess. Pro Des: Allan Cameron. M: Michael Kamen, with music and songs by Queen. (Thorn EMI-Cannon). Rel: 29 August 1986. 116 mins. Cert 15.

High Season. Best in this busy, bustling British film are the marvellous backgrounds of the Greek island viewed through the loving lens of Chris Menges. Otherwise more or less routine stuff about an estranged couple (Jacqueline Bisset and James Fox) and their mutual pal (Sebastian Shaw) who is a Blunt-ish spy character.

Rest of cast: Irene Papas, Kenneth Branagh, Lesley Manville, Robert Stephens, Geoffrey Rose, Paris Yselios, Ruby Baker, Mark Williams, Shelly Laurenti, George Diakoyorgio, Father Bassili, Capt. Stelios. Dir: Clare Peploe. Pro: Clare Downs. Ex Pro: Michael White. Screenplay: Mark and Clare Peploe. Co-Pro: Raymond Day. Ph: Chris Menges. Ed: Gabriella Cristiani. Pro Des: Andrew McAlpine. M: Jason Osborn. (British Screen and Hemdale Film Corp/Film Four International/Curzon Film Dist. Curzon). Rel: 29 May 1987. 92 mins. Cert 15.

The Holy Innocents – Los Santos Inocentes. Strongly political 1984 Spanish film which, in its story of a miserably poor rural family of some 20 years ago contrasted with the aristocratic landowners, draws a terribly disturbing picture of the great divide that was (still is?) a part of Spanish life. Significantly, had the film been made in Franco's times, heads would surely have rolled, so bitter and biased is it. Leisurely paced but with some outstanding scenes.

Cast (all notably good): Alfredo Landa, Francisco Rabal, Terele Pávez, Agustin González, Juan Diego, Maribel Martin, Bélen Ballesteros, Juan and Susana Sanchez, Agata Lys, Mary Carrillo, José Guard-Iola, Manuel Zarzo. Dir: Mario Camus. Pro: Julian Mateos and Pablo Nunez. Screenplay: Camus, Antonio Larreta and Manuel Matji, based on the novel by Miguel Delibes. Ph: Hans Burmann. Ed: José Maria Biurrun. Art: Rafael Palmero. M: Antón Garcia Abril. (Ganesh Pro/Spanish TV-Blue Dolphin). Rel: floating; first shown London (ICA) 13 February 1987. 105 mins. No cert.

Home of the Brave. Ear-drum-assaulting, visually weird, wild and wonderful (let's say) 'showcase' for Laurie Anderson as she appears with her rock band, singing and sometimes just speaking her . . . well . . . yes, witty lyrics, all with a cheery smile and assured front. You have to like Miss Anderson to appreciate the movie, which is surely bound for video release.

The musicians: Joy Askew, Adrian Belew, Richard Landry, Dollette Macdonald, Janice Pendarvis, Sand Won Park, David Van Tyegham, Jane Ira Bloom, Bill Obrecht and William S. Burroughs. Dir and Screenplay:

Sean Connery has some advice to offer Christopher Lambert about his forthcoming battle to the death with the evil Kurgen in the Thorn EMI/Cannon release The Highlander.

Laurie Anderson. Pro: Paul Mazur. Ex Pro: Elliott Abbott. Ph: John Lindley. Ed: Lisa Day. Art: Paul Hoberman. (Talk Normal/Warner-ICA). Rel: floating; first shown London (ICA) 19 June 1987. 90 mins. Cert U.

The Hour of the Star – La Hora da Estrela. Much like *The Lacemaker*, *Hour of the Star* chronicles the life of one of the world's undesirables. Macabea (Marcélia Cartaxo) can't type, can't sing, won't wash, and her conversation is limited to what she has heard on the radio. She's also unattractive, awkward and, at 19, sexually isolated, but dreams of being a film star. She also dreams of men but is most happy when she is left to her fantasies and the music of her tinny wireless. A first film from Brazilian director Suzana Amaral, it's a sad fable, leisurely told and laced with many poetic moments.

Rest of cast: José Dumont, Tamara Taxman, Umberto Magnani, Denoy de Olveira, Sonia Guedes, Lizete Negreiros, Maria Do Carmo Soares, Walter Filho, Fernanda Montenegro. Dir and Screenplay: Suzana

Amaral, based on the novel by Clarice Lispector. Pro: Eliane Bandeira. Ex Pro: Assuncao Hernandes. Ph: Edgar Moura. Ed: Ide Lacreta. M: Marcus Vinicius. (Raiz Pro-Contemporay) Rel: floating; first shown London (Everyman) 1 May 1987. 96 mins. Cert 15.

House II: The Second Story. Like most follow-ups, this one is well below whatever entertainment value the original had. The story is about the 'hero' moving into the home of his murdered parents after a quarter-century lapse, and searching for the magical crystal skull believed to be there. This leads to a struggle in some other world between the 'hero' and the evil spirit who also lusts after the skull . . .

Cast: Arye Gross, Jonathan Stark, Royal Dano, Bill Maher, John Ratzenberger, Lar Park Lincoln, Amy Yasbeck. Gregory Walcott, Dwier Brown, Lenora May, Devin Devasquez, Jayne Modean, Ronn Carroll, Dean Clevedon, Doug MacHugh, Mitzi Kapture, David Arnott, Kane Hodder, Susan Isaac, Gus Rethwisch, Gil Birmingham. Dir and Screenplay: Ethan Wiley. Pro: Sean S. Cunningham. Assoc Pro: A. Z. Davis. Ph: Mac Ahlberg. Ed: Marty Nicholson. Pro Des: Greg Fonseca. M: Henry Manfredini. (Entertainment). Rel: 15 May 1987. 94 mins. Cert 15.

Howard . . . a New Breed of Hero (**Howard the Duck** in America). Somewhat hapless and confused sci-fi fantasy

55

Howard T. Duck, the ducky little visitor from another planet, in earnest conversation with pal Tim Robbins in Universal-UIP's Howard . . . A New Breed of Hero.

(from the generally successful Lucas-film movie factory) about Howard T. Duck being suddenly transported by laser malformation from his cosy duck-world in outer space to Ohio on earth, where he finds things very much as they are. Eventually Howard turns hero when he thwarts some nasty thing from OS in its attempts to take over our planet; but he does so knowing that he'll have to stay here for good . . . which, finding himself manager of the Cherry Bomb all-girl pop troupe, isn't all that unwelcome . . .

Cast: Lea Thompson, Jeffrey Jones, Tim Robbins, Ed Gale, Chip Zien, Tim Rose, Steve Sleap, Peter Baird, Mary Wells, Lisa Sturz, Jordan Prentice, Paul Guilfoyle, Liz Sagal, Dominique Davalos, Holly Robinson, Tommy Swerdlow, Richard Edson, Miles Chapin, Richard McGonagle, Virginia Capers, Debbie Carrington, Jorli McLain, Michael Sandoval, Sheldon Feldner, Lee Anthony, Paul Comi, Maureen Coyne, James Lashly, Tom Parker, Ed Holmes, David Paymer, William Hall, Denny Delk, Martin Genapoler, Tom Rayhall, Gary Littlejohn, Thomas Dolby, Kristopher Logan, Reed Kirk Rahlmann, John Fleck, William McCoy, Steve Kravitz, Anne Tofflemire, Marcia Banks, Nancy Fish, Monty Hoffman, Ted Kurtz, Wood Moy, Wanda McCaddon, James Brady, Carol McElheney, Jeanne Lauren, Margarita Fernandez, Felix Silla and Richard Kiley as the voice of the Cosmos. Dir: Willard Huyck. Pro: Gloria Katz. Ex Pro: George Lucas. Screenplay: Huyck and Katz, based on the Marvel Comics character 'Howard the Duck'. Co-Pro: Robert Latham Brown. Ph: Richard H. Kline. Ed: Michael Chandler and Sidney Wolinsky. Pro Des: Peter Jamison. M: John Barry. (Lucasfilm/Universal-UIP). Rel: 12 December 1986. 110 mins. Cert PG.

Hunter's Blood. Or Hunters-turned-Hunted! The tough adventures of a band of hunters who quickly come into confrontation with a group of outlaw poachers who continue to make life threatening for them from then on, so that before they get out of the woods both sides have been depleted.

Cast: Samuel Bottoms, Clu Gulager, Ken Swofford, Mayf Nutter, Joey Travolta, Kim Delaney, Lee DeBroux, Bruce Glover, Billy Drago, Mickey Jones, Bryan Rasmussen, David Deshay, Joe Verroca, Charles Cyphers, Connie Danese, Gene Glazer, Ray Young, Michael Muscat, Burr Middleton, Billy Million, Allen Lerner, Ron La Pere, Billy Bob Thornton, Beverly Schwarz, Nan J. Seitz, Jerry Ratay, Dennis Dorantes, Daniel McFeeley. Dir: Robert C. Hughes. Pro: Myrl A. Schreibman. Assoc Pro: George Springmeyer and Alexander Beck. Ex Pro: Judith F. Schuman. Screenplay: Emmett Alston, based on the novel by Jere Cunningham. Ph: Tom DeNove. Ed: Barry Zetlin. Art: Douglas Forsmith. M: John D'Andrea. (Cineventure-Palace Pictures). Rel: 26 September 1986. 102 mins. Cert 18.

An Impudent Girl – L'Effrontée. Another sensitive, fluent and subtle French comedy about adolescence, showing marvellous rapport between director/writer Claude Miller and his cast; more especially with Charlotte Gainsbourg, who won a French Academy award for this performance. Set in a small provincial town, it's the story of a restless, stormy and irascible 13-year-old who for a moment sees a promise of freedom, excitement and 'life' when she makes friends with a visiting infant prodigy concert pianist, who casually invites her to become her 'manager'.

Rest of cast: Bernadette Lafont (who also won a 'Best Supporting Actress' award for this performance), Jean-Claude Brialy, Raoul Billerey, Clothilde Baudon, Jean-Philippe Ecoffey, Julie Glenn, Richard Guerry, Simon de la Brosse, Luisa Chafa, Cedric Liddell, Daniel Chevalier, Philippe Baronnet, Chantal Banlier, Armand Barbault. Dir and (with Luc Béraud, Bernard Stora and Annie Miller) Screenplay: Claude Miller. Pro: Marie-Laure Reyre. Dir of Pro: Armand Barbault. Ph: Dominique Chapuis. Ed: Albert Jurgenson. Art: Jean-Pierre Kohut-Svelko. M: Alain Jomy. (Oliane/Films A2/Monthyon Films-Artificial Eye). Rel: floating; first shown London (Lumière and Chelsea cinemas) 4 July 1986. 96 mins. Cert 15.

Inspector Lavardin – Inspecteur Lavardin. Claude Chabrol whodunit bringing back the unconventional cop (Jean Poiret) we first met in *Poulet au Vinaigre*. The crime now is the murder in a small seaside town of a much-detested humbug of a Catholic writer, a crime which in the end Lavardin cynically pins onto a shady night-club owner he dislikes, even though he knows the identity of the real, excusable, killer. All rather routine and below Chabrol's best, but still well worth watching.

Rest of cast: Bernadette Lafont, Jean-Claude Brialy, Jacques Dacqmine, Hermine Claire, Jean-Luc Bideau, Pierre-François Dumeniaud, Florent Gibassier, Guy Louret, Jean Depussé. Dir: Claude Chabrol. Pro: Marin Karmitz. Pro Dir: Catherine Lapoujade. Screenplay: Chabrol and Dominique Roulet. Ph: Jean Rabier. Ed: Monique Fardoulis and Angela Braga-Mermet. Art: Françoise Benoit-Mermet. M: Matthieu Chabrol. (MK2 and Films A2 in co-pro with Television Suisse Romande and Cab Pro-Artificial Eye). Rel: floating; first shown London (Chelsea cinema) 2 January 1987. 103 mins. Cert 15.

Invaders from Mars. More or less straightforward re-make of the imaginative 1953 science-fiction film which, though sometimes listed as being made in 3-D, was switched at the last moment to 'flat' film, and in spite of various production squabbles emerged as something of a minor classic in its genre. About the small boy who sees the Martians land over the hill and has a job convincing the grown-ups he wasn't dreaming . . . was he?

Cast: Karen Black, Hunter Carson, Timothy Bottoms, Laraine Newman, James Karen, Bud Cort, Louise Fletcher, Eric Pierpoint, Christopher Allport, Donald Hotton, Kenneth Kimmins, Charlie Dell, Jimmy Hunt, William Bassett, Virginia Keehne, Chris Hebert, Mason Nupuf, William Frankfather, Joseph Brutsman, Eric Norris, Debra Berger, Eddy Donno, Mark Diardino, Daryl Bartley, Shonda Whipple, Shawn Campbell, Roy Mansano, Amy Fitzpatrick, Brett Johnson, Dale Dye, Douglas Simpson, Lenny Low, Scott Leva, Scott Wulff, Frederick Menslage, Michael McGrady, Lawrence Poindexter, J. Acheson, Matt Bennett, Aaron Scott Bernard, Steve Lambert, Debbie Carrington, Joe Anthony Cox, Matt Bennett, Douglas Simpson, Margarite Fernandez, Salvatore Fondacaro. Dir: Tobe Hooper. Pro: Menahem Golan and Yoram Globus. Assoc Pro: Edward L. Alperson Jr and Wade H. Williams III. Screenplay: Dan O'Bannon and Don Jakoby, based on the screenplay of the 1953 film by Richard Blake. Pro Ex: Mati Raz. Pro Co-Ord: Iya Labunka. Ph: Daniel Pearl. Ed: Alain Jakubowicz. Add Ed: Daniel Lowenthal. Art: Craig Stearns. Pro Des: Leslie Dilley. M: Christopher Young. (Cannon Films/Cannon International-Columbia). Rel: 12 September 1986 (at several Cannon and ABC cinemas). 99 mins. Cert PG.

Iron Eagle. Neatly encapsulated by a *Variety* sub-editor as 'I Was a Teenage Rambo', this to-hell-with-it-all action air-fighting thriller, with its amusing dialogue and breathless pace, never lets up from start to finish, telling a quite incredible story about a daring young lad (who just happens to be able to fly a modern warplane) and a veteran combat ace who against impossible odds rescue the lad's hostage dad from what might be a miniature Libya. But by Jingo it's *fun*.

Cast: Louis Gossett Jr, Jason Gedrick, David Suchet, Tim Thomerson, Larry B. Scott, Caroline Lagerfelt, Jerry Levine, Robbie Rist, Michael Bowen, Bobby Jacoby, Melora Hardin, David Greenlee, Michael Alldredge, Tom Fridley, Rob Garrison, Chino 'Fats' Williams, Jay Footlik, Jacquie Lynn Colton, Shawnee Smith, Heather de Vore Haase, Kathy Wagner, Kevin King, Will Jeffries, David Ward, Terry Wills, F. William Parker, Albert R. Schara, Christopher Bradley, Michael Kehoe, Steve Rabin, Kevin Elders, Tony Becker, Paul O'Brien Richards, Lance LeGault, Max Thayer, Debbie Bloch, Roger Nolan, Jerry Hyman, Uri Gabriel, David Menachem, Yossi Shiloah, Itzik Saydof,

Youngster Jason Gedrick enlists the aid of veteran American Air Force pilot Louis Gossett Jr to rescue his hostage dad in Tri-Star's Iron Eagle.

Arnon Zadok. Dir: Sidney J. Furie. Pro: Ron Samuels and Joe Wizan. Assoc Pro: Lou Lenart. Ex Pro: Kevin Elders. Screenplay: Elders and Furie. Ph: Adam Greenbert. Aerial Ph: Frank Holgate. Ed: George Grenville. Pro Des: Robb Wilson King. M: Basil Poledouris. (Falcons Flight for Tri-Star). Rel: 15 August 1986. 116 mins. Cert: PG.

Jake Speed. Poor relation spin-off from the *Indiana Jones* cycle of all-action spectacle movies with Speed (Wayne Crawford) a pretty dumb macho comic-strip hero, in Africa with tagging-along heroine (Karen Kopins), trying to track down and rescue her sister, abducted in Paris by a white-slaver. And it is surprising, to say the least, to find John Hurt mixed up in all this, playing a villainous vice boss with all stops out and no inhibitions.

Rest of cast: Dennis Christopher, Leon Ames, Roy London, Donna Pescow, Barry Primus, Monte Markham, Millie Perkins, Rebecca Ashley, Alan Shearman, Karl Johnson, Sal Viscuso, Ken Lerner, Peter Fox, Ian Yule, Ken Gampu, Joe Ribeiro, Jean Marc Morel, Bernard Crombey, Thys du Plooy, Jason Ronard, Robert Winley, Lisa Lucas, Wendy Stockle, Jean Pierre Lorit,

The comic-strip, two-dimensional macho hero is the title role of the Entertainment release Jake Speed *(no relation!), seen here in one of his many tight corners. Wayne Crawford is Speed.*

Computer wizard Whoopi Goldberg confronts bogus repairer James Belushi in the Fox comedy thriller Jumpin' Jack Flash.

Vincent Nemeth, Etienne Le Foulon, Franz Rutrovsky, Will Bernard, Sammy Davis, Nancy Riach, Ivan Joseph, June Maforimbo, Mark Orthwaite. Dir: Andrew Lane. 2nd Unit Dir: Grant Pate. Pro: Lane, Wayne Crawford and William Fay. Assoc Pro: Rob Milne and Roy London. Ex Pro: John Roach. Screenplay: Lane and Crawford. Ph: Bryan Loftus. Ed: Fred Stafford. Co-Ed: Michael Ripps. Pro Des: Norm Baron. M: Mark Snow. (New World Pictures/Force Ten Pro/Balcor Film Investors-Entertainment Film Dist.). Rel: floating; first shown London (Cannons at Oxford and Panton Streets) 5 September 1986. 106 mins. Cert 15.

A Judgement in Stone. Britain's Rita Tushingham giving an extremely good, caring performance in an otherwise unremarkable film about a British lady who emigrates to the United States, becomes housekeeper to an American doctor and his wife – and murders anyone who makes disparaging remarks about her literary lack! Incidentally, Shelley Peterson, making her screen debut, is in fact the wife of Ontario's Premier; director Ousama Rawi – also debuting – shows his lack of experience from time to time.

Rest of cast: Ross Petty, Jonathan Crombie, Jessica Steen, Jackie Burroughs, Tom

Quiet housekeeper turned killer Rita Tushingham – with worried American employer Shelley Peterson – in A Judgement in Stone.

Kneebone, Peter MacNeill, Donald Ewer, Joyce Gordon, Aisha Tushingham, Gary Krawford, Wanda Cannon, Layne Coleman, Betty Harris, Sean Collins, Julian Coutts, Eileen Williams, Diane Fabian, Sandra Scott, Jaimie Rainey, Jeffrey Neal, Andy Knott, Gordon Kilner. Dir and (with David Pady) Ex Pro: Ousama Rawi. Pro: Harve Sherman. Screenplay: Elaine Waisglass, based on the book by Ruth Rendell. Ph: David Herrington. Ed: Stan Cole. Art: Reuben Freed. M: Patrick Coleman and Robert Murphy. (Rawifilm/Schulz Pro-Virgin). Rel: floating; first shown London (Odeon Kensington and Cannon Chelsea) 6 February 1987. 92 mins. Cert 15.

Jumpin' Jack Flash. Unlike Richard Pryor or Eddie Murphy, Whoopi Goldberg can transform mediocre material into grand entertainment and comes of age with this helter-skelter comedy involving the CIA, the KGB and the anonymous, amorous computerized voice of a British agent. Whoopi plays a computer expert involuntarily involved in a plot as thick as the actress's accent. Sight gags and corpses litter the screen with gay abandon.

Rest of cast: Stephen Collins, Jonathan Pryce, John Wood, James Belushi, Carol Kane, Annie Potts, Peter Michael Goetz, Roscoe Lee Brown, Sara Botsford, Jeroen Krabbe, Vyto Ruginis, Tony Hendra, Jon Lovitz, Phil E. Hartmann, Lynne Marie Stewart, Ren Woods, Tracy Reiner, Chino Fats Williams, Paxton Whitehead, June Chadwick, Tracey Ullman, Jeffrey Joseph, Caroline Durocq, Julie Payne, Deanna Oliver, Carol LaBove, etc. Dir: Penny Marshall. Pro: Lawrence Gordon and Joel Silver. Screenplay: David H. Franzoni, J. W. Melville, Patricia Irving and Christopher Thompson, based on a story by Franzoni. Ph: Matthew F. Leonetti. Ed: Mark Goldblatt. Art: Frank Richwood. Pro Des: Robert Boyle. M: Thomas Newman. (Lawrence Gordon/Silver Pictures Pro-Fox/UKFD). Rel: 1 May 1987. 105 mins. Cert 15.

Just Between Friends. Some top-class performances in a conventional but consistently interesting 'soap' about a perfect housewife (marvellous Mary Tyler Moore, coming up to 50 but looking and acting like someone 20 years younger) who finds that being perfect is not enough to keep her loving hubbie from having a fling with other women. After his sudden death, half-way through the (over-long) film, a stormy but basically warm relationship develops between wife and – pregnant – mistress.

Looking and acting incredibly youthful, aerobatics pupil Mary Tyler Moore in the Rank release Just Between Friends.

Rest of cast: Julie Payne, Beverley Sanders, Salome Jens, Ted Danson, Read Morgan, Christine Lahti, Sam Waterston, Susan Rinell, Timothy Gibbs, Diane Stilwell, James MacKrell, Chet Collins, Castulo Guerra, Mark Blum, Terry Hanauer, Helene Winston, Gary Riley, Leda Siskind, Joshua Harris, Robert Kino, Lisle Wilson, John Terry Bell, Jane Greer, George D. Wallace, Andra Akers, Robert Rothwell, Darwyn Carson, Lewis Arquette, Brigitte and Tiffany Desper, Dorothy Francis, Suzanne Wishner, Jeannie Elias, Christina Kokubo, Leslie Ann Rieder. Dir and Screenplay: Allan Burns. Pro: Edward Teets and Burns. Assoc Pro: James H. Rascoe. Ph: Jordan Croenweth. Ed: Ann Goursaud. Pro Des: Sydney Z. Litwack. M: Patrick Williams. (MTM Enterprises/Orion-Rank Film Dist.). Rel: floating; first shown London (Cannon Oxford Street) 6 February 1987. 111 mins. Cert 15.

Kangaroo. After several abortive efforts, D. H. Lawrence's difficult-to-adapt story reaches the screen as a well crafted, commendably literate Australian movie considerably adding to that country's celluloid prestige. Disillusioned with post-war Britain in 1918, Lawrence goes to Australia and there finds some fine friendships (even if some of them have ambiguous sexual undertones) as he tries to make up his mind whether to join the labour Left or the smooth-talking fascist Right. Eventually, after a traumatic experience when both sides clash in bloody battle, he decides he will return home after all. Finely acted by a faultless cast, especially Colin Friels as the writer and Judy Davis as his German wife.

Rest of cast: John Walton, Julie Nihill, Hugh Keays-Byrne, Peter Hehir, Peter Cummins, Tim Robertson, Malcolm Robertson, David Hutchins, Victor Kazan, Bill Richardson, Alan Lee, Richard Moss, Howard Priddle, Denzil Howson, Roy Baldwin, Ron Pinnell, Geoff Brooks, Bob Butcher, Don Laughton, David Bickerstaff, Christopher Stevenson, Jack Perry, Phil Sumner, Roderick Williams, Steve Payne, Ian Shrives, Nield Schneider, Steve Hutchinson, John Chu, Roy Edmunds, Terry Trimble, John Mortimore, Kerry Bannister. Dir: Tim Burstall. Pro: Ross Dimsey. Ex Pro: Robert Ward, Mark Josem, Peter Sher-

Colin Friels and Judy Davis in Enterprise's Australian import, Kangaroo, *based on the D. H. Lawrence story.*

Yuji Okumoto (left) and Ralph Macchio meet in unarmed combat in Columbia's The Karate Kid, Part II.

man and William Marshall. Screenplay based on the novel by D.H. Lawrence: Evan Jones. Pro Co-Ord: Jennie Crowley. Ph: Dan Burstall. Ed: Edward McQueen-Mason. Pro Des: Tracy Watt. M: Nathan Waks. (Naked Country Pro-Enterprise Pictures). Rel: floating; first shown London (Cannon Haymarket and Odeon, Kensington) 5 December 1986. 110 mins. Cert PG.

The Karate Kid Part II. With KKI having taken something in excess of £30 million at the US box office by the summer of 1986, KKII, even if somewhat below the standard and appeal (strictly to kidpic audiences, of course), seems inevitably bound for a golden harvest. Noriyuki 'Pat' Morita is the best thing in both movies (he won an Oscar nomination for KKI). Here he is called back to his native Okinawa, where he finds plenty of scope to demonstrate his fighting prowess, often in the defence of his pupil Ralph Macchio.

Rest of cast: Nobu McCarthy, Danny Kamekona, Yuji Okumoto, Tamlyn Tamita, Pat E. Johnson, Bruce Malmuth, Eddie Smith, Martin Kove, Garth Johnson, Brett Johnson, William Zabka, Chad McQueen, Tony O'Dell, Ron Thomas, Rob Garrison, Will Hunt, Evan Malmuth, Lee Arnone, Sarah Kendall, Joey Miyashima, Raymond Ma, George O'Hanlon Jr, Charlie Tani-

moto, Tsuruko Ohye, Arsebio 'Sonny' Trinidad, Marc Hayashi, Robert Fernandez, Natalie N. Hashimoto, Diana Mar, Bradd Wong, Clarence Gilyard Jr, Michael Morgan, Jack Eiseman, Jeffrey Rogers, Aaron Seville, Wes Chong, Traci Toguchi. Dir: John G. Avildsen. Pro: Jerry Weintraub. Assoc Pro: W. J. Cassidy, Karen Trudy Rosenfelt and Susan E. Ekins. Ex Pro: R. J. Louis. Screenplay: Robert Mark Kamen. Ph: James Crabe. Ed: Avildsen, David Garfield and Jane Kurson. Art: W. F. Matthews. Pro Des: Cassidy. M: Bill Conti. (Columbia-Delphi 11-Columbia). Rel: 25 July 1986. 113 mins. Cert PG.

The Keep. Michael (*Miami Vice* producer) Mann's legendary rock-*folie de grandeur* . . . collision of visionary images, pulp narrative and Tangerine Dream's thundering, pulsing score. Which might rightly suggest a film that doesn't fit in any usual pigeon-hole. What plot there is, is quickly tossed off the screen as Mr Mann gets down to his series of strange and often stunning images. Obviously of restricted appeal but likely to appeal mightily to the restricted.

Cast: Scott Glenn, Alberta Watson, Jürgen Prochnow, Robert Prosky, Gabriel Byrne, Ian McKellen, Morgan Sheppard, Royston Tickner, Michael Carter. Dir and Screenplay: Michael Mann. Pro: Gene Kirkwood and Howard W. Koch Jr. Ph: Alex Thomson. Ed: Dave Hoenig. M: Tangerine Dream. (ICA). Rel: floating; first shown London (ICA) 2 February 1987. 93 mins. Cert 18.

The Killing Floor. A story of divided loyalties, with plenty of political and racial edge: a reasonably balanced account of a young black from America's Deep South who ups-and-aways during WWI – leaving his wife and family – for the sake of the money to be had up north while a major part of the US workforce is in uniform. He works in the Chicago abattoirs (memories of Upton Sinclair), resisting but being recruited into the Union, finally becoming a militant. When the war ends and the white men come home looking for their old jobs, the seeds are sown for the terrible Chicago race riots of 1919. In this bitter, excellently made film, based on fact, there's plenty of controversial racial and political truth to ponder.

Cast: Damiel Leake, Clarence Felder, Moses Gunn, Jason Green, Ernest Rayford, Alfre Woodard, Miklos Simon, Wally Taylor, Vernon Schwarz, Mary Alice, James O'Reilly, Henryk Derwenda, Patrick Nugent, Dennis Lane, Nathan Davis, etc. Dir: Bill Duke. Pro: George Manasse. Ex Pro: Elsa Rassbach. Screenplay: Leslie Lee, based on a story by Elsa Rassbach adapted by Ron Milner. Ph (black-and-white and colour): Bill Burch. Sup Ed: John N. Carter. Art: Maher Ahmad. M: Elizabeth Swados. (Public Forum Pro-Cinegate). Rel: floating; first shown London (Gate) 13 March 1987. 118 mins. Cert PG.

The Kindred. Familiar sci-fi stuff about the unfortunate results of a deceased lady scientist's genetic experi-

A shot from Cinegate's The Killing Floor, *a strong drama with political and racial undercurrents.*

Sarah (Jennifer Connelly) and friend in the Tri-Star release Labyrinth, *in which a weird-looking David Bowie plays a sort of Demon King who has captured Sarah's baby brother Toby (Toby Frova).*

ments, leading to a pretty nasty mess her son has to try and clear up.

Cast: David Allen Brooks, Rod Steiger, Amanda Pays, Talia Balsam, Kim Hunter, Timothy Gibbs, Peter Frechette, Julia Montgomery, Bunki Z., Charles Grueber, Bennet Guillory, Edgar Small, James Boeke, Randy Harrington, Ben Perry, Betty Freeman, John Farmer, Steve Conte. Dir: Jeffrey Obrow and Stephen Carpenter. Pro: Obrow. Ex Pro: Joel Freeman. Screenplay: Obrow, Carpenter, John Penney, Earl Ghaffari and Joseph Stefano. Co-Pro: Stacey Giachino. Ph: Carpenter. Ed: Penney and Ghaffari. Art: Becky Block. Pro Des: Chris Hopkins. M: David Newman. (Kindred Ltd-Entertainment). Rel: floating; first shown London (Cannons at Oxford and Panton Streets and Edgware Road) 19 June 1987. 91 mins. Cert 18.

Labyrinth. A sort of modern, high-tech spin-off from *The Wizard of Oz* and *Alice* adventures, with Jennifer Connelly as Sarah, the young girl approaching womanhood who determinedly faces the perils posed by weirdo Demon King David Bowie: he kidnaps Sarah's young brother and tells her she must solve the puzzle of his magic maze leading to his curious castle – and must do it quickly – if she ever wants to see

the bonnie babe again. Along the off-putting, muppetty way, Sarah meets and collects some very curious characters, like the hairy monster, the gnome dwarf and the belligerent terrier. Though laughs are rationed, the marvellous technical effects aren't, and the horde of children at a special preview found the movie worthy of final, babelous acclaim.

Rest of cast (including some voices only): Toby Froud, Shelley Thompson, Christopher Malcolm, Natalie Finland, Shari Weiser, Brian Henson, Ron Mueck, Rob Mills, Dave Goeltz, David Barclay, David Shaughnessy, Karen Prell, Timothy Bateson, Frank Oz, Michael Hordern, Denise Bryer, Steve Whitmire, Kevin Clash, Anthony Asbury, Percy Edwards, Anthony Jackson, Douglas Blackwell, etc. Dir: Jim Henson. Pro: Eric Rattray. Ex Pro: George Lucas. Ex Sup Pro: David Lazer. Screenplay: Terry Jones, based on a story by Denise Lee and Jim Henson. Special Effects Sup: George Gibbs. Ph: Alex Thomson. Ed: John Grover. Pro Des: Elliot Scott. M: Trevor Jones; songs 'Underground', 'Dance Magic', 'Chilly Down', 'Within You' and 'As the World Falls Down' composed and sung by David Bowie. Plus hundreds of other cast and technical credits. (Henson Associates/Lucasfilm Ltd-Tri-Star). Rel: 4 December 1986. 141 mins. Cert U.

Latino. Unashamedly biased film concerned with the Central American civil war in Nicaragua between the left-wing

regime, the Sandinistas, and the USA-backed right-wing rebels, the Contras. This is the background for the somewhat lack-lustre personal story about a Vietnam veteran (Robert Beltran) who is assigned to help the rebels but falls in love and gradually comes to see the light as he experiences the bloody excesses of his own side.

Rest of cast: Annette Cardona, Tony Plana, Ricardo Lopez, Luis Torrentes, Juan Carlo Ortiz, Marta Tenorio, Michael Goodwin, Walter Marin, James Karen, etc. Dir and Screenplay: Haskell Wexler. Pro: Benjamin Berg. Assoc Pro: James Beckett. Ph: Tom Sigel. Ed: Robert Dalva. M: Diane Louie. (Lucasfilm/Latino Pro-ICA). Rel: floating; first shown London (ICA) 23 October 1986. 105 mins. No cert.

Legal Eagles. An inspired piece of casting in the presentation of Robert Redford as a highly successful assistant DA who becomes intimately involved with an attractive young woman (Daryl Hannah) who, he is convinced, is not guilty of the murder of which she so obviously appears guilty. Redford's performance helps this comedy thriller into the top bracket, as does lively acting by initially opposing, soon co-operating fellow legal eagle Debra Winger. Maybe the story is convoluted to the point of complete confusion at times, but a lot of the lines are witty,

the pace is rapid, the slapstick touches are deft and the fiery special effects are really hot.

Rest of cast: Brian Dennehy, Terence Stamp, Steven Hill, David Clennon, John McMartin, Jennie Dundas, Roscoe Lee Browne, Christine Baranski, Sara Botsford, David Hart, James Hurdle, Gary Klar, Christian Clemenson, Bart Burns, Bruce French, Lynn Hamilton, Paul Jabara, Chevi Colton, Annie Abbott, Kristine Sutherland, Everett Quinton, Peter Boyden, Thomas Barbour, Mary Alison Griffin, Vincent Guastaferro, Burke Byrnes, Ken Kliban, Debra Stricklin, Ron Foster, Rudy Will-

Legal Eagles Debra Winger and Robert Redford get together to try to prove that, contrary to the evidence, Darryl Hannah (left) isn't a murderess in the Universal-UIP release.

rich, Robery Benedetti, Grant Heslov, Robert Curtis Brown, Brian Doyle-Murray, Shannon Wilcox, Charles Brown, Kevin Hagan, Jay Thomas, Alex Nevil, Lou Cutell, Olivia Ward, Duitch Helmer, John Marion, Barbara Pallenberg, Gabrielle De-Cuir, Liz Sheridan, Michael Anthony. Dir and Pro: Ivan Reitman. Assoc Pro: Sheldon Kahn and Arnold Glimcher. Pro: Joe Medjuck and Michael C. Gross. Screenplay: Jim Cash and Jack Epps Jr, based on a story by them and Reitman. Ph: Laszlo Kovacs. Ed: Kahn, Pem Herring and William Gordean. Art: Ron Hobbs and David Chapman. Pro Des: John DeCuir. M: Elmer Bernstein, song 'Love Touch' sung by Rod Stewart. (Universal-UIP). Rel: 24 October 1986. 116 mins. Cert PG.

The Legend of Fortress Suram. Highly stylized and specialized, Sergio Paradjanov's film is based on the fairy-tale legends of his country, Georgia, as a tribute to its warriors who down the centuries have died for freedom. Paradjanov's work has not exactly endeared

him to the Soviet authorities; he has in the past been arrested, tried and sentenced to jail on various charges.

Cast: Levan Uchaneischvili, Zurab Kipshidze, Lela Alibegashvili, Dodo Abashidze, Veriko Andjaparidze, Sofiko Chiaureli. Dir: Paradjanov and Abashidze. Screenplay: Vazha Chigashvili. Ph: Yury Klimenko. M: Djansug Kakhidze. (Gruziafilm Studio-Poseidon Films-Artificial Eye). Rel: floating; first shown London (Camden Plaza) 26 September 1986. 87 mins. Cert U.

Let's Get Harry. Robert Duvall as the mercenary hired by some small-town plumbers to lead them on what appears to be a wholly crazy expedition to free one of their fellows, who has been kidnapped by South American terrorists. This five-men-against-the-world story has a moral point to make beneath all the violent action.

Rest of cast: Fidel Abrego, Jere Burns, Gary Busey, Cecille Callan, Terry Camilleri, Elpidia Carrillo, Matt Clark, Rodolfo de Alexandre, Javier Estrada, Glenn Frey, Salvador Godinez, Bruce Gray, Jerry Hardin, Mark Harmon, David Hess, Ben Johnson,

Jonathan Kano, James Keane, Guillermo Lagunes, Pierrino Mascarino, Diane Petersen, Alfredo Ramirez, Guillermo Rios, Rick Rossovich, Michael Schoeffling, Gregory Sierra, Robert Singer, J. W. Smith, Cesar Sobrevals, Jon van Ness, John Wesley, Tom Wilson, Jorge Zepeda. Dir: Alan Smithee. Pro: D. H. Blatt and R. Singer. Assoc Pro: David Shamroy Hamburger. Screenplay: Charles Robert Carner, based on a story by Mark Feldberg and Samuel Fuller. Ph: James A. Contner. Ed: Ralph E. Winters and Rick R. Sparr. Art: Mort Rabinowitz. M: Brad Fiedel. (Tri-Star-Columbia). Rel: 5 June 1987. 102 mins. Cert 18.

Link. Minor, routine British thriller set in the familiar large old house, where primatologist professor – monkey-studier to you – Terence Stamp carries out experiments with the help of pretty assistant Elizabeth Shue. After about an hour things turn sour, deaths occur and Jerry Goldsmith lets the mood music rip loudly. But those chimps are real cute.

Robert Duvall as the hired mercenary leader of a plumbers' army in Tri-Star/Columbia's Let's Get Harry.

Rest of cast: Steven Pinner, Richard Garnett, David O'Hara, Kevin Lloyd, Joe Belcher, Geoffrey Beevers, Caroline John, Daisy Beevers. Dir and Pro: Richard Franklin. Ex Pro: Verity Lambert. Screenplay: Everett de Roche, based on a story by Roche, Zee Slotoff and Tom Ackerman. Co-Pro: Rick McCallum. Ph: Mike Molloy. Ed: Andrew London. Pro Des: Norman Garwood. M: Jerry Goldsmith. (Thorn/EMI-Cannon). Rel: floating; first shown London (Prince Charles and Cannon Haymarket) 12 December 1986. 107 mins. Cert 15.

Little Shop of Horrors. Consistently amusing and thoroughly entertaining adaptation of the stage production which in turn – if distantly – was based on Roger Corman's cheaply made, thorough-going horror movie of 1961. About a mysterious man-eating plant, bought from a Chinese emporium in Skid Row, whose increasing demand for blood as it grows leads to its harassed owner chopping up the – dead – villain in order to satisfy the brute. But the situations are all broadly, farcically funny, the characters most hugely overdrawn and the steady succession of musical interventions bright, breezy and well handled. Some nice perform-

ances, too, especially by Ellen Greene as the dolly-bird heroine, Rick Moranis as the hero and Vincent Gardenia as his boss. A top-class fun film.

Rest of cast: Steve Martin, Tichina Arnold, Tisha Campbell, Michelle Weeks, James Belushi, John Candy, Christopher Guest, Bill Murray, Stanley Jones, Bertice Reading, Ed Wiley, Alan Tilvern, John Scott Martin, Vincent Wong, Mak Wilson, Danny Cunningham, Danny-John Jules, Gary Palmer, Paul Swaby, Mildred Shay, Melissa Wiltsie, Kevin Scott, Barbara Rosenblat, Adeen Fogle, Kelly Huntley, Paul Reynolds, Miriam Margolies, Abbie Dabner, Frank Dux, Peter Whitman, Heather Henson, Judith Morse, Bob Sherman, Doreen Hermitage, Kerry Shale, Robert Arden, Stephen Hoye, Bob Sessions, Michael J. Shannon, the voice of 'Audrey II' by Levi Stubbs of The Four Tops. Dir: Frank Oz. Pro: David Geffen. Assoc Pro: David Orton and Denis Holt. Screenplay and lyrics: Howard Ashman. Ph: Robert Payntner. Ed: John Jympson. Art: Stephen Spence and John Fenner. Pro Des: Roy Walker. M: Miles Goodman. (Geffen Co-

Rick Moranis (right) as the distressed owner of a meat- (and man!) eating plant in Warner's chills-with-music comedy Little Shop of Horrors. *Others involved include Ellen Greene and Vincent Gardenia.*

Warner Bros). Rel: floating; first shown London (Warner) 27 March 1987. 94 mins. Cert PG.

Living on the Edge. The experience of three families – a farmer's, a miner's and one living on a new estate – illustrate the changes in British society since the end of WWII. Producer and director take a pretty dim view of it all, seeing a nation in terminal decline, *very far* from a country fit for heroes. A highly personal and openly partisan view of things.

Dir: Mike Grigsby. Devised and Pro: John Furse. Ph: Ivan Strasburg. Ed: Julian Ware. M: The Blow Monkeys, Herman's Hermits, Pink Floyd and the Ambrose Orchestra. (ICA/BFI). Rel: floating; first shown London (ICA) 29 May 1987. 90 mins. No cert.

A Love Bewitched – El Amor Brujo. Carlos Saura's third Spanish dance film and the one with the most likely popular appeal, in that it is less strictly ballet

Colin Friels as Malcolm, the young man who loves trams and invents odd little electronic gimmicks; an Enterprise-released Australian comedy.

and more equivalent to some of the American 'musicals' (*West Side Story* springs to mind). A combination of folkdance, ballet and a melodramatic, romantic story of passion, murder and sorrow, the whole film is lifted by the amazing dancing of the cast, casting a spell with their virtuosity.

Cast: Antonio Gades, Cristina Hoyos, Laura del Sol, Juan Antonio Jiminez, Emma Penella, La Polaca, Gomez de Jerez, Enriques Ortega, Diego Pantoja, Giovana, Candy Roman, Manolo Sevilla; and singers and dancers of the company. Dir and (with Antonio Gades) Screenplay: Carlos Saura. Pro: Emiliano Piedra. Ph: Teo Escamilla. Ed: Pedro del Rey. Art: Gerado Vera. M: de Falla. (Virgin). Rel: floating; first shown London (Curzon West End) 16 January 1987. 90 mins. Cert PG.

Macaroni – Maccheroni. Two marvellous actors giving marvellous performances in a slight little Italian piece, hardly more than a couple of character studies. Three very important days in the life of an American tycoon (Jack Lemmon) attending a convention in Naples and there learning a lot about life from a delightful Italian (Marcello Mastroianni). A small, gentle masterpiece of cinema.

Rest of cast: Daria Nicolodi, Isa Danieli, Maria Luisa Santella, Patrizia Sacchi, Bruno Esposito, Orsetta Gregoretti, Marc Berman, Jean-François Perrier, Giovanna Sanfilippo, Fabio Tenore, Marta Bifano, Aldo de Martino, Clotilde de Spirito, Carlotta Ercolino, Vincenza Giocoso, Ernest Mahieux, Giovanni Mauriello, Alfredo Mingione, Daniela Novak, Umberto Principe, Giovanni Riccardi, Corrado Taranto. Dir: Ettore Scola. Pro: Luigi and Aurelio de Laurentiis and Franco Committeri. Screenplay: Scola, Ruggiero Maccari and Furio Scarpelli. Ph: Claudio Ragona. Pro Des: Luciano Ricceri. M: Armando Trovaiola. (Filmauro Massfilm Pro/Palace Pictures). Rel: floating; first shown London (Cannon Panton Street) 6 February 1987. 106 mins. Cert PG.

Malcolm. He's a shy, sexually repressed, introverted young man with a passion for tramcars and a genius for inventing extraordinary, if largely useless, high-tech gadgets, like the little trolley he directs to fetch his newspaper. But things hot up when Malcolm takes a criminal and his comfortable – and impressed – lady-friend as lodgers and is inspired by them to

invent some remarkable dustbins with which the trio pull off a large-scale heist! A funny, refreshingly original comedy from Australia, one of the best chucklers of this or any other year. Perfect performances, outstanding direction and technically excellent.

Cast: Colin Friels, John Hargreaves, Lindy Davies, Chris Haywood, Charles 'Bud' Tingwell, Beverley Phillips, Judith Stratford, Heather Mitchell, Tony Mahood, David Lander, David Letch, Mike Bishop, David Johnston, Katerina Tassopoulos, Ian McFayden, Ian Shroves, David Gray, Roy Edmonds, John Raaen, Peter Hoskins, Laurie Dobson, Bill Stacey, John Kazantidis, Antonis Baxevantzidis, Denise Scott, Don Bridges, Don Bishop, Rex Callahan, John Kelly, Peter Nicol, David Bradshaw, Arnold the parrot. Dir and Co-Pro: Nadia Tas. Screenplay, Co-Pro, Ph and mechanical effects: David Parker. Assoc Pro: Timothy White. Ex Pro: Bryan Menzies. Ed: Ken Sallows. Pro Des: Rob Perkins. M: The Penguin Café Orchestra/Simon Jeffes. (Tass/Parker Pro-Enterprise Pictures). Rel: floating; first shown London (Cannons at Bayswater and Tottenham Court Road) 5 December 1986. 86 mins. Cert 15.

The Man Who Mistook His Wife for a Hat. Bound-for-TV film version of the Michael Nyman, ICA-staged 'neurological opera', based on the case study of Oliver Sacks. The story of a doctor who sets his problems to music.

Cast: Emile Belcourt, Frederick Westcott and Pat Hooper. Pro: Debra Hauer. No other credits listed. (ICA/TV). Rel: floating; first shown London (ICA) 5 June 1987. 75 mins. No cert.

Mannequin. Remember that classic story about the sculptor who fell in love with his creation? Well, here's a modernized, vulgarized variation, with the young 'artist' a maker of shop-window dummies who becomes passionately attached to one of his creations, which returns his passion, coming alive at night and whenever they are alone. Likeable, genuinely amusing performances by creator (Andrew McCarthy) and created (Kim Cattrall) considerably atone for all else.

Rest of cast: Estelle Getty, James Spader, G. W. Bailey, Carole Davis, Stephen Vinovich, Christopher Maher, Meshach Taylor, Phyllis Newman, Phil Rubenstein, Jeffery Lampert, Kenneth Lloyd, Jake Jundeff, Harvey Levine, Thomas J. McCarthy, R. L. Ryan, Glenn Davish, Steve Lippe, Lee Golden, Vernon R. DeVinney, Olivia Frances Williams, Charles N. Lord, Ben Hammer, Jane

Kim Cattrall as the shop-window dummy who comes to lively and lovely life, and comforts her creator (Andrew McCarthy), in the Cannon comedy Mannequin.

Moore, Jane Carol Simms, Judi Goldhand, Lara Harris, Dan Lounsberry, Kitty Minehart, Katherine Conklin, Andrew Hill Newman, Bill Greene. Dir: Michael Gottlieb. Pro: Art Levinson. Assoc Pro: Catherine Paura. Ex Pro: Edward Rugoff and Joseph Farrell. Screenplay: Gottlieb and Rugoff. Ph: Tim Suhrstedt. Ed: Richard Halsey and Frank Jimenez. Pro Des: Josan Russo. M: Sylvester Levay. (Gladden Entertainment-Cannon). Rel: 22 May 1987. 90 mins. Cert PG.

Martial Arts of Shaolin. Expensive and expansive Hong Kong/Chinese production that took two years to make and cost some $HK15 million, with no fewer than 300 martial arts experts recruited from all over China to support the Chinese MA film star, Jack Lee, and his Hong Kong rival, Lau Kar Leung. So what matters if the story is thin when the fight spectacles are as good as you'll see, and the fascinating backgrounds include China's Great Wall, the Forbidden City, the Shaolin Temple and the Imperial Palace?

Rest of cast: Jet Lee, Hu Jiang-Qiang, Yu Cheng-Hui, Yu Hai etc. Dir: Lau Kar Leung. Pro: Ann Tse Kai and Liu Yet Yuen. Ex Pro: Fu Chi. Screenplay: Sze

Yeung Pei and Wong Ying Cheong. (Pearl River Pro-Sino Cine). Rel: floating; first shown London (Rio) 24 April 1987. 97 mins. Cert PG.

Masks – Masques. Not the very best Chabrol, but not the worst by a long way. An intriguing psychological thriller about a popular, genial TV host (a brilliant performance by a younger-looking Philippe Noiret) whose façade is pierced and finally destroyed by the brother of a girl he has murdered. Now, greedy for her fortune, he keeps his god-daughter drugged with a view to murdering her, too, eventually.

Rest of cast: Robin Renucci, Monique Chaumette, Anne Brochet, Bernadette Lafont, Pierre-François Domeniaud, Roger Dumas, Pierre Nougaro, Renée Dennsy, Yvonne Decade, Blanche Ariel, René Marjac, Paul Vally, Denise Pezzani, Pierre Risch, Michel Dupuy, Henri Attal. Dir and (with Odile Barski) Screenplay: Claude Chabrol. Pro: Marin Karmitz. Ph: Jean Rabier. Ed: Monique Fardoulis. Art: Françoise Benoit-Fresco. M: Matthieu Chabrol. (MK2 Pro/Films A2-Cannon). Rel: floating; first shown London (Cannons Swiss Centre and Baker Street) 29 May 1987. 100 mins. Cert 15.

Maxie. Pleasantly old-fashioned comedy with plenty of chuckles, a dullish centre and a lively, hilarious final sequence. About the frustrated spirit of a silent-screen actress who returns with

Librarian Nick (Mandy Patinkin) isn't at all happy when his wife Maxie (Glenn Close) tosses her drink at her boss (Valerie Curtin) in the Rank-released Orion film comedy Maxie. *Left: Does Maxie survive this Pearl White situation?*

the idea of proving that it was only her untimely death in an auto accident which prevented her from becoming a great silent movie star. She achieves this by taking possession of a staid librarian's busy (bishop's secretary) wife and changing her into a dizzy, fizzy blonde, the overall effect of the subsequent goings-on being warmly watchable, aided by some nice leading performances.

Cast: Glenn Close (as both serious wife and high 'spirited' star), Mandy Patinkin (as the husband), Ruth Gordon, Barnard Hughes, Valerie Curtin, Googy Gress, Michael Ensign, Michael Laskin, Lou Cutell, Nelson Welch, Leeza Gibbons, Evan White, Harry Wong, Charles Douglas Laird, David Sosna, Hugo Stanger, John O'Neill, Eddie Wong, Pauline Bluestone, Glen Chin, Nanci Kawata, Conan Lee, Cyril Magnin, Michael Jordan, Alan Gin, Rebecca Granfield, Jimaki, Jobyna Phillips, Gayle Vance, Tony Amendola, Nelson the dog. Dir: Paul Aaron. Pro: Carter de Haven. Ex Pro: Rich Irvine and James L. Stewart. Screenplay: Patricia Resnick, based on the novel *Marion's Wall* by Jack Finney. Ph: Fred Schuler. Ed: Lynzee Kingman. Pro Des: John Lloyd. M: Georges Delerue. (Aurora/Carter de Haven-Orion-Rank Film Dist.). Rel: 1 August 1986. 98 mins. Cert PG.

Mélo. The sixth film, all French, to be based on the 1920s play by Henry Bernstein, who was once the rage of Paris but is now neglected and almost forgotten. This time around, under Alain Resnais' always fascinating hand, the film is apparently scrupulously faithful to the original, and so is unavoidably stagey. It's a *ménage à trois* piece; the men, both violinists, are husband and lover, with the husband unaware of the liaison which eventually leads the distraught woman to throw herself into the Seine. Meticulously directed, superbly played and offering plenty of scope for those who will see more than is probably there, *Mélo* offers plenty of interest.

Cast: Sabine Azèma, Fanny Ardant, Pierre Arditi, André Dussollier, Jacques Jacqmine, Hubery Gignoux, Catherine Arditi. Dir: Alain Resnais. Pro: Marin Karmitz. Screenplay: Resnais, based on the Berstein play. Ph: Charlie van Damme. Ed: Albert Jurgenson. Pro Des: Jacques Saulnier. M: Philippe Gérard, Bach and Brahms. (MK2 Pro/Films A2 with participation of the French Ministry of Culture-Artificial Eye). Rel: floating; first shown London (Renoir cinemas) 5 June 1987. 112 mins. Cert PG.

Men – Männer. Amusing, wordy and witty comedy about the male sex and its foibles, made by one of Germany's most successful women writer-directors, Doris Dörrie. About a successful advertising agency executive

A newly divorced couple (Teri Garr and Tom Conti) find themselves unwillingly back together again under threat from their bank robber passenger (Paul Rodriguez) in Orion-Rank's Miracles.

who finds out, on his 12th wedding anniversary, that his wife is having an affair with a penniless amateur artist. Leaving business and home, he lodges with him without revealing his identity, trying to discover what it is the lover has that hubbie hasn't . . . And ends up by becoming the lover's best pal and mentor, transforming him into a mirror image of himself, thus ruining the affair.

Cast: Heiner Lauterbach, Uwe Ochsenknecht, Ulrike Kriener, Janna Marangosoff, Dietmar Bär, Marie-Charlotte Schüler. Dir and Screenplay: Doris Dörrie. Ex Pro: Harald Kügler. Ph: Helge Weindler. Ed: Raimund Barthelmes and Jeanette Magerl. Art: Jörg Neumann, Gabriele Hochheim and Friedrich Natus. M: Claus Bantzer. (Olga Films/ZDF Pro-Artificial Eye). Rel: floating; first shown London (Chelsea and Renoir cinemas and Camden Plaza) 31 October 1986. 100 mins. Cert 15.

The Men's Club.
A group of professional men (psychiatrist, professor, ex-baseball star, etc.) gather for an evening of ribald talk and drinking, and end up exposing their deepest misogynistic feelings. Tempers flare, secrets are revealed, fists fly, and a lot of bull flows under the bridge. A fine ensemble of actors (Roy Scheider, Treat Williams, Frank Langella, Harvey Keitel) give their all for this stagey, offensive and boring piece of claptrap.

Rest of cast: David Dukes, Richard Jordan, Craig Wasson, Stockard Channing, Gina Gallegos, Cindy Pickett, Gwen Welles, Penny Baker, Rebecca Bush, Claudia Cron, Ann Dusenberry, Marilyn Jones, Manette LaChance, Jennifer Jason Leigh, Ann Wedgeworth. Dir: Peter Medak. Pro: Howard Gottfried. Exec Pro: Thomas Coleman and Michael Rosenblatt. Screenplay: Leonard Michaels, based on his novel. Ph: John Fleckenstein. Pro Des: Ken Davis. M: Lee Holdridge. (Atlantic Releasing Corporation presenting an Entertainment Release). Rel: floating; first shown London (Cannon Panton Street) 27 March 1987. 101 mins. Cert 18.

Miracles.
On the day of their divorce bickering doctor (Tom Conti) and lady lawyer (Teri Garr) are literally thrown together and forced to stay that way through a series of events starting with their abduction at gunpoint and continuing with all sorts of unpleasant situations from which they eventually emerge safely, finally to decide, still bickering, to re-marry. The stars' consistently uncomfortable and exhausting comedy performances never quite bring the rewards in terms of the laughter their work deserves.

Rest of cast: Paul Rodriguez, Christopher Lloyd, Adalberto ('Resortes') Martinez, Jorge Russek, Jorge Reynoso, Zaide Silvia Gutierrez, Erika Faraon, Paco Morayta, Alvaro Carcano, Ken Lerner, Charles Rocket, Shelby Leverington, Mae E. Campbell, Susan Wheeler Duff, Barbara Whinnery, John Macchia, Squire Fridell, Ken Hixon, René Pereyra, Guillermo Rios, Tina Romero, Margarita Sanz, Roger Cudney, Joseph Whip, Chris Hendrie, Leopoldo Frances, Bob Nelson, Victor Alcocer Gomez, Eduardo Lugo, Alejandro Bracho, Carlos Vendrell, Douglas Sandoval, Regina Herrera, Jose Chavez Trowe, Dr Francisco Funes, Marie Butler, Paco Pharrez, Miguel Angel Fuentes, Carlos Gonzales, Roberto Sosa, Andaluz Russell, Garardo Moreno, Mario Arevalo, Rodolfo de Alexandre. Dir and Screenplay: Jim Kouf. Pro: Steve Roth and Bernard Williams. Assoc Pro: Lynn Bigelow. Ex Pro: David Greenwalt. Ph:

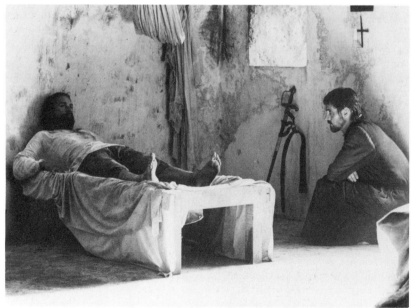

The strong-minded, dedicated Father Gabriel – a fine performance by Jeremy Irons – leads his flock from the burning mission into further dangers in Warner's release of the magnificent British film The Mission. *Left: Father Gabriel visits remorseful mercenary Mendoz (Robert De Niro).*

John Alcott. Ed: Susan Morse and Dennis Virkler. Pro Des: Terence Marsh. M: Peter Bernstein. (Orion-Rank Film Dist.). Rel: floating; first shown London (Cannons at Panton and Oxford Streets) 5 September 1986. 87 mins. Cert PG.

The Mission. Beautifully produced, splendidly directed and, in spite of some dodgy initial lines, smoothly literate and spectacular 16th-century historical drama set in the dense and dripping South American jungle. In mid-century, Spain and Portugal decided to combine against the spreading power and influence of the Jesuits in the border region (eventually to expel them altogether) by sending a military expedition to destroy a thriving mission in the domain of the hitherto intractable (and ill-used) Guarani Indians. A finely sustained and sincere performance by Jeremy Irons as the priest-in-charge, notably supported by Ray McAnally as the conscience-torn Papal envoy forced to make a political rather than humane decision, and by Daniel Berrigan and Liam Neeson as Jesuits. Also firmly supporting is Robert de Niro, as slave-trader turned Jesuit turned defence leader. Impressive work, too, comes from the beautifully bodied local Indians on location in Colombia and Argentina. This fine movie deserves to restore Goldcrest's *Revolution*-dimmed fortunes and status.

Rest of cast: Aidan Quinn, Cheri Lunghi, Ronald Pickup, Chuck Low, Bercelio Moya, Sigifredo Ismare, Asuncion Ontiveros, Alejandrino, Rolf Gray, Alvaro Guerrero, Anthony Lawn, Joe Daly, Carlos Duplat, Rafael Camerano, Monirak Sisowath, Silvestre Chiripua, Luis Carlos Gonzalez, Maria Teresa Ripoll. Dir: Roland Joffé. Pro: Fernando Ghia and David Puttnam. Assoc Pro: Iain Smith. Screenplay: Robert Bolt, based on his story. Ed: Jim Clark. Ph: Chris Menges. Pro Des: Stuart Craig. M: Ennio Morricone. (Goldcrest and Kingsmere/Enigma Pro in assoc with Fernando Ghia-Warner). Rel: 31 January 1987. 125 mins. Cert PG.

Mona Lisa. Bob Hoskins giving another memorable performance (it won him the 1986 Cannes Festival Award for Best Actor) in a neatly tailored British mixture of comedy, drama and social searchlight. The story has two very unusual leading characters: Cathy Tyson plays a coloured hooker trying to struggle up the vice ladder and Hoskins is her short, squat, quick-tempered body-guard, an incredibly naive ex-criminal who falls in love with her.

Rest of cast: Michael Caine (vice boss), Clarke Peters, Kate Hardie, Robbie Coltrane, Zoe Nathenson, Sammy Davis, Rod Bedall, Joe Brown, Pauline Melville, David Halliwell, G. B. 'Zoot' Money, Hossein Karimbeik, John Darling, Donna Cannon, Mandy Winch, Maggie O'Neill, Dawn Archibald, Geoff Larder, Robert Dorning, Helen Martin, Richard Strange, Jeremy Hardy, Bryan Coleman, Raad Raawi, Alan Talbot, Stephen Persaud, Bill Moore, Jack Purvis, Kenny Baker, Gary Cady, Perry Fenwick. Dir: Neil Jordan. Pro: Stephen

Michael Caine as the vice boss with black hooker Simone (Cathy Tyson) in the outstanding Palace Pictures British release, Mona Lisa.

Woolley and Patrick Cassavetti. Ex Pro: Denis O'Brien and George Harrison. Screenplay: Neil Jordan and David Leland. Co-Pro: Ray Cooper and Chris Brown. Ph: Roger Pratt. Ed: Lesley Walker. Art: Gemma Jackson. Pro Des: Jamie Leonard. M: Michael Kamen. (Palace Pro-Handmade Films). Rel: 17 October 1986. 104 mins. Cert 18.

More Bad News. Five years after the disastrous end to their first tour, the

Jane Fonda – is she a murderess? – and Jeff Bridges (as the ex-cop who helps her to find out) in the Lorimar/Fox release of the Sidney Lumet thriller The Morning After.

Group get together again to entertain 70,000 heavy metal fans at a Castle Donington concert. And it isn't all plain sailing . . . Made in two weeks in August 1986, partly in London and partly at the Castle.

Cast: Adrian Edmondson, Peter Richardson, Nigel Planer, Rik Mayall, Jennifer Saunders, Dawn French. Dir and Screenplay: Adrian Edmondson. Pro: Simon Wright. Assoc Pro: Mandy Ruben. Ex Pro: Michael White. Comic Strip Pro: Peter Richardson. Ph: John Metcalfe. Art: Denise Ruben. (Comic Strip Ltd-Palace Pictures). Rel: floating; first shown London (Prince Charles) 13 March 1987. 52 mins. Cert 15.

The Morning After. A minor, slipping, part-time actress and whole-time lush liable to drunken blackouts wakes up in a strange apartment with a very

The Fox family and friend (l. to r. River Phoenix, Conrad Roberts, Jadrien Steele, Helen Mirren, Rebecca Gordon, Harrison Ford and Hilary Gordon) watch the destruction of the ice factory in UIP's The Mosquito Coast.

dead, knifed, man beside her, a man she admits she hates. Who, if not she – and she can't be certain – did the dirty deed, and why? An increasingly interested and involved ex-homicide department cop helps her find out as she flees from arrest on a murder charge. Jane Fonda gives a highly charged, nervous and, as always, fascinating performance (shades of her Oscar-winning *Klute*), while Jeff Bridges gives great back-up as the investigator.

Rest of cast: Raul Julia, Diane Salinger, Richard Foronjy, Geoffrey Scott, James 'Gypsy' Haake, Kathleen Wilhoite, Don Hood, Fran Bennett, Michael Flanagan, Bruce Vilanch, Michael Prince, Frances Bergen, José Santana, Bob Minor, George Fisher, Rick Rossovich, Laurel Lyle, Kathy Bates, Anne Betancourt, Patti Song, Betty Lougaris, Drew Berman, Sam Scarber, Michael Zand, Gladys Portugues, Corinna Everson. Dir: Sidney Lumet. Pro: Bruce Gilbert. Assoc Pro: Wolfgang Glattes and

Lois Bonfiglio. Ex Pro: Faye Schwab. Screenplay: James Hicks. Ph: Andrzej Bartkowiak. Ed: Joel Goodman. Art: Kandy Stern. Pro Des: Albert Brenner. M: Paul Chihara, solo sax by George Howard. (Lorimar/American Filmworks-Fox). Rel: 19 June 1987. 104 mins. Cert 15.

The Mosquito Coast. Harrison Ford turns in an excellent, restrained character performance as an egotistical, physically tireless – and impossible to live with – inventor who, fed-up with the artificiality of modern American life and convinced that the big bomb war is just around the corner, leads his family into a remote African jungle retreat. Here he builds a simple-life community – and, quite incredibly, an ice factory – only to have it all destroyed by the advent of the evil outer world and the rebellion of his own family, who, after initial happiness, begin to hanker for all the things he hates. A sort of modern variation of *The Swiss Family Robinson* which gradually and slyly begins to cast doubts on the very values it initially supports.

Rest of cast: Helen Mirren, River Phoenix,

Jadrien Steele, Hilary Gordon, Rebecca Gordon, Jason Alexander, Dick O'Neill, Alice Sneed, Tiger Haynes, William Newman, André Gregory, Melanie Boland, Martha Plimpton, Raymond Clare, Emory King, Conrad Roberts, Michael Rogers, Tony Vega Sr, Aurora Clavel, Butterfly McQueen, Michael Opoku, Adolpho Salguero, Rafael Cho, Sofia Coc, Margarita Coc, Wilfred Peters, Luis Palacio, Juan Antonio Llanes, Abel Woolrich, Jorge Zepeda. Dir: Peter Weir. Pro: Jerome Hellman. Assoc Pro: Neville Thompson. Ex Pro: Paul Zaenth. Screenplay: Paul Schrader, based on the novel by Paul Theroux. Ph: John Seale. Ed: Thom Noble and Richard Francis-Bruce. Pro Des: John Stoddart. M: Maurice Jarre. (Paul Zaenth Co-UIP). Rel: 27 March 1987. 119 mins. Cert PG.

Murphy's Law. Old-fashioned – apart from the misguided constant introduction of the foulest language, especially by the unattractive 'heroine' – and familiar story of a lonely, hard-drinking Los Angeles cop (Charles Bronson) framed for killing his ex-wife. He has to break out of custody in order to prove his innocence.

Rest of cast: Carrie Snodgress, Kathleen Wilhoite, Robert F. Lyons, Richard Romanus, Angel Tompkins, Bill Henderson, James Luisi, Clifford A. Pellow, Janet Mac-Lachlan, Lawrence Tierney, Jerome Thor, Mischa Hausserman, Cal Haynes, Hans Howes, Joseph Spallina Roman, Chris de Rose, Frank Annese, Paul McCallum, Dennis Hayden, Tony Montero, David Hayman, Lisa Vice, Janet Rotblatt, Greg Finley, Jerry Lazarus, Robert Axelrod, John Hawker, Bert Williams, Daniel Halleck, Randall Carver, Gerald Berns, Don L. Brodie, Graham Timbes, David K. Johnston, Paul McCauley, Brooks Wachtel, Richard Hochberg, John F. McCarthy, Leigh Lombardi, Charlie Brewer, Charles A. Nero, Wheeler Henderson, Frank Bove, Chris Stanley, Linda Harwood, Nancie Clark. Dir: J. Lee Thompson. Pro: Pancho Kohner. Ex Pro: Menahem Golan and Yoram Globus. Screenplay and Assoc Pro: Gail Morgan Hickman. Co-Pro: Jill Ireland. Ph: Alex Phillips. Ed: Peter Lee Thompson and Charles Simmons. Pro Des: William Cruise. M: Marc Donahue and Valentine McCallum. (Cannon). Rel: 31 October 1986. 100 mins. Cert 18.

Murphy's Romance. Simple, warm-hearted and, in the very best sense, old-fashioned, comedy about two guys and a girl in the cowpoke country of Arizona. Sterling, stylish performances from James Garner as the 60-year-old toughie who runs the local store and ice cream parlour, and Sally Field as the tough little divorcée who comes from the East to open a horse ranch and make a new life for herself . . . complicated when her ex-husband turns up and tries to win her back from the increasingly romantically interested Garner.

Rest of cast: Brian Kerwin, Corey Haim, Dennis Burkley, Georgann Johnson, Dorothea Duckworth, Michael Prokopuk, Billy Ray Sharkey, Michael Crabtree, Anna Levine, Charles Lane, Bruce French, John C. Becher, Henry Slate, Tom Rankin, Peggy McCay, Carole King, Ted Gehring, Joshua Ravetch, C. Ray Cook. Eugene Cochran, Gene Blakely, Sherry Lynn Amorisi, Patricia Ann Willoughby, Mike Casper, Hugh Burritt, Michael Friel, Art Royer, Marian Gibson, Irving Ravetch, Michael Hungerford, John Higgenbotham, Drasha Meyer, Ron Nix, Johnny Ray Anthony, Paul E. Pinnt. Dir: Martin Ritt. Pro: Laura Ziskin. Assoc Pro: George Justin and Jim van Wyck. Screenplay: Harriet Frank Jr and Irving Ravetch, based on the novella by Max Schott. Ph: William A. Fraker. Ed: Sidney Levin. Pro Des: Joel Schiller. M: Carole

James Garner and Sally Field, two toughies who find happiness together by the end of Columbia's charm-loaded Murphy's Romance.

King. (Martin Ritt/Fogwood Films Ltd-Warner). Rel: 11 July 1986. 108 mins. Cert 15.

My Life as a Dog – Mitt Liv som Hund. An exquisite (1984) Swedish film: inspirationally directed and produced, and marvellously well acted (by the entire cast but especially by 12-year-old amateur Anton Glanzelius, who is astonishingly mature, very far from the usual screen-cute kid). This smoothly blended anecdotal story tells of a small, lively and fun-loving youngster who has to come to terms with the fact that his loved and formerly loving mother is now suffering from a terminal illness, and with separation from his beloved canine pal. A film to savour and treasure, and inevitably one to linger long in the memory. Winner of Best Film and Best Actor awards at the Swedish Film Awards of 1985.

Rest of cast: Manfred Serner, Anki Liden, Tomas von Brömssen, Melina Kinnaman, Kicki Rundgren, Lennart Hjulström, Ing-

Marie Carlsson, Leif Ericsson, Christina Carlwind, Ralph Carlsson, Didrik Gustavsson, Vivi Johansson, Jan-Philip Hollström, Arnold Alfredson, Fritz Elofsson, Per Ottosson, Johanna Udehn, Suzanna Wetterholm, Vivika Dahlen, Magnus Rask, Tony Rix, Klimpen. Dir: Lasse Hallström. Pro: Waldemar Bergendahl. Screenplay: Hallström in co-operation with Reidar Jönsson, Brasse Brännström and Per Berglund, based on the novel by Jönsson. Ph: Jörgen Persson, Rolf Lindström and Olof Johnson. Ed: Suzanne Linnman and Christer Furubrand. Art: Lasse Westfelt. M: Björn Isfält. (Svensk Filmindustri/Film Teknik-Artificial Eye). Rel: floating; first shown London (Renoir cinemas) 17 April 1987. 100 mins. Cert PG.

My Little Pony. Sugar-coated animation feature, spawned by the TV series, commendably aimed at the youngsters and with the now increasingly rare U certificate. A story set in happy-happy Ponyland – happy, that is, until the evil witch Hydia and her two equally horrid daughters decide to cast some nasty spells upon the equine utopia. The increasingly nasty resultant situation is only finally cleared up by the timely intervention of the tiny Flutter Ponies, with their wonderful high-speed wings

Two of the ponies, and other characters, in the Miracle release of the Sunbow animated feature film My Little Pony.

blowing the wind of change across the country. It is all a neatly done plug for the toys which preceded the movie.

With the voices of Danny De Vito, Madeline Kahn, Cloris Leachman, Rhea Perlman, Tony Randall, Tammy Amerson, Jon Bauman, Alice Playton, Charlie Adler, Michael Bell, Sheryl Bernstein, Susan Blu, Cathy Cavadini, Nancy Cartwright, Peter Cullen, Laura Dean, Ellen Gerstell, Keri Houlihan, Katie Leigh, Scott Menville, Laurel Page, Sarah Partridge, Russie Taylor, Jill Wayne, Frank Welker. Dir and (with Joe Bacal and Tom Griffin) Co-Pro: Michael Jones. Ex Pro: Margaret Loesch and Lee Gunther. Sup Pro: Jay Bacal. Screenplay: George Arthur Bloom. M: Rob Walsh. (Sunbow Pro Inc/Hasbro Industries UK Ltd-Miracle). Rel: 18 July 1986. 100 mins. Cert U.

The Naked Cage. A routine addition to the long line of women's prison movies, with all the routine exploitation and travail (lesbian warden, rapist male guard etc.). Poor little farm gal gets framed for a bank-robbing job and has to suffer a lot before the real culprit owns up and lets little Michelle get back to her farm, her hoss and a life worth living.

Cast: Shari Shuttuck, Angel Tompkins, Lucinda Crosby, Cristina Whitaker, Faith Minton, Stacey Shaffer, Nick Benedict, Lisa London, John Terlesky, Aude Charles, Angela Gibbs, Leslie Huntley, Carole Ita White, Seth Kaufman, Larry Gelman. Dir

and Screenplay: Paul Nicholas. Pro: Chris D. Nebe. Ex Pro: Menahem Golan and Yoram Globus. Ph: Hal Trussell. Ed: Warren Chadwick and Nino de Marco. Art: Alex Hadju. M: Christopher Stone. (Cannon Films/Cannon). Rel: floating; first shown London (Moulin) 30 January 1987. 97 mins. Cert 18.

The Name of the Rose – Der Name der Rose. Consistently grey, grim and gloomy West German/Italian/French co-production, with English dialogue, about murders and other mysteries that occur in an abbey in 14th-century Italy

where a debate is being held as to the future of the Holy Catholic Church: the pomp and power of Rome, or the philosophy of poverty of the Franciscan Order? Refusing to credit the work of the devil in the murders, English delegate Sean Connery (a fine, film-saving performance) doggedly pursues the more reasonable truths.

Rest of cast: F. Murray Abraham, Christian Slater, Elya Baskin, Feodor Chaliapin Jr, William Hickey, Michael Lonsdale, Ron Perlman, Volker Prechtel, Helmut Qualtinger, Valentina Vargas, Michael Habeck, Urs Althaus, Leopoldo Trieste, Franco Valobra, Vernon Dobtcheff, Donal O'Brian, Andrew Birkin, Lucien Bodard, Peter Berling, Pete Lancaster. Dir: Jean-Jacques Annaud. Pro: Bernd Eichinger. Ex Pro: Thomas Schuhly and Jake Eberts. Screenplay: Andrew Birkin, Gerard Brach, Howard Franklin and Alain Godard, based on the novel *Il nome della rosa* by Umberto Eco. Ph: Tonino Delli Colli. Ed: Jane Seitz. Pro Des: Dante Ferretti. M: James Horner. (Eichinger/Schaefer/Constantine/Cristaldifilm/Films Ariane, co-pro in assoc with ZDF-Rank Film Dist.). Rel: floating, first shown London (Cannon Haymarket) 23 January 1987. 131 mins. Cert 18.

Nanou. The very considerable promise of the opening sequences of this Franco-British production – the reactions of an English girl starting out on what she hopes is a working holiday in France – is unfortunately not sustained. Once she meets a slob of a French terrorist and mindlessly slips into his bed and nefarious activities, the fleshing-out begins of two of the most unsympathetic characters to be seen on the screen all year, taking the edge off

Imogen Stubbs as the naive young English girl on holiday in France, and Jean-Philippe Ecoffrey as her unpleasant terrorist lover in Curzon's Nanou.

any pleasure in the fine, authentic backgrounds and the well drawn, and played, supporting characters.

Cast: Imogen Stubbs, Jean-Philippe Ecoffrey, Christophe Lidon, Valentine Pelka, Roger Ibanez, Nathalie Bécue, Dominique Rousseau, Anna Cropper, Patrick O'Connell, Anne-Marie Habraud, Michel Robin, Daniel Day Lewis, Lou Castel, Jean-Marc Maurel, Jean Amos. Dir and Screenplay: Conny Templeman. Pro: Simon Perry and Martin Fuhrer. Co-Pro: Patrick Sandrin. Ed: Tom Priestley. Art: Andrew Mollo. M: John Keane. (Umbrella Films/Arion-Curzon). Rel: floating; first shown London (Curzon Mayfair) 27 February 1987. 105 mins. Cert 15.

The Naples Connection – Camorra: Un Complicato Intrigo di Donne Vicoli e Delitti. A string of brutal murders sparks off panic among the feuding crime lords of Naples. The winner of three Italian 'Oscars' – for Best Actress, Cinematography and Art Direction – *The Naples Connection* arrives in its English incarnation as a catastrophe, owing in part to some dreadful subtitling and an appallingly melodramatic score. Amazingly, Lina Wertmüller directed.

Cast: Angela Molina, Harvey Keitel, Isa Danieli, Paolo Bonacelli, Francisco Rabal, Daniel Ezralow, Vittorio Squillante, Tommaso Bianco, Raffaele Verita, Elvio Porta, Mario Scarpetta, Franco Angrisano, Loffredo Muzzi, Roberto Marafante, Annie Papa, Pino Amendola, Sebastiano Nardone, Gino Carcione, Rosario Campese, Riccardo Perrotti, P. L. Cuomo, Lucio Amelio, Nuccio Pianese, Anna Maria Porta, Mario Porfito, Mietta Albertini, Alberto De Stasio, Elio Steiner, Claudio Ciocca. Dir and (with Elvio Porta) Screenplay: Lina Wertmüller. Pro: Menahem Golan and Yoram Globus. Assoc Pro: John Thompson. Ex Pro: Fulvio Lucisano. Ph: Giuseppe Lanci. Ed: Luigi Zita. Pro Des: Enrico Job. M: Tony Esposito. (Cannon). Rel: floating; first shown London (Cannons Première and Baker Street) 3 April 1987. 106 mins. Cert 18.

Nightmare on Elm Street, Part 2: Freddy's Revenge. Those who found Part 1 of this horror-pic satisfying should find Part 2 equally so, for it is well up to the grisly standard set by the original 'demonic possession' movie; only this time around Freddy selects a male teenager instead of a girl to do his dirty work.

Cast: Mark Patton, Kim Myers, Robert Rusler, Clu Gulager, Hope Lange, Marshall Bell, Robert Englund, Melinda O. Fee,

It's not very pleasant to find your hand turning into a talon, and Mark Patton is understandably shocked when he finds it happening to him in the Palace chiller Nightmare on Elm Street, Part 2: Freddy's Revenge.

Thom McFadden, Sydney Walsh, Edward Blackoff, Chrisie Clark, Lyman Ward, Donna Bruce, Hart Sprager, Allison Barron, Joann Willette, Steve Eastin, Brian Wimmer, Robert Chaskin, Kerry Remsen, Kimberly Lynn, Steven Smith, Jonathan Smith. Dir: Jack Sholder. Pro: Robert Shayle. Ex Pro: Stephen Diener and Stanley Dudelson. Line Pro: Michael Murphy and Joel Soisson. Screenplay: David Chaskin, based on characters created by Wes Craven. Co-Pro: Sara Risher. Ph: Jacques Haitkin. Ed: Bob Brady. Sup Ed: Arline Garson. M: Christopher Young. (New Line/Heron Communictions/Smart Egg Pictures-Palace Pictures). Rel: 31 October 1986. 84 mins. Cert 18.

Nobody's Fool. A bizarre romantic comedy set in a small fictitious town somewhere in Arizona, where Cassie (Rosanna Arquette) goes through a severe identity crisis. One moment she attacks her lover with a fork, the next she's attempting suicide, and then she joins the local drama group. Slowly, ever so slowly, she slides into the lap of Mr Right – only to find that he's as odd as she is. A self-consciously screwball look at small-town Americana, suffering from a deficiency of straightforward plot and a surfeit of sketched-in characters. Of the performers, Mare Winningham (from *St Elmo's Fire*) impresses most as a live-wire barmaid with her mouth on her sleeve.

Rest of cast: Eric Roberts, Jim Youngs, Louise Fletcher, Gwen Welles, Stephen Tobolowsky, Charlie Barnett, J. J. Hardy, William Steis, Belita Moreno, Lewis Arquette, Ronnie Claire Edwards, Anne Hearn, Scott Rosenweig, Cheli Chew, Sheila Paige, Alma Beltran, Budge Threlkeld, Lisa DeBennedetti, Wylie Small, Natalie Golden, Kristy Kennedy, Arwen Nichols, Loraine Wallace, Rod Hart, Mark Atkinson, Derek Barnes, John Hoover, Mark Sanders, Brian West, Jay Dusard, Christopher Michael Johnson, Diane Costa, Marsha Hicks, Walt Zandt, Kat, Barbara Brown, Kay Pasa, Brian Fitzgerald, Bonnie Oda, Dean Ricca, Joe Clarke, Becky Bell Maxwell, Bruce Wright, Frederick Bailey, Melissa Grier. Dir: Evelyn Purcell. Pro: James C. Katz and Jon S. Denny. Ex Pro:

Somebody, but who?, is Nobody's Fool *in the Enterprise release with Eric Roberts and Rosanna Arquette.*

Tracking a killer through the Louisiana swamps with Kim Basinger in tow, Richard Gere finds it hard, and very wet, going in Tri-Star's No Mercy.

Cary Brokaw. Screenplay: Beth Henley. Ph: Mikhail Suslov. Ed: Dennis Virkler. Art: John R. Jensen. Pro Des: Jackson DeGovia. M: James Newton Howard. (Island Pictures/Katy Denny Pro-Enterprise Pictures). Rel: floating; first shown London (Warner) 12 June 1987. 104 mins. Cert 15.

No Mercy. A recently divorced Chicago cop (Richard Gere) sets out to avenge the vicious murder of his colleague (Gary Basaraba) by a merciless crime lord overseeing a giant crime syndicate in New Orleans. A well-researched, good-looking crime thriller which treads old ground with fresh energy. Jeroen Krabbe is a splendid villain and Kim Basinger (breathtakingly sensuous) is the illiterate Cajun woman who draws the two men together. Plenty of atmospheric photography, a first-rate score and telling detail, lifting this out of the run-of-the-mill 'lone cop against the mob' genre.

Rest of cast: George Dzundza, William Atherton, Terry Kinney, Bruce McGill, Ray Sharkey, Marita Geraghty, Aleta Mitchell, Fred Gratton, Dionisio, Ray Brown, Kim Chan, George Dickerson, Raynor Scheine, Carl Gordon, Victoria Edwards, Annalee Jefferies, Ed Nakamoto, John Snyder, Caris Corfman, Pearl Jones, John Schluter, Mike Bacarella, Charles Dutton, Harold Evans, Dave Petitjean, Stephen Payne, Leon Rippy, Bill Hart, Thomas Rosales Jr, Randall Trepagnier, Khon Reid, Helen Yu-Shin McKay, R. G. Martin, Murphy Taylor, Alvin D. Bailey Sr, Nat Emore, Joan Duvalle, Shelton McGee. Dir: Richard Pearce.

Pro: D. Constantine Conte. Ex Pro: Michael Hausman. Screenplay: Jim Carabatsos. Ph: Michel Brault. Ed: Jerry Greenberg and Bill Yahraus. Art: Doug Kraner. Pro Des: Patrizia von Brandenstein. M: Alan Silvestri. (Tri-Star-Columbia). Rel: 8 May 1987. 108 mins. Cert 18.

Nothing in Common. We're all familiar with mixed-up kids, but what about mixed-up movies? Here's a pretty good example. When, as at the beginning, there's plenty of quick-fire fun, it is extremely entertaining, but when it drags in other more serious elements later, it falters and fails. Luckily, to save the day and make it seem all worth while there is Tom Hanks, whose performance as the newly appointed director of a Chicago advertising agency is a joy only dissipated when he gets away from the office and becomes involved in his family's troubles.

Rest of cast: Jackie Gleason, Eva Marie Saint, Hector Elizondo, Barry Corbin, Bess

The madly jealous Otello (Placido Domingo) tries to force – a false – confession from his Desdemona (Katia Ricciarelli) in Franco Zeffirelli's adaptation for the screen of the Verdi opera Otello *(Cannon).*

Armstrong, Sela Ward, Cindy Harrell, John Kapelos, Carol Messing, Bill Applebaum, Mona Lyden, Anthony Starke, Julio Alonso, Jane Morris, Dan Castellaneta, Mike Hagerty, Jeff Michalski, Toni Hudson, Bruce Young, Ben Rawnsley, Vicki Lucachick, Kathi Marshall, Scott Marshall, Kim Genelle, Lynda Goodfriend, Mark von Holstein, Ron Dean, Elma Veronda Jackson, Noelle Bou-Sliman, Andrew Paris, Steve Assad, Vincent Guastaferro, John Antony, Lucinda Crosby, Andra Akers, Tracy Reiner, Harvey Keenan, Sam Denoff, John Yune, Lorna Thayer, Meg Wyllie, Bobbie Jo Burke, Shirley Kirkes, Maxine Dunn, etc. Dir: Garry Marshall. Pro: Alexandra Rose. Assoc Pro: Nick Abdo. Ex Pro: Roger M. Rothstein. Screenplay: Rick Podell and Michael Preminger. Ph: John A. Alonzo. Ed: Glenn Farr. Pro Des: Charles Rosen. M: Patrick Leonard. (Tri-Star-Delphi Pro-Columbia). Rel: floating; first shown London (Warner) 12 June 1987. 119 mins. Cert 15.

Otello. Stagey but artistically impressive Zeffirelli film of his own theatrical production of the highly dramatic Verdi opera, superbly sung and well acted. Apart from all else, it makes the corrosive jealousy of the Moor not only almost credible but certainly moving.

Cast: Placido Domingo, Katia Ricciarelli, Justino Diaz, Petra Malakova, Urbano Barberini, Massimo Foschi, Edwin Francis, Sergio Nicolai, Remo Remotti, Antonio Pierfederici. And additional singing voices of: Ezio Di Cesare, John Macurdy, Constantin Zaharia, Edward Toumajin, Gianncola Pigliucci. Dir and Screenplay: Franco Zeffirelli. Pro: Menahem Golan and Yoram Globus. Assoc Pro: Fulvio Lucisano. Ex Pro: John Thompson. Pro Sup: Mike Hartman and Roberto Giussani. Ph: Ennio Guarnieri. Ed: Peter Taylor and Franca Silvi. Art: Gianni Quaranta. Libretto: Arrigo Boito. (Cannon). Rel: floating; first shown London (ABCs Shaftesbury Avenue and Fulham Road) 23 September 1986. 126 mins. Cert U.

Other Halves – A Dangerous Love Story. Grittily realistic, well acted, tightly directed New Zealand film about some wholly unsympathetic characters: the story of a mature – in years – but otherwise naive and pretty stupid Auckland housewife who suddenly walks out on her husband, and becomes interested in and then sexually besotted with a 16-year-old Maori sneak-thief and mugger. Along with his worthless pals, the lover takes over her home and lives off her. Unfamiliar and fascinating backgrounds help to make this a superior film.

Cast: Lisa Harrow, Mark Pilisi, Paul Grittins, Fraser Stephen-Smith, Clare Gifford, Bruce Purchase, John Bach, Grant Tilly, Temeura Morrison, Raymond Reid, Alan Sio, Olaf Olberg, Emma Piper. Dir: John

Trucker Sylvester Stallone arm-wrestles Rick Zumwalt for the world championship of that odd, unfamiliar sport in Warner's Over the Top.

Laing. Pro: Tom Finlayson and Dean Hill. Screenplay: Sue McCauley, based on her novel. Ph: Leon Narbey. Ed: Harley Oliver. Art: Grant Major. Pro Des: Robert Gilles. M: Don McGlashan. (Oringham-Contemporary). Rel: floating; first shown London

Ill-matched lovers – middle-aged housewife and 16-year-old Maori tearaway thief – played by Lisa Harrow and Mark Pilisi in Contemporary's New Zealand release Other Halves – A Dangerous Love Story.

(Cannon Tottenham Court Road) 10 October 1986. 102 mins. Cert 15.

Over the Top. Sylvester Stallone was paid the record sum of $12 million to write and star in this sentimental truck movie, about as predictable as *Rocky V*. There are the mandatory montages, silhouettes and close-ups of exploding muscle, but this time *Rocky* becomes *The Champ*. A cute kid (David Mendenhall) – the product of a broken home – is forced to spend two days with the father he never knew (Stallone) and whom he thinks he should hate. Meanwhile, Stallone's ex-wife is on her deathbed . . . For excitement, Stallone arm-wrestles in his spare time and has his biceps set for the World Arm-wrestling Championship. The plot weakens . . . I loved every minute of it.

Rest of cast: Robert Loggia, Susan Blakely, Rick Zumwalt, Chris McCarty, Terry Funk, Bob Beattie, Alan Graf, Magic Schwarz, Bruce Way, Jimmy Keegan, John Braden, Tony Munafo, Randy Raney, Paul Sullivan, Jack Wright, Sam Scarber, Richie Giachetti, Michael Fox, Ross St Phillip, Seth Mitchell, Dale Benson, Joe Kiel, Dean Abston, Flo Gerrish, David van Gorder, Kelly Sahnger, Charles M. Wilborn, Terry Burns, William

Nichols Buck, Bob Eazor, Ed Levitt, Andrew Rhodes, Bob Rogers, Reggie Bennett, Joshua Lee Patton, James Mendenhall, Danny Capri, Gregory Braendel, Sly Ali Smith, Rose Dursey, Marion Mickens II, Dave Patton, Alexa Lambert, Ronnie Rondell Jr, James H. Shana, Norman Howell, Rex Pierson. Dir: Menahem Golan. Pro: Menahem Golan and Yoram Globus. Assoc Pro: Tony Munafo. Ex Pro: James D. Brubaker. Screenplay: Stirling Silliphant and Sylvester Stallone, based on a story by Gary Conway and David C. Engelbach. Ph: David Gurfinkel. Ed: Don Zimmerman and James Symons. Pro Des: James Schoppe. M: Giorgio Moroder. (Cannon-Warner). Rel: 3 April 1987. 93 mins. Cert PG.

Oxford Blues. Stereotype teenage romance set against the pleasant background of those 'dreaming spires' and misted river. A pushy young American relentlessly pursues a British aristocrat to Oriel College but ends up with the nicer, patient, commoner gal. It isn't so hard to see all this as a thinly disguised re-make of *A Yank at Oxford*. Made in 1984 but previously unreleased.

Cast: Rob Lowe, Ally Sheedy, Amanda Pays, Julian Sands, Julian Firth, Alan Howard, Gail Strickland, Michael Gough, Aubrey Morris, Cary Elwes, Bruce Payne, Anthony Calf, Pip Torrens, Richard Hunt, Peter Jason, Peter Hugo-Daly, Carrie Jones, Sonia Smyles, Richard Pescud, Jeffrey Per-

Kathleen Turner as the unlikely scholar – well, would you think she's old enough to have two kids and yet be accepted as a schoolgirl? – with divorcing husband (Nicolas Cage) in Tri-Star's Peggy Sue Got Married.

ry, Charles Grant, Laura Francis, Aimée Delmain, Hugh Morton. Dir and Screenplay: Robert Boris. Pro: Cassian Elwes and Elliott Kastner. Assoc Pro: Peter Kohn and David Wimbury. Pro Co-Ord: Valerie Craig. Ph: John Stanier. Ed: Patrick and James Symons. Pro Des: Terry Pritchard. M: John DuPrez and George Romanis. (Winkast Film Pro/ Baltic Industrial Finance Co-Fox). Rel: 17 October 1986. 97 mins. Cert 15.

Parting Glances. Sorrowful little tale of long-standing lovers parting, after six years, the difference here being that the liaison here is an all-male one seen against a background of the 'gay' world of New York during the 24 hours before one of the pair leaves for Kenya.

Cast: Richard Ganoung, John Bolger, Steve Buscemi, Adam Nathan, Kathy Kinney, Patrick Tull, Yolande Bavan, André Morgan, Richard Wall, Jim Selfe, Kristine Moneagle, John Siemans, Bob Kohrherr, Theodore Ganger, Nada, Patrick Ragland, Cam Brainard, Daniel Haughey, Sylvia Hartowicz, Hanna Hartowicz, Nicholas Hill, Lee Greenstein, Jordan McLean, Lori Tirgrath, Elain Swayneson, Marcus Lawson, David Lines, Gardiner Kendall, Victor Rivers, Michael Medeiros, Eric Miller, Al Hughes. Dir, Screenplay and Ed: Bill Sherwood. Pro: Yoram Mandel and Arthur Silverman. Ex Pro: Paul A. Kaplan. Ph: Jacek Laskus. Pro Des: John Loggia. M: No credit. (Rondo Pro-Contemporary). Rel: floating; first shown London (Screen-on-the-Hill) 24 October 1986. 90 mins. Cert 15.

Passing Glory. One of the most promising films in the annual show of work by the National Film and Television School students; a sometimes moving

account of the not always smooth relationship between a doughty old grandmother (a fighter in the Spanish Civil War) and her grand-daughter. With Ida Schuster and Fiona Chalmers. Winner of the Best Newcomer Award in the Celtic Film Festival.

Dir: Gillespie MacKinnon. (NFT and ICA). Rel: floating; first shown London (ICA) 23 February 1987. 40 mins. No cert.

The Passion of Remembrance. A never particularly clear examination of the blacks and their life in Britain, presented in three parts and generally developed by dialogue rather than by action. Obviously destined for TV and video rather than the cinema.

Cast: Anni Domingo, Joseph Charles (female and male speakers), Antonia Thomas, Carlton Chance, Jim Findley, Ram John Holder, Sheila Mitchell, Tania Morgan, Gary McDonald, Janet Palmer, Kelvin Omard, Christopher Tajah, Michael Hughes, Simon Binns, Andrew Powell, David Doyle, Tim Brennan, Marcelle Williams, Derrick Blackwood, Maureen Blackwood, Osaze Ehibor. Dir and Screenplay: Maureen Blackwood and Isaac Julien. Ph: (on 16mm): Steven Bernstein and Nina Kellgren. Ed: Nadine Marsh-Edwards. M: Tony Remy. (Sankofa Films/Video Collective, with financial assistance from Channel 4 and GLC Police Support Committee). Rel: floating; first shown London (Metro) 5 December 1986. 82 mins. Cert 15.

Peggy Sue Got Married. The latest, and most implausible, of time-travel movies, *Peggy Sue* tries to give a more lyrical slant to the genre. Kathleen Turner is, as always, excellent as the mother of two facing divorce from her free-spirited husband (Nicolas Cage); but she never truly convinces that she is either old enough to have a teenage daughter or, later, young enough to be at school. Peggy Sue is miraculously transported 25 years back in time to 1959, and tries to express the love she has for her family which she never showed when she was young. Being courted once again by her oafish husband, Charlie Bodell, is another matter. Can Peggy Sue change the forces of destiny, or will she once again succumb to Charlie's crude charms? An oddly old-fashioned film, *Peggy Sue* never realizes its potential, and is a poor substitute for *Back to the Future*. However, there are some fun lines and a nice, lush score from John Barry.

Julie Walters (as Madam Christine) flanked by Danny Schiller (the 'nurse') and Shirley Stelfox (friend), with erotic angel Lorena Lee and customer Alec McCowen, at a party in her suburban brothel in the UIP British film Personal Services.

Rest of cast: Barry Miller, Catherine Hicks, Joan Allen, Kevin J. O'Connor, Jim Carrey, Lisa Jane Persky, Lucinda Jenney, Wil Shriner, Barbara Harris, Don Murray, Sofia Coppola, Maureen O'Sullivan, Leon Ames, Randy Bourne, Helen Hunt, Don Stark, Marshall Crenshaw, Ken Grantham, Ginger Taylor, Sigrid Wurschmidt, Glenn Withrow, Harry Basil, John Carradine, Sachi Parker, Vivien Straus, Morgan Upton, Dr Lewis Leibovich, Bill Bonham, Joe Lerer, Barbara Oliver, Martin Scott, Marcus Scott, Lawrence Menkin, Dan Suhart, Leslie Hilsinger, Al Nalbandian, Dan Leegant, Ron Cook, Mary Leichtling, Steve Holladay. Dir: Francis Coppola. Pro: Paul R. Gurian. Ex Pro: Barrie M. Osborne. Screenplay: Jerry Leichtling and Arlene Sarner. Ph: Jordan Cronenweth. Ed: Barry Malkin. Art: Alex Tavoularis. Pro Des: Dean Tavoularis. (Tri-Star – Rastar). Rel: 30 January 1987. 103 mins. Cert 15.

Personal Services. Intermittently funny, consistently vulgar, satirically perceptive and often genuinely sad, this surprisingly polished British film is about an astute cockney waitress who becomes a 'madame' and, in a typical suburban villa, sets up a cheerful, harmless brothel catering for kinky as well as 'straight' sex-seekers, giving tea and sympathy while satisfying their carnal desires. With the laughs overlapping the tears, it gives a happily accepted opportunity for Julie Walters to show she's no one-note actress. If it all sounds vaguely familiar, well, there *was* a recent headline-hitting court case about a very similar situation.

Rest of cast: Alec McCowen, Danny Schiller, Shirley Stelfox, Victoria Hardcastle, Tim Woodward, Dave Atkins, Leon Lissek, Benjamin Whitrow, Peter Cellier, Stephen Lewis, Andrew MacLachlan, Anthony Collin, Ewan Hooper, Beverly Foster, Alan Bowyer, Nigel le Vaillant, Antony Carrick, Michelle Collins, Arthur Whybrow, Ron Pember, Pamela Duncan, Sheila Gill, Toni Palmer, Lorraine Brunning, Rupert Holliday Evans, Claire Waugh, Wayne Morris, Renny Lister, Shulie Bannister, Jagdish Kumar, Jason Smart, Jeffrey Daunton, Arnold Brown, Janie Booth, Nick Stringer, Paul Imbusch, Bernard Brown, Andreas Marcos, Peter Wight, John Bailey, Helen Gemmell, Clare Clifford, John Shrapnel, Michael Packer, Stanley Lebor, Suzette Llewellyn, Carolyn Allen, Arthur Hewlett, Joanna Dickens, Ivor Roberts, Arthur Cox, Lorena Lee, Badi Uzzaman, Ian McNeice, Michael Irving, Allan Stirland, Charlotte Seely, Mark Hardy, David Leland. Dir: Terry Jones. Pro: Tim Bevan. Screenplay: David Leland. Ph: Roger Deakins. Ed: George Akers. Art: Jane Coleman. Pro Des: Hugo Luczyc-Wyhowski. M: John Du Prez. (Vestron/Zenith-UIP). Rel: 1 May 1987. 105 mins. Cert 18.

Il Pétomane – The Windbreaker. Only in France could it happen: the naming of a street, Rue Pujol, after a vaudeville performer, Joseph Pujol, who entertained his highly appreciative audiences by musically and otherwise breaking wind! The Italian film about this very successful freak is, surprisingly enough, not at all distasteful. Pujol started life as a baker and finished it, after the war had put an end to the Belle Epoque and his own Moulin Rouge success, as the owner of a biscuit factory. It is certainly amusing and contains another superlative performance by Ugo Tognazzi in the title role, most charmingly supported by the delectable

Almost unrecognizable in hirsute disguise, Walter Matthau as pirate captain Red in Roman Polanski's rollicking Cannon release Pirates; *with the Cap'n, Cris Campion, as faithful companion The Frog.*

Mariangela Melato as his delicate and delicious wife.

Rest of cast: Riccardo Tognazzi, Gianmarco Tognazzi, Flavio Colusso, Stefano Roffi, Giovanni Grimaldi, Vittorio Caprioli, Giulliana Calandra, Anna Maria Gherardi, Peter Berling, Sebastiano Lo Monaco, Sergio Solli, Cesare Rufini, Mila Stanic, Filippo de Gara, Riccardo Perisio Perrotti, Felice Andreasi, Roberto Antonelli, Piero Nutti, Massimo Sarchielli, Raimondo Penne, Enzo Robutti, Adriana Innocenti. Dir: Pasquale Festa Campanile. Pro: Luigi and Aurelio de Laurentiis. Screenplay: Leo Benvenuti, Piero de Barnardi and Enrico Medioli. Ph: Alfio Contini. Ed: Franco Fraticelli. Art: Dario Cecci and Mario Carlini. M: Carlo and Paulo Rustichelli. (Filmauro, Rome-Cannon). Rel: floating; first shown London (Cannon Swiss Centre) 15 May 1987. 101 mins. Cert PG.

Pirates. The result of 12 years' gestation, this Roman Polanski lark turns out, sadly, to be something of a damp if elaborate squib. Almost unrecognizable, sporting lots of hirsute adornment, a wooden leg and a most extraordinary brogue, Walter Matthau plays a scoundrelly, resourceful and often amusing Captain Red the Pirate in a series of win-some, lose-some battles, both of sword and wit, occasionally borrowing a leaf or two out of the late Robert Newton's book.

Rest of cast: Cris Campion, Charlotte Lewis, Damien Thomas, Olu Jacobs, Ferdy Mayne, David Kelly, Anthony Peck,

Anthony Dawson, Richard Dieux, Jacques Maury, Ian Dury, Roy Kinnear, Jose Santamaria, Robert Dorning, Luc Jamati, Emilio Fernandez, Wladislaw Komar, Georges Trillat, Richard Pearson, Georges Montillier, John Gill, Raouf Ben Amor, David Foxxe, Brian Maxine, Eugeniusz Priwieziencew, Roger Ashton-Griffiths, Bill Stewart, Sydney Bromley, Cardew Robinson, Daniel Emilfork, Carole Fredericks, Allen Hoist, Denis Fontayne, Michael Elphick, Angelo Casedei, Bill Fraser, Antonio Spoletini, Bill McCabe, Smilja Mihailovitch, Bernard Musson, Josine Comelas. Dir: Roman Polanski. Pro: Tarak Ben Ammar. Ex-Pro: Thom Mount. Co-Ex Pro: Marc Lombardo and Umberto Sambucco. Screenplay: Polanski and Gerard Brach. Ph: Whitbold Sobocinski. Ed: Herve de Luze and William Reynolds. Art: Henry Sonois, Albert Rajou and Jean-Michel Hugon. Pro Des: Pierre Guffroy. M: Philippe Sarde. (Cathago Films, Paris in assoc with Accent Cominco/Dino de Laurentiis-Cannon). Rel: (at several Cannon cinemas) 10 October 1986. 112 mins. Cert PG.

Platoon. No better than, say, *The Deer Hunter* or *Apocalypse Now*, Oliver Stone's *Platoon* was none the less one of the most numbingly brilliant film experiences of 1987. From the director of *Salvador* and writer of *Midnight Express*, *Platoon* has Charlie (son of Martin) Sheen providing the now-familiar, tortured voice-over. There are the drugs, the Rambo-esque heroes, the lethal efficiency of the Viet Cong – but there are also the bullies, the mindless American jingoism, the torture of Vietnamese peasants, the in-fighting, the incompetence of Western combat . . . *Platoon*, superbly photographed, ferociously acted and expertly plotted, presents the wall-to-wall hell that was Vietnam, but shows *both* sides of the story.

Remarkably, the film was based on actual experiences and characters encountered by Stone in 1967–8. Steel-jawed Tom Berenger plays a brutal mercenary and Willem Dafoe a granite-willed, selfless hero.

Rest of cast: Forest Whitaker, Francesco Quinn, John C. McGinley, Richard Edson, Kevin Dillon, Reggie Johnson, Keith David, Johnny Depp, David Neidorf, Mark Moses, Chris Pedersen, Corkey Ford, Corey Glover, Bob Orwig, Tony Todd, Kevin Eshelman, James Terry McIlvain, J. Adam Glover, Ivan Kane, Paul Sanchez, Dale Dye, Peter Hicks, Basile Achara, Steve Barredo, Chris Castillejo, Andrew B. Clark, Bernardo Manalili, Than Rogers, Li Thi Van, Clarisa Ortacio, Romy Sevilla, Mathew Westfall, Nick Nickelson, Warren McLean, Li Mao Thao, Ron Barracks. Dir and Screenplay: Oliver Stone. Pro: Arnold Kopelson. Ex Pro: John Daly and Derek Gibson. Co-Pro: A. Kitman Ho. Pro Ex: Pierre David. Ph: Robert Richardson. Ed: Claire Simpson. Art: Rodel Cruz and Doris Sherman Williams. Pro Des: Bruno Rubeo. M: Georges Delerue. (Hemdale-Rank). Rel: 8 May 1987. 120 mins. Cert PG.

Playing for Keeps. Humour plus pop (about a dozen numbers) in a lightly frothed mix about a trio of young New Yorkers and their efforts to get the better of the corrupt local authorities and turn a run-down hotel into a sparkling and lively entertainment centre for teenagers.

Cast: Danny Jordano, Matthew Penn, Leon W. Grant, Mary B. Ward, Marisa Tomei, Harold Gould, Robert Millie, Kim Hauser, Jimmy Baio, John Randolph Jones, Raymond Barry, John Bennes, Ruth Judd, Anthony Arcure, Hildy Brooks, Timothy Carhart, Agnes Cummings, Silk's Band, etc. Dir and Screenplay: Bob and Harvey Weinstein. Pro: Alan Brewer and the Weinsteins. Ex Pro: Julia Palau, Michael Ryan and Patrick Wachsberger. Ph: Eric van Haren Noman. Ed: Gary Karr and Sharyn Ross. Pro Des: Waldemar Kalinowski. M: Alan Brewer. (Mirimax-Guild). Rel: floating; first shown London (Cannons Panton and Oxford Streets) 16 January 1987. 107 mins. Cert 15.

Police Academy 3: Back in Training. With the same fortune-making recipe as Nos 1 and 2, this third broad comedy about trainee cops is a collection of gags, jokes and riotous behaviour, with most of the 1 and 2 stalwarts on duty reinforced with a few new recruits. As before, it is really all beyond any serious criticism, but it seems to work, if slightly less so each time.

Cast: Steve Guttenberg, Bubba Smith, David Graf, Michael Winslow, Marion Ramsey, Leslie Easterbrook, Art Metrano, Tim Kazurinsky, Bobcat Goldthwait, George Gaynes, Shawn Weatherly, Scott Thomson, Bruce Mahler, Lance Kinsey, Brian Tochi, Debralee Scott, Ed Nelson, Brandt van Hoffman, Andrew Paris, G. Robertson, Georgina Spelvin, David Huband, R. Christopher Thomas, David Elliott, Arthur Batanides, Jack Creley, Rita Tuckett, Chas Lawther, Lyn Jackson, Mary Anne Coles, Sam Stone, Grant Cowan, Bruce Pirie, Doug Lennox, Teddy Abner, Susan DeRyck, Marcia Watkins, Pam Hyatt, Fran Gebhard, Les Nirenberg, Gloria Summers, Fred Livingstone, Gladys O'Connor, Elias Zarou, Gary Flanagan, Pierre Berube, Peter Colvey, Alex Pauljuk, Anton Tyukodi. Dir: Jerry Paris. Pro: Paul Maslansky. Assoc Pro: Donald West. Screenplay: Gene Quintano, based on characters created by Neal Israel and Pat Proft. Ph: Robert Saad. Ed: Bud Molin. Art: Rhiley Fuller. Pro Des: Trevor Williams. M: Robert Folk. (Warner). Rel: 11 July 1986. 82 mins. Cert PG.

Police Story – Jingcha Goshi. Jackie Chan walks away with considerable acting and directing honours in this express-tempo Hong Kong movie which never pretends to be more than it

The men of Bravo Company restrain their enraged sergeant (Willem Dafoe) in the Orion-Rank Oscar-winning Platoon. *Inset: another sergeant (Tom Berenger) threatens a terrified Vietnamese girl (Li Thi Van) with sudden death.*

is: popular kung-fu entertainment. This time Chan is a special mission cop assigned to protect a vital witness against the local drug king; he fails and has to endure major misfortunes before becoming the hero of the hour. Well, it's fun, and fantastic.

Rest of cast: Maggie Cheung, Ken Tong, Bridget Lin, Cho Yuen, Bill Tung, Lam Kok Hung, Lau Chi Wing, Charles Chao, Kam Hing Yin, Mars, Paul Wong, Wan Fat, Fung Hark On, Danny Chow, Tai Po, Wu Fung, Lau Ai Lai, Money Lo, Winnie Yu, Clarence Ford, Robert Lo. Dir: Jackie Chan. Pro: Leonard Ho. Screenplay: Edward Tang. Ex Pro: Raymond Chow. Ph: Cheung Yiu Joe. Ed: Peter Cheung. Art: Oliver Wong. M: Kevin Bassinson. (Golden Harvest-Palace Pictures). Rel: floating; first shown London (Metro) 23 January 1987. 98 mins. Cert 18.

Poltergeist II: The Other Side. Four years after the horrid happenings at Cuesta Verde – four years of peace and

quiet – a toy telephone rings in the Freeling household and the things that go bump and all else in the night move once more into the Freeling residence to start the grisly game all over again! ('The filthy rain, foul winds, black clouds and malevolent storm', as the synopsis neatly puts it.)

Cast: JoBeth Williams, Craig T. Nelson, Heather O'Rourke, Oliver Robins, Zelda Rubinstein, Will Sampson, Julian Beck, Geraldine Fitzgerald, John P. Whitecloud, Noble Craig, Susan Peretz, Helen Boll, Kelly Jean Peters, Jaclyn Bernstein, Robert Lesser, Ann Louise Bardach, David Beaman, Pamela Gordon, Whitby Hertford, Carrie Lorraine, Jamie Abbott, Syd Beard, Hayley Taylor-Block, Chelsea Hertford, Rocky Krakoff, Kathy Wagner, Bill Schroeder. Dir: Brian Gibson. Pro and Screenplay: Mark Victor and Michael Grais. Assoc Pro: Lynn Arost. Ex Pro: Freddie Fields. Ph: Andrew Laszlo and Bill Neil. Ed: Thom Noble. Pro Des: Ted Haworth. M: Jerry Goldsmith. (MGM-UIP). Rel: 19 September 1986. 91 mins. Cert 15.

P.O.W. The Escape (formerly titled *Behind Enemy Lines*). Routine addition to the Vietnam war movies with Colonel Cooper (David Carradine) leading the usual assortment of GIs through

Social snob James Spader (left) confronts friend Andrew McCarthy about the latter's lower-class girl-friend in Paramount-UIP's Pretty in Pink.

shot and shell from their POW camp to eventual safety just before the fall of Saigon. Lots of action and a real Macho role by Carradine.

Gary Oldman (left) as playwright Joe Orton and Alfred Molina as his very close friend and nemesis, Kenneth Halliwell, in the British Prick Up Your Ears, a Curzon release.

liams, Willy Williams, Avi Karpick, Bill Kipp, Andrew Sommer, Victor Barjo, John Barett, Zenon Gil, Henry Strazalkowski. Dir: Gideon Amir. Pro: Menahem Golan and Yoram Globus. Screenplay: Jeremy Lipp, James Bruner, Malcolm Barbour and John Langley, based on a story by Avi Kleinberger and Amir. Ph: Yechiel Ne'eman. Ed: Roy Watts. Sup Ed: Marcus Manton. Art: Bo Johnson and Ramon Nigado. Pro Des: Marcia Hinds. M: David Storrs. (Golan/Globus-Cannon). Rel: 2 January 1987. 90 mins. Cert 15.

Pretty in Pink. Thankfully well above average 'youth' film from America with a slim and blatantly contrived ending apparently forced on the movie's makers when the star, Molly Ringwald – a charming performance – fell ill, right at the end of shooting. About the girl from the wrong side of the tracks whose life is not made easy by self-doubt and the attitudes of class distinction facing her both in and out of high school . . . Most of the characters seem to be suffering from an inferiority complex of some kind or other.

Rest of cast: Harry Dean Stanton, Jon Cryer, Annie Potts, James Spader, Andrew McCarthy, Jim Haynie, Alexa Kenin, Kate Vernon, Andrew 'Dice' Clay, Emily Longstreth, Margaret Colin, Jamie Anders, Gina Gershon, Bader Howard, Christian Jacobs, Audrey Johnston, Melanie Manos, Maggie Roswell, Dweezil Zappa, Jimmy Podrasky, Tommy Blatnik, Timothy J, Terry Wilson, Bruno, Jeffrey Hollie, Kevin Ricard, David Sutton, Kevin Williams, Rock Deadrick, Karen Laine, Kristy Swanson, K. D. Lindsay. Dir: Howard Deutsch. Pro: Lauren Shuler. Assoc Pro: Jane Vickerilla. Ex Pro: John Hughes and Michael Clinich. Screenplay: Hughes. Ph: Tak Fujimoto. Ed: Jane Schwartz Jaffe. Pro Des: John W. Corso. M: Michael Gore. (Paramount-UIP). Rel: 15 August 1986. 96 mins. Cert 15.

Prick Up Your Ears. Sharply written, witty account of the life and death of anarchic playwright Joe Orton. Orton, born and raised 'in the gutter' in Leicester, moved to London to train as an actor. There he met the sinister, 'cultured' Kenneth Halliwell. Six years older and a good deal more experienced, Halliwell initiated Orton into the ways of the flesh, and from there the young playwright improvised the

Rest of cast: Charles R. Floyd, Mako, Steve James, Phil Brock, Daniel Demorest, Tony Pierce, Steve Freedman, James Acheson, Rudy Daniels, Ken Metcalfe, Kenneth Weaver, Michael James, Irma Alegre, Spanky Manikan, Estrella Antonio, Tony Beso Jr, John Falch, Chris Aguillar, Crispin Medina, Rey Robillard, Leif Eriandson, Brian Tasker, James Gaines, Eric Hahn, Mansour Khalili, Tony Realle, Tony Wil-

rest – mainly in public lavatories. Orton and Halliwell lived together for 16 years but eventually Halliwell's jealousy of his lover's success moved him to murder and suicide. Alan Bennett, who is becoming increasingly obsessed with the scatological in our culture, has fashioned a lucid, gritty screenplay replete with memorable one-liners, most of them far funnier than anything Orton ever thought up. But Gary Oldman (Sid Vicious in *Sid and Nancy*) lacks the necessary charisma to bring Orton to full demonic life, while Vanessa Redgrave, as his agent, is miscast.

Rest of cast: Alfred Molina, Wallace Shawn, Lindsay Duncan, Julie Walters, James Grant, Frances Barber, Janet Dale, Dave Atkins, Margaret Tyzack, Eric Richard, William Job, Rosalind Knight, Angus Mackay, Linda Spurrier, Charlotte Wodehouse, Helena Michell, Sean Pertwee, Liam de Staic, Charles McKeown, Selina Cadell, Bert Parnaby, Antony Carrick, Neil Dudgeon, Richard Wilson, Christopher Guinee, Steven Rimkus, Michael Mueller, Anthony Douse, John Kane, Stevan Mackintosh, Garry Cooper, Roger Lloyd Pack, Joanna Connelly, John Moffat, Philippa Davies, David Cardy, Julie Legrand, Noel Davis, Jane Blackburn, Stella Richman, Neville Phillips, Jonathan Phillips, Richard Ireson, Ahmed El Jheur, Moktar Dagmouni, Sian Thomas, Stephen Bill, Karl Johnson, David Bradley, Simon Adams, James Duggan, Max Stafford-Clark, Mark Brignal, Joan Sanderson, Neville Smith, Spencer Leigh, John Salthouse, Robin Hooper. Dir: Stephen Frears. Pro: Andrew Brown. Screenplay: Alan Bennett, based on the Orton biography by John Lahr. Pro Co-Ord: Lorraine Goodman. Ph: Oliver Stapleton. Ed: Mike Audsley. Art: Philip Elton. Pro Des: Hugo Luczyc-Wyhowski. M: Stanley Myers. (Civilhand/Zenith in assoc with British Screen/Film Four Int-Curzon). Rel: floating; first shown London (Curzon West End) 1 May 1987. 110 mins. Cert 18.

The Princes – Les Princes. French film about gypsies in France, living in pride, poverty and filth. This story concerns one family, of a determined old woman, her small-criminal, violent-tempered, illiterate son, his small daughter – longing for the education he denies her – and her loving mother, thrown out for no explained reason but tagging along, hoping to contact the child. The dismal scene should be authentic in that writer-director Tony Gatlif is a gypsy from Algeria; there he was a thief and a delinquent, but now he is revealed as a fresh, raw talent in

As well as starring in Psycho III *(as he did for Nos I & II) Anthony Perkins assumed the role of director, which in the original film was taken by Alfred Hitchcock.*

the French cinema. A remarkable performance by Gérard Darmon as the savage, proud and passionate gypsy.

Rest of cast: Muse Dalbray, Céline Militon, Concha Tavora, Dominique Maurin, Marie-Hélène Rudel, Anne-Marie Philippe, Farid Chopel, Hagop Arslanian, Tony Gatlif, Tony Librizzi. Dir, Screenplay and M: Tony Gatlif. Pro: Ken and Romaine Legargeant. Dir of Pro: Thierry Barbier. Ph: Jacques Loiseleux. Ed: Claudine Bouché. Pro Des: Denis Champenois. (ACC/Babylone Films Contemporary). Rel: floating; first shown London (Phoenix East Finchley) 28 November 1986. 105 mins. Cert 15.

Psycho III. Anthony Perkins, whose twitchy facial mannerisms were an amusing ingredient in the more seriously intended *PI* and *PII*, repeats them in more tongue-in-cheek mood in this third milking of a story about the macabre and chilling results of a mother fixation. Himself directing the incredible goings-on, Perkins adds some touches of sly humour, but the original vein of gold has now been worked out.

Rest of cast: Diana Scarwid, Jeff Fahey, Roberta Maxwell, Hugh Gillin, Lee Garlington, Robert Alan Browne, Gary Bayer, Patience Cleveland, Juliette Cummins, Steve

Guevara, Kay Heberle, Donovan Scott, Karen Hensel, Jack Murdock, Katt Shea Ruben, Hugo L. Stanger, Lisa Ives, Angele Ritter, Diane Rodriguez. Dir: Anthony Perkins. Pro: Hilton A. Green. Assoc Pro: Donald E. Zepfel. Screenplay: Charles Edward Pogue, based on characters created by Robert Bloch. Pro Co-Ord: Lisa J. Watters. Ph: Bruce Surtees. Ed: David Blewitt. Pro Des: Henry Bumstead. M: Carter Burwell. (Universal-UIP). Rel: 21 November 1986. 93 mins. Cert 18.

Purple Haze. The story of two not very interesting or likeable characters, a long-haired, rebellious drop-out and his high-living pal, growing up against the interesting and well presented back-

Dropout (Peter Nelson) faces up to some hard words from his angry girlfriend Kitty (Susanna Lack) in Cannon-Gala's (Purple Haze).

David Warrilow chats up check-girl Mia Farrow and Diane Keaton sings a nostalgic number in the days when sound was all and TV little more than a glint in inventors' eyes: the background of Woody Allen's Rank-released Radio Days.

ground of the worried America of the 1960s and the threatening shadow of the Vietnam War, with its military call-up. It was a pretty depressing time and it's a pretty depressing picture, embellished by very, very loud musical numbers of the period provided by the likes of Jimi Hendrix, The Animals, Cream etc.

Cast: Peter Nelson, Chuck McQuarry, Bernard Baldan, Susanna Lack, Bob Breuler, Katy Horsch, Joanne Bauman, Heidi Helmen, Jean Ashley, Tomy O'Brien, Dan Jones, Don Bakke, James Craven, John Speckhardt, Sara Hennessy, Michael Bailey, Peter Thoemke, Donna Moen, Spare Change Band, Don Westling, Steve Gjerde, Jake Braziel, Jillian Griffiths, Ky Michaelson, Jane Rogers, Nori Helm, Mary Bea Arman, Bill Tilton, Steve Toakam, Paul Sorensen, Kevin O'Neill, John O'Brien, Gary Geblowitz, Alex Cole, James Newman, Dick Hadlund, Bobby Vandell. Dir: David Burton Morris. Pro: Thomas A. Fucci. Screenplay: Victoria Wozniak, based on a story by Wozniak, Morris and Tom Kelsey. Pro Co-Ord: Marine Davis. Ph: Richard Gibb. Ed: Dusty Nabili. Art: James Johnson. (Cannon-Gala). Rel: floating; first shown London (Cannons Baker Street and Tottenham Court Road) 1 August 1986. 97 mins. Cert 18.

Radio Days. Minor Woody Allen, a deft mixture of Jewish family humour, irreverent comic spots (such as the baseball star who goes on playing after losing a leg, an arm and finally his sight), and nostalgia for the days when radio played a not inconsiderable role in life before TV had come along to dominate it. Worthwhile for the sound track alone: a marvellous collection of popular classics of the 1930s performed by yesteryear's greats, orchestras (Benny Goodman and the like) and soloists (Ink Spots and the like). A gentle little film which almost looks as if Woody made it to fill in time between more major efforts.

Cast (spot the Allen familiars): Mike Starr, Paul Herman, Don Pardo, Martin Rosenblatt, Helen Miller, Daniele Ferland, Julie Kavner, Julie Kurnitz, David Warrilow, Wallace Shawn, Michael Murray, William Flanagan, Seth Green, Michael Tucker, Josh Mostel, Renée Lippin, William Magerman, Leah Carrey, Joy Newman, Hy Anzell, Judith Malina, Dianne Wiest, Fletcher Farrow Previn, Oliver Block, Maurice Toueg, Sal Tuminello, Rebecca Nickels, Mindy Morgenstern, Kenneth Mars, Andrew Clark, Mia Farrow, Lee Erwin, Roger Hammer, Terry Lee Swarts, Margaret Thomson, Tito Puente, Denise Dummont, Dimitri Vassilopoulos, Larry David, Rebecca Schaeffer, Belle Berger, Guy le Bow, Brian Mannain, Stan Burns, Todd Field, Peter Lombard, Martin Sherman, Crystal Field, Maurice Shrog, Marc Colner, Roberta Bennett, Joel Eidelsberg, Danny Aiello, Peter Castellotti, Gina Deangelis, Shelly Delaney, Dwight Weist, Ken Levinsky, Ray Marchica, Jeff Daniels, J. R. Horne, Kuno Spunholz, Henry Yuk, Sydney A. Blake, Kitty Carlisle Hart, Robert Joy, Henry Cowen, Philip Shultz, Mercedes Ruehl, Bruce Jarchow, Greg Gerard, David Cale, Ira Wheeler, Hannah Rabinowitz, Edward S. Kotkin, Ruby Payne, Jacqui Safra, Paul Berman, Richard Portnow, Tony Roberts, Barbara Gallo, Jane Jarvis, Liz Vochecowizc, Ivan Kronenfeld, Frank O'Brien, Yolanda Childress, Artie Butler, Diane Keaton, Gregg Almouist, Jackson Beck, Wendell Craig, W. H. Macy, Ken Roberts, Norman Rose, Kenneth Welsh. Dir, Screenplay and Commentator: Woody Allen. Pro: Robert Greenhut. Assoc Pro: Ezra Swerdlow and Gail Sicilia.

Ex Pro: Jack Rollins and Charles H. Joffe. Ph: Carlo di Palma. Ed: Susan E. Morse. Art: Speed Hopkins. Pro Des: Santo Loquasto. M: Dick Hyman. (Rank Film Dist.). Rel: floating; first shown London (Odeon Haymarket) 26 June 1987. 89 mins. Cert PG.

Ratboy. After *Elephant Man*, *Ratboy* – well, perhaps it was inevitable. Different kinds of 'outsiders' but much the same story, with plenty of heartless, ruthless characters all too ready to exploit a freak of any kind: to them the pitiful half-human, half-rodent creature comes like a gift from . . . well, somewhere. Staying carefully away from tempting melodrama, director-star Sondra Locke keeps things on an even keel and seems mainly concerned with the reactions of various people faced with an opportunity to make a fast buck at someone else's expense.

Rest of cast: Robert Townsend, Christopher Hewitt, Larry Hankin, Sydney Lassick, Gerrit Graham, Louie Anderson, S. L. Baird, Billie Bird, Gordon Anderson. Dir: Sondra Locke. Pro: Fritz Manes. Assoc Pro: David Valdes and Rob Thompson. Screenplay: Thompson. Ph: Bruce Surtees. Ed: Joel Cox. Pro Des: Edward Carfagno. M: Lennie Niehaus. (Malpaso-Warner). Rel: floating; first shown London (Warner) 5 June 1987. 104 mins. Cert 15.

Rate It X. American documentary (partly funded by British TV) about self-obsessed American males. Alternately funny, sad and mad. What a parade of chauvinistic pigs! And made by women!

Dir: Lucy Winer and Paula de Koenigsberg. Pro: de Koenigsberg, Lynn Campbell and Claudette Charbonneau. Ed: Winer. M: Elizabeth Swados. Made on 16mm in both colour and black-and-white. (OTM Productions in assoc with Channel 4–ICA). Rel: floating; first shown London (ICA) 23 January 1987. 95 mins. Cert 18.

Raw Deal. Watch it, Rambo: in Arnold Schwarzenegger you have a real one-man army rival, quite as lethal and equally capable of surviving a hail of lead. Watch him here knocking off so many bad lads it becomes impossible to keep count. He's playing a former FBI agent, now a rural sheriff, who infiltrates the Chicago gang busily knocking off the witnesses against them before their case comes to court. The man directing this comic-strip stuff is none other – you will be astonished to learn –

than John Irvin, who made that intelligent, brilliant British film *Turtle Diary*. Admittedly he gets his moments of fun here . . . but really!

Rest of cast: Sam Wanamaker, Kathryn Harrold, Paul Shenar, Robert Davi, Ed Lauter, Darren McGavin, Joe Regalbuto, Mordecai Lawner, Steven Hill, Blanche Baker, Robey, Victor Argo, George Wilbur, Denver Mattson, John Malloy, Lorenzo Clemons, Dick Durock, Frank Ferrara, Thomas Rosales, Jack Hallett, Leon Rippy, Jay Butler, Norman Maxwell, Tony DiBenedetto, Tom Hull, Cedric Guthrie, Gary Olsen, Brooks Gardner, Pat Miller, Jery Hewitt, James Eric, Ralph Foody, Howard Elfman, Jeff Ramsay, Bill McIntosh, Ted Grossman, Kent Hays, Cliff Happy, Mike Adams, Dean Smith, Alex Ross, Socorro Santiago, Richard McGough, Sharon Rice, R. Pickett Bugg, John Clark, Scott Blount, Phil Adams, Chuck Hart, Larry Holt, Ken Sprunt. Dir: John Irvin. Pro: Martha Schumacher. Screenplay: Gary M. DeVore and Norman Wexler, based on a story by Luciano Vincenzoni and Sergio Donati. Ph: Alex Thomson. Ed: Anne V. Coates. Art: Maher Ahmad. Pro Des: Giorgio Postiglione. M: Cinemascore. (International Film Corps-UKFD). Rel: 23 January 1987. 106 mins. Cert 18.

One-man-army (and Rambo rival?) Arnold Schwarzenegger as a former FBI agent on the warpath in UKFD's Raw Deal.

A Real Genius. Neatly summed up by one American critic as 'a *Police Academy* with brains', this youth-aimed comedy comes as a pleasant surprise after so many moronic college comedies. It's about a couple of bright and brainy youngsters who discover that the advanced laser they are inventing is destined, thanks to their villainous, exploitive Professor, to be offered to the American Air Force for warlike purposes instead of the civilian use they were reckoning on. Swift pace, a reasonably literate script, excellent direction and good performances send this to the top of its class by a mile.

A Real Genius is young Val Kilmer in the Tri-Star release with that title. He invents a laser as his class assignment, not knowing the villains plan to turn it into a weapon for war.

Cast: Val Kilmer, Gabe Jarret, Michelle Meyrink, William Atherton, Jonathan Gries, Patti D'Arbanville, Stacy Peralta, Daniel Addes, Andres Aybar, Louis Giambalvo, Ed Lauter, Charles Shull, Beau Billingslea, Charles Parks, Sean Frye, Joann Willette, Ina Gould, Nadine Vix, Paul Tulley, Joanna Baron, Chip Johnson, Monte Landis, Sandy Martin, Severn Darden, Randolph Dreyfuss, Robert Prescott, John Shepherd, Reid, Tom Swerdlow, Mark Kamiyama, Martin Gundersen, Brett Miller, Dean Devlin, Yuji Okumoto, Lynda Wiesmeier, Penny Baker, Marcia Karr, Isabelle Walker, Marii Mak, Cheri Wells, Catherine MacNamara, Johnny Vasily, Ed Garrabrandt, Isabel Cooley, Robin Stober, Deborah Foreman, David Marvit, Michael Crabtree, Charles Sweigart, Peter Parros, Ronald Taylor, James Carrington, Michael Backes, Corki Grazer, Jeanne Mori, David Ursin, Joe Dorsey, Will Knox, Kevin Hurley. Dir: Martha Coolidge. Pro: Brian Grazer. Assoc Pro: Sam Crespi-Horowitz. Ex Pro: Robert Daley. Screenplay: Neal Israel, Pat Proft and Peter Torokvei, based on a story by Israel and Proft. Ph: Vilmos Zsigmond. Ed: Richard Chew. Pro Des: Josan F. Russo. M: Thomas Newman. (Tri-Star). Rel: 5 December 1986. 104 mins. No cert.

Rebel. Slight and rather mediocre Australian movie based on a straight stage play awash with interpolated musical numbers originally introduced because Olivia Newton-John was pencilled in for the leading *femme* role, now played in a quite commendable debut by Debbie Byrne. A caddish US Marine deserter on the loose in Sydney (a mannered Matt Dillon) is determined to seduce the lonely niterie singer whose husband is away fighting.

Rest of cast: Bryan Brown, Bill Hunter, Ray Barrett, Julie Nihill, John O'May, Kim Deacon, Sherée da Costa, Isabelle Anderson, Joy Smithers, Chris Hession, Annie Semler, Ray Marshall, Beth Child, Cassandra Delaney, Antoinette Byron, Nicky Crayson, Nikki Coghill, Sally Phillips, Betti Summerson, Lisa Ross. Dir: Michael Jenkins. Pro: Phillip Emanuel. Ex Pro: Robyn Campbell-Jones and Bonnie Harris. Screenplay: Jenkins and Bob Herbert, adapted from the latter's stage play. Ph: Peter James. Ed: Michael Honey. Pro Des: Brian Thomson. M: Chris Neal. (Phillip Emanuel/Village Roadshow Corp.-Miracle). Rel: floating; first shown London (Odeon Kensington) 19 September 1986. 93 mins. Cert 15.

Rendez-vous. Minor but fascinating French film about an ambitious young provincial actress who comes to Paris determined to succeed. But her easy attitude to sexual relationships, her turning down the young estate agent who sincerely loves her and her affair with a self-destructive, failed actor lead to the final moment of truth when, unprepared and almost certain to fail, she faces her first night as Juliet without any moral support or affection. A film which takes ghostly appearances in its often erotic stride.

Cast: Juliette Binoche, Lambert Wilson, Wadeck Stanczak, Jean-Louis Trintignant, Dominique Lavanant, Anne Wiazemsky, Jean-Louis Vitrac, Jacques Nolot, Philippe Landoulsi, Caroline Faro, Arlette Gordon. Dir: André Téchiné. Pro: Alain Terzian. Ex Pro: Armand Barbault. Screenplay: Téchiné and Olivier Assayas. Ph: Renato Berta. Ed: Martine Giordana. Pro Des: Jean-Pierre Kohut-Svelko. M: Philippe Sarde. (T.Films/Films A2-Cannon). Rel: floating; first shown London (Cannon Première) 3 October 1986. 83 mins. Cert 18.

The Riveter. About an old drunk who, in an effort to forget his drifting past, goes off to the Western Isles with the idea of starting a new life. This half-hour short was one of the best things in the annual show of work by students of the National Film and Television School. With Andrew Barr and Ewen Bremner.

Dir: Michael-Caton Jones. (NFT and ICA). Rel: floating; first shown London (ICA) 23 February 1987. 33 mins. No cert.

Dexter Gordon, himself a considerable jazz musician, as the famous jazz star Dale Turner (inventor of the 1950s be-bop sound) in Warner's bio-pic 'Round Midnight.

Rosa Luxemburg. An outstanding performance by Barbara Sukowa ('Best Actress' prizes at Cannes and the German Film Awards for 1986) in Margarethe von Trotta's biopic about the Jewish, Polish-born, German-naturalized (by marriage) left-wing agitator of the title, who is presented as a passionately dedicated lady combining untiring work and verbally violent support for the proletarian revolution with an inner warmth and poetic outlook. An ardent pacifist, Luxemburg spent most of WWI in (a reasonably comfortable) prison, only to be murdered by the authorities soon after her release, shot and thrown into the river on 15 January 1919. An interesting lesser-known page of German history.

Rest of cast: Daniel Olbrychski, Otto Sander, Adelheid Arndt, Jürgen Holtz, Doris Schade, Hannes Jaenicke, Jan-Paul Biczycki, Karin Baal, Winfried Glatzeder, Regina Lemnitz, Barbara Lass, Dagna Drozdek, Henryk Baranowski, Patrizia Lazreg, Charles Regnier, Hans-Michael Rehberg, Charles Brauer, Hans Beerhenke, Klaus Abramowsky, Katharina Seyferth, Inge Herbrecht, Lena Birkova, Eva Jaboubkova, Mila Myslikova, Oldrich Vlach. Dir and Screenplay: Margarethe von Trotta. Pro: Eberhard Junkersdorf. Ph: Franz Rath. Ed: Dagmar Hirtz. Art: Bernd Lepel and Karel Vacek. M: Nicolas Economou. (Bioskop/Munich-Artificial Eye). Rel: floating; first shown London (Lumière) 29 August 1986. 124 mins. Cert PG.

'Round Midnight. Like, and yet – thanks to the technical expertise and inspiration of French writer-director

Bertrand Tavernier, a proverbial lover of jazz – completely unlike all those other biopics we've had about jazz 'greats'. This story of a veteran jazz saxophone player is a composite of the heartfelt tribute to the many fine American negro musicians who lived and played in the Paris of the 1930s. The veteran is played to perfection by actual veteran saxophone player Dexter Gordon, 63 years old, a shambling and Armstrong-voiced amateur surrounded by some of today's top jazz talent. Very long (from anyone with less than Tavernier's talent, far, far too long), full of classical jazz, the threading story follows the efforts of a fiery French disciple of the star to bring back the drink- and drug-ridden player-composer to his former glory, a crusade that finally fails.

Rest of cast: François Cluzet, Gabrielle Haker, Sandra Reaves-Phillips, Lonette McKee, Christine Pascal, Herbie Hancock, Bobby Hutcherson, Pierre Trabaud, Frédérique Meininger, Liliane Rovère, Hart Leroy Bibbs, Ged Marlon, Benoit Régent, Victoria Gabrielle Platt, Arthur French, John Berry, Martine Scorsese, Philippe Noiret, Alain Sarde, Eddy Mitchell. Players include: (at Blue Note, Paris) Billy Higgins, Bobby Hutcherson, Eric le Lann, John McLaughlin, Pierre Michelot, Wayne Shorter; (at Davout Studio) Ron Carter, Palle Mikkelborg, Mads Vinding; (at Lyons) Cheikh Fall, Tony Williams, Michel Perez; (at New York) Ron Carter, Freddie Hubbard, Cedar Walton, Tony Williams etc. Dir and (with David Rayfiel) Screenplay: Bertrand Tavernier. Pro: Irwin Winkler. Ph: Bruno de Keyzer. Ed: Armand Psenny. Art: Pierre Duquesne. Pro Des: Alexandre Trauner. M: Herbie Hancock. (Warner). Rel: floating; first shown London (Lumière) 28 November 1986. 131 mins. Cert 15.

Rozinante. British film of good intent but just that bit too pretentious for its own good: it uses the recent coal miners' strike to tilt at too many political windmills (the film's title is taken from Don Quixote's horse). John Hurt is excellent as the 'travelling man' wandering through the English countryside and newcomer Maureen Douglass (a member of the Women's Support Group during the strike) as a lady who believes in physical action.

Rest of cast: Ian Dury, Jimmy Jewel, Carol Gillies, Gillian Heasman, David Travena, Tony Rohr, Nicky Bee, Richard Worthy, Jill Lamede, Adam Daye. Dir and Screenplay: Ann and Eduardo Guedes. Pro: Gustav

Billy Crystal and Gregory Hines as the Chicago cops whose dedicated attempts to bring the drug-runners to justice sometimes lead them into big trouble in MGM/UIP's Running Scared.

Lamche. Ph: Thaddeus O'Sullivan. Ed: Guedes and Richard Taylor. Art: Caroline Amies. M: Jürgen Knieper. (Cinema Action/Channel 4-Artificial Eye). Rel: floating; first shown London (Renoir cinemas) 16 January 1987. 93 mins. Cert PG.

Running Scared. Familiar cops-and-drug-runners stuff, with Gregory Hines and Billy Crystal as the fast-talking undercover Chicago police team whose main aim in life is to bring in mobster boss Jimmy Smits and smash his drugs empire, achieved eventually in spite of sundry hiccups – like suspension, suspicion and official disapproval.

Rest of cast: Steven Bauer, Darlanne Fluegel, Joe Pantoliano, Dan Hedaya, Jonathan Gries, Tracy Reed, John Di Santi, Larry Hankin, Don Calfa, Robert Lesser, Betty Carvalho, Louis Perez, Ron Cummins, Natividad Rios Kearsley, John La Motta, Richard Kuss, Jeff Silverman, Dax Brooks, Jaime Alba, Meg Register, Debbie Johnson, Fred Buch, Ricardo Gutierrez, Frankie Davilla, Ernest Perry Jr, Etel Billig, James Noah, Bob Zrna, Deanna Dunagan, Joe Guastaferro, Mike Bacarella, Johnny O'Donnell, Jim Ortlieb, Julian Pena, Richard Wharton, Tony Zurita Jr, Saralynne Crittenden, Alex Leonard Jenkins, William Lozada, Irma O'Quendo, C. D.

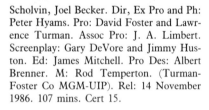

Scholvin, Joel Becker. Dir, Ex Pro and Ph: Peter Hyams. Pro: David Foster and Lawrence Turman. Assoc Pro: J. A. Limbert. Screenplay: Gary DeVore and Jimmy Huston. Ed: James Mitchell. Pro Des: Albert Brenner. M: Rod Temperton. (Turman-Foster Co MGM-UIP). Rel: 14 November 1986. 107 mins. Cert 15.

Ruthless People. Fast-paced, often coarse, indelibly black and very, very funny comedy with lots of sparkling lines and superbly directed farcical action, aided by some meticulously timed performances; all adding up to one of the best comedies of its year.

Cast: Danny DeVito, Bette Midler, Judge Reinhold, Helen Slater, Anita Morris, Bill Pullman, William G. Schilling, Art Evans, Clarence Felder, J. E. Freeman, Gary Riley, Phyllis Applegate, Jeannine Bisignano, J. P. Bumstead, Jon Cutler, Susan Marie Snyder, Jim Doughan, Christopher J. Keen, Henry Noguchi, Janet Rotblatt, Frank Sivero. Dir: Jim Abrahams, David and Jerry Zucker. Pro: Michael Peyser. Ex Pro: Richard Wagner, Joanna Lancaster and Walter Yetnikoff. Screenplay: Dale Launer. Pro Co-Ord: Karen Penhale. Ph: Jan DeBont. Ed: Arthur Schmidt. Art: Donald Woodruff. M: Michel Colombier. (Touchstone-Walt Disney). Rel: floating; first shown London

(Odeon Leicester Square) 7 November 1986. 94 mins. Cert 18.

The Sacrifice – Offret. This was Andrei Tarkovsky's last film, a powerful, ambiguous and visually arresting drama about the war of technology versus spirituality. Tarkovsky tells us that nothing is what it seems, that much is unexplained in this world, and then unfolds a mystery that we are part of but his characters are not. *The Sacrifice* is largely a tale of *malaise*, of lost hopes, of contradiction – told with a leisurely precision and an artistic mind. We are led, unknowing, to the final tragedy, when everything is made clear: an old man has a dream, a terrifying dream, and while asleep he promises God the ultimate sacrifice, that he will destroy his life if only what is happening can be happily resolved. When the old man awakes, everything is back to normal, so he keeps his promise to God.

Cast: Erland Josephson, Susan Fleetwood, Valérie Mairesse, Allan Edwall, Gudrún Gísladóttir, Sven Wollter, Filippa Franzén, Tommy Kjellqvist, Per Kallman, Tommy

Some of those very creditably involved in Touchstone's deep black and very funny comedy Ruthless People: *amateur kidnappers Judge Reinhold and Helen Slater, rumbustious kidnappee Bette Midler, and her ever-hating hubby, Danny De Vito, with his scheming mistress Anita Morris.*

Nordahl. Dir and Screenplay: Andrei Tarkovsky. Pro: Katinka Farrago. Ex Pro: Anna-Lena Wibom. Ph: Sven Nykvist. Ed: Tarkovsky and Michal Leszczylowski. Art: Anna Asp. M: J. S. Bach, Swedish and Japanese folk music. (The Swedish Film Insitute, Argos Films SA in assoc with Film Four International and Josephson & Nykvist HB, Sveriges Television/SVT 2, Sandrew Film and Teater AB, and with the participation of the French Ministry of Culture). Rel: floating; first shown London (Lumière) 9 January 1987. 145 mins. Cert 15.

Salome. One can only imagine Oscar Wilde twirling with fury (or laughter) in his grave at this Franco-Italian assault on his famous play about the lady who demanded, and got, Herod's head on a plate and then danced around with it, shedding veils as she went . . .

Cast: Tomas Milian, Pamela Salem, Tim Woodward, Jo Champa (Salome), Fabrizio Bentivoglio, Jean-François Stévenin, Fabio Carfora, Richard Paul Majewski, Fabiana Torrente, Paul Muller, Feodor Chaliapin, Lorenzo Piani, Valerie Racz, Alex Serra, Andrea Flamini, Nicola D'Eramo, Jorge Krimer, Paolo Paolini, Leslie Thomas, Massimo Sarchielli, Salem Mohamed Badr, Annie Edel, Sergio Doria, Ikky Maas, Cleo Sebastian, Michael Popper, Noel Wallace, David Cameron, Daniele Melani. Dir and Screenplay: Claude d'Anna. Pro: Henry Lange. Ex Pro: Menahem Golan and Yoram Globus. Ph: Pasqualino de Santis. Ed: Roberto Perpignani. Pro Des: Giantito Burchiellaro. M: Egisto Macchi. (Cannon). Rel: floating; first shown London (Cannons Panton and Oxford Streets) 9 January 1987. 95 mins. Cert 18.

Salvador. A raw, rough and in many ways both repelling and compelling political story, of a dissolute, generally unsympathetic (apparently drawn from life) American freelance photojournalist, trying to squeeze a living from the brutal struggle going on in Salvador. At the heart of it is the sudden, out-of-character outburst in which he pillories the United States for helping – or at least doing nothing to stem – the brutal fires of murder, torture and repression carried out by the military regime. Often explosive, overlong, and likely to confuse non-Americans, yet exciting and absorbing, with some good performances headed by James Woods as journalist Richard Boyle.

Rest of cast: James Belushi, Michael Murphy, John Savage, Elpedia Carrillo, Tony Plana, Colby Chester, Cindy Gibb, Will MacMillan, Valerie Wildman, José Carlos Ruiz, Jorge Luke, Juan Fernandez, Salvador Sanchez, Rosario Zuniga, Martin Fuentes, Gary Farr, Giles Milinaire, Ramon Menendez, John Doe, Leticia Valenzuela, Roberto Sosa Jr, Daria Okugawa, Sue Ann McKean, Joshua Gallegos, Maria Rubell, Danna Hansen, Sigridur Gudmunds, Erica Carlson, Kara Glover, Ma Del, Arturo Bonilla, Miguel Ehrenberg, Sean Stone, Tyrone Jones. Dir and (with Richard Boyle) Screenplay: Oliver Stone. Pro: Stone and Gerald Green. Assoc Pro: Bob Morones and Brad H. Aronson. Ex Pro: John Daly and Derek Gibson. Ex in charge of Pro: Brad H. Aronson. Ph: Robert Richardson. Ed: Claire Simpson. Pro Des: Bruno Rubeo. M Sup: Bud Carr. (Hemdale-Virgin). Rel: floating; first shown London (Warner etc) 23 January 1987. 123 mins. Cert 18.

Saving Grace. *Extremities* director, Robert M. Young, at least showing his

Trouble-shooting newsman James Woods (in dark glasses), photographer John Savage and female newshound Cindy Gibb in a tight corner in Virgin's Salvador.

versatility in this odd little tale about a Pope (Leo XIV) who, shut out of his Vatican garden by the wind and a wayward door, decides to take a look at the wider world. He wanders off to a small

Tom Conti, a very unconventional Pope (Leo XIV), in the Embassy-Rank release Saving Grace.

village where his influence brings a new awareness and community ambition to the inhabitants. Though there are a few shafts of ironic criticism of Vatican bureaucracy, the overall tone is one of gentle comedy reminiscent of those similar comedies we had from Italy in the past. Tom Conti as the Pope gives a curious performance, somewhat marred by atrocious 'broken inglese' even though everyone else avoids that pitfall.

Rest of cast: Fernando Rey, Erland Josephson, Giancarlo Giannini, Donald Hewlett, Edward James Olmos, Patricia Mauceri, Angelo Evans, Marta Zoffoli, Guido Alberti, Massimo Sarchielli, Massimo Serato, Agnes Nobercourt, Jorge Krimer, Tom Felleghy, Margherita Horowitz, Domenico Modena, Angelo Panarella, Julian Jenkyns, Peter Boom, Carlo Monni, Claudio Massin, Fernando Cartocci, Tessa Passante, Benito Pucciariello, Francesca Roberti, Mauro Sacripanti, Paolo Merosi, Fabio Caretti, Ettore Martini, Joe Chevalier, Italo Furlan, Phillip Dacchille, Don Sciarrino. Dir: Robert M. Young. Pro: Herbert F. Solow. Assoc Pro: Newton Arnold. Screenplay: Joaquin Montana, based on the book by Celia Gittelson adapted by Richard Kramer. Pro Ex: Michael S. Glick. Pro Sup: Mario Pisani. Ph: Reynaldo Villalobos. Ed: Michael Kelly and Peter Zinner, with Thomas Stanford.

Pro Des: Giovanni Natalucci. M: William Goldstein. (Embassy Film Associates/ Rank). Rel: floating; first shown London (several Cannons) 14 November 1986. 112 mins. Cert PG.

School for Vandals. Another feature – the seventh since 1981 (a remarkable record when you consider that in addition it has made numerous shorts) – from The Children's Film Unit, with the children largely in control on both sides of the camera. This is a comedy-drama with crazy trimmings.

Cast: Anne Dyson, Charles Kay, Peter Bayliss, Jennifer Barrand, Jeremy Coster, Samantha McMillan, Deakin Glyn, Nicholas Mott, etc. Dir and Ed: Colin Finbow. Pro: Joanie Blaikie. Screenplay: Finbow and the children of the Unit. Ph: Titus Bicknell, Orlando Wells, Will Grove-White and Leigh Melrose. M: Dave Hewson. (Children's Film Unit). Rel: floating; first shown London (ICA) 23 May 1987. 80 mins. Cert U.

Secret Admirer. Some nice, talented young players trapped, along with their equally excellent elders, in one of those awful teenager-aimed 'comedies' presenting both, gapless, generations as foul-mouthed, sex-obsessed, amoral and thoroughly unsympathetic.

Cast: C. Thomas Howell, Lori Loughlin, Kelly Preston, Dee Wallace Stone, Cliff de Young, Leigh Taylor-Young, Fred Ward, Casey Siemaszko, Geoffrey Blake, Rodney Pearson, Courtney Gains, Jeffrey Jay Cohen, Scott McGinnis, Cory Haim, Michael Menzies, Michael Moore, John Terlesky, Keith Mills, Ken Lerner, Dermott Downs, Doug Savant, Leslie Allan, Gypsi de Young, Janet Carroll, Mike Toto,

Lori Loughlin and C. Thomas Howell – two of the best things in Orion-Rank's over-familiar, youth-aimed, swearword-loaded Secret Admirer.

Ron Burke, Arvid Malnaa, Ernie Brown. Dir: David Greenwalt. Pro: Steve Roth. Ex Pro: C. O. Erickson. Screenplay: Jim Kouf and Greenwalt. Co-Pro: Kouf. Ph: Victor J. Kemper. Ed: Dennis Virkler. Pro Des: William J. Cassidy. M: Jan Hammer. (Orion-Rank). Rel: floating; first shown London (several Cannons) 18 July 1986. 98 mins. Cert 15.

The Secret of My Success. A sort of sex farce about a country hick in New York whose dream it is to have a lush apartment, a lovely girlfriend and a private plane, but whose reality it is to have nothing but hopes and dreams. Best thing about it is the likeable performance of Michael J. Fox as the innocent abroad; worst, the deafening pop music.

Rest of cast: Helen Salter, Richard Jordan, Margaret Whitton, John Pankow, Christopher Murney, Gerry Bamman, Fred Gwynne, Carol-Ann Susi, Elizabeth Franz, Drew Snyder, Susan Kellermann, Barton Heyman, Mercedes Ruehl, Ira B. Wheeler,

Real-life newlyweds Sean Penn and Madonna in a predicament, and co-star roles, in Handmade-Warner's Shanghai Surprise.

Ashley J. Laurence, Rex Robbins, Christopher Durang, MacIntyre Dixon, Bill Fagerbakke, Jack Davidson, John Bowman. Dir and Pro: Herbert Ross. Assoc Pro: Nora Kay. Ex Pro: David Chasman. Screenplay: Jim Cash, Jack Epps and A. J. Carothers. Ph: Carlo di Palma. Ed: Paul Hirsch. Pro Des: Edward Pisoni and Peter Larkin. M: David Foster. (Rastar/Universal-UIP). Rel: 19 June 1987. 111 mins. Cert PG.

Shanghai Surprise. The completely daft, illogical and further than far-fetched tarradiddle which serves as the story is in reality a big stone tied around the neck of this otherwise often quite amusing, harmless and reasonably acceptable melodrama. The less than charming stars are no great help; it is the several rich supporting performances, fascinating Hong Kong and Macao backgrounds, and high technical standards which are the movie's greatest assets. Sean Penn plays a scruffy tie salesman who becomes mixed up with the most unlikely sexy missionary (played by wife Madonna) and, through her, with a convoluted plot (sic) involving stolen jewels, gorgeous hookers, amusing crooks (one with porcelain hands) and opium.

Rest of cast: Paul Freeman, Richard Griffiths, Philip Sayer, Clyde Kusatsu, Kay Tong Lim, Sonserai Lee, Victor Wong, Professor Toru Tanaka, Michael Aldridge, Sarah Lam, George She. Dir: Jim Goddard. Pro: John Kohn. Assoc Pro: Sarah Romilly. Ex Pro: George Harrison and Denis O'Brien. Screenplay: John Kohn and Robert Bentley, based on the book *Faraday's Flowers* by Tony Kenrick. Pro Ex: Ray Cooper. Co-Pro: Robin Douet. Ph: Ernest Vincze. Ed: Ralph Sheldon. Art: David Minty (Hong Kong) and John Siddall (UK). Pro Des: Peter Mullins. M: Harrison and Michael Kamen. (Handmade Films-Warner). Rel: 17 October 1986. 97 mins. Cert 15.

She's Gotta Have It. Made in a couple of weeks in black-and-white on 16mm stock, this attempt to examine a young woman of the 1980s may have warts, but it is still an impressive work which proves that young movie-maker Spike

Defending her new robot boyfriend 'Number Five' from her more human ex-boyfriend Brian McNamara, a determined Ally Sheedy in the Rank release Short Circuit.

Lee and his photographer Ernest Dickerson both have considerable potential.

Cast: Tracy Camilla Johns, Tommy Redmond Hicks, John Canada Terrell, Spike Lee, Raye Dowell, Joie Lee, Epatha Merkinson, Bill Lee, etc. Dir, Screenplay and Ed: Spike Lee. Pro: Shelton J. Lee. Assoc Pro: Pamm Jackson. Ph: Ernest Dickerson. Art: Ron Paley. Pro Des: Wynn Thomas. M: Bill Lee. (Forty Acres/Mule Filmworks-Pro Recorded Releasing). Rel: floating; first shown London (Screen-on-the-Green) 6 March 1987. 85 mins. Cert 18.

Shoah. Gargantuan French-Swiss documentary, running for almost 10 hours, about Hitler's attempt to exterminate the Jews. Without recourse to the usual horrifying death camp scenes, it emerges as a very powerful, masterly assembled and unforgettable indictment of a regime and those outside it who remained unmoved by the suffering on their doorstep, and reveals that anti-semitism still exists. Altogether a remarkable, disturbing, depressing but stunning cinematic experience which deserves to be shown all around the world. Directed, produced and conceived by French political journalist Claude Lanzmann, ex-Resistance fighter, now editor of *Les Temps Modernes*. It took a dozen years to make but it is a masterpiece in many ways.

Ph: Dominique Chapuis, Jimmy Glasberg and William Lubtchansky. Ed: Ziva Postec. (Les Films Aleph/Historia Films/Curzon Film Dist.). Rel: floating; first shown Lon-

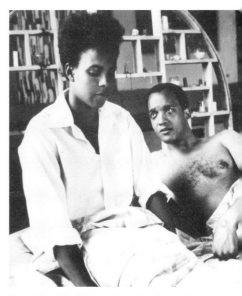

Tracy Camilla Johns as the girl who needs a lotta lovin' in the Recorded Releasing all-black film She's Gotta Have It. *Tommy Redmond Hicks is one of those who provides.*

don (Curzon Mayfair) November 1986. 561 mins. Cert PG.

Short Circuit. A bolt from the blue is what causes it. So starts the fun in this science-fiction send-up comedy in which a nutty professor (Steve Guttenberg) works in a top secret establishment and treats the place like his personal playground, producing a robot – 'No 5' – which the lightning strike brings to life. On the run, the cute No 5 meets a lovely lady (Ally Sheedy – a delicious performance which lights up the film) who takes a fancy to him. Good clean fun.

Rest of cast: Fisher Stevens, Austin Pendleton, G. W. Bailey, Brian McNamara, Tim Blaney, Marvin McIntyre, John Garber, Penny Stanton, Vernon Weddle, Barbara Tarbuck, Tom Lawrence, Fred Slyter, Billy Ray Sharkey, Robert Krantz, Jan Speck, Marguerite Happy, Howard Krick, Marjorie Card Hughes, Herb Smith, Jack Thompson, William Striglos, Mary Reckley, Lisa McLean, Eleanor C. Heutschy. Dir: John Badham. Pro: David Foster and Lawrence Turman. Ex Pro: Mark Damon and John Hyde. Screenplay: S. S. Wilson and Brent Maddock. Pro Sup: Gregg Champion. Co-Pro: Dennis Jones. Ph: Nick McLean. Ed: Frank Morriss. Art: Dianne Wager. M: David Shire. (Tri-Star-Rank). Rel: 13 February 1987. 99 mins. Cert PG.

Sid and Nancy. British-made story of the unattractive Sex Pistols punk star Sid Vicious and his 'romance' with

Gary Oldman as Sid Vicious and Chloe Webb as girlfriend Nancy in Palace Pictures's release Sid and Nancy, *the story of the well-named pop star.*

Nancy Spungen. She was found in a New York hotel room stabbed to death with heroin-high Sid by her side in a junkie trance; he subsequently died from a drug overdose while awaiting trial for her murder . . . but the film seems to suggest that things weren't quite like that.

Cast: Gary Oldman (Sid), Chloe Webb (Nancy), David Hayman, Debbie Bishop, Drew Schofield, Xander Berkeley, Perry Benson, Tony London, Sandy Baron, Sy Richardson, Edward Tudor-Tudor, Biff Yeager, Courtney Love, Rusty Blitz, John Spacely, Coati Mundi, Ed Pansullo, V. J. Isaac, J. S. Markus, Ann Lambton, Sally Anne Field, Kathy Burke, Sara Sugarman, Mark Monero, Michele Winstanley, Andy Bradford, Tom Little, Barbara Coles, Pete Lee-Wilson, Graham Fletcher-Cook, Stuart Fox, Victoria Harwood, Jude Alderson, James Snell, Niven Boyd, Miguel Sandoval, Richard W. Barker III, Patti Tippo, John Jackson, Peter McCarthy, Desirée Erasmus, Gloria Leroy, Milton Selzer, B. W. Magrane, Stephanie Auerbach, Jeffrey Kumer, Bradley Lieberman, Tricia Bartholome,

Jeanny McCarthy, John Snyder, Ron Mosely Jr, Fox Harris, Iggy Pop, Suchi, Dan Wul, Mitch Dean, The Circle Jerks, The Punkettes, The ABC Kids, Al Alu, Bobby Ellis, Peyton Kirkpatrick, Jimmy Emig, Keith Morris, Alexander Folk, Dick Rude, The Dancing Kids. Dir and (with Abbe Wool) Screenplay: Alex Cox. Pro: Eric Fellner. Assoc Pro: Peter Jaques (UK) and Abbe Wool (USA). Co-Pro: Peter McCarthy. Ph:

Roger Deakins. Ed: David Martin. Pro Des: Andrew McAlpine. M: Joe Strummer, The Pogues and Pray for Rain. (Zenith in assoc with Initial Pictures-Palace). Rel: floating; first shown London (Lumière) 25 July 1986. 114 mins. Cert 18.

Smooth Talk. Warm, perceptive and totally convincing story of the delicate change in the life of a 15-year-old Californian girl who, within a few days of an unsettling experience with an older man, changes from giggling kid to young woman. Marvellously correct in feel and detail, and altogether a most impressive debut for director Joyce Chopra and actress Laura Dern (daughter of star Bruce).

Rest of cast: Treat Williams, Mary Kay Place, Margaret Welch, Sarah Inglis, Levon Helm, Elizabeth Berridge, Geoff Hoyle, William Ragsdale, David Berridge, Cab Covay, Michael French, Joy Carlin, Mark McKay, Carl Mueller, David O'Neill, Craig Caddell, Gary Harris, Sally Schwab, William Desmond, Michael Vaughn, Rob Blair, Edgar Kahn, Spenser Mains. Dir: Joyce Chopra. Pro: Martin Rosen. Assoc Pro: Tim Marx. Ex Pro: Lindsay Law. Screenplay: Tom Cole, based on the story 'Where Are You Going, Where Have You Been?' by Joyce Carol Oates. Pro Co-Ord: Kerry Peterson. Ph: James Glennon. Add Ph: Reed Smoot and Michael Santy. Ed: Patrick Dodd. Pro Des: David Wasco. M: Billy Payne, Russ Kunkel and George Massenburg. (Nepenthe Pro in assoc with American Playhouse-Goldcrest-Artificial Eye). Rel: floating; first shown London (Renoir cinemas) 14 November 1986. 92 mins. Cert 15.

Soul Man. Mark Watson (C. Thomas Howell) is a bright, privileged and, above all, white kid from California who is accepted by Harvard Law School. However, his well-to-do father decides to withdraw all financial aid so that his son can utilize his own ingenuity to raise the $54,000 he will need. In desperation, Mark assumes the identity of a negro so that he can qualify for the one scholarship available – for a coloured student. Needless to say, all manner of unexpected problems arise: he falls in love with a coloured girl who only dates blacks; he's chased by a WASP beauty who's into ethnic men; he has to dodge a fellow student who knows his real identity. Along the way, Mark's preconceptions about black

Treat Williams as the unsettling and fascinating stranger who suddenly enters the life of the fifteen-year-old heroine of Artificial Eye's Smooth Talk.

people are radically changed and by the end of his course some of the black rubs off on him. *Soul Man* is not only very funny and moving, it examines racism without being patronizing or resorting to cliché. It also boasts a fine soul soundtrack, with such as Muddy Waters, Nu Shooz, Joan Armatrading, Isaac Hayes, Louis Armstrong and Otis Redding on hand. It's just a pity that the film's conclusion is so contrived. These characters deserved a better funeral.

Rest of cast: Rae Dawn Chong, Arye Gross, James B. Sikking, Melora Hardin, Leslie Nielsen, James Earl Jones, Max Wright, Jeff Altman, Marie Cheatham, Julia Louis-Dreyfus, Mark Neely, Wolfe Perry, Eric Schiff, Ann Walker, Wally Ward. Dir: Steve Miner. Pro: Steve Tisch. Screenplay: Carol Black. Co-Pro: Black and Neal Marlens. Ph: Jeffrey Jur. Ed: David Finfer. Pro Des: Gregg Fonseca. M: Tom Scott. (New World Pictures for Entertainment Film Dist.). Rel: 20 February 1987. 103 mins. Cert PG.

Space Camp. The 'Camp' is a training ground for young would-be astronauts, a fictitious centre inspired by NASA's United States Space Camp at the Space and Rocket Center, Alabama. There, five teenage 'astronauts' are accidentally rocketed into space while sampling the controls of a genuine space shuttle. How they survive – if they *will* survive – creates the drama and tension of this agreeable, vaguely educational 'Kids in Space' adventure. A lush, symphonic score from John Williams and some able playing from the young thesps (especially Lea Thompson, Kelly Preston and Larry B. Scott) make up for some of the film's weaker, duller moments.

Rest of cast: Kate Capshaw, Tom Skerritt, Tate Donovan, Leaf Phoenix, Barry Primus, Terry O'Quinn, Mitchell Anderson, T. Scott Coffey, Daryl Roach, Peter Scranton, Hollye Rebecca Suggs, Terry White, Susan Becton, D. Ben Casey, Kathy Hanson, Ron Harris, Scott Holcomb, Kevin Gage, Saundra McGuire, Bill Phillips, Jon Steigman, Adrian Wells. Dir: Harry Winer. Pro: Patrick Bailey and Walter Coblenz. Assoc Pro: David Salven. Ex in charge of Pro: Herb Jellinek. Ex Pro: Leonard Goldberg. Screenplay: W. W. Wicket and Casey D. Mitchell. Ph: William A. Fraker. Ed: John W. Wheeler and Timothy Board. Art: R. J. Lawrence and L. Harris. Pro Des: Richard MacDonald. M: John Williams. (ABC Motion Pictures-Rank). Rel: 22 May 1987. 108 mins. Cert PG.

C. Thomas Howell as the white youngster who pretends to be black in order to win a (blacks-only) scholarship in Entertainment's racial comedy Soul Man. *Genuinely non-white is Rae Dawn Chong.*

Staircase C – Escalier C. The scene is transposed from Paris to New York, the characters from French to American, in this adaptation of the Elvira

Murail novel which has to its credit the Prix de l'Académie Française as Best French Film of 1985, along with the première award at the Uppsala Festival in Sweden. It's the story of a misogynistic, show-off, generally highly unpleasant young art critic (somewhat incredibly) changed into a more human being by a series of confrontations and experiences taking place in and around the rooming house where he lives and which provides the busy background for a series of character sketches of his neighbours, all of whom have their problems. The intention is good, the realization less impressive in view of Jean-Charles Tacchella's previous direction of the brilliant *Cousin, Cousine*.

Cast: Robin Renucci, Jean-Pierre Bacri, Catherine Leprince, Jacques Bonnaffe, Jacques Weber, Claude Rich, Michel Aumont, Hugues Quester, Catherine Frot, Florence Giorgietti, Fiona Gelin, Gilles Gaston-Dreyfus, Mony-Rey, Constance Schacher, Maite Maille, Petronelle Moss, Olivier Lebeau, Jean-Claude Jay, Dominique Rous-

Adrift in outer space: l. to r., Lea Thompson, Kelly Preston, Tate Donovan and Larry B. Scott, in Rank's SF release Space Camp.

91

Young pals River Phoenix and Will Wheaton surprise and defy the local bullyboys in Columbia's youthful adventure story Stand By Me.

seau, Jean-Marie Bernicat, Pierre Jukien, André Haber, Jacqueline Fontaine. Dir, adaptation and (with Elvira Murail) dialogue: Jean-Charles Tacchella, based on Murail's novel. Pro: Marie-Dominique Girodet. Ph: Jacques Assuérus. Ed: Agnès Guillemot. Art: Georges Levy. M: Raymond Alessandrini. (Films 7/FR3 Films, Paris-Cannon). Rel: floating; first shown London (Cannon Première and other Cannon cinemas) 30 January 1987. 101 mins. Cert 15.

Stand By Me. One has to weigh up the assets of this film – the warmly nostalgic atmosphere of summer 1959 in the small sun-drenched town of Castle Rock, and the truth of the youthful friendship at its heart – against some weighty debits, such as the ceaseless, foullest language used by the town's youngsters as they search to find the body of a missing teenager – and an entirely out-of-context sequence of a pie-eating contest, which is as revolting as anything to be found on the screen in 1987. Also on the credit side are the good performances by the four boys:

Will Wheaton, Jerry O'Connell, Corey Feldman and River Phoenix.

Rest of cast: Richard Dreyfuss, Kiefer Sutherland, Casey Siemaszko, Gary Riley, Bradley Gregg, Jason Oliver, Marshall Bell, Frances Lee McCain, Bruce Kirby, William Bronder, Scott Beach, John Cusack, Madeleine Swift, Popeye, Geanette Bobst, Art Burke, Matt Williams, Andy Lindberg, Dick Durock, O. B. Babbs, Charlie Owens, Kenneth and John Hodges, Susan Thorpe, Korey Scott Pollard, Rick Elliott, Kent Lutrell, Chance Quinn, Jason Naylor. Dir: Rob Reiner. Pro: Andrew Scheiman, Bruce A. Evans and Raynold Gideon. Screenplay: Gideon and Evans, based on the novella *The Body* by Stephen King. Ph: Thomas Del Ruth. Ed: Robert Leighton. Pro Des: Dennis Washington. M: Jack Nitzsche. (Act III Pro-Columbia). Rel: 13 March 1987. 88 mins. Cert 15.

Straight to Hell. Obviously cheaply made, a laboured comic-strip British western farce about three generally inept bank robbers who, having buried their loot in them thar hills, proceed to parody their betters in a small town where their cliché actions end in the conventional shoot-out.

Cast: Sy Richardson, Joe Strummer, Dick Rude, Courtney Love, Dennis Hopper, Elvis Costello, Grace Jones, Jim Jarmusch, Biff Yeager, Zander Schloss, Sara Sugarman, The Pogues, Juan Torres, Shane Mac-Gowan, Spider Stacy, Frank Murray, Terry Woods, James Fearnley, Andrew Ranken, Philip Chevron, Ed Pansullo, Martin Turner, Paul Verner, Xander Berkeley, Cait O'Riordan, Miguel Sandoval, Jennifer Balgobin, Sue Kiek, Kathy Burke, Michele Winstanley, Fox Harris, Jem Finer, Graham Fletcher-Cook, Gloria Ruiz, Juann Uribe, Joe Cashman, Jose Pomedio Monedero, Juan Torres, Anne-Marie Ruddock, Sharon Bailey, Turnham Green, Edward Tudor-Pole, Charlie Braun, Sean Madigan, Paul Wood, Del Zamrora, Luis Contreras, Chalkie Davis. Dir: Alex Cox. Pro: Eric Fellner. Ex Pro: Cary Brokaw and Scott Millaney. Screenplay: Cox and Dick Rude. Ph: Tom Richmond. Ed: David Martin. Pro Des: Andrew McAlpine. M: The Pogues and Pray For Rain. (Initial Pictures/Island Pictures/Commies from Mars Pro-Miracle). Rel: floating; first shown London (Metro and Scala) 12 June 1987. 86 mins. Cert 15.

Street of Crocodiles. Bruno Schulz's *avant garde* 1934 story brought to the screen by Ulica Krokodyli as a 20-minute surrealistic puppet film. A very odd business indeed, with a little bit of spit activating what the synopsis calls 'Myths stalking the streets of this parasitical zone where the mythological ascension of the everyday is charted by a magical interloper who threads himself through this one night of the Great Season. No centre can be reached and the futile pursuit concludes in the deepest rear rooms of a slightly dubious tailor's shop.' Which should make it all crystal clear.

Pro: Keith Griffiths. Animation/Ph: Koninck Quay Brothers. (BFI in assoc with Channel 4 Television). Rel: floating; first shown London (Camden Plaza) 26 September 1986. 20 mins. Cert U.

Streets of Gold. Back to the boxing ring, so long occupied by 'Rocky' Stallone. Klaus Maria Brandauer is a former Soviet amateur champion barred from the ring when his Jewish origins are revealed; so he comes to the US and sinks to drunken dishwasher before an accidental confrontation with two 'hungry' young pugilists results in his return to the canvas. Now, as the couple's manager, he hopes through them to get his revenge by honing his 'boys' well enough for them to play a major part in the US team to beat the Russians when they visit America. All pretty routine, really, but with fine photography, good performances and superbly caught atmosphere of the back-street fight game, it adds up to a very watchable movie.

Rest of cast: Adrian Pasdar, Wesley Sniper (promising young actors as promising young boxers), Angela Molina, Elya Baskin, Rainbow Harvest, Adam Nathan, John Mahoney, Jaroslav Stremien, Dan O'Shea, Mike Beach, John McCurry, Jimmy Nickerson, Jeff Ward, Pete Antico, Dan Nutu, Liya Glaz, Elizbieta Czyzewska, Yacov Levitan, Alexander Yampolsky, Davis S. Chandler, René Rivera, Frances Foster, The Hallelujah Orchestra (Lillian and Henry Covner, Shalom Lovnaytor, Boris Monasrisky, Nathan Isaacson), Bill Cobbs, Gregory Holtz Sr, Grafton Trew, Ramon Rodriquez, Paul Davidovsky, Paul Herman, Frank Patton, John Garcia, Hechter Ubarry, Thomas Mendola, Jud Henry Baker, Luther Rickner, Eddie Mustafa Muhammad, Kevin Mahon, Vern de Paul, Jack Wilkes, James Babchak, Al Bernstein, Gene LeBell, Marty Denkin, Mike Radner. Dir and (with Harry Ufland) Pro: Joe Roth. Screenplay: Heywood Gould, Richard Price and Tom Cole, based on a story by Dezso Magyar. Co-Pro: Patrick McCormick and Magyar. Ph: Arthur Albert. Ed: Richard Chew. Pro Des: Marcos Flacksman. M: Jack Nitzsche. (Roundhouse Pro-Vestron). Rel: 12 June 1987. 96 mins. Cert 15.

A Street to Die. Modest but effective Australian production based on the true story of a Vietnam war veteran who became one of the victims of the cancerous aftermath of exposure to the American-used defloration chemical known as Agent Orange. The battle by himself and, after his death, by his wife, to gain compensation, becomes a battle won. Impressively low-toned and realistic.

Cast: Chris Haywood, Jennifer Cluff, Peter Hehir, Arianthe Galani, Peter Kowitz, Sussanah Fowler, Pat Evison, John Smythe, Robin Ramsay, John Hamblin, Don Crosby, Andrew, Marion and Peter Chirgwin, Steven Shaw, Malcolm Keith, Joy Hruby, Jane Burton-Taylor, Christopher Morton, John Black, Deborah Kramer, Brian Harrison, Dennis McKay, Brett Climo, Matthew O'Sullivan, John Fitzgerald. Dir, Pro and Screenplay: Bill Bennett. Ph: Geoff Burton. Ed: Denise Hunter. Pro Des: Igor Nay. M: Michael Atkinson and Michael Spicer. (Mermaid Beach Pro-Other Cinema). Rel: floating; first shown London (Metro) 5 June 1987. 91 mins. No cert.

Sugar Baby – Zuckerbaby. Original, stylish and memorable West German comedy which without a hint of carica-

With a new aim in life, banned Soviet boxer Klaus Maria Brandauer trains hopeful youngster Adrian Pasdar to international status in the Vestron release Streets of Gold.

ture tells the story of a fat, unlovely – and unloved – undertaker's assistant who decides, while laying out the corpses that she'll lay the underground train driver who has taken her fancy. And she succeeds, luring her willing victim with his favourite sweets. Beneath the bizarre surface this really odd couple generate a real feeling of warmth and wonder. Another of the year's genuine collector's pieces.

Cast: Marianne Sägebrecht, Eisi Gulp, Toni Berger, Manuela Denz, Will Spindler, Hans Stadlbauer. Dir and Screenplay: Percy Adlon. Pro: Eleanor Adlon. Ex Pro: Dietrich von Watzdorf. Ph: Johanna Heer. Ed: Jean-Claude Piroué. Art: Matthias Heller. M: Dreier, etc. (Pelemele Films-Electric Pictures). Rel: floating; first shown London (Everyman) 22 August 1986. 86 mins. Cert 15.

Survivors, the Blues Today. A documentary feature about just that, with lots of good if not famous performers. Made largely during a three-day

session at an apparently famous American blues venue, Wilebski's Blues Saloon in St Paul. Technically good, musically interesting, though the talking does go on a bit . . .

With the Gravebites-Cipollina band, Dr John, Archie Shepp, Ben Sidran, Corky Siegel, Baby Doo Caston, Valerie Wellington, Lady Bianca with the Mark Naftalin Band, Willie Murphy and the Bees, The Minnesota Barking Ducks, John Lee Hooker. Dir: Cork Marcheschi and Robert Schwartz. Ed: Tom de Biaso and Kathleen Laughlin. (Heart Productions-Blue Dolphin). Rel: floating, first shown London (Cannon Charing Cross Road) 8 August 1986. 87 mins. Cert PG.

Sweet Liberty. Intermittently hilarious comedy from writer-director-star Alan Alda, about a film unit which descends on the small town where Alda, as the local college history teacher, has become a best-selling author with his book about the American Revolution, subsequently bought by Hollywood. A lot of the fun – and games – stems from Alda's outraged efforts to prevent his serious historical study from being turned into a costume romp. A deli-

Professor-author Alan Alda gets some reassurance from screenplay writer Bob Hoskins as he watches his serious tome become a period romp in Universal-UIP's Sweet Liberty. *Left: Michael Caine as the star of the movie's movie.*

cious comedy performance by Michael Caine as the larky star, firmly supported by Alda, the marvellous Lillian Gish as his nutty mother, and Bob Hoskins as the scriptwriter who has learned to become 'flexible' and persuades Alda, by the end of the film – and after an affair with the heroine – to be the same.

Rest of cast: Michelle Pfeiffer, Lise Hilboldt, Saul Rubinek, Lois Chiles, Linda Thorson, Diane Agostini, Antony Alda, Alvin Alexis, Christopher Bergman, Leo Burmester, Cynthia Burr, Timothy Carhart, Bryan Clark, Bonnie Deroski, Frank Ferrara, Michael Flanagan, Dann Florek, David Gideon, Katherine Gowan, Terry Hinz, John Leonidas, Christopher Loomis, Kevin McClarnon, John C. McGinley, William Parry, Polly Rowles, Fred Sanders, Robert Schenkkan, Larry Shue, Steven Stahl, Lynne Thigpen, Richard Whiting, Robert Zarem. Dir and Screenplay: Alan Alda. Pro: Martin Bregman. Assoc Pro: Judith Stevens. Ex Pro: Louis A. Stroller. Ph: Frank Tidy. (Ad Ph: George Silano). Ed: Michael Economou. Pro Des: Ben Edwards. M: Bruce Broughton. (Universal-UIP). Rel: 26 September 1986. 106 mins. Cert PG.

Target. Complicated, contrived, consistently fast-paced and gripping espionage thriller about an ex-FBI agent with a new name and life (he's managing a timber yard) forced back into the spy business when his wife is kidnapped during a holiday in Paris. She is being held hostage by a revenge-seeker who has spent years tracing said ex-agent in order to get even with the man he accuses of wiping out his family. Helping dad to dodge death is his increasingly impressed son. Altogether, in spite of the occasional lapse, a very polished and professional job.

Cast: Gene Hackman, Matt Dillon, Gayle Hunnicutt, Victoria Fyodorova, Ilona Grubel, Herbert Berghof, Josef Sommer, Guy Boyd, Richard Munch, Ray Fry, Jean-Pol Dubois, Werner Pochath, Ulrich Haupt, James Selby, Ric Krause, Robert Leinsol, Jany Holt, Catherine Rethi, Tomas Hnevsa, Charlotte Bailey, Véronique Guillaud, Jacques Mignot, Brad Williams, Randy Moore, James Stewart, Robert Ground. Dir: Arthur Penn. Pro: Richard D. Zanuck and David Brown. Screenplay: Howard Berk and Don Petersen, based on a story by Leonard Stern. Ph: Jean Tournier and Robert Jessup. Ed: Steve Rotter. Pro Des: Willy Holt. M: Michael Small. (CBS Productions-Rank Film Dist.). Rel: 29 August 1986. 118 mins. Cert 15.

TerrorVision. A grisly lesson to all inveterate lookers-in. A horrendous Thing is transmitted from another planet into the Putterman family's TV sets, occasionally emerging to gobble up whoever is unlucky enough to be around. Minor sci-fi stuff with plenty of references to more ambitious, previous examples of the genre. Though American, it was actually made in Italy.

Ex-CIA agent Gene Hackman with son Matt Dillon forcibly suggest to their 'tailing' FBI agent that he should return to headquarters in the Rank release Target. *Right: the ex-agent at last comes face to face with his old enemy (Herbert Berghof).*

Cast: Diane Franklin, Gerrit Graham, Mary Woronov, Chad Allen, Jonathan Gries, Jennifer Richards, Alejandro Rey, Bert Remsen, Randi Brooks, Ian Patrick Williams, Sonny Carl Davis. Dir and Screenplay: Ted Nicolaou. Pro: Albert Band. Assoc Pro: Debra Dion. Ex Pro: Charles Band. Ph: Romano Albani. Ed: Tom Meshelski. Pro Des: Giovanni Natalucci. M: Richard Band. (Altare Productions/Empire Pictures-Entertainment). Rel: floating; first shown London (ICA) 1 September 1986. 83 mins. No cert.

That's Life! Apparently a considerably autobiographical 'family' film by Blake Edwards: made in his own Malibu Beach home with a cast headed by wife Julie Andrews, Julie's daughter Emma Walton, his own daughter, Jennifer, and the film's star, Jack Lemmon's son

Chris. Beneath the surface of hilarious comedy we see, or sense, Edwards's very serious misgivings about getting old and never achieving full potential. A wealthy, top-flight hypochondriacal architect faces up – very badly – to his

Hypochondriac architect Jack Lemmon on the eve of his 60th birthday in Blake Edwards' Columbia serio-comedy That's Life! *Inset: The 'family' cast: Lemmon and Julie Andrews (l. to r.) with Jennifer Edwards (Edwards's daughter), Chris Lemmon and Julie's daughter Emma Walton.*

60th birthday, entirely unaware that his patient, ever-loving singer wife is tensely awaiting the results of tests which will show whether or not she has cancer of the throat. Apart from one puzzling (and gratuitously tasteless) sequence which would best be deleted, this is a steadily funny and sometimes very moving film, with a marvellous Oscar-worthy performance by Lemmon.

Rest of cast: Sally Kellerman, Robert Loggia, Rob Knepper, Matt Lattanzi, Cynthia Sikes, Dana Sparks, Felicia Farr, Theodore Wilson, Nicky Blair, Jordan Christopher, Biff Elliot, Hal Riddle, Harold Harris, Sherry P. Sievert, Joe Lopes, James Umphlett, Frann Bradford, Jess G. Henecke, Lisa Kingston, Ken Gehrig, Donna McMullen, Scott L. McKenna, Dr Charles Schneider, Cora Bryant, Robin Foster, Eddie Vail, Deborah Figuly, Larry Holt, Gene Hartline, Ernie Anderson, Harry Birrell, Chutney Walton, Honey Edwards. Dir and (with Milton Wexler) Screenplay: Blake Edwards. Pro: Tony Adams. Assoc Pro: Trish Caroselli and Connie McCauley. Ex Pro: Jonathan D. Krane. Ph: Anthony Richmond. Ed: Lee Rhoades. Set decor (no Art credit): Tony Marando. M: Henry Mancini. (Paradise Cove Ubilam/Columbia). Rel: floating; first shown London (Cannon Shaftesbury Avenue) 15 May 1987. 102 mins. Cert 15.

That Was Then . . . This Is Now. Back to the world of troubled teenagers and the discomforts of growing up, as depressingly portrayed by S. E. Hinton in the four of her books about them that have been adapted to the screen (like *The Outsiders*). As ever, they are an unfortunate, considerably unhappy and unsupported bunch of big kids, many of whom bubble with deep-seated rage against the world.

Cast: Emilio Estevez, Craig Sheffer, Kim Delaney, Jill Schoelen, Barbara Babcock, Morgan Freeman, Frank Howard, Larry B. Scott, Matthew Dudley, Frank McCarthy, Diane Dorsey, Roman Sheen, David Miller, Steven Pringle, Bob Swan, John O'Brien, Paul Lane, Brooks Gardner, Sharon Thomas, Tom Walsh. Dir: Chris Cain. Pro: Gary Lindberg and John Ondov. Ex Pro: Alan Belkin and Brandon Phillips. Screenplay: Emilio Estevez, based on the book by S. E. Hinton. Ph: Juan Ruiz Anchia. Ed: Ken Johnson. Assoc Ed: Mark Lowrie. Art: Chester Kaczenski. M: Keith Olsen and Bill

Pals Craig Sheffer (left) and Emilio Estevez find that growing up can be a painful experience in the Miracle release That Was Then . . . This Is Now.

Promising newcomer Ned Nederlander (left), Chevy Chase and Steve Martin as ¡The Three Amigos! in the Rank-released comedy western with music.

Cuomo. (Media Ventures Inc/Alan Belkin Pro-Miracle). Rel: floating; first shown London (several Cannon cinemas) 31 October 1986. 101 mins. Cert 15.

Thérèse. Carefully underplayed, this tells the true story of Thérèse Martin, who was born in Lisieux in Normandy at the end of the 19th century and became a nun in the strict Carmelite Order. The harsh regime and her own refusal to compromise her passion for Jesus Christ led to her early death from consumption and subsequent canonization in 1925. Alain Cavalier tells the story with uncompromising realism, keeping to convent interiors and concentrating on close- and semi close-ups, dividing many of his scenes with brief black-outs. This unusual film won the Critics' Prize at the 1986 Cannes Film Festival.

Cast (a mixture of professional players and amateurs): Catherine Mouchet (Thérèse), Aurore Priéto, Sylvie Habault, Ghislaine Mona, Hélène Alexandridis, Clémence Massart, Nathalie Berhart, Béatrice de Vigan, Noële Chantre, Anna Bernelat, Sylvaine Massarat, M. C. Brown-Sarda, M. L. Eberschweiler, Josette Lefèvre, Gilbert Laurain, Jacqueline Legrain, Véronique Muller, Jacqueline Bouvyer, Jean Pélegri, Michel Rivelin, Quentin, Pierre Baillot, Jean Pieuchot, Georges Aranyossy, Edmond Levy, Armand Meppiel, Lucien Folet, Pierre Maintigneux, Guy Faucon, Joel Le François. Renée Crétien, Simon Dubocq, Geneviève Fougerat, Bernice Sauvaget, Françoise Janvier, Evy Carcassonne. Dir: Alain Cavalier. Pro: Maurice Bernart. Screenplay: Cavalier in collaboration with Camille de Casabianca. Ph: Philippe Rousselot. Ed: Isabelle Dedieu. Pro Des: Bernard Evein. M: by various composers. (AFC Films/A2CNC-Cannon). Rel: floating; first shown London (several Cannon cinemas) 21 November 1986. 90 mins. Cert PG.

¡Three Amigos! Hit-and-miss Mexican western farce with musical numbers about three unheroic celluloid boots-and-saddle heroes of the 1920s who become involuntarily involved – *à la Magnificent Seven* – in helping the struggle of a small town periodically terrorized and plundered by a band of beastly bandits. The hits are good lines and laughable situations, the misses some blank stretches in between. But always a good fun film with – highly commendably – not a single foul word and only one risqué joke.

Cast: Chevy Chase, Steve Martin, Ned Nederlander, Patrice Martinez, Philip Gordon, Michael Wren, Fred Asparagus, Gene Hartline, William Kaplan, Sophia Lamour, Santos Morales, Joe Mantegna, Jon Lovitz, Philip E. Hartmann, Tino Insana, Craig Berenson, Kai Wulff, Josh Gallegos, Norbert Weisser, Brian Thompson, Hector Elias, Hector Morales, Abel Franco, Betty Carvalho, Benita, Dyana Ortelli, Humberto Ortiz, Jorge Severa, Candy Castillo, Jeff O'Haco, Alfonso Arau, Loyda Ramos, Tony Plana, Carl Lafong, Randy Newman, Rebecca Underwood. Dir: John Landis. Pro: Lorne Michaels and George Folsey Jr. Assoc Pro: Leslie Belzberg. Ex Pro: Steve Martin. Screenplay: Martin, Michaels and Randy Newman. Ph: Ronald W. Browne. Ed: Malcolm Campbell. Pro Des: Richard Sawyer. M: Elmer Bernstein, songs by Randy Newman. (Orion P C in assoc with Home Box Office/L A Films/Lorne Michaels Pro/Landis Folsey Films-Rank Film Dist.). Rel: 12 June 1987. 105 mins. Cert PG.

The US ace fighter pilot rivals for the coveted Top Gun *position (Val Kilmer and Tom Cruise) in Paramount-UIP's box-office topper of that title.*

Three Men and a Cradle – Trois Hommes et un Couffin (American title: *Three Men and a Basket*). Steadily amusing French farce which manages to inject plenty of fresh fun into the tired old story of the reluctant bachelor baby-minders (three in this case) who eventually come to adore their small charge. It's all very simple, modestly made . . . and very successful as a laugh-raiser, with some sparkling performances.

Cast: Roland Giraud, Michel Boujenah, André Dussollier, Philippine Leroy Beaulieu, Dominique Lavanant, Marthe Villalonga, Annik Alane, Josine Comelas, Gwendoline Mourlet, François Domange, Christian Zanetti, Gilles Cohen, Bernard Sancy, Xavier Maly. Dir and Screenplay: Coline Serreau. Pro: Jean-François Lepetit. Ph: Jean-Yves Escoffier and Jean-Jacques Bouhon. Ed: Catherine Renault. Art: Yvan Maussion. M: Schubert. (Flach Films/Sopro Films/TFI Films-Fox). Rel: floating; first

shown London (Odeon Kensington, Chelsea cinema etc.) 22 May 1987. 107 mins. Cert PG.

Top Gun. *Not* a western, but a familiar martial training melodrama (with romantic side-issues and dubious political undercurrent). In this case, we have the final battle training of the *crème de la crème* of naval air force fighter pilots seen through the personal story of a brilliant but too bold candidate, who is brought to earth with a bump when his side-kick navigator is killed in a crash which he survives. Lots of fine aerial dog-fight photography and a deafening soundtrack of engine roar against ceaseless loud-pedal pop music.

Cast: Tom Cruise, Kelly McGillis, Val Kilmer, Anthony Edwards, Tom Skerritt, Michael Ironside, John Stockwell, Barry Tubb, Rick Rossovich, Tim Robbins, Clarence Gilyard Jr, Whip Hubley, James Tolkan, Meg Ryan, Adrian Pasdar, Randall Brady, Duke Stroud, Brian Sheehan, Ron Clark, Frank Pesce, Pete Pettigrew, Troy Hunter, Linda Rae Jurgens, Admiral T. J. Cassidy. Dir: Tony Scott. Pro: Don Simpson and Jerry Bruckheimer. Assoc Pro: Warren Skaaren. Ex Pro: Bill Badalato. Screenplay: Jim Cash and Jack Epps Jr. Ph:

Jeffrey Kimball. Ed: Billy Weber and Chris Lebenzon. Pro Des: John F. De Cuir Jr. M: Harold Faltermeyer. (Paramount-UIP). Rel: 3 October 1986. 110 mins. Cert 15.

Tough Guys. Old-fashioned Hollywood hokum about two train robbers who, after serving 20 years in jail, find life on the outside so sad and degrading that they are finally driven back to trying the old game again. So they hijack the same Gold Coast Flyer (now on its final scheduled run), with excitement rather than loot as their object. It would all be easily overlookable were it not for the vintage, easy comedy performances by veteran stars Burt Lancaster and Kirk Douglas, whose charm, polish and artistry make everything seem worthwhile.

Rest of cast: Charles Durning, Alexis Smith (another top-flight veteran), Dana Carvey, Darlanne Fluegel, Eli Wallach, Monty Ash, Billy Barty, Simmy Bow, Darlene Conley, Nathan Davis, Matthew Faison, Corkey Ford, Rick Garcia, Graham Jarvis, Doyle L. McCormack, Bob Maxwell, Steven Memel, Jeanne Mori, Scott Nemes, Ernie Sabella, Darryl Shelly, Hilary Shepard, Jake Steinfield, Charles Sweigart, Eleanor Zee, Ron Ryan, Ruth de Sosa, John Mariano, Larry

Tough Guys: *out of jail after 20 years within it, train robbers Kirk Douglas and Burt Lancaster find only hit-man Eli Wallach waiting to greet them, and he plans to cut their freedom very short.*

Mintz, Dick Hancock, John Demy, Grant Aleksander, Kenny Ransom, Joe Seely, M. F. Kelly, Jeffrey Lynn Johnson, Hugo Stanger, Jimmy Lennon, Philip Culotta, Donald Thompson, Lisa Pescia, Jeff Levine, Seth Kaufman, Michele Marsh, Todd Hallowell, Steve Greenstein, T. F. Maguire, Ellen Albertini Dow, Scanlon Gail, James Clark, Skip Skellrecht, David M. O'Neill, James Deeth, Harry Hauss, Denver Mattson, Red Hot Chili Peppers. Dir: Jeff Kanew. Pro: Joe Wizan. Co-Pro: Jana Sue Memel and Richard Hashimoto. Screenplay: James Orr and Jim Cruikshank. Ph: King Baggot. Ed: Kaja Fehr. Pro Des: Todd Hallowell. M: James Newton Howard. (Touchstone Pictures-WDP Ltd-UKFD). Rel: 24 April 1987. 103 mins. Cert 15.

The Toxic Avenger. A thin story (not to say a pretty silly one) with lots of laughs and lots of gore and brutality, plus some lurid contributions from the special effects department, all carefully mixed to make the (American) teenage movie-goers happy. And that story: well, it's about a weak and much abused youngster in a body-building establishment who falls into a load of toxic waste and is transformed into a macho avenging angel, setting out to right wrongs and make the world a better, safer place for the bullied and abused. Described by one critic as 'a madcap spoof on *The Hulk*'.

Cast: Andrée Maranda, Mitchell Cohen, Pat Ryan Jr, Gary Schneider, Jennifer Baptist, Cindy Manion, Robert Prichard, Mark Torgi, Dick Martinsen, Chris Liano, David Weiss, Dan Snow, Doug Isbeque, Charles

Lee Jr, Pat Kilpatrick, Larry Sutton, Mike Russo, Norma Pratt, Andrew Craig, Ryan Sexton, Sarabel Levinson, Al Pia, Reuben Guss, Kenneth Kessler, Barbara Gurskey, Donna Winter, Cosmo Wilder, Brigitte Douglaston, Nancy Compansanto, Andrea Suter, Mary Ellen David, Dennis Souder etc. Dir: Michael Herz and Samuel Weil. Pro: Herz and Lloyd Kaufman. Assoc Pro: Stuart Strutin. Screenplay: Joe Ritter, based on a story by Kaufman. Pro Ex: Joe Solomito. Ed: R. W. Haines. Art: Barry Shapiro and Alexandra Mazur. M: Various pop numbers. (Kaufman/Herz Pro/Blue Dolphin). Rel: floating; first shown London (Electric Screen) 20 February 1987. 79 mins. Cert 18.

Trancers. Said by the British releasers to be Charles Band's Empire Films' masterpiece. (Empire are said to make movies 'you can take your brain along to . . . and your sense of humour: low-budget, high concept films'.) This 1984 production was the story of 'Jack Deth pursuing zombie-maker Whistler back through time to Los Angeles in 1985'.

Dir: Charles Band with Tim Thomseson. No other credits. Rel: 4 August 1986. (ICA). 76 mins. Cert 15.

The Transformers – The Movie. This Japanese toy invention has been the motivation of popular book and TV

Sammi Curr as the heavy metal star who comes back from the grave in order to take revenge on his critics in the Palace Pictures release Trick or Treat.

series, so it was only a matter of time before they emerged animatedly on to the large screen. But as the 'players' are constantly changing into something different – transforming in fact – it makes following the thread of the story pretty difficult. Perhaps this isn't really necessary, in view of the fact that one's concentration is on the almost constant battles and vast mechanical destruction. Interesting that this was the last role, albeit a voice-only one, that can be credited to the late Orson Welles.

Other voices include: Eric Idle, Judd Nelson, Leonard Nimoy, Robert Stack, Lionel Stander, the late Scatman Crothers, Clive Revill etc. Dir and Co-Pro: Nelson Shin. Pro: Joe Bacall and Tom Griffin. Ex Pro: Margaret Loesch and Lee Gunther. Screenplay: Ron Friedman. Anim Ph: Matatoshi Fukui. Ed: David Hankins. Sup Ed: Steven C. Brown. M: Vince DiCola. (Sunbow Pro/Marvel-Rank Film Dist.). Rel: 12 December 1986. 85 mins. Cert U.

Transylvania 6–5000. Junior-aimed horror spoof about monsters that aren't! The end of the quest by a couple of investigating reporters sent to Transylvania to get a story about whether the Count is still alive and kicking.

Cast: Jeff Goldblum, Joseph Bologna, Ed Begley Jr, Carol Kane, Jeffrey Jones, John Byner, Geena Davis, Michael Richards, Donald Gibb, Norman Fell, Teresa Ganzel, Bozidar Smiljanic, Inge Apelt, Petar Buntic, Rudy de Luca, Dusko Valentic, Ksenija

Prohaska, Sara Grdjan, Robert F. Lyons. Dir and Screenplay: Rudy de Luca. Pro: Mace Neufeld and Thomas H. Brodek. Assoc Pro: Glenn Neufeld. Ex Pro: Paul Lichtman and Arnie Fishman. Ph: Tomislav Pinter. Ed: Harry Keller. Pro Des: Zeljko Senecic. M: Lee Holdridge. (Mace Neufeld in assoc with Jadran Films-New World Pictures/Dow Chemical Co.-Entertainment). Rel: floating; first shown London (Cannon Panton Street) 3 October 1986. 94 mins. Cert PG.

Trick or Treat. One for the youngsters who like their celluloid horror ration served up with rock music trimmings: the story of a recently demised rock star who rises from the grave when his final, unreleased, recording is played backwards; a chance to get his, horrid, own back on his hated critics. There's heavy metal on the soundtrack and quite a number of amusing macabre effects.

Cast: Marc Price, Tony Fields, Liso Orgolini, Doug Savant, Elaine Joyce, Glen Morgan, Gene Simmons, Ozzy Osbourne, Elise Richards, Richard Pachorek, Sammi Curr, Claire Nono, Alice Nunn, Larry Sprinkle, Charles Martin Smith, Claudia Templeton, Denny Pierce, Ray Shaffer, Brad Thomas, Terry Loughlin, Graham Smith, Kevin Yahger, Amy Bertolette, Leroy Sweet, Barry Bell, Steve Boles, James D. Nelson, Richard Doyle. Dir: Charles Martin Smith. Pro: Michael S. Murphey and Joel Soisson. Screenplay: Murphey, Soisson and Rhet Topham, based on a story by Topham. Ph: Robert Elswit and 'Fastway'. Ed: Jane Schwartz Jaffe. Pro Des: Curt Schnell. M: Christopher Young. (De Laurentiis-Palace). Rel: floating; first shown London (Prince Charles) 13 March 1987. 98 mins. Cert 18.

Troll. The nasty thing of the title 'turns a San Francisco apartment block into a black fairyland peopled with bizarre goblins, battled by an immortal witch with a talking toadstool as a pet'. This odd little movie explores the difference between children's and adults' imaginations cheaply but with some style and lots of amusing borrowings from other movies. Briefly, a silly, youth-aimed story acted by a good cast, a typical example of the Band Brothers' Empire productions.

Cast: Noah Hathaway, Michael Moriarty, Shelley Hack, Jenny Beck, Sonny Bono, Phil Fondacaro, Brad Hall, Anne Lockhart, Julia Louis-Dreyfus, Gary Sandy, June Lockhart, Robert Hathaway, James Beck, Dale Wyatt, Barbara Sciorilli, Viviani Giusti, Jessie Carfora, Debra Dion, Charles Band. Dir: John Buechler. Pro: Albert

Band. Ex Pro: Charles Band. Screenplay: Ed Naha. Ph: Roman Albani. Ed: Lee Percy. Pro Des: Giovanni Natalucci. (Altar Productions for Empire Pictures-Entertainment). Rel: floating; first shown London (ICA) 4 August 1986. 86 mins. Cert 15.

Trouble in Mind. Stylish, very characteristic (of the director), always ambiguous yet consistently fascinating Alan Rudolph film, set in a shadowy, carefully dateless and mysterious Rain City where anything can and generally does happen. It is largely played out between the ex-cop killer just out of jail (Kris Kristofferson), the silly little blonde with the baby (Lori Singer), her punk crook lover looking for loot (Keith Carradine) and the philosophical owner of the café (Genevieve Bujold) which is at the centre of things. Drama, violence, passion and underworld menace end in a ferociously farcical climax of flying bullets, through which the hero and punk walk with casual safety. A real odd mix, wrought by a master of his craft.

Rest of cast: Joe Morton, Divine, George Kirby, John Considine, Dirk Blocker, Albert Hall, Gailard Sartain, Robert Gould, Antonia Dauphin, Billy Silva, Caitlin Ferguson, Allan Nicholls, Debra Dusay, Elizabeth Kay, Rick Tutor, Joanne Klein, Jill Klein, David Kline, William Hall, Andrea Stein, David McIntyre, Steve Danton, Mara Scott-Wood, Robert Kim, Robert Lee, Matt Almond, Tracey Kristofferson, Ron Ben Jarrett, William Earl Ray, Steven Ross, Patricia Tyler, Toni Cross, Sarah Yvonne Murray, Carl Sander, Judy Lynne Gratton, Stuart Manne, B. J. Alexander, Danielle Aubuchon, Nanci Anton, Barry Press, J. Morgan Armstrong, Frank Gargani, Felix Casares, David Quintera, R. Fox, M. James Clark, Raymond Kemp, James Etue, Francis Diamond, Patti Dobrowolski, Pamela Gray, Lee Ann Fuji, Karen Gottberg, Shellee Renee, Susan Catherine, Sheri Ann Nye, Jabus Wesson, J. R. Smith, James Fulgium, Terry Morgan, James Crabtree, Tammy Wolfe, Stephen Sneed. Dir and Screenplay: Alan Rudolph. Pro: Carolyn Pfeiffer and David Blocker. Ex Pro: Cary Brokaw. Ph: Toyomichi Kurita. Ed: Tom Walls. Pro Des: Steven Legler. M: Mark Isham, songs performed by Marianne Faithfull. (Island Alive and Terry Glinwood-Recorded Releasing Co.). Rel: floating; first shown London (ABC Fulham etc.) 19 September 1986. 112 mins. Cert 15.

True Stories. Talking Heads personality David Byrne's very impressive debut as film director in a feature which basically is a warm celebration of the

Dumb blonde waitress Lori Singer captivates ex-cop, killer Kris Kristofferson in Alan Rudolph's typically unusual, very stylish Recorded Releasing Company's release Trouble in Mind. *Right: Keith Carradine (left) as the girl's weak, with-it husband.*

underlying goodness of the people who live in small-town America. A series of sketches done, in a kind of stylish video way, with plenty of music (but only three of the many songs provided by the Heads). An original and charming movie.

Cast: David Byrne, John Goodman, Swoosie Kurtz, Spalding Gray, Alix Elias, Annie McEnroe, Roebuck 'Pops' Staples, Humberto 'Tito' Larriva, John Ingle, Jo Harvey Allen, Matthew Posey, Amy Buffington, Richard Dowlearn, Capucine de Wulf, Cynthia Gould, Kelly Wright; and many, many others, more than 100 in fact, often just flitting across the film, many of them apparently non-actors in the professional sense. Dir: David Byrne. Pro: Gary Kurfirst. Ex Pro: E. R. Pressman. Screenplay: Byrne, Beth Henley, Stephen Tobolowsky. Co-Pro: Karen Murphy. Ph: Ed Lachman. Ed: Caroline Biggerstaff. Pro Des: Barbara Ling. M: D. Byrne and Talking Heads. (True Stories Ventures-Warner). Rel: float-

ing; first shown London (Warner) 14 November 1986. 89 mins. Cert PG.

Twice in a Lifetime. One of a slew of recent films about marital discord which, although brilliantly acted, never realizes its dramatic potential. Gene Hackman stars as an unattractive, unloving husband and father of three who works at a local steel mill. Inexplicably, a very beautiful barmaid (Ann-Margret) falls in love with him, forcing him to re-examine his empty life. He opts to move in with her, leaving behind a wake of hurt and anger. Ellen

The beginning of the end of a good, 30-year marriage: and boredom is the root cause of it. Fine work by Ellen Burstyn and Gene Hackman raised the level of this Miracle release, Twice in a Lifetime.

anger. Ellen Burstyn steals the acting honours as the selfless, loving wife left to fend for herself, with Amy Madigan (who won an Oscar nomination for her role) also good as the tempestuous older daughter. British actor/scenarist Colin Welland (*Chariots of Fire, Yanks*) delivered the screenplay, revealing a keen sense for emotional veracity if not a nose for a good scene. Incidentally, the film was originally set in Manchester, England; the locale was altered to Pennsylvania, and then to Seattle, Washington, once American funds were forthcoming.

Rest of cast: Ally Sheedy, Stephen Lang, Darrell Larson, Brian Dennehy, Chris Parker, Rachel Street, Kevin Bleyer, Nicole Mercurio, Doris Hugo Drewien, Lee Corrigan, Ralph Steadman, Rod Pilloud, Art Cahn, Anne Ludlum, Evelyn Purdue, Gayle Bellows, Kit Harris, George Catalano, Tawnya Pettiford, Mary Ewald, Daniel Mahar,

Sharon Collar, Gary Kowalski, Keith Nicholai, Ken Clark, Audrey Flod, Loretta Adair, Eileen Cornwell, Mary Thielen, Denise Aiumu, Junior Barber. Dir: Bud Yorkin. Pro: Yorkin. Ex Pro: David Salven. Screenplay: Colin Welland. Ed: Robert Jones. Pro Des: William Creber. Ph: Nick McLean. M: Pat Metheny, title song written and sung by Paul McCartney. (The Yorkin Co.). Rel: floating; first shown London (Odeon Haymarket) 9 January 1987. 111 mins. Cert 15.

Under the Cherry Moon. With pop star Prince, this minor musical is strictly for the lad's fans, more so even than his debut picture. A – sort of – story about a poor musician and a rich girl romancing on the Riviera. Shot in colour but, apparently at the insistence of the star, with black-and-white prints.

Rest of cast: Jerome Benton, Kristin Scott-Thomas, Steven Berkoff, Francesca Annis, Emmanuelle Sallet, Alexandra Stewart, Victor Spinetti, Pamela Ludwig, etc. Dir: Prince. Pro and Ex Pro: Bob Cavallo, Joe Ruffalo and Steve Fargnoli. Screenplay: Becky Johnston. Ph: Michael Ballhaus. Ed: Eva Gardos. Art: Damien Lafranchi. Pro Des: Richard Sylbert. M: Prince and The Revolution. (Warner). Rel: floating; first

shown London (Warner) 22 August 1986. 100 mins. Cert 15.

Vamp. Put 'ires' after that title and you'll begin to get the right idea about this deep, deep black (and sometimes gory red) comedy from a new director-writer with an obvious talent for this sort of thing. The background to all the spine-chilling is a night-club catering for bloodsuckers, where Grace Jones' striptease dance is one of the highlights of the proceedings. Neatly summed up by one headline writer as 'a comedy with a bite!'.

Rest of cast: Chris Makepeace, Sandy Baron, Robert Rusler, Dedee Pfeiffer, Gedde Watanabe, Billy Drago, Brad Logan, Lisa Lyon, Jim Boyle, Larry Spinak, Eric Welch, Stuart Rogers, Gary Swailes, Ray Ballard, Paunita Nicholas, Trudel Williams, Marlon McGann, Thomas Bellin, Bryan McGuire, Leila Hee Olsen, Hilary Carlip, Francine Swift, Tricia Brown, Naomi Shohan, Janeen Davis, Ytossie Paterson, Tanya Papanicolas, Robin Kaufman, Hy Pike, Pops, Bob Schott, Adam Barth, Bill Morphew, Simmy Bow, Roger Hampton, Andy Rivas, Julius Leflore, Greg Lewis, Dar Robinson, Mitch Carter, Cathy Cavdini,

The old firm: Leonard Nimoy (right), Jane Wyatt and Mark Lenard in Paramount UIP's The Voyage Home · Star Trek IV. *Right, Nimoy and his crew find their borrowed 'Bird of Prey' spacecraft uncontrollable as it hurtles down towards San Francisco.*

Deborah Fallender, Greg Finley, David McCharen, Jan Rabson, Marilyn Schreffler, Dennis Tufano. Dir, Screenplay and (with Donald Borchers) story: Richard Wenk. Pro: Donald P. Borchers. Assoc Pro: Susan Gelb. Ph: Elliot Davis. Ed: Marc Grossman. Add Ed: Alan Holzman. Assoc Ed: Joe Woo Jr. Pro Des: Alan Roderick-Jones. M: Jonathan Elias. (Entertainment). Rel: 16 January 1987. 93 mins. Cert 18.

The Voyage Home – Star Trek IV. This fourth, Leonard Nimoy-directed, flight into space should please all his TV fans, for it is well up to, if not actually above, the standard of its predecessors, with plenty of fun and frolic, not a little wit, and all the usual spectacular spaceware and special effects. The crew of the SS *Enterprise* are due to come up before the beaks for stealing their spaceship and going off against orders to battle with the nasty Klingons, in the course of which their favourite craft was destroyed.

Cast: William Shatner, Leonard Nimoy, DeForrest Kelley, James Doohan, George Takei, Walter Koenig, Michelle Nichols, Jane Wyatt, Catherine Hicks, Mark Lenard, Robin Curtis, Robert Ellenstein, John Schuck, Brock Peters, Michael Snyder, Michael Berryman, Mike Brislane, Grace Lee Whitney, Jane Wiedlin, Vijay Amitraj, Majel Barrett, Nick Ramus, Thaddeus Golas, Martin Pistole, Scot de Venney, Viola Stimpson, Phil Rubenstein, John Miranda, Joe Knowland, Bob Sarlatte, Everett Lee, Richard Harder, Alex Hanteloff, Tony Edwards, Eve Smith, Tom Mustin, Greg Karas, Raymond Singer, David Ellenstein, Judy Levitt, Teresa A. Victor, James Menges, Kirk Thatcher, Jeff Lester, Joe

Christopher Walken as the American journalist caught up in war-torn Beirut in the Guild release War Zone.

Lando, Newell Tarrant, Mike Timoney, Jeffrey Martin, Joseph Naraddzay. Dir: Leonard Nimoy. Pro: Harve Bennett. Assoc Pro: Brooke Breton and Kirk Thatcher. Ex Pro: Ralph Winter. Screenplay: Bennett, Steve Meerson, Peter Krikes and Nicholas Meyer, based on a story by Nimoy and Bennett, in turn based on the TV series created by Gene Roddenberry. Co-Pro: Industrial Light and Magic. Ph: Don Peterman. Ed: Peter E. Berger. Art: Joe Aubel and Pete Smith. Pro Des: Jack T. Collis. M: Leonard Rosenman. (Paramount-UIP). Rel: 17 April 1987. 119 mins. Cert PG.

Walls of Glass. The story of a New York cabbie who dreams of a Shakespearian acting future but battles against in-built doubt and a feeling of insecurity resulting from his father's addiction to the bottle and inability to provide for the family.

Cast: Philip Bosco, William Hickey, Geraldine Page, Olympia Dukakis, Steven Weber, Brian Bloom, Linda Thorson, Louis Zorich, Philip Astor, James Tolkan, Gwyllum Evans, Pierre Epstein, Jered Holmes, E. R. Davies, Cory Notrica, Theron Montgomery, Ronald Yamamoto, Michael Cullagh, John Stamford, Christine Barker, Diane Davidson-Porter, Heather Fleming, Gretchen Taylor, Dani York, Bonnie Wil-

liams, Don Brockett, George Peck, Loretta Tupper, Isabel Price, Frank Ammarati, Jennifer, Lynne Thigpen, George Zaver, Ibi Kaufman, Brian Kohn, Eddie Castrodad, Tony Mannino, Peter Ratray, Edmond Collins. Dir and (with Mark Slater), Pro and with (Edmond Collins) Screenplay and M: Scott Goldstein. Pro Sup: Peter Repplier. Ph: Ivan Strasburg. Ed: Scott Vickrey. Pro Des: Ruth Ammon. (Tenth Muse Pro-Enterprise). Rel: floating; first shown London (several Cannon cinemas) 16 January 1987. 86 mins. Cert 15.

Wanted: Dead or Alive. Disillusioned ex-CIA agent Rutger Hauer as the modern equivalent of the bounty hunter of the Old West, bringing to justice the villains who have otherwise circumvented the law and the lawmen. Very violent, especially the details of his duel with Los Angeles bomber Malak (Gene Simmons) but with an uproarious climax.

Rest of cast: Robert Guillaume, Mel Harris, William Russ, Susan McDonald, Jerry Hardin, Hugh Gillin, Robert Harper, Eli Danker, Joe Nasser, Suzanne Wouk, Gerald Papasian, Nick Faltas, Hamman Shafie, Tyler Tyhurst, Ted White, Neil Sommers, Dennis Burkley, Deedee Rescher, Jesse Aragon, Tu Thuy, Tu Ban Nguyen, Gary Scott, Tiiu Leek, Bill Smith, R. J. Miller, Charles Shapiro, David E. Boyle, Jeffrey Josephson, Patrick Puccinelli, Jim Edgcomb, Buddy Farmer, Gary Werntz, Rif Hutton, Richard Partlow, Rick Goldman, George Shannon, Ed Brodow, Patrick Gorman, Hubie Kerns Jr, Danny Costa, G. W. Elam, B. R. Scott. Dir: Gary Sherman. Pro: R. C. Peters. Ex Pro: Arthur Sarkissian. Screenplay: Sherman, Michael P. Goodman and Brian Teggert. Co-Pro: Barry Bernardi. Ph: Alex Nepomniaschy. Ed: Ross Albert. Pro Des: Paul Eads. M: Joseph Renzetti. (New World-Entertainment). Rel: floating; first shown London (Cannons Edgware Road and Panton Street) 22 May 1987. 106 mins. Cert 18.

War Zone. An ill-at-ease Christopher Walken stars as a naïve TV correspondent reporting the confused war in Beirut in this worthy but muddled anti-war tract. There are some fine images: a child appearing from the ruins of a bombed house to be met by a battery of reporters; a peasant fleeing on a mule with a TV strapped to its back . . . But the platitudes of screeching car tyres and a heartbeat on the soundtrack deprive the film of greater things. However, there is a fine sense of the chaos and hopelessness of it all, summed up by

The futile attempts by the naïve old country couple to sweep away the after-effects of an atom-bomb attack in Recorded Releasing's ironic animated tragi-comedy, When the Wind Blows.

Hywel Bennett as a jaundiced hack: 'This is Beirut. You don't kill who you want. You kill who you can.'

Rest of cast: Marita Marschall, Arnon Zadok, Amos Lavie, Etti Ankri, Martin Umbach, Moshe Ivgi, Sason Gabay, Shahar Cohen. Dir: Nathaniel Gutman. Pro: Elisabeth Wolters-Alfs. Screenplay: Hanan Peled. Ed: Peter Przygodda. Ph: Amnon Salomon and Thomas Mauch. Art: Yoram Barzily. M: Jacques Swart and Hans Jansen. (A Creative Film Production for Guild Film Dist.). Rel: floating; first shown London 20 March 1987. 100 mins. Cert 15.

When the Wind Blows. A somewhat overblown (presumably to reach feature-length status) British animated feature which, with touches of pawky humour but plenty of obviously sincere and telling truth, depicts a trusting old country couple who, after taking all the daft, official survival advice, sink hopelessly to radiation death after the big bomb has exploded.

With the voices of Peggy Ashcroft and John Mills. Dir: Jimmy T. Murakami. Pro: John Coates. Ex Pro: Iain Harvey. Screenplay: Raymond Briggs. Art, Anim. and Layout Design: Richard Fawdry. Special Effects: Stephen Weston. M: Roger Waters, title song by David Bowie. (Meltdown/TVC-Recorded Releasing). Rel: floating; first shown London (several Cannons and Camden Plaza) 6 February 1987. 85 mins. Cert PG.

High-placed Foreign Office spy John Gielgud is confronted by Michael Caine, a father seeking revenge for the death of his son in the Rank release The Whistle Blower.

The Whistle Blower. Good performances, pace and a nice overall polish, added to a remarkable topicality (in view of its having been initially uncovered at *last* year's Cannes Film Festival) make this a first-rate, more than usually credible spy drama, and outweigh occasional confusion in the storyline and a pretty tame ending. It's about the embarrassed discovery by MI5 of a Russian spy at GCHQ Cheltenham, leading to the even more painful uncovering of a master spy at the top of the British Secret Service. There's a lot more to it than that, with insight into the callous and devious double-dealing by the bowler-hatted wielders of rolled umbrellas down Whitehall way.

Cast: Michael Caine (another fine performance), James Fox, Nigel Havers, Felicity Dean, John Gielgud, Kenneth Colley, Gordon Jackson, Barry Foster, David Langton, Dinah Stabb, James Simmons, Bill Wallis, Andrew Hawkins, Katherine Reeve, Trevor Cooper, Gregory Floy, Peter Hutchinson, Jan Carey, Kim Hicks, Peter Mackriel, Doyle Richmond, Renny Krupinski, Andrew Bradford, David Shaughnessy, Arturo Venegas, Ralph Nossek, Pamela Collins, Susan Porrett, Joe Dunlop, Patrick Holt, Julian Battersby, John Gill, David Telfer, Serilla Delofski, Peter Mikes, Carmel Cryan. Dir: Simon Langton. Pro: Geoffrey Reeve. Assoc Pro: Peter Dolman. Ex Pro: James Reeve, Phillip Nugus and John Kelleher. Screenplay: Julian Bond, based on the novel by John Hale. Ph: Fred Tammes. Ed: Bob Morgan. Art: Chris Burke. Pro

The PM (Peter Cook) outside No 10 with his ministers (Richard Pearson and Richard Wilson) in Miracle/Virgin's satirical British comedy Whoops Apocalypse. Left: the worried US President (Loretta Swit) with Secretaries Daniel Benzau and Shane Rimmer tries to stop the PM from pressing the fatal Go-Go-Go bomb button.

Des: Morley Smith. M: John Scott. (Reeve Enterprises/Portreeve-Rank Film Dist.). Rel: floating; first shown London (Odeon Haymarket) 29 May 1987. 104 mins. Cert PG.

White of the Eye. Beneath the flashy editing and the arty veneer, this British-financed, American-made movie is just a routine thriller about a psychopath killer. An apparently loving husband and father murders and mutilates a local beauty and parcels up her body in cellophane packets, his wife becoming aware of this hobby when she discovers some of the packets hidden under their bath. Once the deed is revealed – quite early on – the thrills come from the wife's frenzied attempts to escape her husband's hunting knife, leading to a chilling finale in which (incredibly opportune, this) the woman's ex-boyfriend arrives on the scene to play a bloody part.

Cast: David Keith, Cathy Moriarty, Alan Rosenberg, Art Evans, Michael Green, Danko Gurovich, David Chow, China Cammell, Danielle Smith, Alberta Watson, Fred Allison, Bob Zache, John Diehl, Marc Hayashi, Jim Wirries, Pamela Seamon, Kaie Waring, Mimi Lieber, William G. Schilling, Donna Barrish, Brad Wyman. Dir: Donald Cammell. Pro: Cassian Elwes and Brad Wyman. Ex Pro: Elliott Kastner. Screenplay: China and Donald Cammell, based on the book Mrs White by Margaret Tracy. Ph: Larry McConkey. Ed: Terry Rawlings. Pro Des: Philip Thomas. M: Nicky Mason and Rick Penn. (Cannon). Rel: floating; first shown London (several Cannon cinemas) 19 June 1987. 111 mins. Cert 18.

Whoops Apocalypse. British feature film spin-off from the TV series. In parts witty, often funny, in parts daft, and certainly with plenty of bad taste in the Monty Python manner, this hodge-podge satirical comedy is of somewhat specialized appeal. A nutty British PM (who issues free red, white and blue umbrellas to everyone as the ultimate protection against the atom bomb and is then quite happy to invite the holocaust) goes to war over a useless little island in the Caribbean, even though the pretty President of the US does her best to stop him. Many of the satirical shafts are shrewdly aimed.

Cast: Loretta Swit, Peter Cook, Michael Richards, Rik Mayall, Ian Richardson, Alexis Sayle, Herbert Lom, Joanne Pearce, Christopher Malcolm, Ian McNeice, Daniel Benzau, Shane Rimmer, Richard Wilson,

Richard Pearson, Stuart Saunders, Graeme Garden, Marc Smith, John Benfield, Ben Robertson, Alex Davion, Phil Marquis, Murray Hamilton, Robert Arden, Blain Fairman, Christopher Muncke, Dan Fitzgerald, Spunky Spaniel, D. L. Blakely, Raymond Forshion, John Sessions, Tristram Jellinek, Christopher Coll, Maria Whittaker, Karen Kelly, T. R. Durphy, Don Wellington, Joy Lynn Frasca, Simon Dormandy, Paul Beech, Nick Copping, Ken Jones, John Cassidy, Manolo Coego, Ruben Rabasa, Robert Blythe, Suzanne Mitzi, Christine Peak, Terry Taplin, Micky O'Donoughue, John Darrell, Ron Webster, Gary Martin, Clifton James, Czeslaw Grocholski, Leon Lissek, Michael Poole, Christopher Rozycki, Ed Bishop, John Archie, Robert Goodman, Harold Bergman, Iris Acker, Richard Murdoch, Barbara Keogh, Elizabeth Proud, Gavin Richards, John Blundell, Daniel Peacock, Robert Bathurst. Dir: Tom Bussmann. Pro: Brian Eastman. Screenplay: Andrew Marshall and David Renwick. Pro Sup: Christabel Albery. Ph: Ron Robson. Ed: Peter Boyle. Pro Des: Tony Noble. M: Patrick Gowers. (ITC-Virgin/Miracle). Rel: 6 March 1987. 91 mins. Cert 15.

Wives, Ten Years After – Hustruer, 2 – Ti ar etter. 'Loosely knit, often witty, meandering but finally in-depth portrait of three rather sluttish young women dissatisfied with the restrictions of their lives but unable to do anything really constructive about it.' That's a quote from *Film Review 1977–8* about the original Norwegian film released in 1976. Here's the sequel, with the same writer-director and cast – and nothing seems to have changed in the interim. The same trio bemoan their fate as they cavort drunkenly round Oslo, quarrel and eventually return to where they started. If the men in their lives seem pretty silly, the three women don't appear much better. But there's enough fun in the film to have made it a Norwegian top-flight success and a popular film for festivals.

Cast: Froydis Armand, Katja Medboe, Anne-Marie Ottersen, Per Frisch, Henrik Scheele, Jon Eiremo, Brasse Brännstrom, Christian Heian, Noste Schwab, Nils Vogt, Svein Wickstrom, Frank Robert, Lise Eger, Eva von Hanno, Karin Haugen, Mona Jacobsen. Dir and (with Knut Faldbakken and the three actresses) Screenplay: Anja Breien. Ex Pro: Bente Erichsen. Ph: Erling Thurmann-Andersen. Ed: Lars Hagstrom. Art: Madla Hruzova. (Norsk Films-Enterprise). Rel: floating; first shown London (Cannon Piccadilly) 13 February 1987. 86 mins. Cert 15.

Working Girls. The 'girls' in question are the prostitutes working in a brothel and the audience of this documentary-style feature is invited to look in, so to speak, to see them working for one day and evening in a New York place of employment. Written, directed, produced and edited by Lizzie Borden, acted by a wholly professional cast, the object appears to be to show that this job is really very much like another, and that when their $50 an hour stint is over the girls go home like any others to domesticity with husband or boyfriend. Miss Borden is non-committal on the subject; she neither tries to add glamour to the job nor to moralize or criticize it: she just presents it for what it is and leaves the viewers to draw their own conclusions.

Cast: Louise Smith, Ellen McEldruff, Amanda Goodwin, Marusia Zach, Janne Peters, Helen Nicholas, Deborah Banks, Liz Caldwell, Boomer Tibbs, Eli Hasson, Tony Whiting, Richard Davidson, Ronald Willoughby, Paul Slimak, Fred Neumann, Patience Pierce, Grant Wheaton, Richard Leacock, Martin Haber, Carla-Maria Sorey, Michael Holland, Dan Nutu, Ron Manning, Fred Baker, Norbert Brown, Benjamin Ehbuna, Chan Lee, Ray Moy, Lu Yu, Roger Babb, Saunder Finard. Dir, Pro and (with Sandra Kay) Screenplay and Ed: Lizzie Borden. Assoc Pro: Margaret Smilow. Co-Pro: Andi Gladstone. Ph: Judy Irola. Art: Kurt Ossenfort. M: David van Tieghem. (Lizzie Borden/Alternate Current Pro-Electric). Rel: floating; first shown London (Metro and Camden Plaza) 20 March 1987. 90 mins. Cert 18.

The Wraith. A movie tailored strictly for hot-rod or other souped-up car enthusiasts: a tale about an angry-looking Dodge Turbo car which mysteriously appears from nowhere to take on a gang of previously triumphant grease-monkey-morons, and defeat them.

Cast: Charlie Sheen, Nick Cassavetes, Randy Quaid, Sherilyn Fenn, Griffin O'Neal, David Sherrill, Jamie Bozian, Clint Howard, Matthew Barry, Chris Nash, Vicki Benson, Jeffrey Sudzin, Peter Mulhouse, Michael Hungerford, Steven Eckholdt, Elizabeth Cox, Dick Alexander, Christopher Bradley, Joan H. Reynolds. Dir and Screenplay: Mike Marvin. Pro: John Kemeny. Ex Pro: Buck Houghton. Ph: Reed Smoot. Ed: Scott Conrad and Gary Rocklin. Art: Dean Tschetter. M: Michael Hoenig and Peter Robinson. (New Century/Visya Films-Medusa Communications/Premier Releasing). Rel: 2 January 1987. 93 mins. Cert 18.

Yellow Earth – Huang Tudi. Slow-moving, technically first-class, visually impressive Chinese film (made 1984) about the tragic result of a soldier's visit to a small, backward community along the Yellow River in the far North Shaanxi province in the course of his mission to collect local folksongs. Marvellous moon-like backgrounds; some excitingly presented spectacular sequences; strange traditional songs set in a modern musical background; altogether an impressive and artistic use of the medium by director and photographer. Winner of the BFI award.

Cast: Xue Bai, Wang Xueqi, Tan Tuo, Liu Qiang and the Peasant Waist-drum Troupe of Ansai County. Dir: Chen Kaige. Pro: Guo Keqi. Screenplay: Zhang Ziliang, based on the essay 'Echo in the Valley' by Ke Lan. Ph: Zhang Yimou. Ed: Pei Xiaonan. Art: He Qun. M: Zhao Jiping, played by the Orchestra and Traditional Music Ensemble of Xi'an Academy of Music. (Youth Production Unit of Guangxi Film Studio-ICA). Rel: floating; first shown London (ICA) 8 August 1986. 89 mins. No cert.

Youngblood. Ice hockey fans should get the greatest kick out of this story, about a Canadian farm boy who dreams of the icy big time and eventually persuades his ailing brother (who until injured was also an ice hockey team member) to stand in for him at home while he goes off to fulfil his frosty destiny; a destiny that includes a nymphomaniac landlady and a pretty girlfriend, as well as his efforts to establish himself.

Cast: Rob Lowe, Cynthia Gibb, Patrick Swayze, Ed Lauter, Jim Youngs, Eric Nesterenko, George Finn, Fionnula Flanagan, Ken James, Peter Faussett, Walker Boone, Keanu Reeves, Martin Donlevy, Harry Spiegel, Rob Sapiensze, Bruce Edwards, Lorraine Foreman, Catherine Bray, Jain Dickson, Barry Swatik, Michael Legros, Murray Evans, Jason Warren, Warren Dukes, Sid Lynas, Jamie McAllister, Jay Hanks, Frank Cini, Greg Salter, Howie McCarrol Jr, Charlie Wasley, Ricky Davis, Joe Bowen, plus 'The Hamilton Mustangs' and 'Thunder Bay Bombers' Ice Hockey Teams. Dir: Peter Markle. Pro: Peter Bart and Patrick Wells. Ex Pro: Jon Peters and Peter Guber. Screenplay: Markle, based on a story by him and John Whitman. Ph: Mark Irwin. Ed: Stephen E. Rivkin and Jack Hofstra. Art: Alicia Keywan. M: William Orbit/Torchsong. (Gubers/Peters Co-Markle Wells for UA-UIP). Rel: 4 July 1986. 110 mins. Cert 15.

The Foreign Language Film

For full details of the films illustrated in this section, see 'Releases of the Year' feature.

Above, Caspar de Boer as Peter, the first of the tragic Steenwijk family to be shot by the Nazis in Fons Rademakers' The Assault – De Aanslag. With the rest of the family executed and the house burned down, the only survivor is the 12-year-old son Anton, who grows up to become a doctor and learns, almost by accident, the full facts of the tragic night in his youth.

Michael Maniatis in the title role of the Greek film Angelos (distributed in Great Britain by Cannon).

Above, a most unlikely wedding: bridegroom Ugo Tognazzi and bride Michel Serrault in the third La Cage aux Folles *film,* The Wedding *released by Tri-Star.*

Right, Peter Wang does some Chinese cooking in Mainline's delightful shoestring Chinese-American film, Chan is Missing.

Alexei Kravchenko as the young peasant boy who experiences the worst of German brutality when, during World War II, his becomes one of the 5000 Russian-Polish villages the Germans burnt down – often along with the peasants living in them. Hard to take in its raw reality and uncompromising starkness, this Cannon Russian import, Come and See, *confirmed director Elem Klimov's stature as one of his country's most outstanding movie-makers.*

Annunziata (Angela Molina) comforts Toto (Daniel Ezralow) in the Cannon-Gala Italian import Camorra: The Naples Connection – Un complicato Intrigo di Donne, Vicoli e Delitti, *a film which marked a new departure for director Lina Wertmüller in that it was a 'straightforward' mixture of mystery – whodunit? – fantasy, drama and melodrama, culminating in a quite extraordinary and spectacular courtroom scene.*

Below, because of the antiquated and morally indefensible local code of 'honour' the brothers Vicario, having – albeit rather unwillingly – murdered the man suspected but never proved to have seduced their sister, seek solace and Holy sustenance from the local priest. The men are played by actual twins, Carlos and Rogerio Miranda in Francesco Rosi's strongly directed film of the turbulent Gabriel Garcia Marquez story of love and death in a small and sleepy Colombian river town, Chronicle of a Death Foretold – Cronaca di una Morte Annunciata *(a Virgin release). This writing-directing combination, with its stern condemnation of brutal moral codes and uncaring human behaviour, produced a memorable movie. Inset: Ornella Muti as the beauty whose virginity, or lack of it, sparks off the tragic events.*

Above left, hard, demanding dad (Trevor Howard) helps by his attitude to drive his mentally rocky daughter (Jane Birkin) to murder him, and thereby to descend further into insanity in the Franco-Belgian ICA release Dust.

Above right: Charlotte Gainsbourg as An Impudent Girl – L'Effrontée, *Claude Miller's sensitive French comedy released in Great Britain by Artificial Eye.*

East Berlin Swiss Embassy's chauffeur Christian Kohlund hides his girlfriend Ursela Monn so that he can smuggle her across the border to taste the delights of West Berlin's livelier lifestyle in Cannon-Gala's Girl in a Boot – Einmal Ku'damm und Zurück.

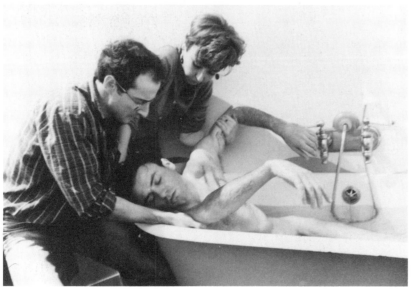

Some of the people who use Staircase C – Escalier C *in this Cannon-Gala French release, about the people and events that occur in a Paris rooming house: this not particularly friendly conversation is between Robin Renucci, Jean-Pierre Bacri and Florence Giorgetti. Left: Jacques Bonnaffe and Catherine Frot are just in time to prevent fellow room-renter Gilles Gaston-Dreyfus from drowning in the bath.*

Above, something of a throwback to his earlier 8½ days, Federico Fellini's Ginger and Fred *(released in Britain by Recorded Releasing) was a romantic and charming film which only lightly satirized TV. A story of a one-show comeback by a former top-of-the-bill dancing duo, it had the advantage of two outstanding performances from Giulietta Masina (Mrs Fellini, of course) and the ever perfectly professional Marcello Mastroianni. Rogers was* not *amused; highly affronted, she took a $1 million-plus claim for damages to the United States courts.*

Inevitably comparable to those classic Jacques Demy musicals like Les Parapluies de Cherbourg, *though with far less impact, Chantal Akerman's Electric Pictures release* Golden Eighties *had a Gallic charm all its own. Love in Miss Ackerman's film is more practical than romantic as it is expressed by the various owners and workers of the shops in the arcade to which the action is confined.*

Above, the return of the Sheik of Araby! Well, maybe not quite, but Gala's French film Harem had a lot in common with that romantic old song and Valentino film. Now the Arab prince – Ben Kingsley – rides a stunning Ferrari instead of a steed, has lots of concubines he neglects, in favour of drugging and abducting pretty New Yorker Nastassja Kinski, whose initial anger turns – what would you expect? – to love.

Marcélia Cartaxo as the unwashed, unkempt and altogether undesirable Macabea, the 'heroine' of Contemporary's Brazilian release The Hour of the Star – La Hora da Estrela. It was a sad, sometimes poetic, leisurely told story of one of the least attractive feminine characters ever to be made the subject of a film.

Left, Wang Xueqi – with Liu Qiang – as the folksong-collecting soldier who unwittingly brings about tragedy when he visits a small backward community, in ICA's Chinese import Yellow Earth – Huang Tudi.

Below left, Jean-Claude Brialy as the man with the odd hobby of collecting glass eyes, who becomes a murder suspect in Claude Chabrol's second film to feature the cases of the unconventional cop Inspector Lavardin – Inspecteur Lavardin, *played by Jean Poiret. The inspector is called in to solve the killing in a small French seaside town of a writer so generally hated that anyone could have murdered him. An Artificial Eye release.*

Below, Jackie Chan doubled up very successfully as both star and director in the Palace Pictures release of Hong Kong's entertaining film Police Story – Jingcha Goshi, *which, while it may not have been of great subtlety, did have plenty of amusing kung-fu and similar action.*

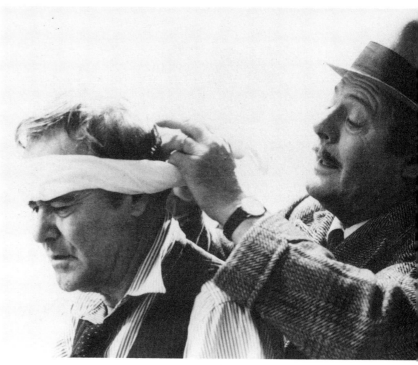

Above left, stylized and of special appeal, Sergio Paradjanov's poetical Legend of Fortress Suram – *an Artificial Eye import – was based on a Georgian legend in similar vein to the same Soviet director's* The Colour of Pomegranates.

Above right, Marcello Mastroianni ministers to his old pal Jack Lemmon in Ettore Scola's Macaroni – Maccheroni. *During their few days together in Italy, the cheerful Italian teaches the go-getting American businessman some useful lessons about the way life should be lived. Two masterly performances made this small, tender gem of a film something to recall with pleasure. A Palace Pictures release.*

Husband (Heiner Lauterbach, left) and his wife's lover (Uwe Ochsenknecht) both lose their trousers in the lift, thus bringing director-writer Doris Dörrie's hitherto wittingly and shrewdly observant comedy Men – Männer *(an Artificial Eye release) to a broadly farcical conclusion. The third feature film from this original and talented German director, the story is about a deserted husband who regains his wife by cleverly changing the unconventional (thus attractive) lover into a mirror image of his own conventional self.*

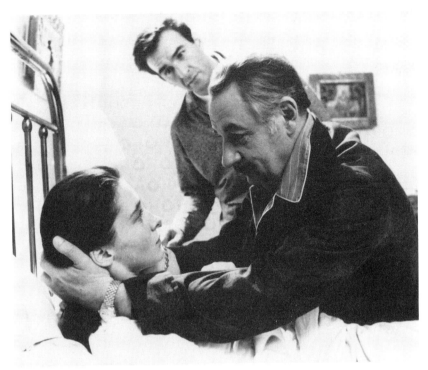

Still wearing the facial bonhomie *which gives the film its title of* Masks – Masques *(a Cannon release), Philippe Noiret stars as Legagneur, a popular programme presenter on French TV whose smile hides a greedy, ruthless character capable of killing for cash. He is planning to drug his god-daughter (Anne Brochet) to death and is only prevented by the intervention of Robin Renucci as the unmasker, who himself wears the false mask of a journalist. Maybe not the very best Chabrol but as stylishly and beautifully directed, with its Hitchcockian allusions, as ever.*

Below, two screen newcomers of outstanding talent are the stars of Fox's French import Betty Blue – 37.2 Le Matin. *Jean-Hugues Anglade and Béatrice Dalle share the acting and erotic honours.*

Above, time for dinner and dalliance for Romaine Belacroix (Sabine Azéma) and Marcel Blanc (André Dussollier) in Alain Resnais's adaptation of Henry Bernstein's 1929 play Mélo (an Artificial Eye release), which has so fascinated movie-makers that it has already been filmed five times. A story crying out for operatic treatment, it's about a triangle between two professional violinist friends and the woman who is wife of one and mistress of the other, a situation leading to an abortive murder attempt and the woman's suicide.

Left, happy and tired ending for Anton Glanzelius and his soccer-playing girlfriend Melina Kinnaman in the exquisite, if somewhat oddly titled My Life as a Dog – Mitt Liv som Hund. We can be grateful to Artificial Eye for the British showing of this story of a captivating 12-year-old boy.

Right, Sean Connery as the English monk turned 14th-century Sherlock Holmes investigating the mysterious deaths of several monks in a Northern Italian abbey and (inset) a young Franciscan novice (Christian Slater), learning the forbidden pleasures of the flesh from a nubile peasant girl (Valentine Vargas) in the Rank release The Name of the Rose – Der Name der Rose, a grey and forbidding drama flickeringly lit by Connery's fine, thoughtful and sincere performance.

Susan Fleetwood, Filippa Franzén, Valérie Mairesse and Sven Wollter dine al fresco by candlelight in Andrei Tarkovsky's last film The Sacrifice – Offret. *He died not long after its completion. A many layered, complex, intellectually fascinating film, its ambiguity asked a lot of the – surely? – enthralled audience. Left, Erland Josephson and Wollter.*

Cop's Honour – Parole de Flic (*released in Great Britain by Guild*) *must have been a busy film for Delon: he starred (with Fiona Gélin), produced, co-scripted and even sang the theme song 'I Don't Know'. And, consciously or not, he included what appear to be all sorts of fascinating allusions to his off-screen experiences. Right, at the receiving end, Guy Viltard.*

Above, Ugo Tognazzi as the French belle époque *music-hall star Joseph Pujol, in the Cannon Italian import* The Windbreaker – Il Pétomane. *It was Pujol's freak ability to bread wind musically and otherwise at will which brought him fame and fortune and private command performances before most of the crowned heads of Europe. The whole thing is based on fact; Pujol was a popular star at the Moulin Rouge. A brilliant performance and careful direction made the film more amusing and far less objectionable than it might have been in other hands.*

Below, Contemporary's The Princes – Les Princes *should at least be authentic in its depiction of life in France for the gypsies, in that the writer-director (and composer of the score) Tony Gatlif is himself a gypsy, originally from Algeria where, he has admitted, he was* something of a junior delinquent. Two outstanding performances, one by Gérard Darmon (left) as the short-tempered gypsy and the other by Muse Dalbray as the indomitable old grandmother, were great assets in an otherwise interesting but uneven film.*

Above, three scenes from Elem Klimov's Farewell – Proshchanie *(an Artificial Eye release) which, although made in 1981, was only premièred in Britain in 1987. Firmly in the old classical Soviet school of movie-making, it is the story of the varied reactions of the inhabitants of a village about to be submerged to make way for a new giant hydroelectric generating station.*

Vincent Gauthier as the man who brings a happy ending to Marie Rivière's less than happy vacation in Eric Rohmer's The Green Ray – Le Rayon Vert. *Released by Artificial Eye. Though entertaining in the manner of this most literate of French directors, it was well below his best standard.*

Above, winner of the Best Actress Award at the Cannes Festival with this performance, Barbara Sukowa was certainly outstanding in Artificial Eye's release of the German biopic Rosa Luxemburg.

Left, Juliette Binoche as the aspiring young French actress who goes to Paris and becomes sexually subservient to a self-destroying failed actor (Lambert Wilson) in Cannon's Rendezvous.

Below, Jo Champa as the seven-veiled lady of the Bible (but shown sporting not even one of the seven) who demanded, and got, a head on a plate as dancing partner. It's doubtful whether Oscar Wilde would have recognized his adaptation of the Salomé story in this Franco-Italian, Cannon-Gala released film.

The sisters watch the hair-cutting ceremony of the new young nun (Catherine Mouchet) in Gala's French import of Alain Cavalier's Thérèse, *based on a true story, that of a young girl's determination to follow her two sisters into the Carmelite Order. Her eventual realization of that ambition led to an early death from tuberculosis, the result of her fervour and neglect of herself, and eventually to her canonization.*

Above right, Marianne Sägebrecht and Eisi Gulp as the odd pair of lovers in Electric Pictures' Sugar Baby, *one of the year's several 'collectors' pieces'.*

Gérard Depardieu and Michel Blanc as a very odd couple indeed – with Miou-Miou as the latter's unfortunate wife – in Bertrand Blier's Virgin Films release Evening Dress – Tenue de Soirée. *Though the ubiquitous Depardieu has played just about everything on the screen from historical drama to broad comedy, this is the first time he's taken the role of a homosexual and it sat rather oddly on him in this, Blier's return to black-and-beastly form after a lapse of several films.*

The Hollywood Year

ANTHONY SLIDE'S annual Letter from America

Hollywood is a community of contradictions. It invites a living legend, Bette Davis, to present the Best Picture Award at the Oscar presentations, and then insults her by refusing to permit her to make her delivery at her own speed. At the same time, film-makers become increasingly agitated at the question of colourization of old black-and-white features.

Few issues have enraged the Hollywood community more than the question of colourization, by which black-and-white films can be converted – on tape, *but not on film* – to colour. Two companies presently offer a colourization process: Color Systems Technology is the leader in the field, with a process invented by Ralph Weinger in 1978, and Hal Roach Studios, Inc. – no longer associated with its late founder – offers a similar system and also owns the exclusive right to use the term 'colourization'.

The impetus behind colourization is that it will increase the value of old black-and-white films by making them palatable for screening on television during peak viewing hours, when colour only is the norm. Additionally, but equally importantly, it will enable the backers of the process to re-copyright old films, such as *It's a Wonderful Life*, which are presently in the public domain in the United States. This last proposition is subject to approval in Congress, and may not necessarily prove correct.

Very few films have actually been seen on television in the colourization process. Some of the first were *Yankee Doodle Dandy*, *Miracle on 34th Street* and *It's a Wonderful Life*, and ratings have so far proved that the addition of colour *has* increased interest, and thus value, in the features. One independent Los Angeles television station, KTLA,

televised *It's a Wonderful Life* on 24 November 1986 and invited its viewers to vote as to whether they were for or against the addition of colour. Some 21,604 viewers telephoned the station to vote 53.5 to 46.5 per cent against colour; but their vote meant little, since the station was already committed to screening additional black-and-white films 'enhanced' with colour.

Those chiefly opposed to colourization have been the directors. The Directors' Guild of Great Britain came out with a curious policy statement, opposing colourization of some films but not others, announcing that it would, in association with the British Film Institute, compile its own list of those films which were 'untouchable'. None of the directors at the Guild seemed willing to explain by what right they could decide which films were worthy of protection as black-and-white masterpieces and which were not.

The Directors' Guild of America took a more general view that no black-and-white films should be colourized. Indeed, the Guild is now sending delegates to speak before Congress (or, to be more precise, the Senate Judiciary Committee's sub-committee on Technology and the Law), urging that black-and-white films be protected from colourization by considering them works of art. Gilbert Cates, president of the Guild, noted that a law in Massachusetts prohibited the altering of works of art and suggested that a similar law be passed by the US Congress.

John Huston called a press conference on 13 November 1986, asking the public to boycott products advertised during television broadcasts of colourized films. His anger was chiefly vented at Ted Turner, whose organization had recently acquired the entire MGM Library and all the pre-1948

Warner Bros. features, and who had made no secret of his plans to colourize everything. Huston began his conference with an old Hollywood joke:

'A couple of generations back, screenwriters used to tell a story about two producers lost in the desert and dying of thirst. About to give up the ghost, they crawl into view of a miraculous spring of pure effervescent water and they go joyously to drink, when one says, "No, wait. Don't drink. Wait till I piss in it." To bring the story up to date one has only to add that, in my opinion, both producers are members of the Turner organization.'

Other members of the Directors' Guild who joined with Huston in condemning colourization in general – and the television screening the previous night of *The Maltese Falcon* in particular – were Karen Arthur, Peter Bogdanovich, Richard Brooks, Arthur Hiller, Ronald Neame, Sidney Lumet, Martin Ritt, Martin Scorsese, Milos Forman and George Schaefer.

The American Film Institute is not an organization to overlook any publicity it might be able to attract to itself, and so it entered the 'game' on 1 October 1986, with a press conference at which James Stewart attacked the colourization of *It's a Wonderful Life*. Former child star and currently chairman of the board of the American Film Institute, Bonita Granville read a statement which said, 'The American Film Institute considers it essential that black-and-white films be presented to

One of the new attractions at Disneyland during the last year was a three-dimensional short subject, directed by Francis Coppola, produced by George Lucas, and starring Michael Jackson. Captain EO was first seen on 19 September 1986 and could be seen nowhere else but at Disneyland.

the public only in black-and-white. To do otherwise is to destroy our national film history and the rich heritage which it represents.' In response, Earl Glick of the Hal Roach organization announced that his company has 'increased and improved on Joe Walker's original photography'. There were boos from the assembled company, which included Stanley Kramer, Nicholas Meyer and Arthur Hiller. A statement was read from Steven Spielberg, which said, in part, that 'It is not the privilege of this generation to overrule our founding fathers because somebody in marketing research discovered that kids today will flip past anything in black-and-white with their TV remotes.'

In response to the Institute's press conference, Roger L. Mayer, president and chief operating officer of the Turner Entertainment Company, issued a statement to the effect that 'It is totally inappropriate for the AFI to take sides in an issue that in my opinion is political in nature and that might have an adverse economic effect on the very companies within the industry which have been most supportive of the AFI and its activities over the years.' In fact, it *was* surprising that the American Film Institute should risk the anger of the major studios, many of the heads of which serve on the AFI's board. A short time later the Institute tried to persuade American film archivists meeting in Los Angeles to support its position on colourization, and failed. The archivists thought it inappropriate for them to take a stand, an attitude which was helped by the Turner organization's positive steps to support film preservation. Whatever one may say of Ted Turner and his company he does understand the value of public relations: MGM would never permit prints of its films to be made available to its former stars, yet Turner has happily supplied videotapes (non-colourized) to such former MGM high flyers as Leslie Caron and Alice Terry.

Most Hollywood organizations, including the American Society of Cinematographers, have opposed tampering with black-and-white films. Columbia Pictures chairman David Puttnam gave assurances that he would not permit the colourization of any Frank Capra feature without the director's permission: 'Certainly the director's voice must be heard and given a great amount of consideration,' he said. The Screen

Actors' Guild, the Costume Designers' Guild, the National Arts Council, and the Writers' Guild of America have all come out in opposition to colourization. One of its few industry supporters has been Tom Pryor, editor of *Daily Variety*, who, rather like the British Directors' Guild, has urged a film-by-film assessment of the process.

The Academy of Motion Picture Arts and Sciences found itself in a curious position. One of its governors is Gilbert Cates of the Directors' Guild, and not surprisingly he introduced a motion at the Academy's 16 December 1986 board meeting urging a stand against colourization. As it happens, also on the Academy's board are Charles Powell, executive vice-president of Color Systems Technology, and Gene Allen, a former Academy president and color consultant to Color Systems Technology. To save itself from an embarrassing internal dispute, the Academy announced that colourization was 'an economic matter', and the organization's by-laws prevented its voting on anything of a political or economic nature.

In time, the colourization dispute may prove to be little more than a storm in a teacup. First of all, an old film is an old film, whether it is in black-and-white or colour, and it will be shunned by the average television viewer. Secondly, it costs approximately $200,000 to colourize one feature, and it seems highly unlikely that the profits from any colourized feature are such that this high price tag can be justified. Finally, and perhaps more importantly, colourization is an electronic process which can only be applied to videotape. There is no way that a film, on film, can be colourized, and thus no way that the integrity of the original negative or viewing prints can be harmed through colourization. If the public wants colourization – and it seems that it does – so be it. For those who prefer to see original black-and-white features in black-and-white on their television screens, it is simply a matter of turning a knob and switching off the colour.

What else has been going on in Hollywood during the past year? Plenty! Lorimar-Telepictures became the new owner of the MGM lot, but the Mayor of Culver City prohibited it from placing its sign above the studio, as rooftop signs are forbidden in Culver City. The question is, will Leo the Lion's sign

remain over a studio which is no longer his?

In July of 1986, Larry Adler finally received his long-overdue Academy Award nomination for the score of *Genevieve*. Because of the McCarthy blacklist, he had never been acknowledged by the Academy as creator of the score; back in 1954, the Academy had credited conductor Muir Mathieson for it. It was not until Adler returned to Hollywood last year to play at the Hollywood Bowl that someone decided to do something about this 'oversight'.

The Academy sponsored the première of the documentary *The Fantasy Worlds of George Pal* on 20 August 1986, and among those present at the screening were Russ Tamblyn, Barbara Eden and Ann Robinson (who starred in *War of the Worlds*). The Fourth Annual George Stevens Lecture on Directing, also sponsored by the Academy, took place on 14 July 1986, and included a screening of the complete version of Stevens' 1939 feature, *Gunga Din*, introduced by Rudy Behlmer.

Among major restoration projects by Robert Gitt of the UCLA Film and Television Archives were the original versions of *A Star Is Born* and *The Bullfighter and the Lady*. The latter is now a full 124 minutes in length, and the newly restored version was given a special screening at UCLA on 18 July 1986, attended by director Budd Boetticher and Robert Stack. *A Star Is Born* is usually seen in poor-quality 16mm prints, but Gitt has now restored full Technicolor to the film and preserved it on 35mm. The first screening of the new print took place on 12 March 1987, again at UCLA, with the last living member of the cast, Lionel Stander, present.

A major film exhibition currently touring the United States is titled 'Before Hollywood: Turn-of-the-Century Film from American Archives'. It includes 69 films from the early years of American cinema selected from the archives of George Eastman House, the Library of Congress, the Museum of Modern Art, and the UCLA Film and Television Archives. The initial presentation took place in New York at the Whitney Museum on 25 January 1987. Very academic in approach, the exhibition 'touts' many films as newly discovered when, in reality, they have been known to many for more than 15 years;

some are discussed in Kevin Brownlow's *The Parade's Gone By* and have only been recently discovered by academics.

The 50th Anniversary of the BBC was celebrated in Hollywood last November with a black-tie dinner at the Ambassador Hotel's Coconut Grove, sponsored by the Academy of Television Arts and Sciences and the International Council of the National Academy of Television Arts and Sciences. Personal reminiscences of the BBC were provided by Coral Browne, Roy Dotrice and Jill Ireland.

The Los Angeles International Film Festival (Filmex) appears dead; in its place, the American Film Institute organized the first annual AFI Festival, held during March. Ken Wlaschin selected the films, all of which were screened at the Los Feliz Theater, the oldest art house in Hollywood. Despite AFI's claims to the contrary, the festival was not a great success, with attendance low at many of the screenings and no great excitement expressed by either audiences or critics. The opening night consisted of a tribute to Hal Wallis which was so badly publicized that, to date, I still don't know where it was held, who participated in it, or whether it was open to the public!

Richard Lamparski, author of the *Whatever Became of . . .?* books, garnered rather more publicity for his party at the newly-restored Hollywood Roosevelt Hotel, last December, celebrating publication of the tenth volume in the series. Among the celebrities present – I use the term very loosely – were Alex D'Arcy, Liz Renay, Madge Bellamy, Betty Rowland, Yma Sumac, Mae Clarke, Cornel Wilde, Curtis Harringon, Rosemary de Camp, Cecelia Parker, Robert Cummings and Irene Manning. Also present was Rose Hobart, one of the better actresses of American stage and screen, who invited me to be her escort to the first annual Pat O'Brien Dinner, on 17 March 1987, at which the first Pat O'Brien Award was presented, by Kevin Dobson, to Dick van Patten. No, I don't really understand why there is a Pat O'Brien Award or why Dick van Patten received it, but it must be important because there was even a tape-recorded message from President Reagan, who, with Nancy, served as Honorary Chairperson.

The City of Hollywood is celebrating

Edith Taliaferro and Tom Forman in the enchanting 1915 feature Young Romance, *one of the films in the 'Before Hollywood' exhibition.*

its 100th anniversary amidst a number of promotional events, usually sponsored by the Hollywood Chamber of Commerce. They commenced in February outside the Hollywood Roosevelt Hotel with the dedication of a star on the Hollywood Walk of Fame to the memory of Natalie Wood; widower Robert Wagner was present.

As part of the initial celebration, an acrylic time capsule was placed on permanent display, to be opened in 2087 on the city's 200th birthday. The capsule contains a special Oscar, struck by the Academy of Motion Picture Arts and Sciences on the condition that it be returned to the organization when the capsule is opened. Also deposited in the capsule were a piece of the Hollywood Sign, a Woody Woodpecker animation cel by Walter Lantz, and a videotape of *Wings*, the first film to win the Academy Award for Best Picture. As videotape has a lifespan of less than twenty years, it appears that *Wings* has less of a chance of making 2087 than the world does. A five-foot-high birthday cake was cut, with Rhonda Fleming leading the crowd in singing 'Happy Birthday'. Miss Fleming's presence was appropriate, or inappropriate depend-

ing on one's point of view; her husband is Ted Mann, who re-named Grauman's Chinese Theater Mann's Chinese Theater in honour of himself. (The Mann theatre circuit was recently acquired by Paramount Pictures, and there is hope that the company's first action will be to give back to the Chinese Theater its original name.)

Celebrations continued. Gene Autry received a fifth star in his honour on the Hollywood Walk of Fame, the only entertainment personality to be so honoured. Autry was one of the last celebrities to receive a star at the old rate of $3,000; the Chamber of Commerce recently raised the price of a star to $3,500, something that makes the whole procedure smack of sleaze, since so many major personalities of the past are still not represented. Yet again, this hint of tawdriness is perhaps appropriate in view of just how shabby Hollywood Boulevard and its environs look. However, let it be noted that the Hollywood Chamber of Commerce is doing its best to bring glamour back to the

Charlton Heston, Bob Hope and Janet Leigh help in the groundbreaking ceremony at the Motion Picture Country House and Hospital. Photo Kevin G. Roznowski

Hal Roach at the same ceremony. Photo Kevin G. Roznowski

occasion, and also presented me with the annual award of the Society of Cinephiles, which sponsors the event. In many respects, Minneapolis organized a far more tasteful salute to the film industry's past than Hollywood could ever accomplish.

Lillian Gish and Anthony Slide with their respective awards at the 1986 Cinecon Convention in Minneapolis. Photo Howard Kolodny

city: there is a big sign now on Hollywood Boulevard to that effect – it announces the opening of a new MacDonald's!

The Motion Picture and Television Fund, of which there can be no criticism, broke ground at its facility in Woodland Hills in December 1986 for a new medical building and additional housing. Among those attending the ceremony were Bob Hope and the late Hal Roach, one of the founders of the Fund. 'When I get so old I can't work, I hope to live right here,' he announced. Bob Hope commented: 'This Home is the one thing of this industry that makes me feel the proudest, but at my age it's a little disturbing to be handed a shovel and told to start digging.'

The Motion Picture and Television Fund is joining with Hollywood for a gala celebration, about which more in next year's report.

On a personal note, I was more than happy to be invited to participate in the annual Cinecon Convention, held this year in Minneapolis and very well orga-

nized by Ron Hall. The main feature of the Labor Day weekend gathering was a multi-film tribute to Dorothy Gish. Her sister Lillian Gish flew in for the

Ten of the Most Promising Faces of 1987

JAMES CAMERON-WILSON

Once again I am faced with this impossible task. For a start, there is no such thing as a 'new' face. Seth Green, the young actor who played Woody Allen's *alter ego* in *Radio Days*, could be described as a new face; but then he did have a prominent part, the role of 'Egg', in *The Hotel New Hampshire*, released four years ago. Some might even argue that Seth Green made his film debut nearly fourteen years ago: his birth was recorded for an industrial film. At two-and-a-half he informed his mother that he wanted to be an actor and at six he was already doing commercials on TV. So how new a face *is* Seth Green? Your answer is probably as good as mine.

The top ten I have selected for 1987 are, I hope, a representative bunch. It would have been a cinch just to list the latest members of the 'Brat Pack': say, Jon Cryer, Kim Delaney, Kevin Dillon, Chad Lowe, Mary Stuart Masterson, Kelly Preston, Francesco Quinn, Alan Ruck, Charlie Sheen, Craig Sheffer – whoever. There's never been so much fresh, promising talent in Hollywood to pick from.

However, I have attempted to avoid the obvious and have opted for **River Phoenix** as the token 'young American actor', a talented 17-year-old who has made some very good films and is destined to go far.

In spite of the plethora of US TV comics migrating to the big screen, I chose **James Belushi** as my sole American comedian because of his supplementary talent as a dramatic actor (witness *Salvador*). Belushi's next film, though, *Real Men*, is definitely a comedy.

Another comic who has proved himself an equally fine dramatic actor is **Paul Hogan**, who took a serious role in Australia's TV war series *Anzacs*. He is now, of course, better known for his *'Crocodile' Dundee*. While Down Under, I thought I'd also elect **Colin Friels** for my list, a very impressive actor with an enormously promising future.

From England I chose stand-up, fall-down comic **Lenny Henry**, and the extraordinarily versatile **Daniel Day Lewis** who, at the time of writing, is starring in his first American comedy, *Stars and Bars*. In it, Day Lewis plays an Englishman endeavouring to shed his British ways in Atlanta, Georgia; Keith Carradine's daughter, Martha Plimpton, co-stars.

From the Continent I selected the actresses **Béatrice Dalle** and **Isabella Rossellini** and, finally, from America, two more promising starlets: **Geena Davis** and **Linda Kozlowski**. I hope you find my pick an interesting mixed bag.

James Belushi. For too long James Belushi (formerly *Jim* Belushi) was just the brother of John. There were bit parts, supporting roles and then cameos, but only last year did the younger Belushi become a star. This was due, in the main, to two films: *About Last Night . . .*, a hit in which Belushi stole the notices as an 'endearing sexist'; and Oliver Stone's stomach-knotting *Salvador*, in which the actor played a straight role as the hedonistic Rock, looking for cheap thrills in a country about to explode. Born and raised in Chicago, Belushi graduated from the University of Illinois and spent two years with the Second City

James Belushi, in Fox's comedy The Man with One Red Shoe.

comedy troupe before playing the Pirate King in *The Pirates of Penzance*, first on tour and then on Broadway. TV's *Saturday Night Live* followed, and then the movies. Filmography: *Violent Streets*; *Trading Places*; *The Man with One Red Shoe*; *Jumpin' Jack Flash*; *The Little Shop of Horrors*. Next: two leads, in *Real Men*, with John Ritter; and *The Principal*, with Rae Dawn Chong.

Béatrice Dalle. Once again the French cinema has unearthed a *femme fatale* of international status. However, I was loath to tip Béatrice Dalle for stardom since she showed little interest in furthering her career, in spite of a devastating debut in Jean-Jacques Beineix's *37.2 Le Matin – Betty Blue*. At the time of the film's release the then 20-year-

Béatrice Dalle, in the Fox release 37.2 Le Matin – Betty Blue.

old actress married a painter and threatened to settle down and do nothing but breed children. However, pressure of fame and a flood of tempting film offers have coerced Mlle Dalle back to the cinema. A stunning, pouting brunette, Dalle exudes a sexuality that out-smoulders any other French actress I can think of. Born in Brest and raised in Mans, the actress left home at an early age to resume a career as punk in Paris. Modelling followed, and then international stardom in one of the most successful French films of all time. The comparisons to Bardot have been numerous and deserve no mention here: Béatrice Dalle is an original.

Geena Davis. Cute, bright, talented, Geena Davis is destined for a healthy career. She actually made her film debut in 1982, in *Tootsie*, as the half-naked TV actress sharing a dressing-room with Dustin Hoffman. Then she had a recurring role in the NBC sit-com *Buffalo Bill* with Dabney Coleman, as

Geena Davis, in Fox's horror-thriller The Fly.

the sweet and dizzy Wendy Killian; she even wrote her own episode, revealing yet further talents. In Michael Ritchie's *Fletch* she played a newspaper morgue chief, a role originally written for a man, and later Karen, the mixed-up housekeeper in TV's *Family Ties*. Ms Davis then snatched her own show on the small screen, *Sara*, a comedy about single life in San Francisco in the 1980s. The TV movie *Elena* followed, then a role as an oversexed vampire in *Transylvania 6–5000*, with Jeff Goldblum. Goldblum and Davis teamed up again for *The Fly*, undoubtedly the actress's greatest achievement to date; besides being a superb movie, *The Fly* gives Ms Davis her first film lead, in which she manages to combine just the right amount of sweetness, kookiness and hard-nosed intelligence. Seldom has the female star of a horror film come off so well. For the record, the Massachusetts actress is also six feet tall, speaks fluent Swedish and is an aspiring cartoonist and inventor. You have to love her. Next up: Tim Burton's *Beetle Juice*, with Michael Keaton.

Daniel Day Lewis. Thanks to a miracle of timing, Daniel Day Lewis astounded New York critics when *My Beautiful Laundrette* and *A Room With a View* opened within eight days of each other. In the former, Day Lewis played a homosexual punk layabout; in the latter, the outrageously stuck-up and pedantic Cecil Vyse, suitor to Lucy Honeychurch. Both performances were perfectly modulated, both films were enormously successful. The actor's pedigree is equally impressive: he is the grandson of film tycoon Sir Michael Balcon and son of Poet Laureate Cecil Day Lewis and actress Jill Balcon. Born in London in 1958, he trained at the Bristol Old Vic, performed a number of plays at the Edinburgh Festival and made several TV appearances, most notably in *How Many Miles to Babylon?* He later established himself in London's West End theatre as Guy Bennett in *Another Country*, going on to play Romeo for the Royal Shakespeare Company. His film roles include parts in *Gandhi*, *The Bounty* (as Mr Fryer, again excellent) and *Nanou*. Day Lewis also starred in Alan Bennett's highly praised *The Insurance Man* for the BBC, and will be seen shortly in his first international film lead, in Phil Kaufman's *The*

Daniel Day Lewis, seen in quick succession in widely differing roles in My Beautiful Laundrette *and* A Room With a View.

Unbearable Lightness of Being. Next: another lead, in the Atlanta-based *Stars and Bars*, a comedy with Harry Dean Stanton.

Colin Friels. In November 1986, Nadia Tass' *Malcolm* swept the Australian Oscars. The production won Best Film, Director, Original Screenplay, Supporting Actor, Supporting Actress, Editing, Sound and, for Colin Friels, Best Actor prizes. The Best Actress award went to Friels' wife, Judy Davis, for *Kangaroo*, in which Friels also starred. Paul Hogan may be box-office champ Down Under, but there is no denying that Mr and Mrs Friels are the home critics' darlings. In *Malcolm*, Friels played a retarded mechanical genius, new to love and crime but a willing learner; avoiding caricature, Friels was moving, real and very funny. In *Kangaroo*, the film based on D. H. Lawrence's experiences in Australia, he was totally different: intense, passionate, intellectual, with a flawless Nottinghamshire accent. Like England's Daniel Day Lewis, Colin Friels proved himself a superb actor in two totally different roles in two excellent films. If he doesn't become Australia's premier film actor, whoever does will have to be an Antipodean Olivier. Friels will next be seen opposite Judy Davis in Gillian Armstrong's *High Tide*. Previous films: *Hoodwink* (with Judy Davis), *Monkey Grip*, *Buddies*, *The Coolangatta Gold*.

Lenny Henry. Comedian, singer, writer, impressionist and now actor, Lenny Henry is one of the most exciting showbusiness forces to emerge from Britain in years. Now he has wowed international critics with his powerful, funny performance as an itinerant DJ in the little-seen BBC film *Coast to Coast*. Little-seen it may have been, but it attracted so much attention at film festivals around the world that a sequel is already planned. Lenny started his career at sixteen when he found himself a winner on the original series of TV's *New Faces*. That led to a string of TV successes – *The Fosters*, *Tiswas*, *OTT*, *Three of a Kind*, *The Lenny Henry Show*,

Colin Friels gave two notable performances in Malcolm *and* Kangaroo.

Lenny Henry has just completed his first American film, The Suicide Club.

Lenny Henry Tonite – punctuated by cabaret appearances and concerts all over Britain. Born in Dudley, one of seven children, Lenny completed his first American film this year, *The Suicide Club*, opposite Mariel Hemingway, and is now contemplating an offer from Hollywood. He is married to the comedienne Dawn French.

Paul Hogan. The most successful comedian to emerge from Down Under since Barry Humphries, Paul Hogan has now secured superstardom in America via *'Crocodile' Dundee*. Before that, he was already an international face thanks to a succession of hugely successful TV commercials. Whether advertising Foster's lager or working (for no payment) for the Australian Tourist Commission, Hogan was a favourite with armchair audiences everywhere; his appearances inter-

rupted and enlivened many a dead TV programme. While working as a rigger on Sydney Harbour Bridge Hogan applied to a TV talent show, describing himself as a tap-dancing knife-thrower from the Outback – available for TV appearances. He got a slot on the show and walked away with the evening. Numerous TV turns followed: guest appearances in *A Current Affair* and his own *The Paul Hogan Show*. Hogan also starred in the critically acclaimed drama series *Anzacs*, and then he developed his own screenplay, *'Crocodile' Dundee*. At the time of writing, the film has grossed over $175 million in the US, and Down Under it has become the most successful film *ever*. Mr Hogan is currently shooting a sequel.

Linda Kozlowski. Not only very beautiful but an accomplished actress, Linda Kozlowski has rocketed to stardom 'overnight'. Graduating from New York's Julliard School in 1981, Ms Kozlowski made her stage debut that year in *How It All Began* at New York's Public Theater. Three years and many plays later, she won a leading role opposite Dustin Hoffman in *Death of a Salesman* on Broadway, repeating her role in the TV production. Hoffman was impressed and recommended her to producer John Cornell, who cast her in *'Crocodile' Dundee*. As the feisty, determined journalist Sue Charlton,

Paul Hogan co-wrote and starred in 'Crocodile' Dundee.

Linda Kozlowski, who came to prominence in 'Crocodile' Dundeee.

Kozlowski matched Paul Hogan's chauvinistic hero tooth for tooth and 'a star was born'. She will next be seen in *Pass the Ammo*, co-starring Tim Curry, and will of course feature in the sequel of *Dundee*.

River Phoenix. The youngest member of the Brat Pack, 17-year-old River Phoenix has shown rare sensitivity in a small number of first-rate films. Born in Madras, Oregon, and raised in Shadow Hills, California, River has had an eventful life up till now. He spent his childhood travelling in South and Central America with his parents, who were then independent Christian missionaries. At the age of ten, he entered the acting profession via a number of TV commercials and a role (Guthrie) in the successful TV series *Seven Brides For Seven Brothers*. The mini-series *Celebrity* and *Robert Kennedy and His Times* followed; then guest spots in *Hotel*, *It's Your Move* and *Family Ties*, and the TV movie *Surviving: A Family in Crisis* (with Ellen Burstyn). At the age of fourteen came his first film, *Explorers*, in which he played Wolfgang Muller, the science prodigy. Next came the 'sleeper' hit *Stand By Me* and the role of narrator in Peter Weir's *The Mosquito Coast*, as Harrison Ford's eldest son. Soon Phoenix will be seen as *Jimmy Reardon* and in the title role of Richard Benjamin's domestic thriller *Little*

The career of River Phoenix is building nicely. Here he is seen in Columbia's Stand By Me.

Nikita, with Sidney Poitier in support. His brothers and sisters, Leaf, Rainbow and Summer, are also actors and have appeared in a number of films. Watch this space.

Isabella Rossellini. Spitting image of Ingrid Bergman, her mother, Isabella Rossellini started out as an actress in, and received decent reviews for, the lead in *The Meadow*, an Italian film. Then, surprisingly, she became a model – one of the highest paid in the world. 'I was surrounded by these beautiful women,' she said, 'and I felt short and fat. Here I was, already 28, and I thought, "This is crazy".' Born in Rome in 1952 to Bergman and the Italian director Roberto Rossellini, Isabella moved to New York at the age of nineteen and worked for Italian TV as an interviewer. She interviewed Martin Scorsese – and they married in 1979. Since then she has married again, to model Jonathan Wiedemann, by whom

Isabella Rossellini, seen most recently in Blue Velvet.

she has a 4-year-old daughter; they, too, are separated. Now she is living with the director David Lynch. In 1985 Isabella returned to the screen in Taylor Hackford's *White Nights*, playing the Russian girlfriend of Gregory Hines. She has also starred in David Lynch's controversial, inspired and erotic *Blue Velvet*, playing a masochistic nightclub singer. The reviews were mixed but never less than ardent, either way. Rossellini will next be seen in Norman Mailer's *Tough Guys Don't Dance*, with Ryan O'Neal; in *Siesta*, with Gabriel Byrne and Martin Sheen; and in Golan and Globus's *Little Red Riding Hood* (as the mother), with Craig T. Nelson. And then she has been lined up for Lynch's long-projected comedy, *Ronnie Rocket*. Previous films: *A Matter of Time* (with Ingrid Bergman), *Pap'occhio*.

A Survey of
the Australian Year

JAMES CAMERON-WILSON

Cinema admissions in Australia are up 14 per cent over last year. Without 'Crocodile' Dundee, admissions would have *plummeted* 2 per cent. Just as Mel Gibson was synonymous with the Australian entertainment industry a year ago, so Paul Hogan is today.

However, the other big earners Down Under were all – predictably – American: *Out of Africa, Rocky IV, Jewel of the Nile, Top Gun, The Karate Kid Part II, The Color Purple* . . . Only *Malcolm*, the tragi-comedy about a retarded genius, also made an impression at the home box-office; it also impressed the critics. Even films directed by Bruce Beresford, Tim Burstall, Graeme Clifford, Paul Cox and George Miller II failed domestically, as did other projects with such reliable stars as Bryan Brown, Judy Davis, Colin Friels, John Hargreaves and Jack Thompson.

Rebel, the story of a Yank GI going AWOL in war-time Sydney, was the only other native feature that made any real impression, and that was no doubt due to the box-office durability of its American star, Matt Dillon. James Coburn was another import, for the well-made, intriguing true-life drama *Death of a Soldier*; but the film's subject matter (should an insane GI have been hanged in 1942?) proved too esoteric for most film-goers, American star or no American star.

Other imports included England's Rupert Everett, in the period drama *The Right Hand Man*; Anthony Andrews, for the epic *The Lighthorsemen*; Donald Pleasence, borrowed for the Melbourne-set thriller *Ground Zero*; and John Lone, in *Promises to Keep*, a love story from Phil Noyce.

But for local thespian talent Paul Hogan was the true hero of Australian cinema. A former rigger on Sydney Harbour Bridge, Hogan became an international face when he extolled the merits of Foster's lager and bolstered Australian tourism (gratis) via a string of hugely successful TV commercials. *'Crocodile' Dundee*, which he co-wrote, was his first film, and it ousted *ET* from the No 1 spot in the Australian charts. With a domestic gross of $A16 million (*ET* clocked up $A11 million), *Dundee* looks like a hard record to beat – even *Star Wars* only grossed $A6 million.

The income from *Malcolm* was a more modest $A628,000, but it nevertheless heralded the rise of another star. Colin Friels was no newcomer but his performance as the retarded mechanical genius won him the Australian Oscar for Best Actor, acting sharply contrasted by his role as D. H. Lawrence in the excellent, literary *Kangaroo*. Both films were well received by the critics, but *Kangaroo* found it even harder-going at the box-office, in spite of the presence of Mr Friels' wife, Judy Davis, as Frieda Lawrence. The acting duo teamed again for Gillian Armstrong's drama *High Tide*, and Friels then starred in *Ground Zero*, alongside Jack Thompson and Donald Pleasence.

At the time of writing, Barry Humphries' first film in eleven years, *Les Patterson Saves the World*, has had a mixed reception from the critics but started fairly well at the wickets, albeit not on the same blockbuster scale as *'Crocodile' Dundee*. The incredible story of Australia's cultural attaché, banished to run the diplomatic corps in Abu Niveah – where the military leader is waging a war on the West via a lethal sexual disease called HELP – *Les Patterson Saves the World* is racist, sexist and decidedly lavatorial. Only Barry Humphries, the most cheerfully brash of

comics, could have come up with the first comedy about AIDS. Patterson, however, being overweight, flatulent and amazingly vulgar, is not an easy character to warm to, unlike Humphries' other creation, Dame Edna Everage, who turned up in a memorable supporting role in the same film. The man in charge was George Miller, better known for his direction of *The Man From Snowy River*, Australia's biggest hit BC (before 'Crocodile').

Miller, incidentally, ought to change his name; more often than not he is confused with that other Australian film-maker, George Miller. To set the record straight, that other Miller came first, and made his name with the original *Mad Max* (1979), followed by *Mad Max 2*, otherwise known as *The Road Warrior*, which made even more money. Then came the 'Nightmare At 20,000 Feet' episode from Steven Spielberg's omnibus *Twilight Zone – The Movie*, the sequence in which John Lithgow usurped the acting honours as a man driven to insanity by his fear of flying; many rated it the best chapter in the film. Miller Mark I then returned to Australia to realize two outstanding TV series, *The Dismissal* and *Bodyline*, before returning to the leather-clad image of Mel Gibson for *Mad Max: Beyond Thunderdome*. With that success behind him, the former doctor revisited America to direct *The Witches of Eastwick*, a big-budget thriller based on the John Updike novel, starring Jack Nicholson, Cher, Susan Sarandon and Michelle Pfeiffer. Miller II also traversed the Pacific but met with less success – his film *The Aviator*, with Christopher Reeve, flopped utterly, and his next film, the Australian *Cool Change*, was equally disastrous, described by kinder critics as a tragedy.

Other Antipodean film-makers working overseas included Peter Weir, possibly still Australia's most famous, who turned in the disappointing *The Mosquito Coast*, based on the Paul Theroux novel. Harrison Ford starred (as he did in Weir's earlier – and better – film, *Witness*). Here he plays an inventor who drags his family off to Central America to escape the corrupting influences of Western society. Ford was good but his character, like Les Patterson, was too unlikeable for audience sympathy.

Fred Schepisi, fresh from his critical success with Meryl Streep in *Plenty*, changed direction with *Roxanne*, an update of the Cyrano de Bergerac story. Steve Martin starred as a Washington fire chief whose love for a beautiful woman (Daryl Hannah) is hampered by his protruding nose.

Russell Mulcahy, director of the stylish Outback thriller, *Razorback*, watched his equally stylish time-warp epic,

Paul Hogan in 'Crocodile' Dundee.

Highlander, with Christopher Lambert, wither in America and reach cult status in Europe. Mulcahy has been tipped to direct *Rambo III*.

Bruce Beresford, recovering from the box-office neglect of *King David* and the critically revered *Fringe Dwellers*, journeyed to North Carolina to produce a wondrous display of acting with *Crimes of the Heart*. The Oscar-laden triumvirate of Diane Keaton, Jessica Lange and Sissy Spacek helped provide the fireworks.

Richard Franklin (*Fantasm*, *Patrick*, *Road Games*) produced *Link*, an unusual thriller about killer apes, but, sadly, the film proved too off-beat for most audiences. Looking to the future, the award-winning director Carl Schultz (*Careful, He Might Hear You*) was invited to America to direct *The Boarder*, a drama from Tri-Star starring Demi Moore, Michael Biehn and Jürgen Prochnow. The film should be released early in 1988.

At home, the most impressive production – besides those already mentioned – was certainly *Cactus*, from the extraordinary Paul Cox. All this director's films differ vastly in style and never conform to any recognizable commerical mode. His latest is no exception, a stylish, languid story of a French girl (Isabelle Huppert) who is partly blinded in a car accident and who, reluctantly, falls in love with a completely blind Australian played by Robert Menzies (a relative of the former Prime Minister). Full of magic moments, detail and wondrous calm, *Cactus* felt more European in texture than Australian, perhaps betraying Cox's Dutch upbringing.

The only other Australian film of any note that surfaced in Britain was the enchanting *Frog Dreaming*. Directed by Brian Trenchard-Smith, better known for his slam-bang shoot-'em-ups (*The Man From Hong Kong*, *Turkey Shoot*), *Frog Dreaming* was an intriguing fantasy for children about the unusual properties of a derelict lake. Henry Thomas (from *ET*) starred as the boy who found out more than he should,

and was well supported by a production that never pandered to its audience, was charming and quite unusual. Unfortunately, the film suffered a miserable release in Britain, helped in no way by critics who didn't seem to notice it or, as is so often the case, didn't bother to view it.

Looking ahead again, there are two major productions that should bring a lot of excitement, if nothing else. The first, *The Time Guardian*, is Australia's first sci-fi extravaganza. Coming in at a staggering $A8 million, the film was financed through government tax concessions on investment in film and TV production, underwritten before reduced write-offs were introduced. $A1 million alone was spent on special effects. The story, we are told, is 'of a futuristic city that travels backwards and forwards through time while being pursued by mutants, until it comes to rest in modern-day outback Australia'. The star role goes to Tom Burlinson (*Phar Lap*, *The Man From Snowy River*), Australia's nearest equivalent to Tom Cruise (at least in popularity), and the film is directed by the writer Brian Hannant.

Another big feature to go before the cameras was *The Lighthorsemen*, at $A10½ million possibly the most expensive Australian film ever made. Directed by Simon Wincer, another of Australia's peripatetic men, the drama stars Anthony Andrews, Gary Sweet and Sigrid Thornton and was shot in Victoria and South Australia. Wincer,

originally known for his small-scale thrillers (*Snapshot*, *Harlequin*) hit paydirt when he produced *The Man From Snowy River* and directed *Phar Lap*. However, his brief foray into international cinema with *D.A.R.Y.L.* was not a success, so it was back to Australia. *The Lighthorsemen*, a World War I cavalry epic, should cover his tracks.

Other promising projects include the sequel to *Snowy River*, coming in at something under $A9 million. America's bulky Brian Dennehy took over from the role originated by Kirk Douglas, while Tom Burlinson and Sigrid Thornton again essayed their earlier chores under Geoff Burrowes' direction. Then there's Phil Noyce's *Promises to Keep*, a romance set in Thailand with the ever-excellent Wendy Hughes falling for John Lone; and Carl Schultz's *Travelling North*, marking the (second) return of Leo McKern to his home country.

Looking at the Australian production scene overall, the climate for making commercially orientated films looks healthier than it has done for years. The generous incentive of a 133 per cent tax write-off (and a guaranteed 40 per cent of the budget supplied through a presale or distribution advance) has been reduced to a 120 per cent write-off and has therefore increased a drive for films that are more likely to get their money back at the box-office. And there has been no lack of funds for investment. Two American production companies, the De Laurentiis Entertainment

Group and New World Pictures, established Australian off-shoots, investing $A107 million between them, while Vestron and Carolco were also reputedly eyeing production bases Down Under. As the prolific producer Anthony Ginnane (*The Lighthorsemen*, *The Time Guardian*) pointed out, 'the industry has turned 21 and picked up its key'. The following twelve months should prove to be an exciting time.

For details of the Australian Institute Awards, see page 184.

Author's Ratings

The year's top films:

1. Frog Dreaming
2. 'Crocodile' Dundee
3. Kangaroo
4. Malcolm
5. The Fringe Dwellers

And their directors:

1. Brian Trenchard-Smith
2. Peter Faiman
3. Tim Burstall
4. Nadia Tass
5. Bruce Beresford

The year's top performers:

1. Colin Friels (*Malcolm*, *Kangaroo*)
2. Paul Hogan ('Crocodile' Dundee)
3. Judy Davis (*Kangaroo*)
4. Bill Hunter (*Death of a Soldier*)
5. Robert Menzies (*Cactus*)

Hollywood at Home

ALAN WARNER in Los Angeles examines the trends in American TV movies and singles out some recent highlights

That fewer American TV movies have been shown on British screens in the twelve-month period of this annual is unfortunate, because the standard of small-screen productions has certainly not diminished, even if their numbers have decreased.

Whereas the main outlets for TVMs just a few years ago were the US networks, the production slates mounted by the cable companies (particularly Home Box Office and Showtime) have increased the overall number of films being premièred each year, indeed HBO finances new movies to show alongside former features.

To explain exactly what differentiates a TV production (also referred to in the business as vidpics) from a feature is a formidable task. Some movies start out on the drawing borad as TV productions, as in the case of the British success *My Beautiful Laundrette*, and there are also feature films with the appearance of a small-screen subject, such as the Meryl Streep–Robert De Niro comedy *Falling in Love* which, for this reporter at least, could have been as effectively played out by Yvette Mimieux and Tim Matheson for TV.

That last statement indicates a preconceived notion of what a TV movie should and does look like, but such instant definition risks undervaluing attempts to broaden the scope of the 'average' TV production designed for the American two-hour slot and also fails to recognize the longer TV movie genre, the mini-series.

One of the currently successful concepts for TVMs is to re-work and extend formulas of vintage TV series; indeed, the taste for old small-screen storylines has also spread into the feature movie business, with both Universal and Paramount recently releasing big-budget big-screen revivals of *Dragnet* and *The Untouchables*.

In April 1986, one of the biggest TV movie hits to date was shown for the first time. Titled *Return to Mayberry*, it starred Andy Griffith and the surviving members of the folksy, long-running series from the 1960s, *The Andy Griffith Show*; among those original co-stars was Ron(ny) Howard, whose current career finds him more often behind the camera. However, while Messrs Griffith and Howard, along with Don Knotts and Jim Nabors, were on hand for the revival movie, not all vintage shows have so many of their original casts available for reunions. For instance, of the leading cast of the memorable *Perry Mason* series, which ran from 1957 to 1966, only Raymond Burr and Barbara Hale remain; continuing their roles as defence attorney Mason and his secretary Della Street, they are starring in a series of

very successful TV movies. Beginning with *Perry Mason Returns* (Ron Satlof, 1985), screened on BBC1 in April, the new format introduces us to private eye Paul Drake Jr, supposedly the son of another member of the old team who was played by the late William Hopper, son of Hollywood gossip columnist Hedda Hopper. The new character is portrayed by William Katt, whose parents are in fact Barbara Hale and retired actor Bill Williams. Rumour has it that a spin-off series is in the works for the Drake Jr character! The BBC will screen all the new TV movies, as they did the original series; based on the first four, they will be every bit as entertaining as their predecessors. Following *Perry Mason Returns*, look for *Perry Mason: The Case of the Notorious Nun*; *Perry Mason: The Case of the Shooting Star*; and *Perry Mason: The Case of the Lost Love*. The latter, again directed by Ron Satlof, boasts a cast of equally familiar faces, including Jean Simmons, Gene Barry and David Ogden Stiers.

Telly Savalas has also donned a former mantle, that of New York Police Department's Lieutenant Theo Kojak, in *Kojak: The Price of Justice* (Alan Metzger, 1986). Television even persuaded George C. Scott to star in a successor to his 1970 *Patton* movie, entitled *The Last Days of Patton*. But one TV re-make stood out head and shoulders above other such attempts, namely *The Defiant Ones* (David Lowell Rich, 1986) with Robert Urich and Carl Weathers in the roles created by Tony Curtis and Sidney Poitier in the 1958 movie.

Reversing the frequent procedure for new TV dramatic series, which often begin with a movie-format pilot episode (good recent examples are *Moonlighting*, which premièred its initial telefilm in ABC's 'Sunday Night Movie' slot in March 1985, and *L.A. Law*, *Dallas* creator David Jacobs turned the tables and gave us a prequel called *Dallas – The Early Years* (Larry Elikann, 1986) which, with commercials, played a three-hour slot on US screens. Other notable one-offs include the occasional Agatha Christie adaptation; you may recall *Murder is Easy* (Claude Whatham, 1981), *A Caribbean Mystery* and *Sparkling Cyanide* (both Robert Lewis, 1983), and a more recent addition is *Agatha Christie's Dead Man's Folly* (Clive Donner, 1986) with Peter Ustinov repeating his big-screen role of Hercule Poirot.

Yet there is one former TV format which cannot find a fresh audience. Though *Bonanza*, *Gunsmoke* and *Wagon Train* are seen in re-runs, almost every attempt to revive the western genre is shot down in flames, even stellar casts being insufficient to breathe successful new life into legends of the

Jennifer O'Neill, Raymond Burr, Lisa Howard and Barbara Hale in The Case of the Shooting Star, *one of several TV films bringing back the famous old series detective, Perry Mason.*

Old West. Honourable mention should, however, be made of *The Last Days of Frank and Jesse James* (William A. Graham, 1985) starring Johnny Cash and Kris Kristofferson, and *Stagecoach* (Ted Post, 1986) with Messrs Cash and Kristofferson again, plus Waylon Jennings, and, in the role of Doc Holliday, Willie Nelson.

Probably the most significant inroad for which the TV movie has been responsible is the small screen's handling of controversial human-interest subjects. *Adam*, the true story of a couple whose son was first kidnapped and then murdered, played to a huge audience and sparked a wave of awareness in America about the plight of missing children. The picture (Michael Tuchner, 1983) starred Daniel J. Travanti and JoBeth Williams as the parents; at the conclusion of its first two network screenings, an on-screen roll call of missing children's names prompted major response from viewers and media alike. The three American networks

(ABC, CBS and NBC) now regularly follow the première broadcasts of such movies with late-night discussions and analyses, emphasizing the increased importance of socially-conscious TV movie-makers.

An Early Frost (John Erman, 1985) starring Ben Gazzara and Gena Rowlands and shown in Britain by ITV, was another breakthrough production, dealing openly with the subject of AIDS virtually for the first time. You may also have seen *M.A.D.D.* (William A. Graham, 1983), subtitled *The Candy Lightner Story* after the woman upon whom it was based, telling of the tragedy that of a driver under the influence of drink caused a mother, and of her subsequent successful crusade to tighten the laws concerning alcohol on the road. Mariette Hartley starred as Candy Lightner.

Although not based directly on fact, a much-honoured movie called *Do You Remember Love?* (Jeff Bleckner, 1985) vividly brought home to viewers the horrors of an incurable illness; the production starred Joanne Woodward as a college professor and poet who contracts Alzheimer's disease, with Richard Kiley as her husband and Geraldine Fitzgerald as her mother. From the 'Hallmark Hall of Fame' (a prestigious series, now in its 35th season, sponsored by Hallmark greetings cards) came *Love is Never Silent* (Joseph Sargent, 1985) starring Mare Winningham in her Emmy

James Woods and Jane Alexander in the NBC drama In Love and War, *one of the series of TV films based on fact, this one about the capture and release of US Naval Commander Jim Stockdale during the Vietnam war.*

Award-winning role as the girl attempting to deal with her parents' deafness. One of the more recent true-life adaptations is *Fight for Life* (Elliot Silverstein, 1987), depicting the struggle of an optometrist (sensitively portrayed by Jerry Lewis) and his wife (Patty Duke) as they discover that their adopted daughter is dying from epilepsy, eventually finding hope in a drug developed by a British doctor played by Barry Morse.

Admirable as movies such as these are, American commercial TV cannot rely on subject matter alone to attract audiences, hence the big-name performers in each production. Although HBO's output has been inconsistently successful there have been outstanding productions, like *Sakharov* (Jack Gold, 1984) with Jason Robards as the Russian dissident and Glenda Jackson as his wife; *Finnegan Begin Again* (Joan Micklin Silver, 1984) uniting Mary Tyler Moore and Robert Preston in a romantic comedy; *Murrow* (Jack Gold, 1985) starring Daniel J. Travanti as the radio and television journalist; and *Act of Vengeance* (John Mackenzie, 1986) bringing together Charles Bronson, Ellen Burstyn and Wilford Brimley in a suspense-packed drama about two rival candidates in a labour union. Indeed, star vehicles play as significant a role on the small screen as on the large, and more and more of the most popular actors in TV series

get the chance to break away and do TV movies; for instance, all the key stars of *Dallas* and *Dynasty* have had their own TV movie starring roles. After Patrick Duffy took his self-imposed sabbatical from Southfork, he teamed with former *Dynasty* star Pamela Sue Martin in a TV movie adaptation of Arthur Hailey's *Strong Medicine* (Guy Green, 1986). Similarly, one of Victoria Principal's first tasks after completing her ninth season stint as Pamela Ewing was to star in a Stanley Jaffe-Sherry Lansing TV movie for the newly revitalized Republic Pictures.

With the Disney 'Sunday Movie' now in its second season of made-for-TV family fare, the networks deliberately contrast this with hard-hitting dramas, such as *The Deliberate Stranger* (Marvin Chomsky, 1985) in which Mark Harmon starred as serial killer Ted Bundy, and *Under Siege* (Robert Young, 1986) starring Peter Strauss, Mason Adams and Lew Ayres in a story about terrorists attacking the USA. This TVM emanated from executive producer Don

Ohlmeyer, whose *Special Bulletin* (Edward Zwick, 1983) stunned audiences on its first showing. On Easter Sunday this year, CBS showed a chilling docudrama based on an actual incident at a Polish death camp: *Escape from Sobibor* (Jack Gold, 1987) starring Alan Arkin, Rutger Hauer and Joanna Pacula. A month earlier, NBC had shown *In Love and War* (Paul Aaron, 1987), starring James Woods in a story depicting the pain and futility of the Vietnam war.

Figures from America's political past have also come under the microscope, firstly with *The Betty Ford Story* (David Greene, 1987) starring Gena Rowlands as the former First Lady and based on Mrs Ford's autobiography *The Times of My Life*; and my own favourite performance of recent years, Randy Quaid as Lyndon B. Johnson in *LBJ: The Early Years* (Peter Werner, 1986), a three-hour account of the President from the beginning of his political aspirations through to the death of John F. Kennedy. New York's *Evita* star, Patti LuPone, played Lady Bird, his wife.

Other noteworthy American TV movies from the recent crop include *Under the Influence* (Thomas Carter, 1986) with Andy Griffith as a father who turns alcoholic; *Barnum* (Lee Philips, 1986) in which Burt Lancaster stars as master-showman P. T. Barnum; *News at Eleven* (Mike Robe, 1986) which examines the American TV news industry, with Martin Sheen as a Californian news anchorman who puts his career on the line by taking a moral stand against a news director's quest for ratings points; and *Something in Common* (Glenn Jordan, 1986) bringing together Ellen Burstyn and Tuesday Weld in a warm-hearted comedy about two mothers and the son of one falling for the other.

Picking one TV movie out from all the rest is a task made easier by a performance by a young black actress called Alfre Woodard. The movie itself is a compelling dramatization of a subject very sensitive in America – the discovery of the effect of the chemical Agent Orange on veterans of the Vietnam war. *Unnatural Causes* (Lamont Johnson, 1986) was written by John Sayles and stars John Ritter (son of cowboy singer Tex Ritter, and a familiar TV comedy actor in the States) as a young vet who is dying but fights on to expose the truth. A sombre and totally absorbing movie. TV productions seldom come this good.

The producers and backers of the mini-series *Amerika* (Donald Wrye, 1987) had hoped to stun audiences over seven evenings. It became the most anticipated mini-series ever but, after its first two episodes, the majority of viewers fell away, though figures rallied for the final part a week later.

In fact, the networks are being forced to re-evaluate the mini-series. Whereas large numbers of viewers seemed initially to be very receptive to these long-form versions of TV movies, there have been more flops than hits in the recent past. Productions that failed to win significant audiences included the four-hour *George Washington: The Forging of a Nation* (William A. Graham, 1986) with Barry Bostwick repeating his role of President in a sequel to the earlier ratings success *George Washington* (Buzz Kulik, 1984); *Fresno* (Jeff Bleckner, 1986) with Carol Burnett and Dabney Coleman in the leading roles, a six-hour spoof of the prime-time soap operas; *Rage of Angels: The Story Continues* (Paul Wendkos, 1986) with Jaclyn Smith as the lawyer she had portrayed in the previous ratings winner *Rage of Angels* (Buzz Kulik, 1983); *Monte Carlo* (Anthony Page, 1986) with

Joan Collins as a Russian-born singer spying for the English; and *Out on a Limb* (Robert Butler, 1986), in which Shirley MacLaine (aided by co-writer Colin Higgins) stars in the teleplay of her own book in which she claims to have been, amongst other things, reincarnated.

By way of complete contrast, CBS came up trumps with consistently high figures for *I'll Take Manhattan* (Douglas Hickox and Richard Michaels, 1986) which premièred in two-hour episodes over four consecutive nights in February 1987. It was the latest Judith Krantz novel to be adapted for TV, this time with Valerie Bertinelli (co-star of a hit sit-com between 1975 and 1984 called *One Day at a Time*), Barry Bostwick and Francesca Annis heading the cast. CBS's print ad campaign ran: 'Seduction. Rapture. Shock. Don't just watch it . . . feel it!' Similar success was notched up by *Fatal Vision* (David Greene, 1984), a two-part docudrama about a Green Beret surgeon accused of murdering both his pregnant wife and his two teenage daughters; the movie, shown a few months ago on BBC1, reunited Karl Malden and Eva Marie Saint, who had previously starred together in the cinema features *On the Waterfront* (Elia Kazan, 1954) and *All Fall Down* (John Frankenheimer, 1962).

Together for the first time were Ann-Margret and Claudette Colbert in the TV movie version of Dominick Dunne's novel, *The Two Mrs Grenvilles* (John Erman, 1986), for which NBC also ran tantalizing blurbs: 'There are only two things they will ever have in common: the family name and murder.' In months to come, NBC has an eight-hour dramatization of James Clavell's *Noble House* in store, while ABC has spent $100 million on Herman Wouk's *War and Remembrance*, the follow-up to their hit mini-series of 1983, *The Winds of War* (Dan Curtis). The projected TV length of *War and Remembrance* is a staggering 30 hours; after the same network's difficulty experienced in maintaining interest in *Amerika*, this must have Capital Cities (the new owners of the American Broadcasting Company) more than a little bit apprehensive.

Two exceptionally successful mini-series were *Kane and Abel* (Buzz Kulik, 1985) with Peter Strauss and Sam Neill, and *The Last Frontier* (Simon Winger, 1986) with Linda Evans. There was also a riveting two-parter called *Blood and Orchids* (Jerry Thorpe, 1986) starring Kris Kristofferson as a Honolulu police detective investigating prejudice and corruption in Hawaii 50 years ago.

But whether the mini-series remains or disappears temporarily, TV movies are here to stay, providing high visibility for a wide range of performers including stars of yesteryear (such as Lew Ayers and Sylvia Sidney) whose faces and names are more readily familiar to the TV audience. Much of today's TV audience is in fact the movie audience of years gone by, when the soaps were referred to as 'women's pictures'. Another important commercial fact about TV movies is that, in the States, a successful TVM or mini-series can spawn two, three or even more financially rewarding lives in syndication, where the product is sold and re-run on independent stations who cannot afford first-run programming.

But whatever their derivation and from whichever part of the industry they come, TV movies are a staple part of small-screen entertainment, and it will be intriguing to spot the new trends as they develop.

Stay tuned!

TV Feature Films of the Year

In this section you will find all the made-for-television movies shown on BBC1 and BBC2, ITV and Channel 4 during the period covered by the annual. The date given in brackets after each title is the year the movie was made. In the case of a repeat broadcast, the date of the previous broadcast is given along with a note of the *Film Review* in which it was listed in detail.

Act of Passion (1983). American TV film based on the German cinema success *The Lost Honour of Katharina Blum*, here re-laundered into a hair-raising indictment of some aspects of American 'justice', so horrifying it surely can't be true? For complainants about British justice, this should be compulsory viewing. Cast: Marlo Thomas, Kris Kristofferson etc. Dir: Simon Langton. Screenplay: Karl Harris. Channel 4, 31 March 1987.

The Adventures of Neeka (1970). Another package of the old TV series with Wonder Dog Lassie. Dir: Dick Moder and Richard Hiveley. No screenplay credit. BBC2, 13 March 1987.

After Pilkington (1986). A pleasant academic background; well observed social mores; some good performances in a neat switch to drama and murder . . . Whatever happened to Professor Pilkington? It's all well above the average. Cast: Bob Peck, Miranda Richardson, Mary Miller etc. Dir: Christopher Morahan. Screenplay: Simon Gray. BBC2, 25 January 1987.

Agatha Christie's Murder in Three Acts (1987). Plump partygoer Hercule Poiret (actually Peter Ustinov) naturally becomes a little curious when guests get knocked off under his nose, so he starts to bring his peculiar powers of investigation into play . . . From the book *Three-Act Tragedy*, under which title this was small-screened in the US. Also featuring Tony Curtis, Emma Samms, Lisa Eichhorn. Dir: Gary Nelson. Screenplay: Scott Swanton. ITV, 17 May 1987.

The Alpha Caper (1973). ITV, 23 October 1986. Previously shown on BBC, 14 September 1983. See *Film Review 1984–5*.

Are You in the House Alone? (1978). ITV, 2 June 1987. Previously shown on same channel, 28 January 1984. See *Film Review 1984–5*.

The Bad Seed (1982). TV film of Maxwell Anderson's (not very good) stage play about an angel-faced little demon with murderous tendencies which was made into a cinema film in 1956. Carrie Wells now plays the horrid girl and her elders include Blair Brown (her worried mother), David Carradine and Lynn Redgrave. Dir: Paul Wendkos. Screenplay: George Ekstein, based on the play by Maxwell Anderson, in turn based on the book by William March. ITV, 11 October 1986.

The Baron and the Kid (1984). Johnny Cash playing himself (with nice support from real-life wife June Carter) in a story about an ex-pool player, suddenly faced with a youngster demanding a game, with a wedding ring, and with memories . . . made all the more interesting by the brilliant debut performance of Greg Webb. Also featuring Richard Roundtree etc. No other credits. Channel 4, 4 November 1986.

Berlin Tunnel (1981). BBC2, 25 October 1986. Previously shown on BBC1, 15 February 1985. See *Film Review 1985–6*.

The Beverly Hills Connection (1985). Formula whodunit with lady Los Angeles cop and male Laramie cop co-operating to find the person who killed the lady's pal. Lisa Hartman, James Brolin, David Hemmings etc. Dir: Corey Allen. Screenplay: Rick Husky. BBC1, 4 May 1987.

Black's Magic (1985). TV movie introduction to a new series about a retired magician turned investigator; in this first case he solves the mystery of a fellow magic-man who is murdered in front of the TV cameras. Hal Linden is magician Black. Dir: John L. Moxey. Screenplay: Peter S. Fischer. ITV, 6 April 1987.

Blinded by the Light (1980). A fictional story which seriously examines the factual tragedy of division in families caused by the religious cults that flourish in America. A more than usually thoughtful TV film. Cast: Kristy McNichol, J. V. McNichol, Anne Jackson etc. Dir: John Alonzo. Screenplay: Stephen Black, Robin Vote and Henry Stern, based on the novel by Robert F. Brancato. Channel 4, 6 January 1987.

Blunt (1986) Fiction and fact woven into the sensational Burgess-Maclean spy case – and not that easy to follow, unless you know the real facts. Cast: Ian Richardson, Anthony Hopkins and Michael Williams. Dir: John Glenister. Screenplay: Robin Chapman. BBC2, 11 January 1987.

The Borgia Stick (1986). Familiar enough story about a couple trying to duck out of the crime gang in which they are involved, and finding it hard-going. But the two leading players perform with zest and, with help from slick direction, make the whole thing fresh and gripping. Don Murray, Inger Stevens etc. Dir: David Lowell Rich. Screenplay: A. J. Russell. Channel 4, 14 April 1987.

Bud and Lou (1978). The private lives – and there were few enough laughs in them – of the classic screen clown duo of Bud Abbott and Lou Costello. Vastly interesting to film buffs and first-class entertainment to others. A highly commendable production. Harvey Korman (Abbott) and Buddy Hackett (Costello) are both splendid. Dir: Robert C. Thompson. Screenplay: George Lefferts, based on the book by Bob Thomas. Channel 4, 11 June 1987.

Burning Rage (1984). Mediocre tale of a lady geologist fighting fires above and below ground, in the mine, and in the town against the mine-owners, as well as the cops and the local newspaper. The starring of Country-and-Western singer Barbara Mandrell doesn't exactly help. Also featuring Eddie Albert, Carol Kane etc. Dir: Gilbert Cates. Screenplay: Karol Hoeffner and Clifford Campion. ITV, 27 November 1986.

Calendar Girl Murders (1984). Routine thriller about a killer who is knocking off the pin-up girls month by month. With both Miss January and Miss February dead and gone, Miss March, yes, *and* Miss April, are worried . . . who's doing it? Cast: Jennifer O'Neill, William Devane, James Blendick etc. Dir: Noel Black. Screenplay: Richard DeRoy. Channel 4, 18 November 1986.

Catholics (1973). Top-drawer TV movie about a rebel abbot who falls foul of the Vatican when he refuses to conform to the old ideas about the Mass in Latin. Featuring a superb performance by Trevor Howard as the rebellious cleric. Also Martin Sheen etc. Dir: Jack Gold. Screenplay: Brian Moore. Channel 4, 28 September 1986.

The Children of Dynmouth (1986). British TV film set in a typical, pleasant seaside resort with the Easter Fair in town – and a horrid teenager spoiling things with his binoculars and evil intent. A sort of dark-edged comedy, well acted. Cast: John Bird, Peter Jones, Gary Raymond etc. Dir: Peter Hammond. Screenplay: William Trevor. BBC2, 19 April 1987.

The Choice (1980). When college girl Lisa reveals her pregnancy problem, her mother recalls her own similar situation just a year previously! Played with the stops more than half out. Cast: Susan Clark, Largo Woodruff etc. Dir: David Greene. Screenplay: Dennis Nemec. Channel 4, 12 May 1987.

Christmas Present (1985). Channel 4, 14 December 1986. Previously shown on same channel, 19 December 1985. See *Film Review 1986–7*.

Coast to Coast (1986). Lenny Henry and John Shea as a couple of 'soul' fanatics on the run from the crooks *and* the cops. Warm but rather weak comedy. Also featuring Peter Vaughan, Cheri Lunghi and a big cast. Dir: Sandy Johnson. Screenplay: Stan Hey. BBC2, 4 January 1987 and BBC1, 20 April 1987.

Coffee, Tea or Me? (1973). BBC1, 12 March 1987. Previously shown on same channel, 24 January 1984. See *Film Review 1984–5*.

A Cold Night's Death (1973). The many chimps involved completely dominate this snow-edged thriller about scientific experiments. Cast: Robert Culp, Eli Wallach, Michael Gwynne etc. Dir: Jerrold Freedman. Screenplay: Christopher Knoff. ITV, 11 May 1987, postponed from 11 March.

Condor (1986). Agent Ray Wise and his beautiful android partner try to track and kill the terrorist they call The Black Widow. Computer-age sci-fi thrills. Dir: Virgil Vogel. Screenplay: Len Janson and Chuck Menville. ITV, 25 June 1987.

Consenting Adult (1985). A family explosion follows the admission by the apparently normal son that he's homosexual. Cast: Marlo Thomas, Martin Sheen, Barry Tubb. Dir: Gilbert Cates. Screenplay: John McGreevey, based on the book by Laura Hobson. Channel 4, 28 October 1986.

Cook and Peary: The Race to the Pole (1983). Based on the long-running and inconclusive controversy as to which of those two explorers actually did put foot on the hypothetical 'pole' first – was it Richard Chamberlain or Rod Steiger? And this time around the story *doesn't* get the documentary treatment. Dir: Robert Day. Screenplay: I. C. Rapoport. ITV, 18 May 1987.

The Corsican Brothers (1984). Somewhat pale remake of the 1941 Douglas Fairbanks rip-roaring version (and the 1960 French version) of the Dumas classic. Cast: Trevor Eve, Geraldine Chaplin, Olivia Hussey, Jean Marsh etc. Dir: Ian Sharp. Screenplay: Robin Miller. ITV, 22 November 1986.

Countdown (1967). Another Lassie adventure: the cute canine gets involved with space exploration, saving another less clever dog from a swampy fate. Dir: Dick Moder. Screenplay: Robert Schaeffer and Eric Friewald. BBC2, 6 March 1987.

The Count of Monte Cristo (1986). French TV film of the famous Dumas story. Jacques Weber plays the title role. Dir: Denys de la Patellière. ITV, 2 May 1987.

Cowboy (1983). Westerns are so rare these days, either on large or small screen, that any outdoor oater is welcome; like this familiar story. A tenderfoot's struggles against the odds to bring a derelict ranch back to life seen in an unfamiliar, modern, setting. Good work from James Brolin, Ted Danson, Randy Quaid etc. Dir: Jerry Jameson. Screenplay: Stanley and Carol Cherry with Dennis Capps. BBC2, 3 March 1987.

Crime Club (1973) BBC1, 14 August 1986. Previously shown on BBC2, 21 February 1984. See *Film Review 1984–5.*

Crisis in Mid-Air (1979). George Peppard as the Air Control officer driven over the edge by his uneasy feelings of guilt about a mid-air collision, about the fact that his marriage is a disaster, and about the fact that some people are saying he's getting too old for the job. Also featuring Karen Grassle, Desi Arnaz Jr etc. Dir: Walter Grauman. Screenplay: Sean Baine. BBC1, 4 October 1986.

Cruise into Terror (1978). Archaeologist Ray Milland trying to prove his theory that the ancient Egyptians had colonies in South America. One of these 'ancients' makes life uncomfortable for Mr Milland and his fellow passengers on board their sarcophagus-bearing cruise liner steaming to Mexico. Also featuring Hugh O'Brian, Lynda Day George, Stella Stevens etc. Dir: Bruce Kessler. Screenplay: Michael Braverman. ITV, 10 July 1986.

A Cry for Help (1975). Unpleasant radio chat show host Robert Culp finds himself unwilling spearhead of an attempt to track down a would-be suicide. Also featuring Elayne Heilveil, Chuck McCann etc. Dir: Daryl Duke. Screenplay: Peter F. Fischer. ITV, 11 September 1986.

Cry for the Strangers (1981) Minor chiller-thriller about the nasty things that happen to peace-seeking psychiatrist Dr Russell (Patrick Duffy) when he stays at a village by the sea. Also featuring Lawrence Pressman, Clair Malis, Jeff Corey etc. Dir: Peter Medak. Screenplay: J. D. Deigelson, based on the book by John Saul. BBC1, 24 September 1986.

A Cry in the Wilderness (1974). ITV, 16 October 1986. Previously shown on Channel 4, 4 June 1985. See *Film Review 1985–6.*

Cry of the Innocent (1980). Frederick Forsyth couldn't have been in top inventive mood when he wrote this story about an American widower walking into danger during a holiday in Ireland when he starts investigating his family's 'accidental' deaths. Cast: Rod Taylor, Joanna Pettet, Cyril Cusack, Nigel Davenport etc. Dir: Michael O'Herlihy. Screenplay: Roy Clark, based on a Forsyth story. BBC1, 23 February 1987.

Dagger of the Mind (1972). Another 1970s series comeback; this time by Peter Falk, as American Police Lootenant Columbo. During a visit to Scotland Yard, Columbo gets involved in a murder mystery. More or less routine whodidit. Also featuring Richard Basehart, Honor Blackman, John Williams, Wilfrid Hyde White etc. Dir: Richard Quine. Screenplay: Jackson Gilles. ITV, 31 May 1987.

A Day for Thanks on Walton's Mountain (1982). Last of several TV films made about the popular series family. Cast: Ralph Waite, Ellen Corby etc. Dir: Harry Harris. Screenplay: Kathleen Hite. BBC2, 25 May 1987.

The Day the Earth Moved (1974). Even in the early 1970s the special effects boys were doing a pretty impressive job, as witness this otherwise unremarkable 'earthquake' disaster

movie. Cast: Jackie Cooper, Stella Stevens etc. Dir: Robert Michael Lewis. Screenplay: Jack Turley and Max Jack. ITV, 3 June 1987.

The Dead Don't Die (1974). George Hamilton as a sailor trying to clear his brother of a murder charge and coming up against some pretty weird situations, with zombies and the like. Set in the 1930s with a cast that stirs the memory, including such bright stars as Ray Milland, Linda Cristal, Ralph Meeker and – ah, nostalgia – Joan Blondell. Dir: Curtis Harrington. Screenplay: Robert Bloch. ITV, 8 April 1987.

Deadly Encounter (1982). BBC1, 26 August 1986. Previously shown on BBC, 11 September 1983. See *Film Review 1984–5.*

Deadly Harvest (1972). BBC1, 14 March 1987. Previously shown on same channel, 17 July 1985. See *Film Review 1985–6.*

A Deadly Puzzle (1982). Made apparently(?) for the large screen in that year, there is no trace of a cinema showing for this story about a widow who is suspicious of her late husband's demise and makes enquiries which soon begin to scare her. Cast: Karen Valentine, Ben Masters etc. Dir: Walter Grauman. Screenplay: Carol and Stanley Z. Cherry. BBC1, 6 July 1986, postponed from 15 June.

Dead Man's Folly (1986). Peter Ustinov as Agatha Christie's amusing sleuth Hercule Poirot, becoming involved in a country mansion murder game which turns into the real thing. First-class AC fun. Also featuring Constance Cummings and Jean Stapleton etc. Dir: Clive Donner. Screenplay: Rod Browning, based on Agatha Christie's book. ITV, 25 December 1986.

Death of a Centrefold (1981). Taking time off from her seemingly endless horror film appearances, Jamie Lee Curtis plays a *Playboy* model promoted by the mean type who finally kills her – apparently a true story with some fictional trimmings. If it appears familiar it's because this story of P. Pet Dorothy Stratton was made as a cinema movie by Bob Fosse in 1984. Also featuring Bruce Weitz, Tracy Reed etc. Dir: Gabrielle Beaumont. Screenplay: Donald Stewart. BBC1, 23 March 1987.

Death Race (1973). World War II – and the Eighth Army are winning. But that's small consolation to the US Air Force plane crew shot down by one of Rommel's tanks in the desert; able only to taxi along the ground, they are relentlessly pursued by the tank's nasty Nazi captain, Lloyd Bridges. Also featuring Doug McClure, Roy Thinnes etc. Dir: David Lowell Rich. Screenplay: Charles Kuemstle. ITV, 18 September 1986.

Death Stalks the Big Top (1986). Angela Lansbury, as series sleuth Jessica, spreads her investigation to movie length when she saves her circus star brother-in-law from a murder rap. As unlikely but entertaining as ever. Also featuring Jackie Cooper, Lee Purcell, Alex Cord etc. Dir: Seymour Robbie. Screenplay: Paul Savage. ITV, 20 June 1987.

Detour to Terror (1980). And terror comes to coach driver O. J. Simpson as he takes the Adventure Club members on a trip around Las Vegas, suddenly to realize he is being followed by some very unpleasant people! Also featuring Arte Johnson, Anne Francis, Lorenzo Lamas. Dir: Michael O'Herlihy. Screenplay: Sidney Glass and Mark Rodgers. ITV, 26 August 1986.

The Dirty Dozen – the Next Mission (1985). Lee Marvin leading another suicide mission behind enemy lines. A TV follow-up to the original cinema movie of this title – and not half as good, although with the same stars and a reliable director. Also featuring Ernest Borgnine, Ken Wahl, Richard Jaeckel etc. Dir: Andrew V. McLaglen. Screenplay: Michael Kane. BBC1, 29 August 1986.

The Dollmaker (1984). Most impressive production, introducing Jane Fonda to the medium of TV movies and winning her an 'Emmy' in the process for her performance as the gallant little lady who dreams of one day having her own farm but instead finds herself coping with life in the bricks-and-mortar world of wartime Detroit. Also featuring Geraldine Page, Levon Helm, Amananda Plummer etc. Dir: Daniel Petrie. Screenplay: Susan Cooper and Hume Cronyn, based on the novel by Harriette Arnow. BBC2, 5 May 1987.

Dr Max (1974). The always-worth-watching Lee J. Cobb as an old-fashioned, dedicated doctor whose Baltimore practice brings him plenty of headaches, especially when the demands of patient and family conflict. Also featuring Janet Ward, Robert Lipton etc. Dir: James Goldstone. Screenplay: Robert L. Joseph. BBC2, 25 February 1987.

Drop-out Father (1982). Nice to see Dick Van Dyke again, especially in this superior TV comedy about an advertising executive who opts out of the rat race – and most of his family – to start a new life in a loft! Also featuring George Coe, Mariette Hartley, William Daniels etc. Dir: Don Taylor. Screenplay: Bob Shanks. BBC1, 10 August 1986.

East of Ipswich (1986). Michael Palin wrote this British comedy about a family holiday in Suffolk-by-the-sea, getting plenty of mild fun out of familiar situations. Cast: Phyllida Hewat, John Nettleton and Pat Heywood etc. Dir: Tristram Powell. Screenplay: Palin. BBC2, 1 February 1987.

Escape from Sobibor (1987). Really top-class movie based on the familiar theme of the German extermination camps. Cast: Alan Arkin, Joanna Pacula, Rutger Hauer. Dir: Jack Gold. Screenplay: Reginald Rose, based on the book by Richard Rashke. ITV, 10 May 1987.

Family Flight (1972). Family friction turns out actually to be beneficial when the chips are down in a fatal air flight. Dominating family and film, tough dad Rod Taylor. Also featuring Dina Merrill, Janet Margolin, Gene Nelson, Ed Begley Jr etc. Dir: Marvin Chomsky. Screenplay: Guerdon Trueblood. ITV, 25 September 1986.

The Family Rico (1972). BBC2, 22 August 1986. Previously shown on BBC, 1 November 1983. See *Film Review 1984–5*.

Flight 90: Disaster on the Potomac (1984). In 1982 a Florida-bound airliner fell out of the winter skies and crashed through the ice on the Potomac river. This is the story of that disaster. Cast: Richard Masur, Stephen Macht etc. Dir: Robert Lewis. Screenplay: John McGreevey. ITV, 26 May 1987.

Flight of the Cougar (1976). U-certificate-type TV movie about that quite remarkable canine, the indomitable Lassie. Obviously a collection of episodes from the 1960s series. Cast: Les Brown Jr, Burt Douglas etc. Dir: Jack Hiveley, Dick Moder and William Beaudine. No screenplay credit. BBC2, 23 January 1987.

Flood (1976). BBC2, 7 January 1987. Previously shown on BBC, 16 January 1984. See *Film Review 1984–5*.

For Ladies Only (1981). The sad tale of a young actor who, initially reluctant, turns male stripper and climbs to stardom in the business. Cast: Gregory Harrison, Marc Singer, Viveca Lindfors etc. Dir: Mel Damski. Screenplay: John Riley. Channel 4, 7 April 1987.

Games Mother Never Taught You (1982). Loretta Swit fighting to combine marriage and career and finding it hard going; familiar but quite good fun. Also featuring Sam Waterston, David Spielberg etc. Dir: Lee Philips. Screenplay: Liz Coe, based on the book by Betty Lehan Harragan. Channel 4, 9 June 1987.

Going Home. (1986) About the Canadian soldiers of World War I in their Welsh transit camp; made with Welsh-Canadian co-operation. Cast: Nicholas Campbell, Sioned Mair etc. Dir: Terry Ryan. Screenplay: Christopher Green. BBC2, 15 March 1987.

Guilty Conscience (1985). Well out of, and far above, the general run of films about murder. Anthony Hopkins is as ever superb as a famous lawyer who plans the perfect murder – of his wife. But, as ever, plans can go wrong . . . splendid stuff. Also featuring Blythe Danner (as the wife). Dir: David Greene. Screenplay: Richard Levinson and William Link. BBC1, 31 May 1987.

Hadley's Rebellion (1983). About a college boy obsessed with the sport of wrestling. Good performances by a largely youthful cast, plus Charles Durning as the fallen idol. Dir and Screenplay: Fred Walton. Channel 4, 26 May 1987.

Handford's Point (1970). Dogs may decease but good ole Lassie (screen debut in the 1940s) never dies. Here she is in another wholesome adventure with Bonita Granville (yes, the ex-child star extraordinaire) doubling up as co-star and TV producer. Very pleasant it is, too. Dir: Jack Hiveley. No screenplay credit. BBC2, 14 November 1986.

Happy Endings (1983). Familiar stuff about a girl and a fellow whose unhappy breaks from their respective former partners lead them to turn to each other for comfort. Neighbours who become good friends . . . as the Australian series title song goes. Cast: John Schneider, Catherine Hicks etc. Dir: Noel Black. Screenplay: Christopher Canaan. BBC2, 7 April 1987.

Hardhat and Legs (1980). Channel 4, 25 November 1986. Previously shown on ITV, 2 August 1984. See *Film Review 1985–6*.

Hauser's Memory (1970). Weird little piece set in Germany, at a time when the Cold War was freezing. About one man getting an injection from another's brain and made to go back in memory . . . no fun, it seems. Cast: David McCallum, Susan Strasberg, Lilli Palmer etc. Dir: Boris Sagal. Screenplay: Adrian Spies, based on the book by Curt Siodmak. ITV, 3 July 1986.

Heaven on Earth (1986). Apparently it took ten years to get this lesser-known chapter of British-Canadian history on to the screen. The result is certainly worth while: it follows the fortunes of four of the 100,000 (yes, *that* many) orphans sent from Britain to Canada between 1870 and 1930 in order to make good in that part of the New World. Very watchable. Cast: R. H. Thomson, Sian Leisa Davies, Amos Crawley etc. Dir: Allan Kroeker. Screenplay: Margaret Attwood and Peter Pearson. BBC2, 1 March 1987.

Hedgehog Wedding (1987). Make what you like of that title; in fact it's one of those get-togethers in which a lot of drink, a lot of talk and a lot of exposure of what has been hidden keeps the party going, if not smoothly. Cast: Frederick Treves, Sheila Allen etc. Dir: Tim King. Screenplay: Elizabeth Spender. BBC2, 17 April 1987.

Helen Keller . . . the Miracle Continues (1983). A sort of sequel to *The Miracle Worker*, originally titled *Helen and Teacher* and concerned with the later life of the marvellous Helen. Cast: Blythe Danner, Mare Winningham, Peter Cushing, Alexander Knox etc. Dir: Alan Gibson. Screenplay: John McGreevey. Channel 4, 30 June 1987.

His Mistress (1984). Routine but nicely polished tale about the unhappy result of a clandestine affair between the boss and a pretty member of his staff. Mainly interesting in that it marks the screen debut of Sachi Parker, Shirley MacLaine's daughter. Also featuring Robert Urich, Julianne Phillips etc. Dir: David Lowell Rich. Screenplay: Beth Sullivan. ITV, 22 November 1986.

Hitchhike! ITV, 6 November 1986. Previously shown on same channel, 9 December 1984. See *Film Review 1985–6*.

Homeward Bound (1980). Tear-flecked tale of a 14-year-old lad facing up to a terminal illness. Mercifully, there's more than tears here and it does give David Soul the chance to show that he is much more than a pretty face. Dir: Richard Michaels. Screenplay: Burt Prelutsky. Channel 4, 19 May 1987.

Horror at 37,000 Feet (1972). BBC2, 23 August 1986. Previously shown on BBC1, 12 November 1984. See *Film Review 1985–6*.

The House That Would Not Die (1980). Another haunted house movie. This time the strange voices and eerie events take place in an 18th-century home near Gettysburg. Involved in the ghostly mystery, Barbara Stanwyck and

Richard Egan. Routinely entertaining, with a good climax. Dir: John Llewellyn Moxey. Screenplay: Henry Farrell, based on the book *Annie Comes Home* by Barbara Michaels. ITV, 28 May 1987.

How Awful About Allan (1969). If you have any shivers you'd better warn your spine they'll be running up and down during this grim thriller about a house fire survivor, now blind, who hears voices and becomes involved in some very unpleasant and mysterious accidents . . . Good acting, especially Julie Harris, and strong direction by Curtis Harrington. Also featuring Anthony Perkins, Joan Hackett etc. Screenplay: Henry Darrell. ITV, 24 March 1987.

Hunter. After the success of the *Mission Impossible* and *Mannix* series, they obviously hoped for a nice follow-up from this showcase by the same producer, but it was not to be. After agent Hunter's defeat of a 'foreign' agent's plan to spread a deadly virus across the States, we neither heard nor saw more of him. Cast: John Vernon, Steve Ihnat, Fritz Weaver etc. Dir: Leon Horn. Screenplay: Cliff Gould. BBC1, 1 August 1986.

Inappropriate Behaviour (1987). About an American 'behaviour expert' let loose in an English countryside school; more especially, the relationship between her and one of the less easy pupils. Quite well done and nicely acted. Cast: Jennifer Landor and Charlotte Coleman etc. Dir: Paul Seed. Screenplay: Andrew Davies. BBC2, 8 March 1987.

The Incredible Hulk (1977). This was one of two films that launched the series about a gamma-rayed scientist whom anger transforms into a seven-foot-tall, immensely powerful character in tasteful green. Popular strip-cartoon stuff. Cast: Bill Bixby, Susan Sullivan etc. Dir and Screenplay: Kenneth Johnson. ITV, 4 April 1987.

In Love with an Older Woman (1982). He'a a marriage-shy bachelor lawyer and she's a much older divorced lady investigator with a daughter her wooer's age. That threadbare theme get's good enough script and performances to make it very watchable. Cast: Karen Carlson, John Ritter etc. Dir: Jack Bender. Screenplay: Michael Norell. BBC2, 13 January 1987.

Invitation to Hell (1984). Explaining why you should be very careful about joining an American country club; heaven – sorry, hell – only knows what you'll find you've got yourself into. A competent thriller from a director who knows his job. Cast: Robert Urich, Susan Lucci, Joanna Cassidy. Dir: Wes Craven. Screenplay: Richard Rothstein. BBC1, 20 October 1986.

Isn't It Shocking? (1973). Vintage comedy thriller. Small-town sheriff gets a shock when he starts to investigate the mysterious deaths of some of the townsfolk. This one comes out of the TV movie top-drawer. Cast: Alan Alda, Louise Lasser, Edmond O'Brien, Ruth Gordon, Lloyd Nolan etc. Dir: John Badham. Screenplay: Lane Slate. BBC2, 16 June 1987.

Jealousy (1984). Portmanteau film with Angie Dickinson playing three varying roles in three different tales based on the dire results of jealousy: a woman who believes her daughter has seduced her husband; a millionaire's wife who gets upset about her husband's odd interests; and a singer having to choose between career and possessive boyfriend. Also featuring Paul Michael Glaser, David Carradine, France Nuyen etc. Dir and Screenplay: Jeffrey Bloom. BBC1, 17 November 1986.

Jimmy B. and André (1980). Simple little movie about a Greek restaurateur and his efforts to adopt a small black boy (the son of a junkie) who wins his affection. Based on a true story. Cast: Alex Karras, Susan Clark, Eddie Barth etc. Dir: Guy Green. Screenplay: Douglas Graham and Charles Johnson. Channel 4, 9 December 1986.

Joyous Sound (1972). Another Lassie episode, or episodes rather, for once again it's several of the TV series carefully stitched into a full-length movie. Cast: Larry Pennell, Pamela Ferdin etc. Dir: Jack Wrather. Screenplay: Robert Schaeffer and Eric Fretwald. BBC2, 20 March 1987.

The Kid with the 200 I.Q. (1983). About a 13-year-old genius who leapfrogs into university. Cast: Gary Coleman, Robert Guillaume, Dean Butler etc. Dir: Leslie Martinson. Screenplay: George Kirqo and Martin Cohan. ITV, 4 May 1987.

Kids Don't Tell (1985). Delicately and sincerely directed feature about a documentary movie-maker who finds his film on the evil of child molestation becomes too difficult for him to handle. Cast: Michael Ontkean, JoBeth Williams etc. Dir: Sam O'Steen. Screenplay: Peter Silverman and Maurice Hurley. Channel 4, 28 April 1987.

Killer By Night (1972). ITV, 16 June 1987. Previously shown on BBC1, 7 August 1984. See *Film Review 1985–6*.

Kung Fu II (1986). David Carradine back to the mystic-with-muscles role he played in the early 1970s series. Note the debut of Bruce's son, Brandon Lee. Also featuring Martin Landau etc. Dir: Richard Lang. Screenplay: Durrell Royce Crays. ITV, 5 December 1986.

Lady With a Badge (1981). BBC1, 10 December 1986. Previously shown on BBC, 30 April 1984. See *Film Review 1984–5*.

Lassie: The Miracle (1975). That remarkable collie canine to the rescue once more, this time saving a boy from a lion. Cast: Robert Rockwell, Skip Homier, James Wixted etc. Dir: Dick Moder and Jack Hiveley. No screenplay credit. BBC2, 20 February 1987.

Lassie: The Road Back (1970). You know that old story about someone being knocked down and losing their memory? Change human for dog, Lassie, and you have this addition to the famous canine saga. Jed Allen and Jack de Mave among the human support. Dir: Dick Moder. No screenplay credit. BBC2, 21 November 1986.

Lassie: The Voyager (1966). Some unlikely adventures of Wonder Dog Lassie. Surviving a cyclone, she is brought before the courts for theft – of, suitably, a turkey! Human members of the cast include Macdonald Carey and Robert Bray. Dir: Dick Moder and Jack Hiveley. No screenplay credit. BBC2, 31 October 1986.

A Last Cry for Help (1979). About a teenager who seems to have it made, when she suddenly tries to kill herself with a drug overdose. Why, oh why? Very serious stuff. Cast: Linda Purl, Shirley Jones etc. Dir and Screenplay: Hal Sitowitz. Channel 4, 2 June 1987.

Linda (1973). Stella Stevens, as the deceived wife planning to murder the mistress and implicate her faithless husband in the crime, gives such a powerful performance that this thriller becomes an altogether superior splendidly directed TV film. Also featuring Ed Nelson, John McIntire, John Saxon etc. Dir: Jack Smight. Screenplay: Merwin Gerard. ITV, 30 October 1986.

Lisa and Tshepo (1981). German TV movie about a white secretary who falls in love with a black South African. Cast: Pia Hanggi and Dumisani Mabaso etc. Dir and Screenplay: Erika Runge. Channel 4, 25 June 1987.

A Little Game (1971). Another thriller featuring a horrible child with a satanic character. The worried parents of this one (played by Mark Gruner) hire a private eye to see if he *is* a murderer. We've seen it all before, and better done. Also featuring Diane Baker, Ed Nelson. Dir: Paul Wendkos. Screenplay: Carole Sobieski, based on the book by Fielden Farrington. ITV, 17 February 1987.

The Loneliest Runner (1976). BBC1, 21 January 1987. Previously shown on BBC2, 8 September 1985. See *Film Review 1986–7*.

Lost Flight (1969). Familiar story about a group of ill-assorted people under stress – in this case, crash-landed aeroplane passengers on an island – showing their true colours; and routine they are, too. Cast: Lloyd Bridges, Anne Francis, Ralph Meeker, Billy Dee Williams etc. Dir: Leonard J. Horn. Screenplay: Dean Riesner. ITV, 7 September 1986.

M.A.D.D.: Mothers Against Drunk Drivers (1983). Another true story adapted to a TV film: about a woman who, after her daughter is killed by a drunken driver while on bail for a previous d.d. charge, goes to war when she learns the motorist may get off with a comparatively short jail sentence. Highly professional. Cast: Mariette Hartley, Paula Prentiss etc. Dir: William A. Graham. Screenplay: Michael Braverman. Channel 4, 13 January 1987.

Mae West (1982). Ann Jillian as the large lady of the sex innuendo in a questionable bio-pic. Cast: James Brolin, Piper Laurie, Roddy McDowall etc. Dir: Lee Philips. Screenplay: E. A. Kean. BBC1, 12 November 1986.

The Magician (1974). ITV, 13 November 1986. Previously shown on same channel, 25 August 1984. See *Film Review 1985–6*.

The Magic of Dr Snuggles (1984). A charming TV animated film from Holland about a kindly old inventor and his animal companions. Dir: Tim Terry. No other credits. ITV, 23 December 1986.

Malice in Wonderland (1985). Elizabeth Taylor and Jane Alexander as the bitchy rival Hollywood columnists of the film colony's golden period, Louella Parsons and Hedda Hopper, and their frantic feud over some 20 years. An acid eye-opener for British newspaper and magazine readers. Dir: Gus Trikonis. Screenplay: Jacqueline Feather and David Seidler. BBC2, 3 February 1987.

Man of Letters (1984). Warren Mitchell casts off his coarse and crude cockney image to play an elderly professor with teenage ideas and ambitions about sex. A made-in-Australia TV comedy. Also featuring Dinah Shearing, Carol Raye etc. Dir: Chris Thomson. Screenplay: Alma de Groen, based on the novel by Glen Tomasetti. ITV, 6 October 1986.

Matlock: Diary of a Perfect Murder (1986). Introduction to a series centred on a rural Georgian lawyer (Andy Griffith) who may be unconventional but is certainly successful with his methods in court as he defends a man accused of killing his wife. Dir: Robert Day. Screenplay: Dean Hargrove. ITV, 24 April 1987.

May (1982). Pretty sad and sombre piece from Denmark about the country lass who comes to the big city (Copenhagen) and finds life anything but sugar and spice: she becomes mistress to a married man, has a baby and goes through the usual routine of this kind of moral tale. Featuring: Mette Munk Plum. Dir and Screenplay: Bille August. Channel 4, 11 June 1987.

Mayday: 40,000 ft! (1976). BBC1, 29 June 1987. Previously shown on BBC, 23 June 1984. See *Film Review 1985–6*.

Men of the Dragon (1974). Routine martial arts movie set in Hong Kong, with Jared Martin and his side-kick determined to rescue the former's abducted sister, Katie Saylor, another kung fu expert. Also featuring Robert Ito, David Chow, Joseph Wiseman etc. Dir: Harry Falk. Screenplay: Denne Bart Petitclerc. ITV, 2 October 1986.

The Migrants (1974). Small-screen adaptation of the Tennessee Williams story about the exploitation of America's migrant farm workers, seen through the eyes of one such family in the New Jersey farm belt. Some fine performances by a starry cast including Sissy Spacek, Cloris Leachman, Cindy Williams, Ed Lauter etc. Dir: Tom Gries. Screenplay: Landford Wilson. BBC1, 26 March 1987.

The Miracle of Kathy Miller (1981). Heart-stirring story of a youngster who, after a horrific accident which seems likely to cripple her completely, fights back to something like a normal life by sheer guts and wonderful family support. Superior stuff, finely acted. Cast: Sharon Gless, Frank Converse, Helen Hunt etc. Dir: Robert Lewis. Screenplay: Mel and Ethel Brez. Channel 4, 21 April 1987.

The Miracle Worker (1979). A new adaptation of William Gibson's powerful and moving play about Helen Keller, the blind, deaf and dumb girl saved from a life in an asylum and coached into understanding, and more, by her dedicated teacher. Always a remarkable and almost incredible real-life story. Cast: Melissa Gibert (Helen), Patty Duke Austin (teacher) etc. Dir: Paul Aaron. Screenplay: William Gibson. BBC1, 5 November 1986.

Mother's Day on Walton's Mountain (1982). Another TV spin-off from the popular Walton series which ended its run the year before this was made. All about Mary Ellen's tragic honeymoon, and the aftermath. Cast: Judy Norton-Taylor, Ralph Waite, Jon Walmsley etc. Dir: Gwen Arner. Screenplay: Juliet Packer. BBC1, 2 April 1987.

The Movie Murderer (1977). Arthur Kennedy as the insurance company investigator who suspects arson when a series of fires occur, all of them involving the destruction of film stock. Warren Oates as the fire-raiser. Also featuring Tom Selleck, Jeff Corey, Elisha Cook etc. Dir: Boris Sagal. Screenplay: Stanford Whitmore. ITV, 9 June 1987.

The Munster's Revenge (1981). Monsters from a wax museum sparked into a crime wave by the nasty Dr Diablo, alias Sid Caesar. Also featuring Fred Gwynne, Yvonne de Carlo etc. Dir: Don Weis. Screenplay: Arthur Alsberg and Don Nelson. Channel 4, 31 December 1986.

Murder on the Waterfront (1985). Carroll O'Connor, New York cop, is assigned the twin tasks of catching a very elusive killer and preventing the newspapers having a field day with the case. It was hoped this would be good enough to launch a new series. Also featuring Lois Nettleton, Vincent Gardenia etc. Dir: Corey Allen. Screenplay: Alvin Bortez and Matt Harris. ITV, 14 September 1986.

Murder With Mirrors (1985). Three bodies line the path of Miss Marple's (Helen Hayes) way to solving the mystery of the threat to her old schoolfriend's (Bette Davis) life in this recent American TV movie. Helen Hayes as the sleuth and a brave effort by stroke-afflicted Miss Davis, as the friend, after being told by her medics that she would never work again. Also featuring John Mills, Leo McKern, Dorothy Tutin etc. Dir: Dick Lowry. Screenplay: George Eckstein, based on the whodunit by Agatha Christie. ITV, 1 September 1986.

Naming the Names (1986). The Irish 'Troubles' brought back to the screen by writer Anne Devlin, telling the story of one woman's involvement in them between 1969 and now. Cast: Sylvestra Le Touzel and plenty of Erse names, including Michael Maloney, Mick Ford, Ian McElhinney etc. Dir: Stuart Burge. BBC2, 8 February 1987.

Nightmare in Badham County (1976). Two stranded, vacationing girl students become victims of the local corrupt sheriff and are sent to the local horrid prison farm: Cast: Deborah Raffin, Lynne Moody, Chuck Connors, Ralph Bellamy. Dir: John Llewellyn Moxey. Screenplay: Jo Heims. ITV, 23 June 1987.

The Night Stalker (1971). Generally considered to be among the very best TV movies ever turned out; a thriller with comedy trimmings about the Las Vegas cops *v.* the vampire killer. Cast: Darren McGavin, Carol Lynley, Ralph Meeker etc. Dir: John Llewellyn Moxey. Screenplay: Richard Matheson. BBC2, 19 May 1987.

Nobody's Child (1986). Award winning, based-on-truth TV movie about an abused mental institution victim who fought her way back to normality. Dramatic and moving . . . and very good. Cast: Marlo Thomas etc. Dir: Lee Grant. Screenplay: Mary Gallagher and Ara Watson. BBC2, 23 June 1987.

No Man's Land (1984). BBC1, 1 June 1987. Previously shown on BBC1, 6 July 1985. See *Film Review 1986–7.*

Northanger Abbey (1987) A neat performance by Katharine Schlesinger as the over-romantic heroine with lots to learn about life in this let's-get-on-with-it version of Jane Austen's early but meaty novel. Set in 18th-century Bath and the fictional stately home of the title. Also featuring Peter Firth, Googie Withers and Robert Hardy. Dir: Giles Foster. Screenplay: Maggie Wadey. BBC2, 15 February 1987.

Not Just Another Affair (1982) BBC1, 3 December 1986. Previously shown on BBC, 3 June 1984. See *Film Review 1984–5.*

Obsessed with a Married Woman (1985). Routine mistress and marriage drama. Cast: Jane Seymour, Tim Matheson etc. Dir: Richard Lang. Screenplay: C. O'Brien, Dori Pierson and Marc Rubel. Channel 4, 27 January 1987.

The Old Man Cried Wolf (1970). Apparently the only TV movie Edward G. Robinson ever made. He plays the Old Man determined to prove to the cops that his old friend was murdered . . . and the murderer doesn't like his determination. Also featuring Martin Balsam, Diane Baker, Ruth Roman, Sam Jaffe etc. Dir: Walter Grauman. Screenplay: Luther Davis. ITV, 20 April 1987.

On the Palm (1987). Pretty depressing tale of an out-of-work steelworker whose initially cheering job (a sort of super errand boy) for a shady businessman turns sour. Cast: Peter Martin, Philip Jackson etc. Dir: Michael Whyte. Screenplay: David Sheasby. BBC2, 5 April 1987.

The Ordeal of Bill Carney (1981). In spite of all that's going for it, this is a singularly uninvolving film about a paraplegic's fight against his handicap as he also fights his divorcing wife for the custody of their two sons. Cast: Richard Crenna, Ray Sharkey etc. Dir: Jerry London. Screenplay: Tom Lazarus. Channel 4, 24 February 1987.

The Other Victim (1981). Another TV movie based on the theme of rape, only this one takes a somewhat different line by presenting the view of the raped woman's husband. Cast: William Devane, Jennifer O'Neill etc. Dir: Noel Black. Screenplay: Richard DeRoy. Channel 4, 18 November 1986.

The Outlaws (1984). This jolly little comedy about a couple of young guys and a girl tryng to evade the chasing cops is

good enough to make one regret that the hoped-for follow-on series never came to fruition, while less talented ideas took off. Cast: Christopher (Jack's son) Lemmon, Charles Rocket, Joan Sweeny, M. Emmet Walsh etc. Dir: James Frawley. Screenplay: P. M. Belous and Robert Wolterstorff. ITV, 11 December 1986.

Parole (1982). Superior story about the relationship between a paroled prisoner (Mark Soper), whose experiences during his three-and-a-half years in a top security jail have been horrific, and his patient parole officer (James Naughton). Also featuring Lori Cardille, Ted Ross etc. Dir: Michael Tuchner. Screenplay: Edward Hume. Channel 4, 20 January 1987.

Passion Flower (1985). You are likely to find the Singapore backgrounds more entertaining than this somewhat convoluted murder melodrama about a girl who hates her rich dad. There are some nice performances even though they come from the baddies. Cast: Bruce Boxleitner, Barbara Hershey, Noel Williamson etc. Dir: Joseph Sargent. Screenplay: R. A. Guttman. ITV, 15 June 1987.

The Patricia Neal Story (1981). Glenda Jackson superb in the true fairy story of actress Patricia Neal, who survived three strokes. A moving and gripping TV film, well above the norm. Dir: Anthony Harvey and Anthony Page. Screenplay: Robert Anderson, based on the book by Barry Farrell. ITV, 16 January 1987.

Perry Mason Returns (1985). Years after Raymond Burr and Barbara Hale (regrettably) ended that famous and fascinating detection series, they make a very welcome return in a movie. Mason sheds the legal robes he now wears and gets down to the defence of his late secretary when she is arraigned on a murder charge. More Perry please! Dir: Don Satlof. Screenplay: Dean Hargrove. BBC1, 17 April 1987.

The Phantom of the Opera (1982). The fourth screen adaptation of the famous horror story – three large screen ones (starting with the famous Lon Chaney silent) and one TV spectacular have preceded it. Now down to pretty routine handling, with Maximilian Schell as 'Scarface'. Also featuring Jane Seymour, Michael York, Jeremy Kemp etc. Dir: Robert Markowitz. Screenplay: Sherman Yellen. ITV, 8 November 1986.

A Piano for Mrs Cimino (1982). BBC1, 26 November 1986. Previously shown on BBC, 5 September 1983. See *Film Review 1984–5.*

The Plumber (1978). This one doesn't leave his tools at home. In fact, this Mad Max progenitor does a pretty thorough job on the house *and* on the lady of the house, over five days of ordeal for her . . . a deep black comedy from now-famous Australian director Peter Weir. Cast: Judy Morris, Ivor Kanis etc. No screenplay credit. Channel 4, 14 February 1987.

Policewoman Centrefold (1983). Could it happen here? A lady cop appearing in the altogether in a girlie magazine?: What *would* her Inspector say, after inspecting it? Incredible? Well, it actually happened in a New Mexico precinct, if maybe not *quite* as shown here. Cast: Melody Anderson, Ed Marinaro, David Spielberg. Dir: Reza S. Badiyi. Screenplay: Jan Worthington. ITV, 16 May 1987.

Portrait of a Showgirl (1982). Lesley Ann Warren finds life isn't all roses even after finding some sort of fame as a dancer at Caesar's Palace in Vegas. Also featuring Tony Curtis, scene-stealing Rita Moreno etc. Dir: E. W. Swackhammer. Screenplay: Jim Barnett. ITV, 13 June 1987.

The Priest Killer (1971). It's nice to see old Ironside (Raymond Burr) back again, here collaborating with an ex-cop now priest (George Kennedy), in order to put their collective hand on the shoulder of a triple killer. The duo make it a 'must'. Dir: Richard A. Colla. Screenplay: Robert van Skoyk and Joel Oliansky. ITV, 29 March 1987.

Private Sessions (1985). Kelly McGillis takes this story about some of the customers of a popular psychiatrist by the neck, and, as a nymphomaniac client, out – but never quite over-plays everybody else. *What a performance!* No wonder they gave her the co-star role in *Top Gun*. Also featuring Robert Vaughn, Maureen Stapleton, Mike Farrell, Hope Lange etc. Dir: Michael Pressman. Screenplay: Thom Thomas. Channel 4, 3 February 1987.

Professor Poopsnaggle's Steam Zeppelin (1986). The first of four made-in-Australia comedy films for the kids, with Gerry Duggan as the Prof. Dir: Howard Rubie and Russell Webb. Screenplay: Ken Talbot and Justine Clarke. ITV, 25 April 1987.

Professor Poopsnaggle's Steam Zeppelin: Island Adventure. (1986). The second. Same credits. ITV, 2 May 1987.

Quartermaine's Terms (1987). Smoothly made, beautifully acted and very talkative drama set in the professorial staff room of a language college. What a joy to listen to stage-trained eloquence instead of the too-often cinema-trained mumbling. Cast: Edward Fox, John Gielgud, Eleanor Bron etc. Dir: Bill Hays. Screenplay: Simon Gray. BBC2, 29 March 1987.

A Question of Honour (1981). BBC1, 25 July 1986. Previously shown on same channel, 16 July 1984. See *Film Review 1985–6*.

Reckless Disregard (1985). Very topical TV film examination of the freedom of the press and television, and the point when investigative journalism becomes invasion of personal privacy. Seen in the fictional case of a libel action against a star reporter. Good stuff, nicely directed and well acted by Tess Harper and Leslie Nielsen etc. Dir: Harvey Hart. Screenplay: Charlie Haas. Channel 4, 11 November 1986.

Reflections (1983). Channel 4, 29 January 1987. Previously shown on same channel, 5 July 1984. See *Film Review 1985–6*.

Relentless (1977). BBC1, 6 September 1986. Previously shown on BBC, 28 January 1984. See *Film Review 1984–5*.

Return of the Gunfighter (1967). A nice, comfy old western with Robert Taylor on the trail of the killers of some friends who sent him a call for help . . . too late. Also featuring Chad Everett, Lyle Bettger, Ana Martin etc. Dir: James Neilson. Screenplay: Robert Buckner, based on a story by Buckner and Burt Kennedy. BBC2, 17 December 1986.

Right to Kill (1985). More social conscience problems in a serious and satisfactory film (based on a true story) about an ill-treated teenager who eventually turns on his dad. In the painful circumstances did the lad have the right of the title? Cast: Frederic Forrest, Christopher Collet etc. Dir: John Erman. Screenplay: Joyce Eliason. BBC2, 26 May 1987.

The Runaway Train (1973). Not, of course, the more recent large-screen film of that name, but an American made-for-TV film originally titled just *Runaway*. It is claimed this was actually shown in British cinemas with the above title, but no trace of it in *Film Review*. All very confusing! Cast: Ben Johnson, Vera Miles, Ed Nelson etc. Dir: David Lowell Rich. Screenplay: Gerald Dipego. ITV, 9 October 1986.

Sacred Hearts (1984). Channel 4, 5 February 1987. Previously shown on same channel 16 May 1985. See *Film Review 1985–6*.

Savages (1974). Murder in the desert, with young guide Sam Bottoms finding the expedition he leads turning into a nightmare experience. Also featuring Andy Griffith, Noah Beery, James Best etc. Dir: Lee Katzin. Screenplay: William Wood. ITV, 17 December 1986.

The Scarlet Pimpernel (1982). ITV, 27 December 1986. Previously shown on same channel, 27 December 1983. See *Film Review 1984–5*.

The Secret Drawer (1986). Long and star-flecked TV film from France, originally made as a mini-series in six parts, now condensed. Michèle Morgan goes a-sleuthing in order to delve into her late husband's mysterious past. Also featuring Marie-France Pisier, Daniel Gélin, Michael Lonsdale. Dir: Edouard Molinaro, Nadine Trintignant, Michel Boisrond and Roger Gilioz. Screenplay: Daniele Thompson. BBC2, 1 January (Part 1) and 2 January (Part 2) 1987.

Secrets of a Married Man (1982). Frothy little comedy about the seven-year itch, with William Shatner as the itchy one and Cybill Shepherd as a glamorous irritant. Dir: William A. Graham. Screenplay: Dennis Nemec. BBC1, 1 December 1986.

Seduced (1985). Superficial, polished and smooth murder mystery with stock scandal and romantic trimmings. Cast: Cybill Shepherd, Gregory Harrison, José Ferrer and Mel Ferrer. Dir: Jerrold Freedman. Screenplay: C. Robert Carner. ITV, 4 January 1987.

The Seduction of Miss Leona (1979). Lynn Redgrave lights up this otherwise pretty familiar romance about a girl who finds her determination not to love again, after a romantic disaster, being undermined by the nice, but married, house repairer who comes to repair her house but stays to repair her heart. Anthony Zerbe, Brian Dennehy etc. Dir: Joe Hardy. Screenplay: Dan Wakefield. BBC1, 9 April 1987.

The Shadow Riders (1982). BBC1, 2 June 1987. Previously shown on BBC, 14 October 1983. See *Film Review 1984–5.*

Sins of the Father (1984). Pretty, aspiring lawyer Kevan Harris allows the boss to sweep her into his bed, then switches to his less forceful son and jumps between the sheets with *him*! Also featuring Glynnis O'Connor, James Coburn, Ted Wass etc. Dir: Peter Werner. Screenplay: Elizabeth Gill and Jeff Cohn. Channel 4, 24 March 1987.

Sky Heist (1975). BBC2, 6 April 1987. Previously shown on BBC, 30 June 1984. See *Film Review 1985–6.*

Skyway to Death (1974). It all starts to happen when a cable car comes to a halt . . . and not everyone gets down to *terra firma*. One of the 'disaster' movies that marched across big and small screens around this period. Cast: Ross Martin, Stefanie Powers. Dir: Gordon Hessler. Screenplay: David Spector. ITV, 29 August 1986.

The Snowman (1982). Channel 4, 25 December 1986. Previously shown on ITV, 29 December 1985. See *Film Review 1986–7.*

Someone's Watching Me! (1978) ITV, 30 June 1987. Previously shown on BBC1, 2 November 1985. See *Film Review 1986–7.*

Something About Amelia (1984). BBC2, 12 May 1987. Previously shown on same channel, 12 June 1985. See *Film Review 1985–6.*

A Song for Europe (1984). Channel 4, 15 January 1987. Previously shown on same channel, 23 May 1985. See *Film Review 1985–6.*

Squaring the Circle (1983). Channel 4, 22 January 1987. Previously shown on same channel, 31 May 1984. See *Film Review 1984–5.*

Street Cop (1982). The true (at least, based on fact) story of a New York undercover cop's successes, and her final inner struggle between duty and domestic responsibilities when called upon to trap a rapist. Cast: Karen Valentine, John Getz, Vincent Gardenia etc. Dir and Screenplay: Sandor Stern, based on the book by Mary Glazle and Evelyn Fiore. BBC1, 5 August 1986.

Summer of My German Soldier (1978). BBC2, 2 June 1987. Previously shown on BBC, 16 April 1984. See *Film Review 1984–5.*

Sunshine (1973). Cristina Raines as a young woman very much in love who has to face up to some pretty nasty decisions . . . and it is all based on a true story. Also featuring Cliff de Young, Meg Foster, Brenda Vaccaro etc. And as a bonus, a series of songs sung by John Denver. Dir:

Joseph Sargent. Screenplay: Carol Sobieski. BBC1, 8 August 1986.

Swan Song (1980). TV's well-known cop David Soul shows another side of his prowess in this story about a world-class ski-star on the slide, who decides he'll go against the slopes and climb back to the top. If you like snow it's fine. Also featuring Bo Brundin, Slim Pickens, Jill Eikenberry etc. Dir: Jerry London. Screenplay: Michael Mann, Ron Koslow and Jeffrey Bloom. BBC1, 18 February 1987.

Terror on the 40th Floor (1974). The small screen's answer to the large screen's 'disaster' cycle success *The Towering Inferno*, with the same situation of people trapped at the top of a burning skyscraper. Cast: John Forsythe, Anjanette Comer, Pippa Scott etc. Dir: Jerry James. Screenplay: Jack Turley. ITV, 5 July 1986.

This is Kate Bennett (1981). Janet Eilber as the girl TV reporter who finds some nasty problems at home (a custody struggle) and away (a threat to her life). Dir: Harvey Hart. Screenplay: Sue Milburn. Channel 4, 30 May 1987.

The 3,000-Mile Chase (1977). ITV, 11 April 1987. Previously shown on BBC, 13 August 1983. See *Film Review 1984–5.*

Thursday's Child (1983). Heart transplant drama based on fact, with Rob Lowe as the young man whose alternatives are a heart transplant or death. Also featuring Gena Rowlands, Don Murray etc. Dir: David Lowell Rich. Screenplay: Gwen Bagnidubov, based on the book by Victoria Poole. Channel 4, 16 December 1986.

Topper (1979). Pale shadow re-make of the 1937 classic about a couple killed in a car smash whose ascent to heaven is held up, pending the good deed passport they need to enter through the pearly gates. Cast: Kate Jackson, Jack Warden, Andrew Stevens etc. Dir: Charles S. Dubin. Screenplay: George Kirgo, Maryanne Kascia and Michael Scheff. Channel 4, 10 March 1987.

The Toughest Man in the World (1984). Mr T, of TV's *A-Team* series, shows just how tough he is – for the $100,000 he needs to set up a youth centre in Chicago. Cast: Dennis Dugan, Peggy Pope etc. Dir: Dick Lowry. Screenplay: Jimmy Sangster and Richard Guttman. ITV, 22 December 1986.

Two of a Kind (1982). Don't be misled, this *isn't* the John Travolta musical of that title: in fact it is George Burns as a withdrawn widower brought back to an interest in life by his mentally retarded grandson. Also featuring Cliff Robertson, Robby Benson, Barbara Barrie. Dir: Roger Young. Screenplay: James Sadwith. BBC2, 10 March 1987.

Valentine (1979). Move over, you young things . . . romance can still flourish in the seventies, as it does in this story of a loving couple in an old folks home. It marks Mary Martin's return to the studios after a 20-year absence. Also featuring Jack Albertson, Danny De Vito etc. Dir and (with Merrit Maloy) Screenplay: Lee Phillips. Channel 4, 10 February 1987.

The Victim (1972). More or less routine thriller. Storm; empty house; terrified girl, who becomes aware she is next on the list of a killer. Cast: Elizabeth Montgomery, George Maharis etc. Dir: Herschel Daugherty. Screenplay: Merwin Gerard. ITV, 20 November 1986.

Victims for Victims: The Theresa Saldana Story (1984). A true story, with the added authenticity of the victim playing herself. A young actress is attacked on a Hollywood boulevard in 1982 and almost knifed to death. But she did survive, and she went on to form the organization of the title for others who have suffered similar savagery. And the horrifying fact – with its echoes in our own legal system – is that the would-be killer is due to be released in 1988. Dir: Karen Arthur. Screenplay: Arthur Heinemann. Channel 4, 3 March 1987.

Visions of Death (1972). ITV, 13 May 1987. Previously shown on BBC, 7 February 1984. See *Film Review 1984–5*.

Visitors (1987). Dennis Potter's TV film adaptation of one of his typical dark stage comedies, *Sufficient Carbohydrate*. In a villa by an Italian lakeside a quintet of vacationing sun worshippers (three American, two British) find plenty of grounds for diverse argument. Cast: Michael Brandon, John Standing, Nicola Paget etc. BBC2, 22 February 1987.

The Wall (1982). *Not* the Turkish cinema film shown in Britain, but an overlong story about the walled-in Jews of the Warsaw ghetto and their brave but unavailing struggle to avoid their fate. Cast: Lisa Eichhorn, Tom Conti, Eli Wallach, Rachel Roberts etc. Dir: Robert Markowitz. No other credits. Channel 4, 29 March 1987.

A Wedding on Walton's Mountain (1982). One of three features that followed the popular TV series about the Waltons. Up-to-earth story of simple Appalachian mountain folk. Cast: Ralph Waite, Ellen Corby, Jon Walmsley etc. Dir: Lee Phillips. Screenplay: Marjorie Fowler, based on the stories by her and Claylene Jones. BBC1, 7 January 1987.

Welcome Home, Bobby (1986). The travails of a homosexual teenager, his kith and kin. A very talkie talkie, with Tony Lo Bianco and Timothy Williams. Dir: Herbert Wise. Screenplay: Conrad Bromberg. BBC2, 30 June 1987.

Well of Love (1970). Lassie playing the canine healer when a small boy loses his beloved dog. With supporting humans Bruce Bennett, Sean Kelly, Robert Samson etc. Dir: Jack Hiveley. Screenplay: Robert Schaefer and Eric Freiwald. BBC2, 5 December 1986.

Wet Gold (1984). Poor relation TV re-make of the classic cinema movie *The Treasure of the Sierra Madre*. Why *do* they take this sort of liberty? Cast: Brooke Shields, Burgess Meredith, Tom Byrd, Brian Kerwin. Dir: Dick Lowry. Screenplay: David Sherwin and Joyce Eliason. BBC1, 4 October 1986.

When Every Day Was the Fourth of July (1978). Murder in small-town America in the late 1930s. Is the killer that harmless deaf-mute? Things look black for him . . . but at least some think he's innocent. Cast: Dean Jones, Louise Sorel, Henry Wilcoxon etc. Dir: Dan Curtis. Screenplay: Lee Hutson, based on a story by Curtis and Hutson. BBC2, 17 February 1987.

The Wild Wild West Revisited (1979). Ten years after this apparently popular series ended, this (and one other) feature was launched with the hope that the fun and thrills could be brought back to popularity. They couldn't. Robert Conrad (as agent West) and Ross Martin as his team-mate saving the world from the super villain. Wild, indeed, but fun. Dir: Burt Kennedy. Screenplay: Bill Bowers. BBC1, 20 June 1987.

William the Conqueror (1986). A really international TV movie if ever there was one, with Swiss, French, West German, Belgian and Romanian fingers in the production pie. Made in English, it seems that the studios used were in East Germany and, according to *TV Times*, the sound was done in Hollywood. And all to relate the way Norman Willy gave Saxon Harold one in the eye and took us over in 1066. No wonder it takes three-and-a-half hours to unroll. Hervé Bellon (Willy), John Terry (Harold) and a supporting cast with names like Szilagyi. Dir: Gilles Graingier and Serge Nicolaesco. Screenplay: Serge de la Roche. ITV, 25 April 1987.

Will You Love Me Tomorrow? (1987). 'Screen Two' British TV movie about two young girls, escaped from jail, sampling the grey-toned pleasures of freedom in a wintry East-coast town. Made with gritty realism but at times quite affecting. Joanne Whalley and Tilly Vosberg as the girls on the run. Also featuring Phil Daniels, Iain Glen etc. Dir: Adrian Shergold. Screenplay: Shergold and David Snodin. BBC2, 18 January 1987.

The Women of Wilmar (1983). Documentary-style true story of the long fight against sex discrimination by a group of women employed in a small-town bank in Minnesota. Less a Women's Lib lesson than a stirring human story. Cast: Jean Stapleton, Dinah Manoff, Judge Reinhold etc. Dir: Lee Grant. Screenplay: Joyce Eliason. Channel 4, 17 March 1987.

The Young Visiters (1974). Channel 4, 22 December 1986. Previously shown on same channel, 25 December 1984. See *Film Review 1985–6*.

The Zany Adventures of Robin Hood (1984). Hollywood's George Segal came to Britain to don Robin's feather-bedecked hat in this rather heavily underlined jokey version of the old Sherwood Forest legend. From the pen of the writer of that large-screen success, *Love at First Bite*. Also featuring Roddy McDowall, Janet Suzman, Michael Hordern, Fenella Fielding etc. Dir: Ray Austin. Screenplay: Robert Kaufman. BBC1, 2 August 1986.

Video Releases

ANTHONY HAYWARD

About 2½ million budget-price videos were sold in the last quarter of 1986, with *Cabaret*, on the VideoGems label, selling 25,000 copies. The massive success of these budget-price cassettes, pioneered by The Video Collection and Channel 5, has already had an impact on another part of the British video industry. Dealers reported that tape rentals fell by up to 30 per cent over Christmas 1986, and also blamed a strong line-up of films on TV.

But it was a full-price cassette that won the top honour in the British Videogram Association's first annual awards ceremony, in October 1986: *Beverly Hills Cop*, released by CIC, was the most popular tape during the previous year.

CBS/Fox and Warner were the most successful video distributors of 1986 in Britain, according to the trade magazine *Video Business*, with CBS/Fox's own releases and distribution of videos for other labels accounting for one-third of the market. Both companies joined forces in January 1987 to promote *Commando* and *Cobra* with a £250,000 national press campaign. Joint promotion is a growing trend in Britain, and other distributors watched with interest.

Piracy was also on the increase by the beginning of 1987. The Federation Against Copyright Theft (FACT), Britain's trade-backed anti-piracy organization, revealed that illegal cassettes accounted for a quarter of the £400 million annual rental market. In 1986, 46,500 pirated videos were seized, compared with 20,600 the previous year. Many counterfeit films, including *Rambo: First Blood Part II* and *Friday the 13th – A New Beginning*, were imported from the Lebanon and South East Asia even before their British cinema release. FACT also reported that piracy was conducted mainly by small-time operators, not organized crime syndicates, and that cable and satellite TV had given crooks a new source of illegal taping.

A legal move prevented video dealers boosting their income by up to one-fifth when the High Court stopped them opening on Sundays, in a ruling of February 1987. An Essex dealer claimed unsuccessfully he was running a video club rather than a store, thus was not breaking the trading laws. In the last quarter of 1986, 65 per cent of tapes were hired from specialist dealers and only 7 per cent from newsagents, according to a Gallup survey for the British Videogram Association.

In America, films were being released on video quicker than ever before, and the major studios feared they would not be able to meet the demand expected by the end of the 1980s. This has led to an increase in original programming for the video market. It is estimated there will be more than 50 million video recorder owners in America by 1990, compared with almost 37 million – 42 per cent of TV households – in early 1987. This is already more than double the number of regular cinema-goers.

But sales of films on video had fallen by about 15 per cent by mid-1986 because of the success of cable TV services offering top movies at 3 am for subscribers to record for later play-back. About 2.5 million homes, paying $5 for each film, had subscribed by then.

Particularly hard-hit by the age of video are American sex cinemas. There are now only 300 to 400 of these compared with 800 to 1,200 in 1981, as Americans watch 16 to 20 million blue films a week at home. Pornographic cassettes generated $600 million in 1986 – one-tenth of the video market – compared with $50 million in 1980.

JULY 1986

American Commandos (Frontier)

A Billion for Boris (PolyGram)
Bingo Bongo (RCA/Columbia)
Blame It on the Night (CBS/Fox)
Born Free (RCA/Columbia)

Darlings (Warner)
The Day of the Dolphin (Channel 5)

Easy Money (Rank)
Explorers (CIC)

Final Justice (Vestron)
Flight of the Doves (RCA/Columbia)

Follow the Fleet (Video Collection)

Go for Gold (Vestron)

How to Pick Up Girls (Impact)

Johnny Guitar (Video Collection)

Killjoy (PolyGram)
Krush Grove (Warner)

Lost in America (Warner)

Misfits of Science (CIC)

No Surrender (Palace Premiere)

Penny Serenade (Video Collection)
Poison Ivy (RCA/Columbia)

The Producers (Channel 5)

The Quiet Earth (CBS/Fox)

Rancho Deluxe (Warner)
Run for Your Life (Impact)
Run Wild Run Free (RCA/Columbia)

Scandal Sheet (CBS/Fox)
Searchers of the Voodoo Mountain (Frontier)
Sky Pirates (Vestron)
The Story of David (RCA/Columbia)
The Stuff (CBS/Fox)

Thunder Alley (MGM/UA)
To Hell and Back (CIC)

Welcome to LA (Warner)

AUGUST

Age of Consent (RCA/Columbia)
Alamo Bay (RCA/Columbia)
Among Wolves (RCA/Columbia)

Black Narcissus (Video Collection)
Bless This House (Video Collection)
Blind Justice (CBS/Fox)
Blood Relatives (reissue) (Virgin)
Breaking Glass (reissue) (Virgin)
Bridge at Remagen (Warner)
The Butcher (reissue) (Virgin)

Ceasefire (Odyssey)
Chapter Two (RCA/Columbia)
The Chinatown Kid (Warner)
The Cop Killers (Ariel Films/CBS Records)

Deadringer (Cannon)

Five Superfighters (Warner)
Flying High (Impact)
The Fog (Channel 5)
Foreign Correspondent (Video Collection)
40 Carats (RCA/Columbia)

The Hireling (RCA/Columbia)

Interlude (RCA/Columbia)
It's a Wonderful Life (Video Collection)

Killer (Warner)

The Life and Death of Colonel Blimp (Video Collection)
Lovelines (CBS/Fox)

Merrill's Marauders (Warner)
Mishima (Warner)
Moving Violations (CBS/Fox)

On Golden Pond (Channel 5)

Paradise Motel (PolyGram)

Rappin' (MGM/UA)
Revolution (Warner)

Sessions (reissue) (Virgin)
She Wore a Yellow Ribbon (Video Collection)
Silverado (RCA/Columbia)
The Stepford Wives (reissue) (Virgin)
The Sure Thing (Embassy)

Take a Girl Like You (RCA/Columbia)
That Lucky Touch (Video Collection)
Tomorrow Never Comes (reissue) (Virgin)

The Violent Breed (Guild)
Volunteers (Cannon)

Women of San Quentin (MGA/UA)

SEPTEMBER

Abducted (RCA/Columbia)
Absolute Beginners (Palace)

The Bikini Shop (PolyGram)
Black Moon Rising (Cannon)
Blood Tracks (Avatar)

City Limits (PolyGram)

D.A.R.Y.L. (RCA/Columbia)
Death Wish 3 (Guild)
Defence of the Realm (Rank)

Down by Law (Palace)

Evil Dead II (Palace)

Fandango (Warner)
Flaming Star (CBS/Fox)

Girl in the Empty Grave (MGM/UA)
Grace Quigley (Guild)

Hollywood Vice Squad (Medusa)
Hostage Dallas (Virgin)
Hot Target (RCA/Columbia)
Hunter's Blood (Palace)

The Image Maker (Medusa)
Incident at Crestridge (MGM/UA)

The Journey of Natty Gann (Walt Disney/Rank)

Legend (Cannon)
Lost (Avatar)
Love Me Tender (CBS/Fox)

Macaroni (Palace)
The Man with One Red Shoe (CBS/Fox)
Mixed Blood (Embassy)
Mr Love (Warner)

Nobody's Fool (Palace)

Prizzi's Honour (Embassy)
The Protector (Warner)

Quicksilver (RCA/Columbia)

Return of the Living Dead (Vestron)

The Slipper and the Rose (Video Gems)
Subway (CBS/Fox)
The Supergrass (Recorded Releasing/CBS/Fox)

Terror's Edge (PolyGram)
They Shoot Horses Don't They? (Video Gems)

Up the Academy (Warner)

Victory at Entebbe (Warner)
The Vindicator (PolyGram)

Warning Sign (CBS/Fox)
Wild in the Country (CBS/Fox)

OCTOBER

Bad Medicine (CBS/Fox)
The Boys Next Door (CBS/Fox)

A Chorus Line (CBS/Fox)
Comin' at Ya (Castle/IVS)
The Cop and the Girl (Castle/IVS)

The Delta Force (Rank)
Dream Lover (MGM/UA)

Fright Night (RCA/Columbia)

Goodbye New York (Guild)

Hell Hole (MGM/UA)

Indiana Jones and the Temple of Doom (CIC)

The King of Friday Night (Cannon)

The Little Green Man (Cannon)

Marie (Cannon)

Once Bitten (Vestron)

Spies Like Us (Warner)
The Sword in the Stone (Walt Disney/Rank)

Year of the Dragon (Cannon)

NOVEMBER

Biggles (CBS/Fox)

A Case of Deadly Force (Cannon)
Children of the Night (MGM/UA)
Choices (Cannon)
Clan of the Cave Bear (Embassy)
Copacabana (CBS/Fox)

Fever Pitch (MGM/UA)
Force of Darkness (Cannon)

Hear No Evil (MGM/UA)
Hostage Flight (CBS/Fox)

Jagged Edge (RCA/Columbia)

Killer Party (MGM/UA)
King Solomon's Mines (Rank)

The Last Starfighter (Channel 5)
The Lightship (CBS/Fox)
Lorca and the Outlaws (PolyGram)

The Muppet Movie (Henson/Virgin)

One Magic Christmas (Walt Disney/Rank)
One on One (Warner)

Rainbow Brite and the Star Stealer (Warner)
Recruits (Medusa/CBS/Fox)
Remo – Unarmed and Dangerous (Rank)
Rocky IV (Warner)

Santa Claus (Cannon)
Silver Bullet (Cannon)
The Snowman (reissue) (Palace)
Sparkle (Warner)
Spookies (Palace)
Sylvia (Odyssey)

To Live and Die in LA (Vestron)
Turtle Diary (CBS/Fox)

Under the Cherry Moon (Warner)
Under Siege (Guild)
Up Your Anchor (Guild)

Waterloo (RCA/Columbia)
White Nights (RCA/Columbia)

DECEMBER

Act of Vengeance (Guild)
American Flyers (Warner)

Clockwise (Cannon)
Crimes of Passion (Rank)

Death in California (Guild)
Dreamchild (Cannon)

Echo Park (Vestron)
The Edge of Terror (PolyGram)

Gimme an F (CBS/Fox)

Heated Vengeance (CBS/Fox)

The Last Valley (VideoGems)

My Little Pony (Vestron)

9½ Weeks (CBS/Fox)

Relatives (Odyssey)
Runaway Train (MGM/UA)

Smooth Talk (Odyssey)
Strike Commando (Cannon)

JANUARY 1987

Apology (Medusa/CBS/Fox)
The Assignment (Odyssey)

Blood Sisters (Cannon)
Bridge to Hell (Cannon)

Charlie Chan and the Curse of the Dragon Queen (Warner)
Christine (reissue) (RCA/Columbia)
Cobra (Warner)
Commando (CBS/Fox)
Confessions of a Window Cleaner (reissue) (RCA/Columbia)

The Deliberate Stranger (CBS/Fox)
Doing Life (Odyssey)

Escape From New York (reissue) (Channel 5)

The Far Side of Paradise (Odyssey)
For Lovers Only (MGM/UA)
French Quarter Undercover (Cannon)

Halloween II (EPS)
Highlander (Cannon)
The Howling (reissue) (Channel 5)

Intimate Strangers (Guild)
Iron Eagle (RCA/Columbia)

Jo Jo Dancer Your Life is Calling (RCA/Columbia)

Karate Kid I (reissue) (RCA/Columbia)
Kramer vs Kramer (reissue) (RCA/Columbia)
Krull (reissue) (RCA/Columbia)

Naked Vengeance (Vestron)
The Nesting (Warner)

Of Pure Blood (Warner)
Oliver! (reissue) (RCA/Columbia)

Police Story (Palace Premiere)
Possession (EPS)

Real Genius (RCA/Columbia)
Rebel (Vestron)
Reuben, Reuben (reissue) (Channel 5)
Right of the People (CBS/Fox)

The Sicilian Connection (MGM/UA)
Sid and Nancy (Embassy)
Static (Vestron)
Stir Crazy (reissue) (RCA/Columbia)
Stripes (reissue) (RCA/Columbia)

Tootsie (reissue) (RCA/Columbia)
The Toy (reissue) (RCA/Columbia)

Underground Aces (Capital)

White Lightning (Warner)
Wise Guys (MGM/UA)

A Zed and Two Noughts (Palace)

FEBRUARY

After Hours (Warner)
Agnes of God (RCA/Columbia)
At Close Range (RCA/Columbia)

Banzai Runner (Medusa/CBS/Fox)
Beer (Orion)
Bill (Video Collection)
Black Caesar (Capital)
Booby Trap (Medusa/CBS/Fox)
Born to be Bad (Video Collection)
The Bridge on the River Kwai (RCA/Columbia)
Broken Mirrors (Cannon)

Carve Her Name With Pride (Video Collection)

Day of the Dead (EV)
Death of a Snowman (Screen Indoors)
Dirty Harriet (Vestron)
Disconnected (Studio International)
Donovan's Kid (Walt Disney)

Emanon (Embassy)

Family and Honour (Avatar)
Fire in the Night (Cannon)
A Fistful of Dollars (Warner)
Fool for Love (Rank)
Futureworld (Video Collection)

The Good Father (Virgin/PVG)
Good to Go (CBS/Fox)
Gunpowder (Vestron)

Hanlon: In Defence of Minnie Dean (CIC)
Hardbodies (Vestron)
Head Office (Cannon)
Hercules in New York (VPD)
Highpoint (Missing in Action)
The Hitcher (Cannon)

In a Colt's Shadow (VPD)
Iron Fist Boxer (VPD)

The Jewel of the Nile (CBS/Fox)
A Judgement in Stone (Virgin/PVG)

La Cage aux Folles 3: The Wedding RCA/Columbia)
The Last Days of Patton (CBS/Fox)
The Last Electric Knight/2½ Dads (double-bill) (Walt Disney)
Like Father and Son (PolyGram)

Macao (Video Collection)
Mafia Princess (Braveworld/IVS)
The Malta Story (Video Collection)
The Man Who Fell to Earth (MGM/UA)
The Master Ninja (Ninja Theatre)
Mountaintop Motel Massacre (New World)
Murder By the Book (Capital)

Nightmare Weekend (Avatar)
Ninja Champion (Ninja Theatre)
Ninja Dragon (Braveworld/IVS/
No Blade of Grass (MGM/UA)

Oceans of Fire (Castle/IVS)
Out of Africa (CIC)
Oxford Blues (Guild)

Party Stooge (EV)
The Prey (Trans World)

Reform School Girls (New World)
Richard III (Video Collection)
The Rocking Horse Winner (Video Collection)
A Room With a View (Embassy)

Second Serve (Guild)
The Sex O'Clock News (VIP Premiere)
Snake and Crane – Arts of Shaolin (AVR)
Stripper (Sony)
The Substitute (CBS/Fox)
The Sword and the Rose (Walt Disney)

This Property is Condemned (CIC)
The Treasure of the Sierra Madre (Warner)
The Trip to Bountiful (Vestron)

Underwater (Video Collection)
Union City (Missing in Action)
Unmasking the Idol (Medusa/Guild)

Vengeance – The Story of Tony Cimo (New Media Entertainment)
The Visitor (Warner)

The Way Ahead (Video Collection)
Werewolf Shadow (Screen Indoors)
The White Buffalo (Video Collection)
Wildcats (Warner)
Witness for the Prosecution (MGM/UA)

Yellow Pages (Medusa/Guild)
Young Again (Walt Disney/Rank)

MARCH

Aerobicide (IVS)
An American in Paris (MGM/UA)
Assignment Munich (MGM/UA)

Basket Case (Palace)
Blood Brothers (Elephant)
Boat House (Mogul)
Body Snatchers (Video Vision/AVR)
The Boy Who Had Everything (Sony)
Brigadoon (MGM/UA)

The Care Bears Movie 2 (RCA/Columbia)
Chain Gang (Medusa)
Concrete Hell (Cannon)

The Eight Diagram Pole Fighter (Clockwork)
Eleni (Embassy)
Enemy Mine (CBS/Fox)

Fear in the City (Elephant)
The Fearless Hyena (Jackie Chan Collection/AVR)
A Fine Mess (RCA/Columbia)
Flight of the Angry Dragon (Clockwork)
Fortress (CBS/Fox)
For Your Height Only (ABC)

The Girl Who Spelled Freedom (Walt Disney)
The Go-Kids (ShowChannel/PVG)

The Hills Have Eyes (Palace)

In the Shadow of Kilimanjaro (Guild)
The Iron Fist Adventure (Senator Releasing)

Jack and Mike (MGM/UA)
Jailhouse Rock (MGM/UA)

The Karate Kid 2 (RCA/Columbia)
Kentucky Fried Movie (VPD)
Killing Cars (MGM/UA)

Leonora (VIP)
Lifespan (Vestron)
Love Streams (Guild)

Master Ninja 2 (Ninja Theatre)
Miles to Go (Odyssey/PVG)
Miracles (Orion)
Mona Lisa (Cannon)
Monster in the Closet (VPD)
Murphy's Law (MGM/UA)
My Chauffeur (Vestron)

National Lampoon's European Vacation
 (Warner)
Necropolis (EV)
Ninja Hunt (Cannon)

The Patriot (RCA/Columbia)

Return of the Demons (Clockwork)
Revenge of the Drunken Master (VPD)
The Richest Cat in the World (Walt Disney)

Sexual Deviants (Clockwork)
Shadey (Virgin/PVG)
Shaft (MGM/UA)
Shattered Spirits (IVS)
She Was Fair Game (Embassy)
Singin' in the Rain (MGM/UA)
Switchblade Sisters (Stateside)

Terror in the Swamp (Impact/PVG)
3.15 (Virgin)
Thunder Squad (Mogul)
To Kill With Intrigue (Jackie Chan
 Collection/AVR)
Trouble in Mind (CBS/Fox)

The Ultimate Ninja (Ninja Theatre)

Warrior Queen (Vestron)
When Father Was Away on Business (Cannon)
The Wraith (Medusa)

Yes Giorgio (MGM/UA)
Youngblood (Warner)
*Young Sherlock Holmes and the Pyramid of
 Fear* (CIC)

APRIL

About Last Night . . . (RCA/Columbia)
Aliens (CBS/Fox)
An Almost Perfect Affair (CIC)
Armed Response (EV)

The Bedford Incident (RCA/Columbia)
Blood Ties (Palace)
The B.R.A.T. Patrol (Walt Disney)
Buckaroo Banzai (Cannon)

City Limits (PolyGram)
Claudia (Sony)
Club Med – The Movie (Capital)
Cop's Honour (Guild)
The Cotton Club (Channel 5)

The Danger Zone (RCA/Columbia)
Dead-End Drive-In (New World)

Desert Hearts (Vestron)
Dreamslayer (AVR)
Dr Strangelove (RCA/Columbia)

Equalizer 2000 (New Dimension)
Extra-Terrestrial Visitors (AVR)

Fail Safe (RCA/Columbia)
A Fire in the Sky (RCA/Columbia)
Fire With Fire (CIC)
Flesh and Blood (Orion)
Free Ride (New Dimension)
Friday the 13th (reissue) (Warner)

Ghetto Warriors (AVR)
Grandview USA (CBS/Fox)
The Great Gold Swindle (Nickelodeon)

Hero in the Family (Walt Disney)
The Hound of the Baskervilles (Channel 5)
The Hustler (CBS/Fox)

I.F.O. (Virgin)
Invaders from Mars (Rank)

Keeping Track (Medusa)
Koyaanisqatsi (Channel 5)

The Liquidator (MGM/UA)
Lucky 7 (HBL)

Marriage Italian Style (Channel 5)
Mask (Hollywood Nites)
Masterblaster (New Dimension/Guild)
Mesmerized (Cannon)·
Monster in the Closet (VPD)

Neon Maniacs (New Dimension/Guild)
*A Nightmare on Elm Street 2: Freddy's
 Revenge* (Warner)
Ninja Holocaust (Mogul)
Nothing Underneath (Avatar)

On the Edge (Vestron)
Only Love Defies (Clockwork)
Out of Bounds (RCA/Columbia)

Panic on the 5.22 (Turbophase)
The Phantom of the Park (IVS)
Poltergeist 2: The Other Side (MGM/UA)
Pretty in Pink (CIC)

Robbery (Nickelodeon)

Saturn 3 (Channel 5)
Screwball Academy (Braveworld/IVS)
Secrets of a Door-to-Door Salesman
 (Stablecane)
The Sign of Four (Channel 5)
Silent Witness (IVS)
Sour Grapes (Medusa)
South Bronx Heroes (AVR)
Stagecoach (Mogul Plus)
Swamp Thing (Warner)

The Terminal Man (Warner)
That Was Then, This is Now (Embassy)
Theatre of Blood (Warner)
Tiger Claw Death Kick (Clockwork)
Trespasses (Embassy)

Ultimax Force (Avatar)

Vamp (New World)
Victims of Passion (Cannon)

The Warboy (Cannon)

When Dreams Come True (Guild)
When Night Falls (MGM/UA)
Who is Julia? (CBS/Fox)
Women of Valour (Virgin)

MAY

Adam: His Son Continues (Virgin)
Amazons (Medusa)
Armed and Dangerous (RCA/Columbia)

Beverly Hills Madam (Orion)
Boys and Girls Together (Clockwork)

The Cheque is in the Post (AVR)
Corleone (MGM/UA)
Crossroads (RCA/Columbia)

The Dark Power (Atlas)
Dog Tags (Rank)

The Empty Beach (Sony)

The Flying Misfits (CIC)

Ghost Fever (Virgin)
The Graveyard Shift (Medusa)

Heavenly Pursuits (CBS/Fox)
High Midnight (CIC)
Howard . . . A New Breed of Hero (CIC)

Jungle Wolf (IVS)

The Lie (Action Channel)
Little Spies (Walt Disney)
Lucan (MGM/UA)

Making Contact (MGM/UA)
Marine Issue (Warner)
Meatballs, Part 2 (EV)
The Men's Club (EV)

No Dead Heroes (Vestron)
No Time to Die (Embassy)

Party Climax (Clockwork)

Rage of Honor (VPD)
Ran (CBS/Fox)
Ruthless People (Touchstone)

Salome (Rank)
Savage Harvest (Warner)
Secret Admirer (Orion)
Sex Appeal (Vestron)
Shanghai Surprise (Warner)
Shaolin Red Master (Clockwork)
Slow Burn (CIC)
The Snake Strikes Back (VPD)
Spot Marks the X (Walt Disney)
Stagefright (Avatar)

Target (CBS/Fox)
Terminal Exposure (PolyGram)
Thinkin' Big (IVS)
Trick or Treat (Palace)
Twice in a Lifetime (Vestron)

Valentino (Warner)
Vanishing Act (CBS/Fox)

Wanted: Dead or Alive (New World)
Wardog (Avatar)
Windrider (Vestron)

JUNE

Appointment With Fear (Medusa)
The Avenger (Embassy)

The Berlin Affair (Rank)
Big Trouble in Little China (CBS/Fox)
Biohazard (Virgin/PVG)
Blue City (CIC)

C.A.T. Squad (Braveworld)
Charley Hannah's War (Guild)
Club Paradise (Warner)
The Color Purple (Warner)
Crawlspace (Vestron)

Dangerously Close (Rank)
Deadly Prey (Avatar)
Death Wave (Embassy)
The Dirty Dozen: the Deadly Mission (MGM/UA)
Down by Law (Palace/PVG)
The Dragon, The Hero (VPD)

Easy Prey (New World)
Eat the Peach (RCA/Columbia)
The Everglade Killings (Motion Pictures On Video)

The Fantasist (PolyGram)
Farrell for the People (MGM/UA)
Fatherland (Palace/PVG)
Force of Death (Artic)
Friday the 13th, Part 2 (CIC)
Friday the 13th, Part 3 (CIC)
F/X: Murder by Illusion (RCA/Columbia)

The Great Skycopter Rescue (MGM/UA)
The Gun (CIC)

Heartbreakers (Orion)

Invincible Pole Fighter (Warner)
It Lives Within Her (Artic)

The Leftovers (Walt Disney)
Legendary Weapons of Kung Fu (Warner)
Let's Do It (Ariel)
Lucas (CBS/Fox)

Malcolm (Virgin/PVG)
Mankillers (Avatar)
Mayhem (Castle/IVS)
Mutant Hunt (EV)
My American Cousin (Vestron)

The Ninja Murders (Motion Pictures On Video)

One Police Plaza (CBS/Fox)

Parent Trap 2 (Walt Disney)
Pink Nights (Sony)
Planet Earth (Warner)
Playing for Keeps (Guild)
The Prodigal (Rapid Video Distribution)

Radioactive Dreams (New Dimension)
Raiders of the Living Dead (Braveworld/IVS)
Ricky 1 (EV)

Scanners (reissue) (Virgin/PVG)
Shaolin Temple (Warner)
Soul Man (New World)
Stocks and Blondes (Vestron)
Strange New World (Warner)
Sweet Liberty (CIC)

Tantrums (Motion Pictures On Video)
That Secret Sunday (CBS/Fox)
The Toxic Avenger (New Media Entertainment/PVG)
Twilight People (Atlas)

Valet Girls (Vestron)

In Memoriam

A list of the stars, directors and producers who have died during the year, with biographical details and, in many cases, a tribute to their contribution to the cinema.

Walter Abel, who died, aged 88, on 26 March 1987, was one of those busy feature players whose face is probably much more familiar to movie-goers than his name. A 1917 graduate from the American Academy of Dramatic Art, he made his professional debut in a tiny role in *Out of a Clear Sky* in 1918, and two years later had a somewhat larger part in *The North Wind's Malice*. But during these early years it was the stage that kept him busy, after his New York debut in 1919; he appeared in London in 1929 in *Coquette*. Frank Borzage gave him a small role in his 1935 film *Liliom* and he actually starred in *The Three Musketeers* that same year. From then on he was constantly busy in the studios, in spite of a long succession of stage roles. Some of those movies included *Arise My Love*, *Miracle on Main Street*, *Hold Back the Dawn*, *Holiday Inn*, *Star Spangled Rhythm*, *Mr Skeffington*, *The Affairs of Susan*, *The Kid from Brooklyn* and *13 Rue Madeleine*. His many 1950s films included *Island in the Sky*, *The Indian Fighter* and *Raintree County*; his 1960s films included *The Confession* (starring Ginger Rogers and Elliott Gould – the latter's screen debut, but the film was never released), and *Mirage*. His final screen appearance was in the 1983 (released 1985) Katharine Hepburn film *The Ultimate Solution of Grace Quigley* (also shown as just *Grace Quigley*). Abel appeared quite often on the small screen; as late as 1986 he appeared in the TV documentary *Eugene O'Neill*.

Walter Abel.

Yves Allégret, the French director (who in his early career sometimes used the name of Yves Champlain) died in Paris on 31 January 1987 at the age of 79. Allégret learned his trade largely from his brother Marc, who appointed him his assistant on several of his productions (a post Yves was later to fill under Jean Renoir). Allégret achieved his first feature direction with the ill-fated *Tobie est un ange*, the negative of which was destroyed by fire before it could be shown to the public. His next film, *Les Deux Timides*, completed in 1942, was luckier, and during the 1940s his work began to be critically acclaimed, the films of this period undoubtedly helped by his collaboration with the screenwriter Jacques Sigurd and the performances of his actress wife Simone Signoret during their five-year marriage (1944–9). This combination produced several classics of the screen, including *Les Démons de l'Aube* (1946) and a trio of outstanding *films noirs: Dedée – Dedée d'Anvers* (1948), *Riptide – Une Si Jolie Petite Plage* (1949) and *Ménages – The Cheat* (1950). A few of his later films (he made a total of 25) were of high quality, too, even if they lacked some of the brilliance of his earlier work: notable were his adaptation of a Jean-Paul Sartre story, *Les Orgueilleux – The Proud and the Beautiful* (a Venice Festival Bronze Lion award winner in 1953), and the screen version of Emile Zola's *Germinal*, made in Hungary in 1963. Allégret's final film was *Mords pas t'aime* completed in 1976, the plans for a feature which he tried to launch some years later falling through. He died just a month before he was to be honoured by a prestigious César award for 'career achievement'.

Heather (Grace) Angel had some 50 films to her credit when she died (from cancer) in Santa Barbara on 13 December 1986 at the age of 77. A graduate of the London Polytechnic of Dramatic Art, she joined the Old Vic Co. at the age of seventeen and for the next two years toured the world with them. Miss Angel made her screen debut at the age of 21 in *City of Song* (alternative title: *Farewell to Love*), going on to appear in many British films including *The Hound of the Baskervilles*. In 1931 she went to Hollywood, where she co-starred with Leslie Howard in *Berkeley Square* (1933), was in *The Mystery of Edwin Drood* in 1935 and also appeared in several John Ford films including *The Informer*. Also around this time she appeared in several *Bulldog Drummond* films and *The Orient Express*, gradually moving from star status to that of sup-

Fred Astaire.

Fred Astaire (real name Frederick Austerlitz) died, aged 88, on 22 June 1987. Starting his professional career on the American vaudeville circuit when he was only seven, he made his Broadway debut with sister Adèle in *Over the Top* in 1917. With fellow newcomer Ginger Rogers, he really made his debut on screen in the classic musical *Flying Down to Rio* in 1934 (though in fact he had previously that year been given a small part in Joan Crawford's *Dancing Lady*). The success was instant and, to quote a phrase, the rest is history: certainly screen history, for it presaged that marvellous string of Astaire–Rogers classics. Switching to straight acting for *On the Beach* – that classic about the end of atom-bombed humanity – Astaire continued to make the occasional screen appearance up to *Ghost Story* in 1977, appearing in some 40 films in all. One of his partners complained that Astaire, a stickler for perfection, rehearsed her until her feet were bleeding. A more complete record of his career and a more lengthly tribute to him will appear in next year's *Film Review*.

Ill since suffering a stroke in July 1986, **Hermione Baddeley** died in Los Angeles on 19 August that year aged 79. A student of the Morris School of Dance and Drama, Miss Baddeley had made her stage debut at the age of six and her London debut when she was twelve . . . at sixteen she was already a star and she made her first film, *The Guns of Loos*, when she was eighteen. A

Hermione Baddeley, as Mrs Grogan in MGM's The Unsinkable Molly Brown.

porting player, appearing as such in Hitchcock's *Lifeboat* in the 1940s. She also supplied the voices for a number of Disney cartoon characters and did a considerable amount of TV work. Her last film, in 1962, was *Premature Burial*. She suffered a tragic loss when in 1970 a burglar stabbed and killed her third husband, director Robert B. Sinair, in front of her.

Far better known for his radio and TV work – the latter including one of the most successful series ever made, *I Love Lucy* – Cuban-born **Desi Arnaz** (real name Desiderio Alberto Arnaz de Acha) started out as a singing guitarist with a rumba band, and it was not long before he had his own orchestra. Repeating his stage role in the 1940 film of *Too Many Girls*, he met Lucille Ball on the set and married her. After four

more films (of which *Bataan* was the best) and two years in the US Army, Arnaz launched a big show band and also became musical director of Bob Hope's radio shows. When Lucille Ball's radio show was transferred to TV, Arnaz joined it and so began the *I Love Lucy* series. Shrewd businessman that he was, Arnaz built a TV empire on the strength of it, with 35 sound stage studios. This property was divided when the couple divorced in 1960, but eventually Arnaz sold his interests to Miss Ball, who in turn sold the lot to Gulf + Western, who made it the basis of their Paramount Television. Arnaz made only eight movies, of which the last two were *The Long, Long Trailer* in 1954 and *Forever Darling* two years later. He died from cancer on 2 December 1986 at the age of 69.

Arguably the most talented, certainly the most dedicated of the whole line of the cinema's song-and-dance stars,

short retirement for motherhood was followed by stage successes in London and New York. Though she excelled in comedy roles, Miss Baddeley occasionally revealed her versatility in more serious parts. During the 1940s she made a number of films including *Brighton Rock*, *Passport to Pimlico* and *Quartet*. These were followed by many others during the 1950s and 1960s including *Tom Brown's Schooldays* (1951), *The Pickwick Papers* (1952), *The Belles of St Trinians* (1954), *Room at the Top* (1959) *Mary Poppins* (1964) and *The Happiest Millionaire* (1967). In the 1970s she made *The Black Windmill* (1974) and *C.H.O.M.P.S.* (1979). Apart from films and plays, Miss Baddeley (whose full surname was Clinton-Baddeley) had a successful TV career including a three-year stint in *Maude*. Her autobiography had the title *The Unsinkable Hermione Baddeley*.

Gunnar Bjornstrand, born 1909, was one of Sweden's most distinguished actors, achieving international success with his impressive appearances in several of Ingmar Bergman's films. He died on 6 June 1986.

Looking more like a rugby player than an actor, with his stocky, powerful build, **Colin Blakely**, who died from blood cancer on 7 May 1987 at the age of only 56, gave one of his most memorable screen performances in the British classic *This Sporting Life* as just such a player. It was only his second screen role, the first having been in another British classic, *Saturday Night and Sunday Morning*, made in 1960. Born in Bangor, Northern Ireland, it was as an assistant in the family sports goods shop there that Blakely began to take an interest in amateur theatricals, and in 1958 after some success in them he turned professional. A very versatile actor, who played drama and farce with equal facility, Blakely had many successes on the stage with such prestigious companies as the English Stage Company, the National Theatre and the Royal Shakespeare Company. He appeared with considerable credit in many British movies including *A Man for All Seasons* (1966), *The Private Life of Sherlock Holmes* (as Dr Watson, 1970), *Young Winston* (1972), *Murder on the Orient Express* (1974), *The Pink Panther Strikes Again* (1976), *It*

Shouldn't Happen to a Vet (same year), *Equus* (1977), *The Big Sleep* (1978) and *Nijinsky* (1979). His last stage appearance was in the London production of Alan Ayckbourn's *A Chorus of Disapproval* and he was also seen in 1987 in the TV production of John Mortimer's *Paradise Postponed*.

Like a number of other European directors, **Alessandro Blasetti**, who died in Rome on 2 February 1987 at the age of 86, began his career as a film journalist and critic. Appointed film critic of the daily *L'Imperomand*, he later started his own monthly film magazine *Lo Schermo*, which became the *Cinematografo* in 1928. That same year Blasetti joined a newly formed film production co-operative for whom he made his directing debut with *Sole*, a story of conflict engendered by Mussolini's grandiose plans to drain the Pontine Marshes. A number of feature films followed, culminating (in 1934) with *1860*, the film most critics consider his masterpiece. But in Britain Blasetti will probably be best recalled for his 1942 film *Quattro passi fra le nuvole – Four Steps in the Clouds*, a comedy with some bitter undercurrents in which he also acted, and which is generally considered to have signalled the advent of Italy's famous neo-realist movies. Blasetti went on to prove his easy versatility of style and content with films like *Un giorno nella vita – A Day in the Life*, a drama about the destruction of a convent during World War II (1946), the historical spectacle *Fabiola* (1949) and the unashamedly sentimental *Prima communione – Father's Dilemma* (1950). Doubling as an actor – he had roles in several of his own films – his most memorable performance was the one he gave with Anna Magnani in *Bellissima* (1951). During his 41 years in the film business, Blasetti made 35 films, the last of which was *Simon Bolivar* in 1969. For some obscure reason, however, Blasetti liked to consider his semi-autobiographical *Io, Io, Io . . . egli altri – Me, Me, Me . . . And the Others* (1965) as his final work. In his own country, and by many critics in others, Blasetti was respected as one of Italy's greatest and in many respects most innovative movie-makers.

Sadly, Hollywood never seemed capable of appreciating and exploiting the

Ray Bolger.

full potential of comedian and eccentric dancer **Ray Bolger**, who died at the age of 83 in Los Angeles on 15 January 1987. After vaudeville and Broadway musical successes, Bolger arrived in Hollywood in 1936 to appear in *The Great Ziegfeld*, staying on to appear in *Rosalie* (1937) and *Sweethearts* the following year. It was when MGM cast him in the role of the Straw Man in *The Wizard of Oz* (now accepted as a screen classic, though critically panned when first shown) that Bolger reached the height of his film career, although his subsequent playing of Charley's 'Aunt' in 1952's *Where's Charley?* ran a pretty close second. In all Bolger made only sixteen films between *The Great Ziegfeld* and his last, *The Runner Stumbles*, in 1979, though he did contribute to the spoken commentary in *That's Dancing!* ten years later. Included in the sixteen were *The Harvey Girls* in 1945, *April in Paris* in 1952 and *Babes in Toyland* in 1961. Though making no more movies, Bolger continued to be a stage success until trouble with one hip forced him into retirement in 1984. It is interesting to note that Bolger always saw himself as a comedian rather than as the masterly dancer he was.

Sue Cabot (real name: Susan Cabot Roman) was at the age of 59 beaten to death on 10 December 1986. Her son was later charged with the crime. She used to be called Roger Corman's B-Movie Queen, for she was his favourite actress. She made her debut in 1950 in *On the Isle of Samoa* and went on to appear in some fourteen films, ending with the co-star role in *Surrender – Hell!* in 1959.

James Coco, the rotund, balding actor who, although he made only a total of some dozen movies, was always very popular and busy on stage and the small screen, died in New York after a heart attack on 25 February 1987. He was 56. Coco made his New York debut in 1957 at the age of 27, and his screen debut in 1964 in *Ensign Pulver*, following this with *End of the Road* (1969), *Tell Me That You Love Me, Julie Moon* (1970) and *Murder By Death* (1975). One of his most memorable performances was in *The Wild Party* in 1974, in which he played a character easily recognizable as the tragic Fatty Arbuckle.

For mature movie-goers, the name of **Jerry Colonna**, who died on 21 November 1986 at the age of 82, will surely bring to mind that great big

Jerry Colonna.

walrus moustache, the bulging eyes and the vocal eccentricity of being able to hold a piercing note for well over a minute. Born Gerald Colonna in Boston, Jerry started out as a dance band trombonist but soon switched to the role of comic when he found the audience applauding his fun. His appearance on the *Bing Crosby Show* introduced him to Bob Hope, who used him on radio, TV and in his films over a period of some 30 years and was at Colonna's bedside when he died. After some 1,500 shows and 4 million

miles of travel with Hope, Colonna largely stopped working when he suffered his first stroke in 1966, although he did appear in a Hope TV show ten years later. He was in several of the Hope-Crosby 'Road' films including the first, *Road to Singapore*, and last, *Road to Hong Kong*. In all he made a score of movies including *52nd Street* (his screen debut), *Naughty But Nice*, *Coming Round the Mountain*, *Star Spangled Rhythm* and *Meet Me in Las Vegas*. One of his many discs, *Ebb Tide*, sold a half million copies and he also wrote two successful books, *Who Threw That Coconut?* and a novel, *The Loves of Tullio*.

Benjamin Sherman 'Scatman' Crothers, the American negro jazz player who became an endearing featured player in movies and on TV, died of lung cancer on 26 November 1986 at the age of 76. Crothers began his professional life playing and singing in local speakeasies while still at school, and by the mid-1930s was fronting his own band. Moving to Los Angeles in 1948, he became the first black performer to appear on local TV there and, following his considerable personal success in the 1953 movie *Meet Me at the Fair*, film and TV offers poured in; thereafter he was seldom idle. Some of his best recalled, more recent performances were in *The Shining* in 1980, *Hello Dolly!*, *One Flew Over the Cuckoo's Nest*, *The Shootist*, *Bronco Billy* and, more particularly, as the warm,

'Scatman' Crothers.

black philosopher in the Spielberg segment of *Twilight Zone – The Movie*. Incidentally, the name 'Scatman' apparently came about in 1932 when a TV director demanded a shorter name than his real one. It was a quick reaction as, Crothers explained, he was doing a lot of 'scat' singing at that time.

London-born **Hugh Dempster**, who died in America, aged 86, on 30 April 1987, was best known as a stage actor: he appeared in some 40 London shows and created something of a record by staying with the touring company of *My Fair Lady* for six years. But he did have a number of roles in films, including *The Saint*, *Moulin Rouge* and *Anna Karenina*.

Seen quite recently in the TV series *Hi-de-Hi* but not on the screen for some time, **Leslie Dwyer** died on 29 December 1986 at the age of 80. Dwyer's screen career dated back to the silent

Leslie Dwyer.

days. Known for his cheerful cockney characters, he contributed some delightful character parts to such films as *The Way Ahead*, *In Which We Serve*, *Night Boat to Dublin*, *Laughter in Paradise*, *The Goose Steps Out* and *The Fifth Form of St Dominic's*. He also chalked up some theatrical successes and contributed some telling characters to TV. Those who have seen Leslie Dwyer in one of his roles, however minor, will never forget him, for he always made his characters more than one-dimensional.

You will find plenty of people, including professional critics, who consider that Argentinian director **Hugo Fragonese** – whose trademark was generally violence set against breathtakingly beautiful backgrounds – was always critically under-rated and given few opportunities to reveal his full talent. A medical student, cowboy and journalist, he became a technical adviser on Latin American films while studying at Columbia University. Back in Argentina in 1938 he did various jobs in the local studios before his first feature, *Pampa Barbara*, in 1943. Returning to Hollywood in 1949, Fragonese began a long string of generally excellent B movies, specializing in westerns and gangster stories. Among his 1950s output were *One-Way Street* (with James Mason), *Apache Drums*, *My Six Convicts* (producer was Stanley Kramer), *Black Tuesday* (which some critics regard as his best work), *Decameron Nights*, *Blowing Wild* (with Gary Cooper and Barbara Stanwyck), *The Raid* (co-starring Van Heflin and Anne Bancroft) and *The Man in the Attic* (a Jack the Ripper variation with Jack Palance as the killer). Failing to get suitable offers in the US in the late 1950s, Fragonese came to Europe, where he made some British films – *Harry Black and the Tiger*, with Stewart Granger, filmed in Africa, and *The Beast of Marseilles* (alternative title: *Seven Thunders*) – as well as directing others in Italy, Germany and Spain. In the 1970s he returned to Argentina and made a number of films including *Mas aalla del Sol* and, his last, *Hot Hand* in 1975. He died in Buenos Aires in mid-January 1987 at the age of 78.

Hermione Gingold, who died in New York on 24 May 1987 at the age of 89, was a fine dramatic actress (playing in a number of Shakespearean productions at the Old Vic and elsewhere) who became an outstanding comedienne. The change of direction came after her enormous success in the London wartime revue *Sweet and Low*. Born in London, her professional career began when she was eleven; three years later she appeared with Noel Coward in a production of *Where the Rainbow Ends*. Though it was on the stage that she achieved her greatest successes, Miss Gingold did appear in a number of films, most notably in *Gigi* with Maurice Chevalier (with whom she sang the

Cary Grant.

classic duet 'I Remember It Well'). A master (or mistress) of the *double-entendre*, she could, with that unique voice and subtle facial expression, make even telephone directory entries seem to be in questionable taste. Later she had as great, if not greater, success in New York and lived on the other side of the Atlantic for many years. Her first film was *Someone at the Door* in 1936; later screen roles included *The Pickwick Papers* in 1952, *Around the World in 80 Days* in 1956, *Gigi* in 1958, *Munster Go Home!* in 1966 and *A Little Night Music* in 1971. She also supplied one of the voices in the animated feature with Judy Garland, *Gay Purr-ee*, in 1962. Her final film was *Garbo Talks*, 1984.

Cary Grant (real name Archibald Alexander Leach), died suddenly on 29 November 1986 at the age of 83, when about to present a one-man show of his film clips to an audience in Iowa. He was born into a poor Bristol family and at the age of thirteen ran away from home to join a vaudeville troupe. The fling lasted ten days, after which, located by his father, he was hauled back to school for another two years. But the show business dream persisted and he re-joined the company of clowns and acrobats, going with them to New York in 1920. When the company returned to Britain, Grant stayed on in America, earning a meagre living as a lifeguard during the summer and as a billboard man and occasional one-night-stand song-and-dance man in the winter. Three years later Grant returned to Britain and picked up some bit parts in musical shows, but in 1927 went back to New York and had some success in the 184-performance musical *Golden Dawn*. After several more stage shows and an unsuccessful screen test, Grant decided in 1932 to try once more to break into films. This time he was more successful, landing a Paramount contract worth $450 a week and appearances in no fewer than seven films during his first year and six the next. These included *This is the Night* (his debut), *The Devil and the Deep, Blonde Venus, I'm No Angel* and *Alice in Wonderland*. But it was in *Sylvia Scarlett*, with Katharine Hepburn, that he gave his most assured and impressive screen performance to date. In 1937, contracted to both RKO Radio and MGM, Grant began to reveal his gift for crazy comedy in films like *The Awful Truth, Holiday* and *Bringing Up Baby*; in different style were his roles in *Gunga Din* and *Only Angels Have Wings*. His chirpy, evergreen, debonair personality won him a warmly faithful audience and kept him at the top long after many of his contemporaries had slid down the hill. In fact, Grant was at the height of his prowess and popularity when, in 1966, he announced his retirement from show business, switching to successful business executive with the famous cosmetic firm of Fabergé. His private life was more chaotic than any of his film roles: married five times (he fathered his first child when he was past 60), he was accused by one wife of beating her up and being a drug-taker, and was also said to have dabbled in the supernatural. But his popularity survived all this and more, and in 1970 his peers awarded him an Oscar, something which had always eluded him for specific performances, for his entire career. Grant made 72 films in all. It is difficult to pick out just a few titles from among so many successes, but certainly movies like *His Girl Friday, I'm No Angel, The Philadelphia Story, I was a Male War Bride, Arsenic and Old Lace, Father Goose, Operation Petticoat, Mr Blandings Builds His Dream House* and the Hitchcock films *North By Northwest* and *To Catch a Thief* are among his vintage performances. His last screen appearance, in 1966, was in *Walk Don't Run*. Cary Grant's personality and charm far outweighed his talent as a serious actor, though that shouldn't be discounted too easily. With his usual honesty he once summed it all up by saying: 'I play myself to perfection.' But whatever he had to offer, it was enough to take him to the very top of the celluloid tree and keep him there, quite deservedly, for a very long time and a great many movies.

When the guests arrived at **Joan Greenwood**'s London home on 28

Joan Greenwood.

February 1987, they found their hostess dead of a sudden heart attack; she was 65. One of Miss Greenwood's greatest assets was her 'special' husky, smoky voice, and the winning way she used it. Born in Chelsea, trained at RADA, Joan Greenwood made her London stage debut in 1938 in Molière's *Imaginary Invalid*, and appeared on screen in the 1940 film *John Smith Wakes Up*. Seen by Leslie Howard in a subsequent stage production – *The Women* – she was invited to join the cast of his *The Gentle Sex* in 1942, the

Rita Hayworth.

beginning of a career which mixed films and stage with great success. In all, Miss Greenwood made some 30 films, including appearances in several of those great old Ealing comedies like *Whisky Galore* (1949), *Kind Hearts and Coronets* (same year) and *The Man in the White Suit* (1951). Her other films included *Saraband for Dead Lovers* (1942), *Young Wives' Tale* (1951), *The Importance of Being Earnest* (1952), *The Amorous Prawn* (1962), *Tom Jones* (1963) and *The Water Babies* (1979). Latterly Miss Greenwood had been enjoying success on TV reviving what had at one time seemed to be a career in decline.

One of the great Hollywood glamour stars and foremost 'love goddess' of the 'forties, **Rita Hayworth** (real name: Margarita Carmen Cansino, and billed as such in her first few films) died after a long illness in the home of her daughter, Princess Yasmin Aga Khan, on 14 May 1987 at the age of 68. The daughter of a well-known Spanish dancer father and a former Ziegfeld Girl mother, Margarita made her professional debut as a dancer with her father when she was fourteen, going with him to Mexico where for the next eighteen months they performed at the top-ranking Club Tijuana. It was at a subse-

quent engagement in Agua Caliente that Margarita was seen and offered a contract by Fox, for whom she made her screen debut in 1935 in a quartet of movies including *Dante's Inferno*. Minor, mostly dancing, roles followed for some nine films, after which Fox dropped her. It was at this point that she was taken in hand by a shrewd car salesman, Edward Judson, who changed her appearance, altered her hair from jet black to auburn, persuaded her to take elocution lessons and organized a publicity campaign which helped her to win a contract from Columbia. She married Judson in 1937. A number of forgettable roles in forgettable films led up to her first real chance when she was cast opposite Cary Grant in *Only Angels Have Wings* in 1939. But nothing much came of this, and it was only after another run of minor film roles that in 1941 she leapt to stardom when she partnered Fred Astaire in *You'll Never Get Rich*. The result was a highly coveted *Time* cover photograph and another role opposite Astaire – who is on record as saying she was his favourite dance partner – in *You Were Never Lovelier*. In 1943, while engaged to Victor Mature, Rita married Orson Welles, with whom she had her first daughter, Rebecca, in 1945. But though they were to remain close friends for the rest of their lives, their marriage lasted for only five years. Success continued with films like *Tales of Manhattan* (1942), *Cover Girl* (1944), *Tonight and Every Night* (1945) and *Gilda* (1946), in which she performed her sensationally sexy number 'Put the Blame on Mame, Boys' (though *Variety* and other sources have always claimed that in every case where Rita sang in films, the voice was not actually hers). In 1948, although divorce was looming, Rita appeared with considerable impact in husband Welles' classic thriller *Lady from Shanghai*. In 1949 Rita Hayworth was married to Aly Khan, father of her second daughter Princess Yasmin, but the marriage lasted only two years, after which she returned to the studio to make the successful *Affair in Trinidad* and a number of other, less successful, productions, including *Salome* (1953). Another marriage followed, to Dick Haymes this time, but this, too, lasted only two years. In 1957 she had another big success in *Pal Joey* and in the following year gave a good straight performance as an older woman in

Separate Tables followed by an even more untypical, certainly nonglamorous, performance in *They Came to Cordova*, which earned her some of the best critical notices she had in her entire career. After her divorce from Haymes, she continued to work in a number of now almost forgotten movies like *The Rover, The Poppy is Also a Flower* and *Sons of Satan*. Her last three films were *The Road to Salina* (1970), *The Naked Zoo* (1971) and *The Wrath of God* (1972). It was continually whispered during the 1970s that her inactivity was due to alchoholism, and it was only comparatively recently that her daughter revealed she was suffering from Alzheimer's disease. One of the greatest film glamour stars of her own or any other time, Rita Hayworth in later years demonstrated she had been honed into a quite considerable actress. They don't make 'em like that any more.

Born in South Australia, **Robert Helpmann** died in Sydney, after a long illness, on 28 September 1986 at the age of 77. He studied under and danced with Anna Pavlova in the 1920s, then, moving to London in 1933, he became the leading male dancer with the Sadler's Wells Ballet from 1934 until 1950.

Danny Kaye.

During that time he made several appearances in films, including his first, *One of Our Aircraft is Missing* (in 1942), and *Henry V* (in 1944). In 1948 Michael Powell chose him to choreograph and star in his famous ballet film *The Red Shoes*, a double credit he repeated in *The Soldier's Tale* in 1964. In 1972 he played the Mad Hatter in the film of *Alice in Wonderland* and two years later co-directed (with Rudolf Nureyev) and played the title role in *Don Quixote*. In all, he appeared in fifteen films, the last of which was *Patrick* in 1978. Apart from his films he consistently worked in straight plays, appeared on TV (as late as 1985 he was still earning credits in top-rating productions), and continued dancing, producing and choreographing to the end.

Brian Desmond Hurst died on 4 October 1986. The Irish-born director learned his trade as John Ford's assistant. His 25 films include *Dangerous Moonlight, Hungry Hill, The Malta Story, Simba* and *The Playboy of the Western World*.

Danny Kaye (real name: Daniel Kominski) was born and raised in Brooklyn, the son of Russian émigrés. His original choice of profession was that of doctor, but when his mother

died during his youth he had to change direction, and formed a vaudeville act called 'Red and Blackie' with his friend Louis Eisen, doing one-night stands while working as soda-jerk and insurance salesman during the day. When the act broke up, Kaye carried on on his own. It was during a tour in the Far East that Danny developed his miming, in order to bridge language difficulties. Various on, and off, Broadway stage work followed and then, in 1940, he met and married Sylvia Fine, a composer and lyric writer who was responsible for some of his best numbers and, in a number of ways, had a big effect on his career from then on. Kaye made his screen debut in 1943 in Goldwyn's *Up in Arms*, the first of several movies tailored to his cheerful, many-sided song-dance-comic talents. *Wonder Man* (1945), *The Kid from Brooklyn* (1946) and his big hit performance in *The Secret Life of Walter Mitty* (1947) followed, establishing Kaye as a great entertainer. Others in his total of eighteen films included *The Inspector General* (1949), *On the Riviera* (1951), *Hans Christian Andersen* (1952), *Knock on Wood* (1954) and *White Christmas* (same year). In 1959 he played the role of famous jazz musician Red Nicholls in *The Five Pennies*, and made his final screen appearance in *The Madwoman of Chaillot* after a six-year interval during which he concentrated on the charity work, mostly for UNICEF, which was to take up a large amount of his time from then on. Although he couldn't read a word of music, Danny conducted some of the world's finest symphony orchestras at one time or another, raising more than $10 million for orchestral musicians' charities by so doing. He was one of Britain's most popular entertainers; he was visited by royalty, won compliments from Sir Winston Churchill, was entertained at home by George Bernard Shaw, received 100,000 fan letters, and became the London Palladium's golden boy. He received a special 'Oscar' in 1954, following a special Tony Award the previous year. He also won two entries in *The Guinness Book of Records*, one for conducting 'the world's biggest' band (3,500 musicians in the Dodger Stadium) and the other for visiting 65 US and Canadian cities in 5 days – piloting his own jet aeroplane – for UNICEF. His various international honours included France's Chevalier of the Le-

gion of Honour and the Danish Knight's Cross. He was still appearing on the TV screen as late as 1986; he died of a heart attack in Los Angeles on 1 March 1987, aged 74. Looking back at Danny's prestigious career, perhaps one can best recall him for the number which had originally brought him fame, his tongue-twisting 'Tchaikovsky' song which called for him to reel off the names of 50 Russian composers (both real and imaginary) within a 38-second time span.

Madge Kennedy, who died on 9 June 1987 at the age of 96, had enjoyed some stage – including Broadway – success when in 1917 Samuel Goldwyn persuaded her to sign a three-year contract which resulted in some 21 films for him, an association ending only when, after a running argument with him as to the kind of roles she should play, she returned to the theatre. Later she founded her own film company, for which she made two features, *The Purple Highway* and *Three Miles Out*, in 1923–4. But after four more films (*Scandal Street*, *Bad Company* and *Lying Wives* in 1925, and *Oh Baby* the following year) she retired from the screen – and almost as completely from the stage – for the next 25 years. George Cukor in 1952 persuaded her to return to the studios for his *The Marrying Kind*. After that Miss Kennedy appeared in quite a number of movies in character roles, more notably in *Lust for Life* (1956), *Let's Make Love* (1960), *They Shoot Horses Don't They?* (1969), *The Day of the Locust* (1975) and, her final screen appearance, *Marathon Man*.

The **Esmond Knight** story is a brave one: blinded in action while serving

Esmond Knight.

with the British Navy in World War II (during the battle with Germany's *Bismarck*), he refused to give up his acting career and was soon back on the boards when his sight began to return (though it never returned to normal). Born in East Sheen, Knight made his professional stage debut in *The Wild Duck* in 1925, the first of a long succession of fine performances in the classics (with the Old Vic etc.) and in contemporary plays, like *The Cocktail Party* and *The Caine Mutiny Court-Martial*. He appeared in a considerable number of films during an acting career spanning more than 60 years, including *The Ringer* (his screen debut in 1931), *The Silver Fleet* (1943), *Henry V* (1944), *Black Narcissus* (1947), *Hamlet* (1948), *The Red Shoes* (same year), Renoir's *The River* (his finest screen performance, in 1951), *Sink the Bismarck* (they could hardly have left him out of *that* one; 1960), *The Spy Who Came in from the Cold* and *Anne of the Thousand Days* (1969). Knight worked up to the day of his death, 23 February 1987, when he was on location in Egypt on *The Balkan Trilogy*; he was just 80.

Elsa Lanchester (real name: Elizabeth Sullivan), famous for her playing of odd and eccentric roles (like her famous title role creation in 1935's *The Bride of Frankenstein*) died, aged 84, in a California hospital from bronchial pneumonia, on Boxing Day 1986; she had in fact been ailing ever since she suffered a stroke in 1983. Born in Lewisham, London, she started her professional career with Isadora Duncan's dancers in Paris and by the age of sixteen was appearing with a children's theatre group in Soho. Her debut on the screen was in *One of the Best* in 1927 – the first of the 50 films she made in her career. After a success in *The Constant Nymph* in 1928, a year later she married Charles Laughton, a marriage which lasted more than 30 years in spite of his earlier, hidden, homosexuality. Although she never won an Oscar, she was twice nominated for one: for *Come to the Stable* in 1949 and again for *Witness for the Prosecution* in 1958. But there were many who considered she should have won an award for her playing of Anne of Cleves opposite Laughton in his famous *The Private Life of Henry VIII* in 1933. Among her films were *Ghost Goes West*, *Vessel of Wrath* and *Rembrandt* (three classics of

Elsa Lanchester.

British cinema) and the American *Ladies in Retirement* (1941), *Tales of Manhattan* (1942), *The Spiral Staircase* (1946), *The Razor's Edge* (same year), *The Big Clock* (1948), *Les Misérables* (1952), *Bell, Book and Candle* (1958), *Mary Poppins* (1964), *That Darn Cat* (1965), *Terror in the Wax Museum* (1973) and, her final screen appearance, *Murder By Death* in 1976. She wrote two books: *Charles and I* in 1939 and *Elsa Lanchester Herself* in 1983.

Fulton Mackay, the Scottish actor, whom millions of TV viewers knew best for his marvellous, dry comedy performance as the chief prison warden in the five-year-long series *Porridge*, died on 6 June 1987 in London at the early age of 64. Few of his multitude of fans knew anything about his versatility: he was a successful painter (in oil) and under the name of Aeneas Mac-Bridge was also a successful writer of both radio and TV plays. Mackay was a practising surveyor at the outbreak of war, volunteering for the RAF in 1941. On being demobbed, he decided to switch career and enrolled in RADA. Founder of the Scottish Actors' Company (for whom he both acted and directed), he spent nine years with the Glasgow Citizens' Theatre. Down south, he appeared in both Old Vic and Royal Shakespeare Company productions. In films he will be remembered for his marvellous performance in *Local Hero*, though he gave sound performances in *Gumshoe* and *Defence of the Realm*. His was the voice of the Gryphon in *Dreamchild*. He once revealed his true self in a memorable TV interview: a splendid actor and an intelligent man.

Siobhan McKenna, who died some time after a lung cancer operation in Dublin on 16 November 1986 at the age of 63 was a splendid Belfast-born actress who devoted most of her time to stage work, appearing with distinction in Dublin, London and New York productions. After a period at the Abbey Theatre (in English and Gaelic plays) she came to London and had a great success in Shaw's *St Joan*. She made only a few films, her first being *Hungry Hill* (a tale of Irish family feuds)

in 1946. She played The Virgin in *King of Kings* (1961), and in the following year appeared in the film *The Playboy of the Western World*; her other films were *Of Human Bondage* in 1964 and *Doctor Zhivago* in 1965, her last screen role, although she had been signed up by John Huston in 1986 to play a role in his film of James Joyce's *The Dead*.

Pioneering Scots animator **Norman McLaren**, who died in Canada on 27 January 1987, at the age of 72, was born in Stirling and started to make films while still attending classes at the Glasgow School of Art. At the age of 21 he made his first animated film; when his work was shown at an amateur film festival it so impressed John Grierson – the erudite movie-maker said to have invented the word 'documentary' as applied to the film – that he invited McLaren to work with him at the then prestigious GPO Film Unit, which turned out some of the finest documentaries ever made. During this period, McLaren continued experimenting with his own unique method of making camera-less animated films by drawing the image directly on to celluloid. Later he also experimented with synthetic sound, stop-action and 3-D cartoons. In 1939 McLaren emigrated to the United States but when, two years later, John Grierson arrived in Canada to set up that country's Film Board, he sent for McLaren to join him, eventually appointing him to head the Board's animation department. But, despite all his other work, McLaren will always be best known for his drawn-on-film animated shorts, often dazzling in their colour and effects, the celluloid equivalent of the abstract school of painting, which remained unequalled to this day. Among the many awards McLaren won was the 1952 Oscar for his film *Neighbours*.

Though differing sources during his lifetime listed his birthdate as varying between 1910 and 1913, *Variety* came down firmly on 83 as the age at which **Vincente Minnelli** died at his Beverly Hills home during his post-dinner nap on 25 July 1986. Vincente's father had been a musician and his mother an actress who often appeared in her uncle's touring tent show theatre. Vincente made his first public appearance with her, at the age of three, in a

167

production of *East Lynne*, and continued to do so until he was eight and went to school. He left school at sixteen but details of his initial working life seem as indefinite as his age, with various sources claiming he was apprenticed to a photographic studio, and others that he held a similar position in a shop window display firm. Certainly, having later worked as a theatrical costume designer secured Minnelli a similar position with Paramount Theatres in 1931. After several productions he became art director for the New York Radio City Music Hall stage shows, and two years later was designing costumes and sets for several Broadway musicals, including *At Home Abroad*, starring Bea Lillie and Eleanor Powell. It was as a result of his big success with *The Ziegfeld Follies* that Paramount issued their abortive invitation to Hollywood. After more New York stage successes, Minnelli went to Hollywood in 1940 at the request of MGM, who gave him a contract and careful training for the next two years, during which he contributed sequences to several films, such as *Strike Up the Band*. In 1943 he was given his first film to direct, the black musical *Cabin in the Sky*, and two years later he made the Judy Garland musical *Meet Me in St Louis*; soon afterwards he and Judy were married. Their daughter, Liza, was born a year later. After several routine features Minnelli scored a big surprise success with his direction of the straight comedy *Father of the Bride* in 1950. In 1951 he made the classic musical *An American in Paris* – and was divorced from Judy. Another memorable musical, *The Band Wagon*, appeared in 1953, then a string of movies such as *Brigadoon* (1954), *The Cobweb* (1955), *Kismet* (same year), *Lust for Life* in 1956 and, his own favourite amongst all his productions, *Tea and Sympathy*. There followed *Designing Woman* and *The Seventh Sin* (which he took over without credit from an ailing Ronald Neame), the evergreen masterpiece *Gigi*, *The Reluctant Debutante* and *Bells Are Ringing*, all of which, though in varying degress, helped to fill the MGM coffers. Minnelli remained happily under contract for more than a quarter of a century to MGM, though his next film, the disastrous remake of *The Four Horsemen of the Apocalypse* in 1962, must have shaken them somewhat. After that

came *The Bad and the Beautiful* and the now forgotten *The Courtship of Eddie's Father*, after which he at last moved from Metro to Fox, for whom in 1964 he made *Goodbye Charlie*. Minnelli returned to the famous growling lion to make *The Sandpiper* (1965) but in 1966 he left MGM for good. It was more than four years before he made his next movie, *On a Clear Day You Can See Forever*, and in 1976 he directed his disappointing last film *A Matter of Time*, though in this he achieved his own ambition of working with daughter Liza. Minnelli is on record as saying that he never catered to audiences, that he always worked to please himself. Doubtful as to whether films were an art form, he said in his biography (*I Remember It Well*, published in 1974): '. . . if they are not, then let it be inscribed on my gravestone what they could say about any craftsman who loves his job: "Here lies Vincente Minnelli. He died of hard work." ' Married four times, he had another daughter, singer Christina Miro, by his second wife. Possibly more successfully than any other director, Minnelli was able with good taste and consistent artistry to integrate musical numbers into the flow of a film's story line. The result was a number of unforgettable and evergreen screen musicals.

The French personality **Moustache** (real name: François-Alexandre Galepides) died in Paris on 28 March 1987, after being involved in a motor car accident. One-time restaurateur, jazz drummer, orchestral leader, night-club star, composer (of songs) and Monte Carlo Rallyist, as well as actor, he played in many films including *Irma La Douce*, *Mayerling*, *A Flea in the Ear* and *Zorro*. He was 58.

British movie-goers may best recall **Anny Ondres**, the Czech actress whose real name was Anna Sophie Ondrakowa, as the centre of controversy when she starred in Alfred Hitchcock's first talkie, *Blackmail* (which was planned as a silent but was switched to sound midway through production). Her English was so impossible Hitchcock decided she should mouth the lines while off-camera Joan Barry actually spoke them. The wife of champion boxer Max Schmeling, Miss Ondres made something like 70 films in Europe and in Britain; apart from *Blackmail* she starred in *The Manxman*

for Hitchcock and also appeared in two other British silents the same year, *God's Clay* and *Glorious Youth*. She died on 28 February in Hamburg, Germany, at the age of 83.

Film-goers will best recall **Geraldine Page**, who died, aged 62, on 13 June 1987, for her marvellous, moving performance in the 1985 release *Trip to Bountiful*, which so deservedly brought her the Best Actress Oscar. A very independent-minded lady, Miss Page was very choosy about her roles and turned down many lucrative stage and film offers. A doctor's daughter, she made her professional debut when she was seventeen and in the same year (1952) that she made her Broadway stage debut appeared in two films, *Taxi* and *Hondo*. (Her first screen role had been a small one in 1947 in *Out of the Night*.) Her *Trip to Bountiful* Oscar was the culmination of seven previous nominations for either Best Actress or Best Supporting Actress in *Hondo*, *You're a Big Boy Now*, *Pete 'n' Tillie*, *Summer and Smoke*, *Sweet Bird of Youth*, *The Pope of Greenwich Village* and *Interiors*, a remarkable record for someone who made not much more than a score of movies in all. She has not been and now never will be seen in her final film role, for *Single Room*, co-starring Don Ameche, remains unfinished. Other films in which Miss Page appeared include *Walls of Glass* (also known as *Flanagan*), *My Little Girl*, *Native Son*, *Honky Tonk Freeway* and *White Nights*.

Robert Preston (real name: Robert Preston Meservey), who died on 21 March 1987 in Santa Barbara aged 68, from lung cancer, was a rugged actor with a broad, special smile whose greatest achievements came in the theatre although he served the cinema well, first with a long series of featured roles and then as a star in his own right. He made appearances in something in excess of 40 movies, among them *King of Alcatraz* (his screen debut in 1938), *Union Pacific* (1939), *North West Mounted Police* (1940), *Reap the Wild Wind*, *This Gun for Hire* (two of four films he made in 1942), *Blood on the Moon* (1948), *The Sundowners* (1950), *How the West Was Won* and *The Music Man* in 1962, *Junior Bonner* and *Child's Play* in 1972, *Mame* (1974) and, his final screen appearances, *The Last Star-*

Robert Preston.

fighter, *S.O.B.* and *Victor, Victoria.* In the last two, directed by Blake Edwards, he gave notable performances. Preston later appeared in a number of TV feature films. His successful stage career was capped by his performance in *The Music Man*, in which he starred on Broadway for two years, repeating the role, against some pretty fierce opposition, when the film was made. There's a story in Hollywood that among those given first chance to star in the movie *The Music Man* was Cary Grant; his reported reaction was, 'Not only won't I play the part but if anyone other than Preston plays it I won't even go to see the film.'

A Pinewood Studios trainee (later teamed with director Alexander Mackendrick at the old Ealing Studios, where together they made such marvellous pictures as *The Maggie* and *The Lady Killers*) American-born screenwriter **William Rose** died at his Jersey home on 10 February 1987 at the age of 68. After collaborating with other writers on several scripts, Rose got his first solo assignment with that wonderful comedy *Genevieve*. Other British and American credits include *The Smallest Show on Earth*, *The Russians Are Coming, It's a Mad, Mad, Mad, Mad World* and *Guess Who's Coming to Dinner*, for which he won an Oscar.

Randolph Scott (real name: Randolph Crane) retired in 1962 as one of the richest men in Hollywood, with a fortune reputed to be at the $100 million mark (the majority resulting from shrewd investments in oil and property). The popular cowboy star died in his sleep at his Los Angeles home on 2 March 1987. He was 89, and had been in ill health for some years. Born into a wealthy family, Scott studied engineering at the University of North Carolina, where he was one of the University's football stars. Enlisting in the Army in World War I (he was actually under age) he shocked his parents on demob by announcing that he was going to make acting his career: an accidental

meeting with Howard Hughes on the golf course led to his venturing into films as a bit player in 1929; *The Far Call* in that year was the first of his 100 films. For the first twenty years of his career Scott played in all kinds of films (including westerns, of course), in 1933 hitting a personal record of eleven movies within twelve months. He twice appeared with Fred Astaire and Ginger Rogers (in the musicals *Roberta* and *Follow the Fleet*) and was Shirley Temple's co-star in *Rebecca of Sunnybrooke Farm*. He also starred in the Mae West film *Go West, Young Man* and appeared in the Mamoulian musical *High, Wide and Handsome*, as well as in Rider Haggard's *She*, and *The Road to Reno*. But it was the last 30-odd films he made that brought him his greatest successes. They were all westerns, many of them made for his own company that he had formed with Harry Joe Brown, and under the direction of either Budd Boetticher or André de Toth, with both of whom he developed great working partnerships. After a short retirement at the end of this era Scott made a brief but outstanding return in 1962 (opposite that other great western star, Joel McCrea) in Sam Peckinpah's *Ride the High Country*. One of the greatest tributes ever paid to Scott – according to *Variety* – was made by Michael Curtiz at the completion of *Virginia City*: 'The man is a complete anachronism. He's a gentleman. And so far he's the only one I've met in this business full of self-promoting sons of bitches.'

Randolph Scott, in The Texans *with Joan Bennett.*

Though primarily known in his native America as stage actor and cabaret performer, **Dick Shawn** (real name: Richard Schulefand) appeared in more than a score of films including *The Opposite Sex* (debut in 1960), *It's a Mad, Mad, Mad, Mad World* (1961), *The Producers* (1968), *The Happy Ending* (1969), *Love at First Bite* (1969) and several others which have never reached Britain. He died while performing his act at the University of California on 17 April 1987. In his American obituaries his age was variously given as anything between 57 and 63 (the latter, according to the usually very dependable *Variety*, being correct). In Britain he will be best recalled for the role which was almost certainly his best (in films), the Hitler character in Mel Brooks' *The Producers*.

Douglas Sirk (real name: Detler Sierk) was something of a movie magician: given an indifferent or even poor script and by normal standards a tiny budget, he could still turn out a movie of some distinction, an ability which led to his becoming Universal's favourite director. Born in Hamburg of Danish parents, Sirk by the age of 22 had already had his German translations of Shakespeare's *Sonnets* published. Turning to the theatre, he was soon installed as director of the Kleines Theater in Chemnitz, subsequently holding similar posts in Bremen and Leipzig, directing well over 100 plays betwen 1922 and 1936. In 1934 he made three short films for UFA; he made some nine feature films for them before fleeing Germany in 1937, worried about the political situation there. He made a French and a Dutch film before arriving in Hollywood where, in spite of his considerable European reputation, he had to start at the bottom of the ladder; it was only in 1943 that he was given his first American directorial chance with *Hitler's Madness*. Sirk then went on to direct a string of routine movies, such as *Summer Storm* (1944), *A Scandal in Paris* (1946) and *Shockproof* in 1949, the year which saw him given his Universal contract. With them, after a series of easily forgettable films, he came into full flower in the 1950s with such notable productions as *Magnificent Obsession* (1954), *All That Heaven Allows* (1956), *The Tarnished Angels* (1958) and – his own favourite film of his output – *Written on the Wind* (1957).

A Time to Live and a Time to Die came in 1958 and his final feature *Imitation of Life* the following year. After completing this film he moved back to Europe; though plagued by illness, he taught cinema at the Munich Film School and made several interesting short films there. He later moved to a village in Switzerland and died in Lugano aged 86 on 14 January 1987. Sirk was above all else a master craftsman; he had impeccable taste, visual style and the occasional flash of inspiration, able to turn celluloid dross into something very near cinematic gold.

Though the bulk of his work and his greatest achievements were in TV – he ended up with no fewer than twenty Emmy awards to his credit – ex-press agent, ex-talent scout, sometime actor and talk show host **Walter Susskind**, who died in his native New York at the age of 66 on 22 February 1987, nevertheless produced a number of memorable movies during his career, among them his first, *Edge of the City*, in 1957, *Lovers and Other Strangers* (1970), *All Creatures Great and Small* (1974), *Alice Doesn't Live Here Anymore* (which he co-produced in 1975), *It Shouldn't Happen to a Vet* (1976) and *Buffalo Bill and the Indians* (same year), his final work for the cinema.

(Sarah) Blanche Sweet, who died from a stroke at her New York home on 6 September 1986 at the age of 90, began her theatrical training at the tender age

Blanche Sweet.

of eighteen months (both her parents were in show business). So when she began her film career at the age of thirteen she justifiably claimed that she was by then an 'old trouper'. Initially at the old Biograph studios, she worked with the major stars of the period like Mary Pickford and the Gish sisters. But it was under D. W. Griffith's direction that she began to show her full potential, in films like *The Lonedale Operator* (1911) and *Judith of Bethulia*, the movie which lifted her to major stardom in 1913. In 1915 she moved across to the Lasky Company and is generally reckoned to have given two of her best performances for them in 1923's *Anna Christie* and *Tess of the D'Urbervilles* in the following year. In 1928 she came to Britain to appear in Herbert Wilcox's *The Woman in White*. Of more than 100 films that she made, only three were talkies: *Always Together* in 1929 and *The Woman Racket* and *The Silver Horde* in 1930. She left the film studios that year to go back to the theatre and it was not until Danny Kaye offered her a small role in his *The Five Pennies* in 1959 that she again appeared before the cameras. After that she devoted herself to the preservation of old movies, as well as serving on the National Board of Review of Motion Pictures and as consultant for the Film Section of the Museum of Modern Art. In contrast to most of her contemporaries and in spite of her name, Blanche Sweet did not play the sweet, ultra-feminine heroines of the period; in fact just the opposite, usually being cast in strong character roles and even, on occasion, as something of a villainess.

A great cinema stylist whose films were always fascinating but often judged obscure, open to different interpretations and lacking in accepted storyline, Moscow-born **Andrei Tarkovsky** died of lung cancer in Paris on 29 December 1986 at the age of 54, on the eve of the British première of his acclaimed 1985 film *The Sacrifice*, about a nuclear holocaust. Prior to his enrolment in the Soviet State Institute for Cinema in 1956, Tarkovsky had studied Arabic and worked as a geological prospector. He graduated after four years at the Institute, and two years later took the Golden Lion first prize at the Venice Film Festival with his *Ivan's Childhood*. His second film, *Andrei Rublev*, completed in 1967, had its world première at the Cannes Film Festival of 1969, where it took the International Critics' Prize. Not a great favourite of his own country's regime, Tarkovsky's film was not seen in Russia until 1971. His next movie, *Solaris*, made in 1972, was supposedly a science-fiction story but was in fact a dense parable about love and life – and again drew official Russian criticism while it was winning the Jury Prize at Cannes. The next film, *The Mirror*, was another 'difficult', highly personal film with unorthodox production technique which once more upset the Soviets but brought him international acclaim. Tarkovsky's output was small, but important; every one of his seven films is a classic in its own right. It is sad that his work was cut short at such an early age.

A consistently liberal-minded man, **John Trevelyan**, who for thirteen years up to 1971 was head of the British Board of Film Censors, died in London on 15 August 1986, aged 83. Coming to the Board – originally as one of its staff examiners – in 1950 from an educational background, Trevelyan was consistent in his opinion that children should be shielded from adult films of possible bad influence, and once he went on record accusing the Board of not taking enough care to prevent this. Notwithstanding his views, he often passed films containing sequences which before his time would never have been allowed to be screened.

Best remembered by tele-viewers for his stint in the *Dr Who* series, **Patrick Troughton**, who died at the age of 67 on 28 March 1987 during an American *Dr Who* publicity tour, was one of those reliable British feature players who, while never achieving stardom, appear in a remarkable number of films with considerable success. London born and bred, Troughton won a scholarship to the Long Island Leighton Rollins Studio for Actors; after serving in the British Navy during World War II, he became a member of the Old Vic Co. His long list of film appearances includes *Hamlet*, *Chance of a Lifetime*, *Treasure Island*, *Richard III*, *The Curse of Frankenstein*, *The* (1962) *Phantom of the Opera*, *The Gorgon*, *Sindbad and the Eye of the Tiger*, *The Omen* and, in 1978, *A Hitch in Time*. He was seldom absent from the small screen, appearing in series, such as *Dr Finlay's Casebook*,

and plays, like *The Norman Conquests*. His most recent appearances were in the 1985 series *Knights of God*.

Playing heroes or villains came equally easy to 6′ 4″ toughie **Forrest Tucker**, who died aged 71 on 21 October 1986. After a spell with a Washington theatrical company (which ended when it was discovered he was under age) Tucker joined the US Army. Settling his age was always a problem: it's variously quoted as any year between 1915 and 1919. However, two years later and a civilian again, he returned to the theatre, and after appearing in a number of shows, was tested and then signed by Samuel Goldwyn, who launched him on his film career with a role in his 1940 production *The Westerner*. The following year Tucker made two films, *Emergency Landing* and *New Wine*, then re-joined the Army as a private, serving for three years. Back to filming in 1946, he made four movies that year, including *The Yearling*. Films that followed included *Fighting Coastguard*, *Pony Express*, *Bugles in the Afternoon*, *The Quiet Gun*, *Auntie Mame* and *Fort Massacre*. Tucker also appeared in a number of British films, including *Laughing Anne*, *Trouble in the Glen*, *Break in the Circle* and *The Abominable Snowman*. For three-and-a-half years he toured in *The Music Man* and in 1964 made his Broadway debut in *Fair Game for Lovers*. From 1968, when he appeared in *The Night They Raided Minsky's*, he divided his time pretty equally between filming and TV. His

Forrest Tucker.

final two films, in 1985, were *Thunder Run* and *Out-take*.

Popular British feature player **Patrick Waddington** started his film career in the old silent films and took the talkies in his stride, appearing in a large number of them, including *The Wooden Horse* and *School for Secrets*. He died on 4 February 1987 at the age of 86.

Hal B(rent). Wallis was one of Hollywood's most successful, prolific and completely professional producers, with more than 400 films to his credit – 32 of which won Oscars in various categories. Born in Chicago, Wallis had to cut short his schooling in order to help support his family; starting as an office boy, he graduated to the position of travelling salesman for an electrical firm. When he was 23 the family moved to Los Angeles and Wallis quickly succeeded in being appointed manager of one of the city's largest cinemas, a situation which brought him to the notice of the Warner brothers; impressed by him, they offered him the job as head of publicity for their studio. In 1928 they promoted him, first to Studio Manager and then Production Executive. But one morning in 1933 when he arrived at the studio, Wallis found a workman changing the name on his office door: without prior notice, the studio had brought in Darryl Zanuck to take over his job (the story goes that Wallis's reaction was amusement!). When Zanuck moved on to Fox two years later, Wallis was reinstated in his old job. During his time with Warners, he produced some of their best films and greatest hits, starting with classics like *Dawn Patrol* and *Little Caesar* in 1930 and continuing with such famous titles as *I Am a Fugitive from a Chain Gang*, *G-Men*, *Anthony Adverse*, *Jezebel*, *Four Daughters*, *Dark Victory*, *Now, Voyager*, *Sergeant York*, *Juarez*, *King's Row*, *The Maltese Falcon*, *Casablanca*, *Yankee Doodle Dandy*, *High Sierra*, *The Old Maid* and *Roaring Twenties*. In 1944 he left Warners to form his own Hall Wallis Productions, continuing to make outstanding movies like *Gunfight at the O.K. Corral*, *Barefoot in the Park*, *Mary Queen of Scots*, *True Grit* and, his last production, in 1975, *Rooster Cogburn*. During the fifty years of his career he launched many subsequently famous stars, such as Burt Lancaster, Kirk Douglas, Charlton Heston, Shirley MacLaine . . . and so many others. Always honest and modest, he is on record as saying he was 'a pretty lucky fellow' – but it is obvious that with the luck went a very considerable talent. Always conscious of costs, Wallis kept a tight rein on his budgets; lavishly spending or wasteful directors soon found that out when they went to work for him. He expected value for money, and some found him on the cool, even cold, side because of that. In poor health for several years, he died in his sleep at his Californian home on 5 October 1986 aged 88. The perfect professional, Wallis will need no elaborate tombstone to keep his memory green: 400 films, without one dud among them, will be an everlasting memorial.

High Priest of Pop Art and maker (in one way or another) of a large number of films and non-films, **Andy Warhol** died suddenly and unexpectedly in New York on 22 February 1987 at the age of 59. Famous for his silkscreen work – who hasn't seen his pictures of the Campbell's soup can or his portrait of Marilyn Monroe? – Warhol went enthusiastically into films in 1963. He produced a number of long, dreary and utterly boring movies such as his *Sleep* – in which the camera remained fixed on a man sleeping for an interminable eight hours – and his equally ridiculous and wholly static film of the Empire State Building. Originally the sound he used in his productions was as crude as his 'scripts' were nebulous, but in his later works this became more professional; eventually his action and story on occasion bore some resemblance to normality. The casts he used were often pretty repellent, though: transvestites, oddballs, eccentrics, with names like Candy Darling and Ingrid Superstar. Warhol's most commercial films came in the early 1970s, highlighted by his fright duo *Flesh for Frankenstein* and *Blood for Dracula* in 1974. Another of his more commercial efforts, *Flesh*, in 1968, made a star of Joe Dallessandro. One of his strangest films, made in 1967, was his '★★★★' which ran for 25 hours and had two quite separate, simultaneous reels of film superimposed on the screen. About the same time he made his controversial *Nude Restaurant*, in two versions, in one of which the players were completely nude and in the other had minimal

covering. His *Blue Movie* in 1969 was the first time that explicit sex had been shown on the screen (an erotic novelty which undoubtedly paved the way for the more daring scenes in many movies of the 1970s). Warhol's output was so prodigious – literally hundreds of films between the ludicrously long to the snappily short – combined with his 1,000-plus paintings and prints, his magazine publishing and his TV talk shows, that it is quite impossible to do more than include this thumbnail notice about him here. Whatever one may think of the quality and worth of his art, in several media, Warhol's influence on all of them has been considerable, and can certainly be seen in many of the commercial films produced today.

Maker of some of Britain's finest short and feature documentaries, **Harry Watt** died on 2 April 1987 at the age of 80. Born and bred in Scotland, Watt, after a number of jobs, joined the Empire Marketing Board's film unit in 1931, working under John Grierson. After learning the ropes, Watt became Robert Flaherty's assistant in the making of the classic *Man of Aran* in 1934. Then, working alone, he made some outstanding wartime documentaries including *Night Mail, Target for Tonight, North Sea, London Can Take It* and

Keenan Wynn.

Dover: Front Line. Joining Ealing Studios towards the end of World War II, he made several features for them including *Fiddlers Three* (1944), *The Overlanders* (1946), *Eureka Stockade* (1949), *Where No Vultures Fly* (1951) and, in 1959, *The Siege of Pinchgut*, which had the sad distinction of being the last film to be made at Ealing before the studios were handed over to the BBC.

Keenan Wynn (real name: Francis Xavier Aloysius Jeremiah Keenan Wynn) died from cancer at his home, aged 70, on 14 October 1986. He certainly had showbiz in his blood: his father was the famous comic and actor Ed Wynn, his mother, Hilda Keenan, was an accomplished actress, and his grandfather, Frank Keenan, was a Broadway actor and silent film star. Keenan's output was quite extraordinary: he appeared in something over 220 films, 100 stage productions and 250 TV series and movies. Starting as prop boy at the age of seventeen in a Maine theatre summer season, he made his acting debut in repertory, appearing with more than 70 companies during the next five years. He was already something of a veteran (having by then appeared in 21 Broadway productions) when in 1942 MGM signed him up and gave him his first film role in *Northwest Rangers*. Screen roles followed in quick succession until his contract expired and he freelanced, as busily as ever, in movies like *The Man in the Grey Flannel Suit, The Abominable Snowman, Dr Strangelove, The Great Race, Finian's Rainbow* and *Nashville*. Musicals, comedies, dramas, thrillers and westerns, as hero or villain – Wynn went from one picture to another without a break. His final film appearance in *Hyper Sapien* had yet to be shown at the time of his death. Strangely, in spite of his succession of brilliant supporting roles and critical acclaim, Keenan was never even nominated for an Oscar. The small screen was his favourite medium and he was a familiar figure, latterly in *Dallas*. In later years hard of hearing (the result of his aeroplane, speedboat, motorcycle and motor racing: he held the Manhattan hydroplane speed record between 1934 and 1951), he spent a lot of time lecturing on hearing matters. A versatile, reliable and often brilliant supporting player, Keenan Wynn will be hard to replace.

Film Books of the Year

IVAN BUTLER

Included in this year's list are a number of earlier titles which, owing to an unavoidable lack of space, had to be excluded from *Film Review 1986–7*.

The following is a purely personal choice, in alphabetical order, of a dozen books which seem of particular interest in various aspects of the cinema:

The American Film Industy – a Historical Dictionary, Anthony Slide;
Filming Literature, Neil Sinyard;
The Films of René Clair, 2 vols, R. C. Dale;
The Great Spy Pictures, vol. 2, James Robert Parrish and Michael R. Pitts;
Hollywood – Legend and Reality, ed. Michael Webb;
Horror, ed. Phil Hardy;
The Illustrated History of the Cinema, ed. Ann Lloyd and David Robinson;
Images of Children in American Film, Kathy Merlock Jackson;
A Life in Movies, Michael Powell;
Orson Welles – a Celebration, John Russell Taylor;
People Will Talk, John Kobal;
The United Artists Story, Ronald Bergen.

A welcome to two volumes of a very promising new series: *Poland*, Frank Bren, and *Sweden*, Brian McIlroy.
Stop press: Welcome news, too, is that Denis Gifford's unique and indispensable *British Film Catalogue* (first published in 1972 and long out of print) is now available from David & Charles in a new edition revised and updated to 1985, covering 90 years and 16,500 films, price £45.

Alec Guinness – The Films, Kenneth von Gunden; McFarland & Co, dist. Bailey Bros. & Swinfen, £25.95
This is the first fully detailed study of Sir Alec's films, and a splendid one it turns out to be. Apart from synopsis and discussion of each film in chronological order, the author gives biographical and other information on dozens of the actors and directors with whom Guinness has worked, providing a living and colourful background. An excel-

lent filmography gives cast-and-credit lists extending in several cases over a full page, and an unusually interesting appendix gives similar details of other players concerned, together with awards received by the films in question. The commentaries and criticisms throughout are lively and informative, and there are a good number of fine stills. It is pleasant to think that from America should come so warm and appreciative a study of a leading British film actor.

Alfred Hitchcock and the British Cinema, Tom Ryall; Croom Helm Books, £13.95
After a somewhat heavy-going introductory chapter on 'Hitchcock and Criticism', this develops into an interesting examination, mainly of his British films, so often given short shrift in comparison with the Hollywood output. It is good to find them given due attention here, particularly as much is included about their relationship to the British cinema scene of the period. Despite its modest size, this is solid reading, aimed at the serious student rather than the more casual film watcher, with many very lengthy paragraphs and detailed theorizing; but for anyone really interested in Hitchcock it has something new to say. Full notes are given to each chapter, and there is a modest section of illustrations.

The American Film Industry – A Historical Dictionary, Anthony Slide; Greenwood Press, dist. Westport Publications Ltd, £49.95
The scope of this excellent reference book is far wider than its title may suggest. Not only does it contain all the expected business entries, including concise histories of every studio, but it deals also with *genres* (musicals, horror, westerns, *film noir*), series (*Andy Hardy*, *Thin Man*), technical terms and dozens of associated subjects. In other words it is not only essential for libraries, historians and other students, but of interest to anyone concerned with the cinema. Well worth the admittedly rather high price, as it is both comprehensive and packed with fascinating details.

The American Films of Michael Curtiz, Ron Kinnard and R. J. Vitone; Scarecrow Press, dist. Bailey Bros. & Swinfen, £15
Perhaps because he has made so many purely commercial successes – from Errol Flynn's *Robin Hood* to *Casablanca* – Michael Curtiz has not had as much serious critical attention as many other directors. This excellent, concise but detailed study makes handsome amends. The author takes us through the entire body of Curtiz's American films (the first of these being No 79 in the list of his enormous, complete output, including the Hungarian, Austrian and German productions), covering the most important ones at some length. The filmography is exemplary in its comprehensiveness; there are two indexes (Names and Titles) and a number of excellent stills. A biographical introduction completes an important addition to the film reference bookshelf.

The American Indian In Film, Michael Hilger; Scarecrow Press, dist. Bailey Bros. & Swinfen, £18.50
This is a useful handbook on a specialized subject. Each chapter (Silent; Early Sound; 1950s and 1960s; 1970 and 1980s) starts with an essay on certain key productions, followed by a chronological list with title, production company and brief comment. Cast lists are mainly restricted to Indian characters, a full Names index indicating whether the player is an Indian or a non-Indian actor. In addition, a detailed 'Topical' index is sub-divided into sections such as Bad or Good Indians, Companies, Criticisms, Historical Events and Figures, Literary Sources, Love and Marriage, Studios, Tribes, etc., an unusual and would-be useful aid to investigation, though apt to tail off on occasion into a mass of unspecified page numbers. There is a small section of illustrations – not quite up to the usual Scarecrow standard.

Australian Cinema, 1970–1985, Brian McFarlane; Secker & Warburg, £9.95
A useful handbook on the remarkable recent years of Australian film, which include such

widely known productions as *Picnic at Hanging Rock*, *Walkabout* and *Caddie*, in addition to such disappointments as *The Year of Living Dangerously*. Some of the stills are rather poorly reproduced and one would have welcomed (in this quite highly priced paperback) more reference material, such as a list of directors' filmographies; but this is still a recommendable and well-documented survey of an astonishing success story.

Backstory, Pat McGilligan; University of California Press, £23

Interviews with, analyses and lives of the great directors are numerous – dare one say on occasion more numerous than necessary – so it is good to welcome for a change a first-class book of interviews with the often under-credited *writers* of the Golden Era. Most of them, interviewed by a variety of fellow writers, prove themselves as articulate in speech as on paper; the result is a very revealing and informative collection, with amusing and often trenchant comments on their craft, their lives and their associates. They include Charles Bennett (known for his work with Hitchcock), W. R. Burnett, James M. Cain and Donald Ogden Stewart. Credit lists, often difficult to compile accurately in this field, are given as fully as possible; biographical paragraphs, a double index and a number of photographs round off a useful reference book and an entertaining volume of reminiscences.

The Best of Rob Wagner's *Script*, ed. Anthony Slide, Scarecrow Press, dist. Bailey Bros. & Swinfen, £15

An entertaining oddity, In addition to various other activities connected with the cinema, Wagner ran a Beverly Hills journal he named *Script* from 1929 until he died in 1942, when it was taken over by members of the family. Anthony Slide has collected about 50 articles, short stories and poems, most of which are short. Included among the contributors are Charlie Chaplin (several articles and a poem), Eddie Cantor, Ernst Lubitsch, William Saroyan, Ray Bradbury and Lillian Gish. From Gene Lockhard, there is a poem entitled 'Little Orson Annie' and a brilliant 1942 *Mikado* skit aimed against the Axis Powers.

Bette Davis – A Celebration, Alexander Walker; Pavilion, £12.95

Another in the Celebration series of large-format illustrated biographies, well up to standard with plenty of good stills, portraits and production photographs, written in Alexander Walker's usual lively style. An illustrated filmography of 95 films (including TV) up to 1983 and a short list of stage work round off a handsome volume.

Brian De Palma, Michael Bliss, Scarecrow Press, dist. Bailey Bros. & Swinfen, £15.00

De Palma's films may not be everybody's cup of tea (or draught of blood, perhaps) but there is no denying his magnificent visual power – as Anthony Slide, editor of this Film-makers series, points out. Who could forget, for instance, the deeply uneasy feeling conjured up by the first view of the 'memorial' in *Obsession*, or the apocalyptic vision of the avenging *Carrie* in the film of that name? Mr Bliss has written an excellent analysis of De Palma's films up to and including *Blow Out* (1983), together with a lengthy interview and a full filmography.

Cagney, Doug Warren with James Cagney; Robson Books, £4.95

A paperback edition of the 'authorized biography' reviewed in *Film Review 1984–5*. Sound, straightforward, appreciative, not unduly adulatory. Filmography, and two good sections of illustrations.

Cary Grant – A Celebration, Richard Schickel; Pavilion, £8.95

Cary Grant joins Orson Welles, Alec Guinness and other notables in this prestigious series (in paperback this time), with a lively and perceptive text accompanying a vast number of fully captioned, excellent illustrations. The detailed filmography also is well up to standard, with an additional still for each movie.

A Cast of Killers, Sidney Kirkpatrick; Hutchinson, £10.95

No sooner did I recommend (in *Film Review 1986–7*) Jonathan Goodman's fascinating book of screen and stage crime, *Acts of Murder*, for the fullness of its account of the William Desmond Taylor case in Hollywood 1922, than along comes this enthralling story of the director King Vidor's exhaustive investigation with a view to making a film of it. This is, surely, the very final word on a mystery that has intrigued the curious for years. Vidor's solution seems incontrovertible: apart from setting out the appallingly complicated details with admirable clarity, Mr Kirkpatrick paints a vivid picture of life in the film colony at the time – not quite the Age of Innocence, after all. Among the 'cast' are Mabel Normand, Mary Miles Minter and her mother; Antonio Moreno, Douglas MacLean and his wife in minor parts; the Los Angeles Police Department; and of course Taylor himself. Helping Vidor in his searchings after truth was the indestructible and unforgettable Colleen Moore, great jazz-age star. The period of Vidor's investigations was the late 1960s; at the end of his book Sidney Kirkpatrick describes her some twenty years later 'as young, vibrant, ambitious and loving at age eighty-four as she was

when she took Hollywood by storm at the age of seventeen'.

Caught in the Act, Richard Todd; Hutchinson, £12.95

A very enjoyable, genial and generous autobiography covering the author's life of the 1950s. The main part of the book is devoted to his war-time experiences, and very amusing and at times exciting they are. But there are also accounts of his early stage work, in particular with the Dundee Repertory Company, and after the war of his films such as *The Hasty Heart* and in particular working with Hitchcock in *Stage Fright*. A second volume is apparently on its way.

Charlton Heston: the Epic Presence, Bruce Crowther; Columbus Books, £7.95

Suggesting that, with few exceptions (notably *Will Penny*), Heston has not really essayed a role that fully realized his potential, the author follows his career in an excellently detailed study, making the point that the ultimate test of *King Lear* might – and should – lie ahead. He also underlines the error of regarding Heston as mainly a star in epic films simply because his best-known roles have been such – Moses in *The Ten Commandments*, and *Ben-Hur*. Every production from the early *Peer Gynt* (1942) to *Nairobi* (1984) is covered, demonstrating an unexpectedly wide range of characterizations, with only too many occasions on which Heston's ability to display his full power has been cramped by the confines of the script, in particular where comedy is concerned. It is an interesting and entertaining account with plenty of good stills and an adequate filmography.

The Columbia Comedy Shorts, Ted Okuda with Edward Watz; McFarland & Co, dist. Bailey Bros. & Swinfen, £29.95

Between 1933 and 1958 the Columbia Studios produced over 500 two-reel comedy shorts, of which probably the 'Three Stooges' series is most often seen on TV screens today. Other names, often well-known from the silent days, are the George Sidney/Charlie Murray team, Harry Langdon, Andy Clyde, the much underrated Charley Chase and – sadly – Buster Keaton. Sadly because, as the author says, these short comedies were the worst films he ever appeared in – only a few years after the matchless *The General*. This book has an invaluable collection of hitherto little-known information and unseen stills. It includes accounts, synopses and casts of every film, and over 50 pages of biographical details, mainly concerning the lesser-known players.

Courtroom's Finest Hour in American Cinema, Thomas J. Harris; Scarecrow Press, dist. Bailey Bros. & Swinfen, £17.50

At first glance this somewhat clumsily titled book might seem to indicate a haphazard dip into an overflowing bran barrel to pick out such movies as come to hand. The author's contention, however, is that the hundreds of courtroom scenes in earlier films were merely 'diverting entertainments' and that it was only in the past 30 years or so that they began to show what he describes as 'redeeming social significance'. He also makes the valid point that such films have resulted in some of the best acting and direction from those participating in them. As examples he selects eight key productions, from *Twelve Angry Men* to *The Verdict*: the first seven having been made in the four years from 1957 to 1961 and the last (significantly) after an interval of 21 years, in 1982. He discusses all of them (and refers to many more) cogently and vividly, causing the reader to look forward to the next courtroom appearance in the cinema or on TV; and his book is well documented, illustrated and indexed.

Curtis Bernhardt, interviewed by Mary Kiersch; Scarecrow Press, dist. Bailey Bros. & Swinfen, £19.50

This is one of a series issued, in conjunction with the Directors' Guild of America, as 'oral histories', in which book-length interviews are conducted with film-makers. With the exception of King Vidor, the first seven in the list are comparatively lesser-known names. The advantages of this method are that the discussions of their work are mainly in their own words; and the breaking-up of pages into Question and Answer paragraphs makes for easier assimilation than in the case of weightier tomes. One disadvantage – in this case at any rate – is that the questioner is apt to interrupt an interesting answer by abruptly switching to another subject, resulting in a series of *non-sequiturs*; another is that some of the longer questions appear to have almost a didactic approach, putting answers into the speaker's mouth. They are in fact statements rather than questions. This may well be due to the fact that the words can only be read; could we actually hear the interview, it would doubtless sound different. It starts off with a rather charming personal exchange, and has quite a few moments of humour as well as information. Indexes of film titles and of subjects are provided – but no illustrations (except for a frontispiece portrait) in a book that surely cries out for them.

The Dead That Walk, Leslie Halliwell; Grafton Books, £12.95

Leslie Halliwell, staunch champion of 1930s and 1940s movies, breaks new ground here rather surprisingly with a detailed and painstakingly researched examination of the Emperors of Horror: Dracula, Frankenstein and the Mummy, with a note on Zombies as runners-up. It is much more than a mere discussion of the films; he digs deep into the underlying reasons for their deathless popularity, and that of their literary and dramatic counterparts, including long extracts from novels and films. His own writing has all its usual gusto and humour. Plenty of stills, together with portraits of Conan Doyle, W. W. Jacobs and other practitioners.

Debrett Goes to Hollywood, Charles Kidd; Weidenfeld & Nicolson, £9.95

This wholly fascinating coffee-table book traces the family trees of famous Hollywood dynasties with the aid of numerous genealogical tables, including the ingenious and recently invented 'lateral tree'. Among the names to be found in it are the Barrymores, Norma Shearer, Elizabeth Taylor, Tyrone Power and the Marquis de la Falaise; but there are also many surprises cropping up among the branches, perhaps the most unexpected being the linking of Sir Winston Churchill and Groucho Marx (courtesy of Howard Hawks). The author suggests a British book may follow; in the meantime this is constantly entertaining, researched and written by the editor of the august *Debrett's Peerage and Baronetage*, and embellished with numerous good illustrations and a full index.

D. W. Griffith and the Biograph Company. Cooper C. Graham, Steven Higgins, Elaine Mancini and Joao Luiz Vieira, Scarecrow Press, dist. Bailey Bros. & Swinfen, £29.50

Without surprise, one learns that it took the compilers six years to complete this mammoth reference work, which lists every film that Griffith made at the Biograph Company from 1908 to 1914. The first section gives the film credits, dates, length, etc, and cast list (including, where possible, the characters played); the second section comprises a filmography of those involved, technically and/or creatively. When one considers that many actors appeared in well over 100 productions *per year* (for instance, in the case of cameraman Billy Bitzer, the list fills over three pages), the scale of research involved can be appreciated. An appendix gives the names of many (including some as well-known as the Talmadge sisters) whose claims to have appeared in Biograph pictures cannot be verified: 'a guide for future research' say the authors, should anyone have the courage to embark on it!

It may be argued that so much work on such films – of which most of us will only ever see a fraction – is 'purely academic', but this is a question of the evolution of an art form. To any student, the mere fact that, for instance, Mack Sennett played 'A Drunkard' in a 1910 film entitled *The Gold-Seekers* will probably be a matter of interest; and it is surprising to read that *all* Biograph films exist in some form, even if all are not accessible as positive reference prints.

A superb addition to early film history, this is No. 10 in the *Film-makers* series, under the editorship of the indefatigable Anthony Slide.

Film As Film, V. F. Perkins; Pelican Books, £2.95

Described as 'an introduction to appreciation and criticism of the cinema', this is a reprint of the book first published in 1972 (at 35p!) and recommended in *Film Review 1973-4* for its clarity and freedom from pretentious obscurity. The author deliberately does not dwell only on the famous and the masterpieces; his examples range from *Psycho* to *House of Wax*, from *Elmer Gantry* to *The Courtship of Eddie's Father*, and his remarks and conclusions are as relevant today as they were when his book originally appeared.

Filmfront, annotated by Anthony Slide; Scarecrow Press, dist. Bailey Bros. & Swinfen, £15

Filmfront was a fairly extreme left-wing magazine which lasted for five issues during 1934-5. These have been collected together and reprinted here in their entirety and almost exactly in their original mimeographed form, even to the use of the original typed symbols. The book contains many and varied articles, comments, criticism, information and some rather elementary practical advice on technical problems of film-making. It is of interest both as a piece of sociological record and as representing a particular, if limited, aspect of the cinema of the period, though the assessment of almost every film on the basis of how closely it does or does not coincide with the Party line makes for a certain rather depressing monotony – particularly as much of the invective is somewhat juvenile. During its short life, however, *Filmfront* obviously represented the viewpoint of a small number of film-goers, and Anthony Slide has done a useful job in disinterring it.

Filming Literature – The Art of Screen Adaptation, Neil Sinyard; Croom Helm, £12.95

This is surely a model of what a work of film analysis should be; clear, concise, illuminating, almost wholly free of the woolly theorizing and pseudo-profundities that so often render such studies almost unreadable. A large number of 'films of the book' are discussed in relation to their originals, the authors covered ranging from Shakespeare to L. P. Hartley. Two final chapters deal with 'bio-pics', those generally dreadful travesties, limited here to lives of writers, and with filmed plays, including an opening paragraph setting out the essential differences between theatre and cinema. Mr

Sinyard is particularly interesting in his opening chapter on Shakespeare; on Orwell's *1984*, Dickens' *Great Expectations*, Henry James' *The Turn of the Screw*; and above all in a special section on *The Go-Between*, which should increase the reader's and viewer's appreciation of both film and novel. The whole book is stimulating, shot through with some splendidly pithy comments, essential reading for anyone seriously interested in either film or literature.

The Films of Alfred Hitchcock, Neil
Sinyard; Admiral, £9.95
Perhaps inevitably, with so much already written about the life and work of Hitchcock, much of the ground travelled in Mr Sinyard's book is familiar territory. Nevertheless, he casts a fresh and penetrating eye on his subject and has numerous interesting points to make: if his book is as much a summing-up as a new investigation, it is still stimulating, enthusiastic and eminently readable. The photographs are excellent, in many cases rare, and very well arranged. The huge double-page spread of *Marnie* for instance (pp. 126–7) takes full advantage of the central division to illustrate one of Hitchcock's most exciting moments of suspense. It is a pity, however, that in the caption on p. 22 the author perpetuates the error that the girl is Anne Grey – it is, in fact, Ann Casson, daughter of Dame Sybil Thorndike. A brief final section deals with the influence of Hitchcock on other directors – such as Truffaut, Chabrol and Brian de Palma – rounding off a welcome addition to the literature on the Master of Suspense.

The Films of René Clair, I & II, R. C.
Dale; Scarecrow Press, dist. Bailey Bros. & Swinfen, £79.50
This two-volume examination of Clair's entire output (filling together over 1,000 pages) must be one of the fullest single-handed accounts of any director's work. It is divided into two separate approaches. The first, Exposition and Analysis, contains brief synopses of all the films, biographical details, cast lists and various notes; the second, Documentation, consists mainly of far more detailed relation of the stories – almost shot by shot – together with excerpts from Clair's writings. Each volume is fully illustrated and has its own index. The author was in touch with the director, by interview or correspondence, for ten years. Despite the scholarly tone and purpose of the book, his style is light and lucid enough to make for easy reading, even in the extremely detailed story-telling of the second volume. This is an essential guide for any close study of René Clair's work.

The Films of the Seventies, William J.
Palmer; Scarecrow Press, dist. Bailey Bros. & Swinfen, £25
A social history in which, as the author says,

the films are the stars – not the actors nor the critics. Many films are referred to and several, regarded as of special significance, are discussed in great detail. These include *Chinatown*, *Network*, *The Conversation* and *Blow-Up*. The latter, of course, was made in the mid-1960s and is often regarded as *the* film which reflects the spirit of that crucial decade; but the author considers that in terms of film history the 1970s begin with its appearance: the long examination of it is one of the most interesting parts of his book. Not unexpectedly, much space is also devoted to the cinema's attitudes to the Vietnam war, and a final section deals with Australian war films. A useful study both for the serious film buff and the social historian. A couple of stills are used to illustrate particular points; a few more would have been welcome.

Columbus Filmmakers series:
Alfred Hitchcock, Gene D. Phillips; Columbus Books, £5.95
Chaplin, Julian Smith; Columbus Books, £5.95
Steven Spielberg, D. R. Mott and C. M. Saunders; Columbus Books, £5.95
New German Cinema, James Franklin; Columbus Books, £5.95
These are the first four volumes in an enterprising new series of paperbacks on filmmakers. The first two cover well-trodden paths, but manage to find something fresh to say about their subject. In these, and in the Spielberg book, the approach is straightforward, dealing with every film in chronological order, nicely combining entertainment with scholarship. *New German Cinema* is rather heavier going, analysing the work of seven directors and dealing on the whole with less familiar films. The author of *Hitchcock* is rightly severe in pointing out the errors of other writers but substitutes several of his own, e.g.: 'Rachel' Low (for Rachael), Daphne du Maurier as Gerald du Maurier's 'niece' (she was his daughter) and, in the still on p. 69, 'Anne Grey' (it is in fact Ann Casson). Illustrations and stills are rather sparse (non-existent in *Spielberg*), but all four books are thoroughly documented and could form the nucleus of a useful library of introductory studies.

The First Tycoons, Richard Dyer
MacCann; Scarecrow Press, dist. Bailey Bros. & Swinfen, £22.50
This is the first of a five-volume series dealing with the earliest years of American cinema – the fifth will cover the films of the 1920s. This one consists of extracts from a large number of histories, autobiographies and memoirs from those concerned directly or indirectly with a period of often frenzied wheeling and dealing. It may be a book for the specialist rather than the general reader, with few illustrations, but it is skilfully put

together to form a coherent picture, and has sufficient human interest to hold the attention of any keen student of cinematic history. Appendices include a useful bibliography.

Five Screenplays by Preston Sturges, ed.
Brian Henderson; University of California Press, £15.95
This stout paperback contains photocopies of the final shooting scripts of *The Great McGinty*, *Christmas in July*, *The Lady Eve*, *Sullivan's Travels* and *Hail the Conquering Hero*, together with exhaustive notes and analyses in each case, a lengthy Introduction and some illustrations. Essential for the historian and the student, and, since the scripts are very clearly set out and easy to follow, for the 'ordinary buff' also.

Franklin J. Schaffner, Erwin Kim,
Scarecrow Press, dist. Bailey Bros. & Swinfen, £35
This is No. 9 in the excellent *Film-makers* series, edited by Anthony Slide, in what might be described as the 'Scarecrow Uniform Edition' of cinema books. This volume is a long one, close on 500 pages. The first part deals with Schaffner's extensive television career; the second and much longer part is devoted to his films. As there are only about a dozen of these, it means that far more space than usual can be given to the examination of each one – among the best-known being *Planet of the Apes*, *Patton*, *Papillon* and *The Boys from Brazil*. It is a scholarly and thoroughly researched work, with copious notes and a large bibliography. Despite his comparatively small output, Schaffner (born in Tokyo in 1920) is definitely a character in the cinema world, (a fact that is brought out in this well-written study containing plenty of interesting ancillary information).

The Golden Gong, Quentin Falk;
Columbus Books, £8.95
In this account of the Rank Organization and Pinewood Studios, published as a companion to a BBC documentary with the same title, the author takes us briefly and painlessly through the complications of the business side, then devotes most of his space to the films and cinema personalities themselves, covering dozens of productions, from the fiasco of *Cleopatra* to the fun and games of the *Carry On . . .* series. This is a lighter-weight book than his excellent study of the cinema of Graham Greene (*Travels in Greenland*), but it is informative as well as entertaining, with a useful filmography as well as a wealth of anecdotes – very evidently a celebratory undertaking. Excellent (and lavish) stills, both black-and-white and coloured, attractively presented in glossy soft-cover.

The Goldwyn Touch, Michael Freedland;
    Harrap, £9.95

This is a lively biography of Sam Goldwyn, full of good stories, familiar with not so familiar, with plenty of references to the notorious malapropisms. Some myths also are debunked; his name, for instance, was not originally Goldfish, nor even Goldfisch, but Gelbfisz. Life in Hollywood is covered from the earliest days – the famous first feature of Lasky, Goldwyn and DeMille, *The Squaw Man* – to 1974 when Sam, as he was universally known, died at the age of 91. In addition to the lighter side, full emphasis is given to his great and valuable contribution to the cinema. He may have said (as the author repeats several times) 'include me out', but he also produced, among many others, such films as *The Best Years of Our Lives*, *Dodsworth*, *The Little Foxes* and *Dead End*. Despite an occasional jokiness in style that becomes a little wearing at times, this is an entertaining and informative biography.

The Great Spy Pictures, vol. 2, James
    Robert Parrish and Michael R. Pitts;
    Scarecrow Press, dist. Bailey Bros. &
    Swinfen, £39.50

The second volume of this excellent reference book brings the coverage from 1974 to 1985, but it also includes a great deal more. A vast number of earlier films omitted from the previous volume (recommended in *Film Review 1976–7*) are to be found here, from the silent years on. All receive comprehensive cast-and-credits list, brief but adequate commentary and, in many cases, a contemporary review. TV movies and serials (such as *Tinker, Tailor, Soldier, Spy*) are also covered, together with foreign-language productions. An invaluable bonus is the enormous bibliography, single novels and series, which fills over 60 pages. There are a number of good illustrations. Taking the two volumes together, the spy *genre* must now be almost as well documented as horror, musical and western.

Harrison Ford, Minty Clinch; New English
    Library, £12.95

This is a standard showbiz biography, but written in a pleasantly lively and entertaining style, presenting an attractive portrait of a modest but forthright film star who regards his astonishing rise to superstardom with unassuming clearsightedness. His unusual name undoubtedly caused many older film-goers to wonder whether there was any relationship with the very well-known (not 'long-forgotten') silent star who died as recently as 1957. This, it appears, is not the case – though he states disarmingly that he would be happy to share the 'old guy's' concrete footprint in the Hollywood Boulevard rather than have one of his own. It is cheering to read of his hatred for the appalling 'Indy' hat he was compelled to wear in

Raiders of the Lost Ark – a hatred surely shared by most of his audience.

Harrison Ford, Paul Honeyford; Sidgwick
    & Jackson, £9.95

It may at first sight seem rather premature for a full-length biography on Harrison Ford, but it is perhaps surprising to realize that he has been in films for some 20 years. Starting as a bellboy in *Dead Heat on a Merry-go-round* (1966), he has in that period appeared in five of what are claimed to be among the most profitable movies ever made. He is also nearer 40 than 30 years old. His rise, in fact, was not as meteoric as is generally imagined, and for some time he found his skill at carpentry a useful alternative to making movies! This is a brief but business-like showbiz biography. Good stills and filmography – but no index.

Heart to Heart with Robert Wagner, Diana
    Maychick and L. Avon Borgo; Robson
    Books, £8.95

As implied in the title, a punning reference to Wagner's TV series *Hart to Hart*, this is biography somewhat in the 'soap' style, but pleasantly readable, the first full account of an actor equally well-known in the cinema (36 titles in the filmography) and on TV. There is also, of course, much about Natalie Wood, including a moving account of her tragic death. Tragedy again affected Wagner a few years later when young Samantha Smith, the schoolgirl who became world-famous after visiting the USSR at the invitation of Chairman Andropov, was killed in an air crash during the making of the TV series *Lime Street*, in which he was playing her father.

Henry King's America, Walter Coppedge;
    Scarecrow Press, dist. Bailey Bros. &
    Swinfen, £17.50

This is another of Anthony Slide's Filmmakers series which concentrates usefully on the less 'written-up' workers in the medium. King's film career, first as actor and writer but mainly as sensitive director of so many aspects of American life, lasted from 1915 to the early 1960s. Five major productions from his large output are selected here for special treatment: the silent *Tol'able David* and *Stella Dallas*, the enchanting early sound version of *State Fair*, and two westerns, *Jesse James* and the unforgettable *The Gunfighter*. The book, a warm and welcome tribute to this fine director, concludes with a useful reference section in the form of a full chronology of life and work; but, regrettably, there is no index.

Hollywood – Legend and Reality, ed.
    Michael Webb; Pavilion, £25

This sumptuously produced book deals with all the main activities of film-making, with

separate chapters on Production, Design, Cinematography, Costume, Special Effects, etc., based largely on extracts from the writings of, or interviews with, those chiefly involved. An introductory section gives a brief history of the growth of Hollywood, and another examines the popular myths that have grown up around it. The whole is embellished with a lavish and unique collection of superb illustrations – in colour and black-and-white – depicting the various activities, as well as stills and historical photographs. Also included is a fine reproduction of Edward Hopper's wonderfully evocative painting, *New York Movie, 1939*. Derived from an American museum exhibition opened in 1986 by the Smithsonian Institute, this is a celebratory volume to decorate the most illustrious coffee-table.

The Hollywood Murder Casebook,
    Michael Munn; Robson Books, £10.95

Thirteen notorious cases are covered, including William Desmond Taylor, Sharon Tate, and the mystery of Marilyn Monroe's final hours. At least four accounts of the Taylor killing have recently appeared, including the exhaustive study by Sidney Kirkpatrick (apparently too recent for mention in this volume) of the investigations carried out by veteran director King Vidor and silent star Colleen Moore. The grim stories are told in good straightforward style and, though most have already been recorded elsewhere, this is a convenient collection of tales from the seamier side of stardom, together with an interesting final round-up of less familiar items. Among the latter, incidentally, Munn repeats the story that Milton Sills committed suicide because of his failure to adapt to the coming of sound; other reports, however, state categorically that he died of a heart attack while playing tennis with his wife, and this is confirmed in the official obituary in *Variety*. There are some good illustrations, but no index.
Note: Roman Polanski was not Sharon Tate's 'vampire lover' in *Dance of the Vampires*, but the young assistant of the professor tracking them down.

Hollywood Tricks of the Trade, Alan
    McKenzie and Derek Ware; Admiral,
    £9.95

Learning 'how it was done' is a seemingly inexhaustible attraction, and this large-format, lavishly illustrated book should satisfy a lot of curiosity. The explanations of stunt feats, special effects secrets and monster make-up miracles are set out clearly, without being overloaded with technical details, from Fred Astaire dancing on the ceiling, to the leaps and falls of Douglas Fairbanks and Yakima Canutt, and the creation of the fearsome faces of horror. An entertaining (and possibly disillusioning) book, which would have benefited from an index.

Horror, ed. Phil Hardy; Aurum Press,
£17.95

Following science-fiction and the western,
the Aurum Film Encyclopedia turns its
attention to the most difficult of film *genres*
to define. The problem of the borderline
between horror and science-fiction has been
solved (or evaded) by including examples of
each type of film. The result is a truly
gargantuan volume of some 1,300 titles.
Every film is given a commentary, brief cast
list and other details. The range is wide,
including crime and mystery, as well as the
to-be-expected monsters and vampires, and
there are many foreign productions. In fact,
with so extensive a range, it is perhaps
surprising that, for instance, Polanski's *Cul-
de-Sac* and the much underrated Hitchcockian *And Soon the Darkness* (directed by
Robert Fuest) are omitted; but even in so
comprehensive a survey some selection in
inevitable. The commentaries, apart from
occasional clumsiness of style (see the last
sentence on Polanski's *Repulsion*) are in
general lively and often entertainingly critical, though the writer on *Witchfinder General*
misses (as did the film itself) the true horror
of the story, which is that in real life the
infamous Matthew Hopkins, far from being
gorily hacked to death, retired to his own
home and later died in bed. Appendices, a
huge index and over 150 stills, including a
magnificent colour section, round off an
essential addition even to this well-
documented subject.

Horrorshows, Gene Wright; David and
Charles, £15

Another reference book on the horror film
with, on the credit side, an intelligent introduction and commentaries, excellent and
often unhackneyed illustrations, wide coverage, and a double index of titles and authors;
on the debit side somewhat skeletal cast-
and-credit lists, particularly the former. The
films are grouped under subjects (Mad Sci-
entists, Monsters, Vampires, Splatter, etc.)
with a useful section on Anthologies. There
are references to TV, radio and stage excursions into horror, and a final chapter is
devoted to brief biographies of horror practitioners. This is an attractive and serviceable
addition to the *genre* literature, even if it
covers much familiar ground.

Illustrated Directory of Film Stars, David
Quinlan; Batsford, £17.50

The second edition of this indispensable
reference book includes 300 new names in
fewer pages, made possible by slightly smaller (but easily readable) print, and by the
recent transfer of numerous people, such as
Margaret Dumont, Raymond Huntley,
George Zucco, to the same author's *Directory
of Film Character Actors* where they more
properly belong. The borderline between
star and character actor is sometimes a hazy
one, but David Quinlan defines it deftly

enough. The new entries in the present book
belong mainly to the 1930s and the present
day. Each star is given a photograph, film
lists are *complete*, including important TV
appearances and Oscar awards and nominations, and the whole first edition has been
re-checked and updated. In addition to the
regular reference photographs there are a
number of attractive half-page stills. Essential for reference, browse, or even nostalgia.

The Illustrated History of the Cinema, ed.
Ann Lloyd and David Robinson; Orbis,
£14.95

To have compressed this vast subject into
about 430 lavishly illustrated pages is quite a
feat. Inevitably critical judgements are cur-
tailed and many films have to be mentioned
only in mere listings, so it would be unfair to
carp at various odd omissions or unduly
severe constraints; indeed, an astonishing
amount of detail and commentary is included. The early days, often unduly
skimped in such studies, are given fair
prominence and the structure of the whole is
well proportioned. Stills and other illustrations are in the main excellent, even if some
are rather too familiar and others are not
particularly well reproduced. The index is
sometimes careless: James Cruze has no
reference, though he is mentioned in the
text, and his famous western is misspelt as
The Covered Waggon; Robbe-Grillet's *L'Im-
mortelle (The Immortal Woman)* is not to be
found under either title; nor is LeLouche's
Vivre pour Vivre (Live for Life); Bunuel fares
badly; several of his films, though commented on in the text, are not entered.
There also seems to be some confusion in
regard to foreign and translated film titles –
the latter are printed in the text sometimes
in roman type, sometimes in italics. On the
whole this is a useful potted guide as an
introduction to more detailed study.

**Images of Children in American Film – A
Socio-Cultural Analysis**, Kathy
Merlock Jackson; Scarecrow Press, dist.
Bailey Bros. & Swinfen, £22.50

It would be a pity if the somewhat daunting
title gave a wrong impression of what is in
fact a wholly interesting and indeed fascinating study. The author traces the changing
representations of children in the American
cinema from the earliest years to the present,
against the equally changing background
of American cultural and historical events
and social attitudes. From the sunshine-
spreading little Miss Fix-its of the 1920s and
1930s (Mary Pickford, Baby Peggy, Shirley
Temple, Margaret O'Brien), she moves
through the darker post-Hiroshima era of
fear and uncertainty (films such as *The Bad
Seed*), to the monster-children of *The Exor-
cist*, *The Omen* and *It's Alive*, to the tough,
self-reliant youngsters (Tatum O'Neal in
Paper Moon) and finally to the wonder-eyed
child of *Close Encounters of the Third Kind*.

Throughout all these changes, she argues,
the essential innocence of children has,
whether to a greater or lesser extent, been
preserved. Using a wealth of examples, she
has produced a lucid, authoritative and never ponderous examination of an important
aspect of the cinema as social history. Highly
recommended.

International Film Guide 1987, ed. Peter
Cowie; Tantivy Press, £7.95

This renowned Guide proceeds on its unique
and all-embracing way (a quarter of a century old next year) with no lowering of its
high standard. A specialist reference work it
may be, with numerous films from all over
the world which we are unlikely ever to see,
but in its 500 packed and fully illustrated
pages there is something to interest everyone; and the final part of the book, following
the World Survey, covers every aspect of the
cinema. This year's 'Dossier' – a welcome
recent feature – is concerned with the Canadian output.

International TV and Video Guide, ed.
Richard Paterson; Tantivy Press, £7.95

The borderline between TV, video and cinema is becoming so hazy that mention of this
excellent yearly Guide is relevant here. It
surveys TV and video throughout the world,
with interesting statistics for each country
showing some surprising variations. In addition, there are a number of general articles
(including a special feature on *Doctor Who*)
and useful lists of dealers, schools, magazines, etc. This is an admirable companion
to the much older *International Film Guide*.

**Intrepid Laughter – Preston Sturges and
the Movies**, Andrew Dickos, Scarecrow
Press, dist. Bailey Bros. & Swinfen,
£15

It was time that the director of such notable
films as *The Lady Eve*, *Sullivan's Travels*,
The Palm Beach Story and *Hail the Conquering Hero* had a full-length study of his work,
and this neat book, though modest in size,
offers a concise but very adequate survey.
Apart from the perceptive examinations of
individual films, there are a number of good
illustrations, a detailed filmography, an
annotated bibliography and a life chronology
– Sturges died in 1959. Though not one of
the *Film-makers* series, this could well stand
beside them on the film-book shelf.

James Dean Revisited, Dennis Stock;
Plexus, £8.95

The 'legend' appears imperishable. Dennis
Stock met James Dean in 1954, and during
the following months travelled around with
him taking innumerable photographs; re-
visiting his home town, in New York, in
Hollywood, at work, at play, having his hair
cut, attending Katherine Dunham's dance
class, acting in *Rebel Without a Cause*, en-

gaged in other activities great and small. A brief text accompanies these illustrations, but they themselves are the chief attraction. The final impression is interesting but glum. Not once is there a smile on the subject's face; indeed, the final photograph seems to bear out Elia Kazan's words on the star he directed: '. . . actually, he was a pudding of hatred.'

Keep Watching the Skies – Volume II, Bill Warren; McFarland & Co, dist. Bailey Bros. & Swinfen, £39.95
Though covering fewer years than the first volume (see *Film Review 1983–4*) this is a vastly larger book, discussing every American science-fiction film between 1958 and 1962. It is also, as the author states, a sadder survey, the *genre* being then in decline. It follows much the same lines as its predecessor: lengthy essays, good reference section, vast index, a number of illustrations (though more would have been welcome). It is clearly a book for the fanatic, as a large proportion of the films are of very little merit; but for comprehensiveness in regard to its period it will surely never be bettered and, despite the considerable library already available on the subject, it should be welcomed as a necessary addition to the true buff's bookshelf.

Kiss Kiss Bang Bang, Pauline Kael; Arena, £5.95
Taking It All In, Pauline Kael; Arena, £5.95
Two handsome paperback reprints of 'Film Writings', covering the years 1965–7 and 1980–3 respectively. Pauline Kael is one of the liveliest critics; as I remarked in an earlier *Film Review*, it is stimulating even to disagree with her. Some 450 films in all are covered, ranging far beyond the years mentioned. Also included are a number of general essays, notably a trenchant piece on the effects of transfer to TV on films made for cinema viewing.

The Last Hero – Gary Cooper, Larry Swindell; Robson Books, £5.95
This is the paperback edition of the biography first published in 1981 and recommended in *Film Review 1981–2* as a soundly written history of a large part of cinema through one of its most famous figures. It is even better value in its new form.

Laurel and Hardy, Bruce Crowther; Columbus Books, £9.95
The great asset of this amiable study of 'The Clown Princes of Comedy', to quote the subtitle, is the large number of rarely seen stills, posters and photographs from the earliest days to the final years. Two interesting inserts in the generally chronological survey are a section entitled 'Our Relations' (on Keaton, Chaplin and Lloyd), and another on some famous L. & H. associates, such as Charley Chase, Edward Kennedy,

Mae Busch and – of course – Jimmy Finlayson. There is also a list of British theatres visited by the pair in 1932 and 1954, a warm-hearted foreword by fellow comedian Ernie Wise, and the whole text is informed and entertaining.

Leading Ladies, Don Macpherson and Louise Brody; Conran Octopus, £12.95
This is a companion volume to *Leading Men* (see *Film Review 1986–7*) covering some 120 stars from the silent days (Theda Bara) to the present (Greta Scacchi), stunningly photographed in studio portraits and film stills. The general introduction and those to the various periods are lively and interesting, the comments on individuals frank and, where necessary, critical. Perhaps one might have wished that a curtailment of the several pages expended on the favoured and much photographed few might have afforded room for the inclusion of more Leading Ladies from the earlier years (the silent era, for instance, is given only 20 out of 200 pages) but otherwise the range is generously wide. A handsome volume, eminently suitable for a good browse.

Legends – Joan Crawford, ed. John Kobal; Pavilion, £6.95
Legends – Clark Gable, ed. John Kobal; Pavilion, £6.95
Two further volumes in the attractive series of which the first two were covered in *Film Review 1985–6*: collections of about 100 full-page studio portraits and stills from the famed Kobal Collection. Biographical introductions are by Anna Raeburn (Crawford) and James Card (Gable), and in each case there is an additional note on the photography. Interspersed between the illustrations (which are superb) are brief comments from friends, associates and film magazines. The general production quality is high, and the price reasonable.

Leni Riefenstahl and Olympia, Cooper C. Graham; Scarecrow Press, dist. Bailey Bros. & Swinfen, £32.50
This is No. 13 in the enterprising Filmmakers series edited by Anthony Slide. In over 300 crowded pages the famous (or notorious) Nazi record of the 1936 Olympics is described and discussed in exhaustive detail – its background and planning, filming, editing, and post-release history. It is a fascinating account which can be read, studied and enjoyed on several levels: as the story of the production of a mammoth film masterpiece; as a brilliant piece of political propaganda; as a portrait of an extraordinary and indomitable personality; as a sinister picture of the growing shadow of Nazism over the world of the mid-1930s; or even as a mere record of a series of sporting events. Despite the mass of involved and often

intractable material with which he has to deal, the author brilliantly succeeds in keeping his story lucid and gripping, totally involving the reader throughout. Fully documented with copious notes and appendices for the serious student.

A Life in Movies, Michael Powell; Heinemann, £15.95
Though filling 670 pages, this mammoth autobiography only takes us up to the 43rd year of the author's life of over 80 years. It's not a page too long, however, for he has a great deal to tell. His 'life in movies' started with work for the notable Rex Ingram, director of *The Four Horsemen of the Apocalypse*, the silent *Prisoner of Zenda*, *The Arab* and *Mare Nostrum*; continued through several years of directing British 'quota quickies'; and mounted to such brilliantly original – and often flamboyant – masterpieces as *The Life and Death of Colonel Blimp*, *A Matter of Life and Death*, *Black Narcissus* and *The Red Shoes*, with its complete original ballet integrated into the plot. With the latter film this volume, full of interest and charm, tantalizingly comes to an end; but he has promised to tell the rest 'if I am spared' – an outcome every film-goer will agree is devoutly to be wished.

Marilyn – A Never-Ending Dream, Guus Luijters; Plexus, £6.95
The difference between this and the many other photographic compilations is that the text consists almost wholly of Marilyn Monroe's own words, culled from a wide variety of interviews and other sources, and quoting an equally wide variety of subjects, opinions, comments and biographical details. A vast number of illustrations form the greater part of the book, from posed portraits to candid camera shots, record sleeves and dust jackets. Incidentally, the compiler/editor accepts briefly and unequivocally the suicide version of her death.

The Motion Picture Guide, Jay Robert Nash and Stanley Ralph Ross; Cinebooks/Information Publications International, 12 vols, £750
There is no doubt that this enormous work is an impressive addition to the film reference library. More than 50,000 English-speaking and notable foreign sound feature films are covered, and more than 3,000 silent films appear in Vol. X, together with a 'miscellaneous' list. A further claim is made for no fewer than 35,000 'in-depth' entries on films of the silent period plus an 'appendix-compendium' of an additional 10,000 silents, which is truly remarkable; even the American Film Institute Catalog for the peak years 1921–1930 contains only 6,606 titles. (Understandably, in view of the cost, the publishers were able to supply only one volume for review, but this may be

taken as representative of the whole.) Each film receives the customary treatment: cast-and-credit lists, date, length, 'star' and other ratings, etc., together with video-cassette availability, synopsis and commentary ranging from a few lines to a full column.

Extremely high claims (*the only definitive and all-encompassing film encyclopedia in the world*, etc.) are 'justifiably and proudly' made in a Foreword almost a quarter of which is given up to contemptuous dismissal of other similar publications; something which in my view is not wholly justified. Fuller cast-and-credit lists can often be available elsewhere – particularly when the inclusion of 'roles played' is taken into consideration – even though the *MPG* states that 'your authors have seen the films'. Despite the claim 'all-encompassing', there are, inevitably, gaps. Commentaries and criticisms, though naturally subjective, seem at times almost perversely prejudiced. On at least one occasion in this volume the authors allow their hatred of a film (highly regarded elsewhere) to betray them into inaccuracies: the 'anaemic-looking' Hemmings in Antonioni's *Blow-Up* spends only a few moments (not 'most of the film') 'frolicking with nudes'; they are not in fact 'models' (an important point), nor is he in bed.

With these small reservations, however, this is a remarkable achievement, essential for all libraries and mouth-watering for every film enthusiast.

Note: Minor errors in spelling, etc., are inevitable in so large an undertaking and should not be unduly stressed, but to refer to 'BRITTANIA' HOSPITAL not only in the bold-type heading, but three times during the ensuing commentary, is the sort of mistake which might have been spotted.

My Husband, My Friend, Neile McQueen
Toffel; Columbus Books, £9.95
This is another 'intimate biography' written to quash false rumour and set records straight, but this time, thankfully, written with affection and regard rather than resentment or wish for revenge. The authoress was McQueen's first wife (1955–71): their relationship, through all the usual ups and downs, lasted beyond separation and they remained close friends until his death. Her story is well and simply told, often humorous and occasionally moving, and should interest everyone who has enjoyed McQueen's lively and action-packed films. With two good sections of attractive photographs, but no index.

The Nine Lives of Mickey Rooney, Arthur
Marx; Robson Books, £10.95
It is perhaps surprising that no full life of Mickey Rooney has been available before, but this warm and entertaining biography adequately fills the gap. Private life and

public career are given due proportionate prominence, and the illustrations are good – though the straight procession through eight wives induces a certain sense of satiety. The book is not without its carelessnesses. The index, for instance, though at first glance very full, omits such significant early films as *Not to be Trusted* (Rooney's first appearance, in 1926) and *Orchids and Ermine*, with Colleen Moore in 1927. The latter film, in fact, receives particularly poor treatment: in the list of photographs the star is referred to as 'Coleen More' and in the caption to the still as 'Coleen Moore'; the film itself is dated 1932 in the caption and (correctly) as 1927 in the text. The inclusion of a filmography would have been welcome.

Olivier – in Celebration, ed. Garry
O'Connor; Hodder & Stoughton, £12.95
This attractively produced 80th-birthday tribute consists of 22 brief essays on Olivier – as Actor, Director and Man – by well-known people who knew him in these various capacities. The 'cast' includes Dilys Powell, J. C. Trewin, Peter Ustinov, Sheridan Morley, Michael Caine, Peter Hall, Douglas Fairbanks Jr, Melvyn Bragg and Peggy Ashcroft. Garry O'Connor, who earlier published a notable life of Ralph Richardson, has edited the collection with skill, requesting contributors to concentrate on a particular aspect, and encouraging frankness. Some events in Olivier's history are, inevitably, repeated several times, but only add to the interest to be given the varying comments on, for instance, the famous Gielgud/Olivier – Romeo/Mercutio exchange production of 1935. There are a number of magnificent portraits by photographer Angus McBean, and a jacket and frontispiece illustration by Antony Sher depicting Olivier in some of his best-known parts.

Olivier – The Complete Career, Robert
Tannich, Thames & Hudson, £12.95
This handsome, large-format book is accurately subtitled 'a visual record'. Every part Olivier has ever played – on stage, film, television and radio – every play he directed, and every production he was involved in on the management side is listed in chronological order. Practically every performance is illustrated in the 182 superb photographs – a few familiar but many newly published. Brief comments, reviews and, in some cases, personal tributes from actors, directors and other associates accompany the illustrations, which extend from a portrait of Olivier as a ten-year-old Maria in *Twelfth Night* at All Saints Choir School in 1917 to one as Rudolf Hess in *Wild Geese II* in 1985. This splendid collection is an essential companion to Olivier's autobiography and to the book based on his famous television interview with Melvyn Bragg.

Orson Welles – A Celebration, John
Russell Taylor; Pavilion, £14.95
Another excellent volume in this excellent series, presenting in pictures and text as complete a portrait as possible of the elusive genius and creator of *Citizen Kane*. Photographs and stills are lavish in number and well reproduced; in the text Mr Taylor tackles his formidable subject with the requisite combination of frankness, sympathy and understanding in spirited style. The cast lists in the filmography are exemplary in their fullness.

**Orson Welles – The Rise and Fall of an
American Genius**, Charles Higham;
New English Library, £12.95
In *Film Review 1986–7* I described Barbara Leaming's biography of Orson Welles as probably definitive; this now appears to have been premature. Mr Higham's 'life' is not only livelier and easier reading than the solid but somewhat stolid earlier book, but gives a more fully rounded portrait. It tells a riveting if at times harrowing story with often devastating frankness, but equally with warm admiration and sympathy. The appalling struggles to raise money, the overbearing rudeness, the ruthlessness, disregard of others, chicanery, lies and evasions are all frankly faced, but the irresistible charm and the sheer professional genius that aroused intense loyalty in so many who came into contact with him shine through. In the end one is left with a sense of both triumph and tragedy. 'Rise and Fall' it may have been, but, judging by the story told here, the particular world in which Welles lived and worked would have been a duller place without him. Note: Though 'easy reading', the book shows signs here and there of over-hasty writing: the final paragraph on p. 162, for instance, should surely refer to Welles, not – as printed – to Robert Wise.

People Will Talk, John Kobal; Aurum
Press, £14.95
A bumper book of interviews (or Conversations, to use the author's term), 41 in all, with people connected with movie-making in the great days: players, directors, choreographers, designers and others. As a sample – Arletty, Joan Blondell, Hermes Pan, John Engstead, Louise Brooks, Colleen Moore, Anita Loos, Henry Hathaway and Barbara Stanwyck. The Conversations are lengthy, filling in all over 700 pages; under Kobal's gentle but subtle prompting the subjects are encouraged to talk fully and freely, following a brief introduction in each case. The accompanying illustrations – as might be expected from one of the leading photographic archivists – are excellent. The result is entertainment, information, gossip and, on occasion, the pathos of a time that is past.

Poland, Frank Bren; Flicks Books, £11.95
Sweden, Brian McIlroy; Flicks Books, £11.95

A new publisher makes a welcome appearance on the cinema book scene with the first two volumes, in a series entitled World Cinema, which belie the firm's somewhat jokey name. They are, in fact, informed, detailed and thoroughly documented studies, attractively presented, and set out in short, clearly headlined sections that make it unusually easy for the reader to find his or her way around. In each case a straightforward history is followed by a useful chronology, bibliography and comprehensive index, complete with cross-references between foreign and British titles. *Poland* has interviews with Wajda and Zanussi; *Sweden* has an excellent major section on Ingmar Bergman. Both are well illustrated.

Producers Releasing Corporation, ed. Wheeler Dixon; McFarland & Co, dist. Bailey Bros. & Swinfen, £19.95

The increasing interest in the work of the smaller Hollywood studios in the 'golden years' (for example Monogram, Republic) is well served in this compact and thorough history of a company that flourished – if that is the word – during the 1940s. Few of the titles will be remembered today except by 'B-feature' buffs, but quite a number of well-known names appear in the cast lists, and even some of the films may turn up on less-than-prime-time TV. This is a book for the specialist, perhaps, but none the less useful for that: a thorough survey of both the business and the creative activities. Included are an introduction by William K. Everson and an interview with the best-known PRC director, Edgar G. Ulmer, together with an interesting essay on the 'B-movie' structure.

The Real Walt Disney, Leonard Mosley; Grafton Books, £12.95

A good straightforward biography, eminently 'readable' and particularly good in disentangling the financial side of the huge and multiform organization. Due attention is paid to the 'real life' films as well as the cartoons and animated features more popularly associated with his name. A fanciful conclusion to the book envisages the possibility that Disney may have had himself frozen and will return to clear up the confusion caused by the successors to his kingdom! Appendices include a useful 'film history' and a note on the animators. The index is excellent.

Red – The Tempestuous Life of Susan Hayward, Robert LaGuardia and Gene Arceri; Robson Books, £10.95

This is one of the best of the Robson biography series, a study which is both uncompromisingly frank and deeply sympathetic. Apart from the interest it may hold as a 'portrait of a famous star' (and there is plenty about her performances, her admirably professional attitude towards her work, her sometimes acerbic relations with her associates), it is a remarkable study of character. Whatever opinion one may hold of Susan Hayward's extraordinary mixture of cruelty and thoughtfulness, generosity and sometimes incredible meanness, occasional brashness probably concealing deep insecurity – one can only feel appalled at the horror of her final months when her brain was invaded by malignant tumours, and moved by the fierce determination and anger with which she faced and fought the inevitable end. The story has been told before, but never so powerfully.

Rex Harrison, Roy Moseley; New English Library, £14.95

Described as the first biography (though a book on Harrison by Allen Eyles was published in 1985), this is a solid, workman-like job, presenting a well-rounded and authentic-seeming portrait of a complex and unconventional personality, with plenty of information about his career and a sympathetic but clear-sighted account of his not uneventful private life. Full lists of his theatre and screen appearances are included, together with a detailed bibliography, a good index and a section of stills and portraits, in one of which one may see a resemblance to, of all people, John Wayne.

Robert Taylor, Jane Ellen Wayne; Robson Books, £10.95

This is a pleasant, anecdotal story of a popular star but often underrated actor, with lots of invented dialogue and dramatized situations. Among the most interesting items is the brief account of his working with Garbo in *Camille*. An excellent and well presented filmography fills over 60 pages, but even this does not excuse the lack of an index.

Screen World 1986, John Willis; Muller, Blond and White, £14.95

This fine long-running series (37 volumes, only narrowly beaten by *Film Review* itself, to which it is complementary rather than rival) continues in its usual form: no articles, commentaries or criticism, but exceptionally full cast lists and credits, several good stills per film (1,000 in all), obituaries and other useful reference material, all attractively presented. This year's volume is dedicated to Claudette Colbert.

Sherlock Holmes – A Centenary Celebration, Allen Eyles; John Murray, £10.95

A large part of this beautifully produced tribute to the Great Detective (who made his debut in 1886) is devoted to his many screen appearances. Opinions may differ as to which actor, on stage or screen, represents THE Holmes (for many, Basil Rathbone – though acceptable when in period – puts himself beyond the pale by his connivance in the appalling 'up-dated' travesties in which the original creator had no hand), but all are fully discussed here in a lively and painstakingly researched text, which includes many fascinating minor details, such as the origin of Holmes' *curved* pipe. Allen Eyles has also gathered together an astonishing collection of rare illustrations, all excellently reproduced in black-and-white or colour. Whether the reader's interest is Holmes or Hollywood, this is a book to treasure.

Slapstick, Tony Staveacre; Angus & Robertson, £9.95

With almost every conceivable aspect of the entertainment world already chronicled, it is strange that until now nothing has been devoted solely to so basic an ingredient of comedy as slapstick – knockabout action involving 'comics who make their living by falling down, not standing up'. In his thorough and affectionate survey, the author covers the whole field, from ancient Greece, through the *Commedia dell' Arte*, to the pantomime, circus, seaside entertainers, modern theatre, cinema and TV. All the famous, and many not so famous, names are here, and the cinema not unexpectedly comes in for a large share of attention. The book is packed with illustrations from all ages and places, and with numerous hilarious script extracts. A short selection of brief biographical paragraphs rounds off an entertaining and informative book.

Spanish Film Directors, 1950–1985, Ronald Schwartz; Scarecrow Press, dist. Bailey Bros. & Swinfen, £20

A very useful survey dealing briefly but pithily with the work of 21 directors. Many of the films, of course, may not have been seen on British screens, but a number have or have also appeared on TV; for example the unforgettable *Spirit of the Beehive*, here given a full analysis. Familiar names also appear, such as Geraldine Chaplin and Anthony Quinn. Excellently illustrated with stills, and well documented, this handbook whets the appetite for a larger taste of Spanish fare. Note: *Oh, What a Lovely War!* was not a Richard Lester film, but the first to be directed by Richard Attenborough.

Stanwyck – The Untold Biography, Jane Ellen Wayne; Robson Books, £9.95

A brisk, business-like and interesting, if somewhat superficial, biography. Unfortuntely it is apt to get bogged down in too many tedious 'romantic details' of the ins and outs and ups and downs of Stanwyck's private life, in particular her marriage to Robert Taylor, including quite unnecessary intimate revelations which do nothing to raise the level of these pages. For many years, after all, she has been one of the most highly regarded actresses in Hollywood for her versatile artistry and unfailing professionalism, whatever the personal failings that seem to be suggested here. The book includes good illustrations and a filmography, but is sometimes carelessly written: how on earth did its three final words get passed – 'Veni, vide, vici'? There is no index, perhaps an indication of the general approach.

Trick Cinematography, R. M. Hayes; McFarland and Co, dist. Bailey Bros. & Swinfen, £25.95

This covers all the films that have received Academy Award nominations from the start in 1927 – *Wings*, *The Jazz Singer*, *The Private Life of Helen of Troy* – to 1984. The chief feature of the book is the gargantuan cast-and-credit lists; those for *The Return of the Jedi* and *Superman*, for example, each cover five closely packed pages. Apart from the Special Visual Effects, Scientific and Technical Awards are also detailed. One could perhaps have wished for fuller and more explanatory 'how-it-was-done' introductions, but this is obviously a book for the specialist, and the coverage of reference material is unsurpassed. An enormous index fills over 60 3-column pages.

Unfinished Business, John Houseman; Chatto & Windus, £14.95

John Houseman's previous books were what might be described as professional autobiographies; this one, as indicated by its subtitle 'A Memoir', is a more personal account of a very long and varied career. And a fascinating story it turns out to be, its 492 pages not one too many for the multifarious activities, plots and schemes, failures and successes, friendships and at times violent disagreements that fill a life of over 80 years. Born of British/Alsatian Jewish parents and educated at Clifton College, Bristol, Houseman became widely known through his appearances as the formidable college professor in *The Paper Chase* series, having won an Oscar for his performance in the film (his first except for a 'bit' part in *Seven Days in May*), the role having been turned down by several stars such as Edward G. Robinson and James Mason. A remarkable story of a remarkable character.

The United Artists Story, Ronald Bergen; Octopus, £14.95

This sixth volume of the Octopus studio history series is well up to the standard of its forbears, covering every one of the films (1,581, we are assured) with a brief commentary, cast list, name of director and, in all except minor cases, an excellent still. Each decade opens with a historical summary, and appendices include British and

foreign releases, documentaries, awards and other relevant details, together with two enormous indexes. Readers familiar with the author's brief but pithy *A–Z of Movie Directors* (*Film Review 1983–4*) will find the same forthright and often witty approach in this large and handsome account of the corporation founded by Mary Pickford, Douglas Fairbanks, D. W. Griffith and Charles Chaplin – which caused R. A. Rowland, President of Metro Pictures, to exclaim, 'The lunatics have taken charge of the asylum!'

Views from the Hollywood Hills, Julian and Carey More; Pavilion, £12.95

This small but elegant book is a collaboration between father and daughter, the former being responsible for the text and the latter for the photographs. It might be described as a kaleidoscopic view of modern Los Angeles – Dreams and Realities, as indicated by the section headings. The text is a rather rambling mixture of impressions, historical facts, comments and conclusions, interesting but at times confusing. The photographs, over 100 in colour, are remarkable for their clarity and originality. Many of them appear to have been taken in the early morning or at sunset, one or two bearing a distinct resemblance to the paintings of Edward Hopper. It is an attractive book to look at and handle, but surely offers little incentive to visit the human scenes it presents in all their vulgarity and brashness, set against – and often overpowering – the natural beauty of the backgrounds.

Vivien, Alexander Walker; Weidenfeld & Nicolson, £12.95

Without doubt this moving and riveting biography of Vivien Leigh merits the often misused description 'definitive'. Thoroughly researched, well documented, and written with a balanced mixture of unsparing frankness and deep compassion, it holds the attention from the first page to the last, providing not only a vivid account of her meteoric career, unfailing courage and eventual personal tragedy, but also an equally sympathetic portrait of Laurence Olivier and their brilliant but in the end sadly doomed life together. The book is well illustrated, with a useful chronology and a good index.

Warren Beatty – A Life And A Story, David Thomson; Secker & Warburg, £14.95

This is an extraordinary hybrid – half-biography, half-fiction – the first written mainly in the present and the latter in the past tense. The style is often strained and not easy to read; and one may close the book not much the wiser. It is well documented as regards quoted speech, etc., and much of

the picture of Hollywood life and work is interesting – but how much of it is the reader intended to believe? The brief final chapter, a sort of 'open letter' to Beatty containing, among other things, advice not to run for political office, seems somewhat pointless and verging on impertinence. The book is handsomely produced and well illustrated: it all depends on what you want from a *Life* and a *Story*.

Western Movies, A TV and Video Guide to 4,200 Genre Films, Michael R. Pitts; McFarland & Co, dist. Bailey Bros. & Swinfen, £39.95

This gargantuan reference work forms a good companion to the two-volume *Science Fiction, Horror and Fantasy Credit Lists* from the same publisher. Each film is given a good cast list, date, production company, director, video availability, etc., together with a brief but pithy comment. The range, to use the apt word, is wide, the author including not only the conventional 'shoot-'em-up' movie but all aspects of the *genre*, together with foreign productions, and musicals such as *Naughty Marietta* and *Rose-Marie*; there are also a number from the often disregarded silent period. Lists of screen names, famous cowboy horses, etc., plus an enormous index complete a 625-page book of essential reference material.

Woody Allen – Beyond Words, Robert Bénayoun; Pavilion, £12.95

An analysis of Allen's unique style and films, presented with a wealth of magnificent illustrations, much of the text being in the form of captions. Some of Allen's jokes are feeble, such as the series of fake photographs showing him with various notable people – no more amusing than family pictures taken on a seaside pier – but there is much else to entertain his devotees in this spacious collection, translated and introduced by Alexander Walker.

Zeffirelli, Franco Zeffirelli; Weidenfeld & Nicolson, £14.95

Though Zeffirelli's main work has been in the theatre and the opera house, his few films, such as *The Taming of the Shrew* with Richard Burton and Elizabeth Taylor, his 'juvenile' *Romeo and Juliet*, and his filmed operas *La Traviata* and *Otello*, have aroused considerable interest and critical heat – both pro and con. This lengthy and very 'readable' autobiography, packed with interesting details, ranges from his alarming war-time experiences with the partisans, to his directorial career and his association with such figures as Visconti, Anna Magnani, Olivier, Burton and Taylor, Leonard Bernstein and, of course, Maria Callas.

Awards and Festivals

While this feature cannot pretend to cover all the many and ever-increasing lists of national awards, you will find listed most of the major ones. Likewise, it is not practical to list every prize at every Festival (of which again there are now considerable and continually proliferating numbers) but all the major results are given, together with the prize lists of some of the more interesting minor ones. Incidentally, for those of you who would like a really complete list of Festivals, competitive, non-competitive and specialized ones, Variety periodically publishes such a list – and it has become a very long one indeed.

The Academy of Canadian Cinema and Television 1987 Genie Awards, March 1987

Best Film: *The Decline of the American Empire*, produced by René Malo and Roger Frappier. Also Best Direction: Denys Arcand; Best Supporting Actor: Gabriel Arcand; Best Supporting Actress: Louise Portal; Best Editing: Monique Fortier; Best Original Screenplay: Denys Arcand.

Best Actor: Gordon Pinsent, in *John and the Missus*. Also: Best Music Score: Michael Conway Baker.

Best Actress: Martha Henry, in *Dancing in the Dark*. Also: Best Adapted Screenplay: Leon Marr; Best Art Direction: Lillian Sarafinchan.

Best Cinematography: Pierre Mignot, for *Anne Trister*.

The Air Canada Award for Outstanding Contribution to the Business of Filmmaking in Canada: Garth H. Drabinsky.

The American Academy of Motion Picture Arts and Sciences Awards, March 1987

Best film: *Platoon*. Also Best Direction: Oliver Stone.

Best Actor: Paul Newman, in *The Color of Money*.

Best Actress: Marlee Matlin, in *Children of a Lesser God*.

Best Supporting Actor: Michael Caine, in *Hannah and Her Sisters*.

Best Supporting Actress: Dianne Wiest, in *Hannah and Her Sisters*.

Best Original Screenplay: Woody Allen, for *Hannah and Her Sisters*.

Best Screenplay Adaptation of material from another medium: Ruth Prawer Jhabvala, for *A Room With a View*.

Best Editing: Claire Simpson for *Platoon*.

Best Cinematography: Chris Menges, for *The Mission*.

Paul Newman, who won the 1987 Best Actor Oscar for his performance in The Color of Money.

Best Foreign Language Film: Fons Rademakers' *De Aanslag – The Assault* (Dutch).

Best Art Direction: Gianni Quaranta, Brian Ackland-Snow, Brian Savagar and Elio Altramura, for *A Room With a View*.

Best Musical Score: Herbie Hancock, for *'Round Midnight*.

Best Documentary Feature: shared between Brigitte Berman's *Artie Shaw: Time Is All You've Got* and Joseph Feury and Milton Justice's *Down and Out in America*.

Best Documentary Short: Vivienne Vernon-Roe's *Women – For America, For the World*.

183

Best Short Films: *A Greek Tragedy* (Animated) and *Precious Images* (Live Action).

The Irving G. Thalberg Award went to Steven Spielberg.

Special Honorary Award to Ralph Bellamy for 'his unique artistry and his distinguished service to the profession of acting'.

The Animation Festival Awards, Annecy, June 1987

Grand Prizes: *L'Homme qui plantait des arbres – The Man Who Planted Trees*, by Frederic Back (Canada) and *Smatchkan Sviat – A Crushed World*, by Boyko Kanev (Bulgaria).

Best Feature Film: *When the Wind Blows*, by Jimmy Murakami (Great Britain).

Special Jury Prizes: *Setltanzer*, by Raimund Krumme (West Germany); for editing and rhythm, *Girls' Night Out*, by Joanna Quinn (Great Britain); and for art direction *Dver – The Door* by N. Shorina (USSR).

The Australian Film Awards, October 1986

Best Film: *Malcolm*. Also: Best Director: Nadia Tass; Best Original Screenplay: David Parker; and Best Editing: Ken Sallows.

Best Actor: Colin Friels, in *Malcolm*.

Best Actress: Judy Davis, in *Kangaroo*.

Best Supporting Actor: John Hargreaves, in *Malcolm*.

Best Supporting Actress: Lindy Davies, in *Malcolm*.

Best Screenplay Adaptation: Bruce and Rhoishin Beresford, for *The Fringe Dwellers*.

Best Cinematography: Peter James, for *The Right-Hand Man*.

The Berlin Film Festival Awards, March 1987

Golden Bear for Best Film: *The Theme*, by Gleb Panfilov (USSR).

Special Jury Prize: *The Sea and Poison*, by Kei Kumai (Japan).

Best Direction: Oliver Stone, for *Platoon* (USA).

Best Actor: Gian Maria Volonte, in *The Moro Case* (Italy).

Best Actress: Ana Beatriz Nogueira, in *Vera* (Brazil).

Silver Bear for 'Best individual achievement' shared by: *The Year of Awakening*, by Fernando Trueba (Spain) and *Diary for My Loves*, by Marta Meszaros (Hungary).

Silver Bear for 'The handling of a specific theme in a popular and sensitive way': *Children of a Lesser God*, by Randa Haines (USA).

The Alfred Bauer Prize: *Bad Blood*, by Léos Carax (France).

Best Film in the Children's Festival: *Henri*, by François Labonte (Canada).

The British Academy of Film and Television Arts Awards, 1986

Best Film: *A Room With a View*, by James Ivory.

Best Direction: Woody Allen, for *Hannah and Her Sisters*. Also: Best Original Screenplay: Woody Allen.

Best Actor: Bob Hoskins, in *Mona Lisa*.

Best Actress: Maggie Smith, in *A Room With a View*.

Best Supporting Actor: Ray McAnally, in *The Mission*.

Best Supporting Actress: Judi Dench, in *A Room With a View*.

Best Screenplay Adaptation: Kurt Luedtke, for *Out of Africa*.

Best Musical Score: Ennio Morricone, for *The Mission*.

Best Short Film: (director) *La Boule* (France).

Best Foreign Language Film: Akira Kurosawa's *Ran* (Japan).

The British Critics' Circle Film Awards, 1986

Best English Language Film: *A Room With a View*.

Best Foreign Language Film: *Ran*.

Best Direction: Akira Kurosawa, for *Ran*.

Best Screenplay: Woody Allen, for *Hannah and Her Sisters*.

Best Acting Performances: Bob Hoskins in *Mona Lisa* and *Sweet Liberty*, and William Hurt in *Kiss of the Spider Woman*.

Film Music Award: John Barry.

Special Awards: Lillian Gish; photographer Chris Menges; and French set designer Alexandre Trauner.

The 40th Cannes Film Festival Awards, May 1987

Golden Palm for Best Film: *Under the Sun of Satan*, by Maurice Pialat (France).

Special Jury Prize: *Repentance*, by Tengiz Abuladze (USSR).

Best Direction: Wim Wenders, for *The Sky Over Berlin* (West Germany).

Best Actor: Marcello Mastroianni, in *Black Eyes* (Italy).

Best Actress: Barbara Hershey, in *Shy People* (USA).

Best Artistic Contribution: Stanley Myers, for his music in *Prick Up Your Ears* (Great Britain).

Jury Prize shared by: *Brightness*, by Soulemane Cisse (Mali) and *Shinran: Path to Purity*, by Rentaro Mikuni (Japan).

Special 40th Anniversary Prize to Federico Fellini.

Caméra d'Or, Best First Feature Prize: Nana Dzhordzhade, for *Robinson My English Grandfather* (USSR).

Prize of the Commission for Technical Excellence: *Cinema in the Eyes*, by Gilles and Laurent Jacob (France).

The Chicago International Film Festival Awards, October 1986

Golden Hugo for Best Film: *Welcome in Vienna*, by Axel Corti (Austria).

Silver Hugo shared by: *The Decline of the American Empire*, by Denys Arcand (Canada), and *Thérèse*, by Alain Cavalier (France).

Special Jury Prize: *Rhosyn a Rhith – Coming Up Roses*, by Stephen Bayly (Wales).

Best Performance: Anna Linden, in *Love Me* (Sweden).

The 15th Fantasy Film Festival, Avoriaz, January 1987

Grand Prize: *Blue Velvet*, by David Lynch (USA).

Special Jury Prize: *The Fly*, by David Cronenberg (USA).

Critics' Prize: *The American Way*, by Maurice Phillips (USA).

'Fear' Category Prize (accent on the 'gory'): *Bloody Bird*, by Michele Soavi (Italy).

The French Academy César Awards, March 1987

Best Direction: Alain Cavalier, for *Thérèse*. Also: Best Film; Best Photography: Philippe Rousselot; Best Editing: Isabelle Dedieu.

Best Actor: Daniel Auteuil, in *Jean de Florette*.

Best Actress: Sabine Azéma, in *Mélo*.

Best Foreign Film of the Year: Jean-Jacques Annaud's *Der Name der Rose – The Name of the Rose*.

The 11th International Festival of India, New Delhi, February 1987

Golden Peacock for Best Film: *Farewell Green Summer*, by Illior Ishmukhamedov (USSR).

Silver Peacock for Best Film: *The Outcast*, by Yao Shougang (China).

Silver Peacock for Best Direction: Jesus Diaz, for *Lejania: Parting of the Ways* (Cuba).

Silver Peacock for Best Actress: Anoja Weerasinghe, in *Maldeniy Simion* (Sri Lanka).

Silver Peacock for Best Actor: Regvuhir Yadez, in *Massey Sahib* (India).

The 9th International Women's Film Festival Awards, Paris, April 1987

Grand Prize for Best Film shared by: *Loyalties*, by Anne Wheeler (Canada) and *Seppan*, by Agneta Fagerstrom-Olsson (Sweden).

Best Actress shared by: Lena T. Hansson, in *Ester* (Sweden) and Suzanne Osten, in *The Mozart Brothers* (Sweden).

Best Actor: Hendrick Toompere, in *Children's Games* (USSR).

Best Child Actor: Zoltan Nagy, in *Elysium* (Hungary).

The Association of Women Journalists' Prize: *Dirigenterna*, by Christina Olofson (Sweden).

The Italian David Di Donatello Awards, Rome, April 1987

Best Film: *The Family*. Also: Best Direction: Ettore Scola; Best Actor: Vittorio Gassman; Best Screenplay: Scola, Ruggiero Maccari and Furio Scarpelli; Best Editing: Francesco Malvestito; and Best Music: Armando Trovajoli.

Best Actress: Liv Ullmann, in *Farewell, Moscow*.

Best Photography: Tonino Delli Colli, for *Der Name der Rose – The Name of the Rose*. Also Best Art Direction: Dante Ferretti.

Best Foreign Film: *A Room With a View*. Also Best Direction: James Ivory.

The Luchino Visconti prize went to Alain Resnais.

The 29th Leipzig International Documentary and Short Film Festival Main Awards 1986

Golden Dove for Best Feature Film: *Joe Polowsky – An American Dreamer*, by Wolfgang Pfeiffer (West Germany).

Silver Dove shared by: *Acta General de Chile*, by Miguel Littin (Spain) and *Half Life*, by Dennis O'Rourke (Australia).

Golden Dove for Best Short Film: *Children of Fustat*, by Heiki Partanen (Finland).

Silver Dove shared by: *Mariska's Band*, by Peter Krelja (Yugoslavia) and *Hippocrates' New Oath*, by Gisela Schulz and Walter Heinz (German Democratic Republic).

Golden Dove for Best Animated Film: *Break!*, by G. Bardin (USSR).

The Locarno International Film Festival, August 1986

Golden Leopard for Best Film: *Jeziore Bodenskie – The Lake of Constance*, by Janusz Zaorski (Poland).

Silver Leopard: *40m Deutschland*, by Tevfik Baser (West Germany).

Bronze Leopard shared by: *Lamb*, by Colin Gregg (Great Britain) and *Moj Drug Ivan Lapchin – My Friend Ivan Lapchin* (USSR).

Special Mentions: *Kali Patridha Syndrophe – Happy Homecoming, Comrade*, by Lefteris Xanthopoulos (Greece); *Diapason*, by Jorge Polaco (Argentine); and Fernanda Torres for her performance in *Com Licenca eu vou a Luta – I'm Taking Off* (Brazil).

The London Evening Standard Awards, January 1987

Best Film: *A Room With a View*.

Best Actor: Ray McAnally, in *The Mission* and *No Surrender*.

Best Actress: Coral Browne, in *Dreamchild*.

Best Screenplay: Robert Bolt, for *The Mission*.

The Peter Sellers Award for Comedy: John Cleese, in *Clockwise*.

Most Promising Newcomer: Gary Oldman in *Sid and Nancy*.

Outstanding Technical Achievement: Tony Pierce-Roberts, for the photography in *A Room With a View*.

Special Award was give to Jake Eberts of Goldcrest Films, for his 'Contribution to British Cinema'.

The Montreal Festival, September 1986

Grand Prix of the Americas: *37.2 Le Matin – Betty Blue: 37.2 in the Morning*, by Jean-Jacques Beineix (France).

Special Jury Award: *My Sweet Little Village*, by Jiri Menzel (Czechoslovakia).

Jury Award: *Laputa*, by Helma Sanders-Brahms (West Germany).

Best Actress: Krystyna Janda, in *Laputa*.

Best Actor: Dennis Hopper, in *Blue Velvet* (USA).

A Special Award was given to Carlos Saura, for his dance film trilogy.

The New York Critics' Circle Awards for 1986

Best Film: Woody Allen, for *Hannah and Her Sisters*. Also: Best Direction: Woody Allen.

Best Actor: Bob Hoskins, in *Mona Lisa*.

Best Actress: Sissy Spacek, in *Crimes of the Heart*.

Best Supporting Actor: Daniel Day Lewis, in *A Room With a View* and *My Beautiful Laundrette*.

Best Screenplay: Stephen Frears, for *My Beautiful Laundrette*.

Best Cinematography: Tony Pierce-Roberts, for *A Room With a View*.

Best Foreign Film: *The Decline of the American Empire*, director (Canada).

The 3rd International Film Festival of Cinema, TV and Video Awards, Rio de Janeiro, November 1986

Golden Toucan for Best Film: *My Beautiful Laundrette* (Great Britain).

Best Direction: Ruy Guerra, for *Opera Do Malandro* (Brazil).

Best Actress: Sabine Azéma, in *Mélo* (France).

Best Actor: Peter Thiel in *Manden I Manen – Man in the Moon* (Denmark).

Jury Prizes((1) *La Mansion de Araucaime* (Colombia); (2) *Baixo Gavea – Gavea Woman* (Brazil); (3) *La Femme de ma Vie – The Woman of My Life* (France).

The San Sebastian Film Festival Awards, September 1986

Gold Shell for Best Film: *La Mitad Del Cielo – Half of the Sky* (Spain).

Silver Shell shared by: *27 Horas – 27 Hours* (Spain) and *Ninguen No Yakusoko – The Promise* (Japan).

Special Jury Prize: *A Nagy Generacio – The Great Generation* (Hungary).

Best Direction: Axel Corti, for his *Welcome to Vienna* (Austria).

Best Actor: Ernesto Gomez Cruz, in *El Imperio de la Fortuna – The Empire of Fortune* (Mexico).

Best Actress: Angela Molina, in *La Mitad Del Cielo – Half of the Sky* (Spain).

The Sitges Film Festival, October 1986

Best Film: *Blue Velvet* (USA).

Best Direction: Sergio Paradjanov and Dodo Abashidze, for their *The Legend of Suram Fortress* (USSR).

Best Actor: Juanjo Poigcorbe, in *Mes Enlla de la Paseio – Beyond Passion* (Spain).

Best Actress: Caroline Williams, in *The Texas Chainsaw Massacre Part II* (USA).

Best Cinematography: Frederick Elmes, for *Blue Velvet*.

The 1st Spanish Academy of Motion Pictures Arts and Sciences Awards, April 1987

The first Spanish Academy handouts, the Goyas, was a celebration for producer-director-writer-actor Fernando Fernan-Gomes who picked up Best Picture and Best Screenplay prizes for his *Viaje a Ningana Parte – Voyage to Nowhere* and was voted Best Actor for his performance in *Mambru se fue a la guerre – Mambru Went to War*.

Best Actress: Amparoro Rivellas, in *Hay que deschacer la casa*.

Best Cinematography: Teo Escamilla, for *El Amor Brujo*.

The 32nd Taormina Film Festival Awards, July 1986

Gold Charybdis for Best Film: *Rih Essed – Man of Ashes*, by Nouri Bouzid (Tunisia).

Silver Charybdis: *Malayunta – The Incompatibles*, by Jose Santiso (Argentine).

Bronze Charybdis: *Eat the Peach*, by Peter Ormrod (Great Britain).

Gold Polyhymina Mask for Best Performance: Tom Conti, in *Heavenly Pursuits* (Great Britain).

Silver Polyhymina Mask: Micheline Presle, in *Beau temps mais orageux en fin de journée – Clear Skies and Evening Storms* (France).

Bronze Polyhymina Mask: Marian Rolle, in *Almacita of the Desolado* (Dutch Antilles).

Italian Film Critics' Association Award shared by: *Desert Bloom*, by Eugene Corr (USA) and *The Decline of the American Empire*, by Denys Arcand (Canada).

Italian Film Journalists Association Award shared by: *Beau temps mais orageux en fin de journée – Clear Skies and Evening Storms*, by Gérard Frot-Coutaz (France) and *F/X*, by Robert Mandel (USA).

City of Taormina Awards: Franco Bruno (director) and Gianni Garko (performance), in *Black Tunnel* (Italy); and Alessandro Haber, for his performance in *Tomasso Blu* (Germany).

The Valladolid Festival Awards, November 1986

Golden Sheaf for Best Film shared by: *Mona Lisa*, by Neil Jordan (Great Britain) and *Offret – The Sacrifice*, by Andrei Tarkovsky (Sweden).

Silver Sheaf: *El Disputado Voto del Señore Cayo – The Disputed Vote of Mr Cayo*, by Antonio Gimenez-Rico (Spain).

Best Actor: Bob Hoskins, in *Mona Lisa* (Great Britain).

Best Actress: Meryl Streep, in *Heartburn* (USA).

Best Cinematography: Sven Nykvist, for *Offret – The Sacrifice*.

The Venice Film Festival Awards, September 1986

Golden Lion Grand Prix for Best Film: *Le Rayon Vert – The Green Ray*, by Eric Rohmer (France).

Silver Lion for Best First Film: *La Pelicula del Rey – A King and His Movie* by Carlos Sorin (Argentine).

Best Actor: Carlo Delle Piane, in *Regalo di Natale – Christmas Present* (Italy).

Best Actress: Valeria Golino in *Storia d'Amore – Love Story* (Italy).

A Special Award was given to Oddvar Einarson, for his *X* (Norway).

International Critics' Prize: *Le Rayon Vert – The Green Ray*.

Special Awards of the Jury: *Storia d'Amore*, by Francesco Maselli (Italy) and *Cuzaja, Belaja I Rjaboj – Wild Dove*, by Sergei Soloviev (USSR).

The Vevey International Festival of Film Comedies, August 1986

Golden Cane for First Prize: *Männer – Men*, by Doris Dörrie (West Germany).

Best Actor: Bernard Ménez, in *Main Ocean*, by Jacques Rozier (France). Special mention to Susan Dey, in *Echo Park* (Austria-USA).

Best First Feature: *Rhosyn a Rhith – Coming Up Roses*, by Stephen Bayly (Great Britain).

Index

Page numbers in *italic* refer to illustrations